# Credits

National Geographic Guide To
America's HIDDEN CORNERS

**Published by**
THE NATIONAL GEOGRAPHIC SOCIETY

John M. Fahey, Jr.
    President and Chief Executive Officer
Gilbert M. Grosvenor
    Chairman of the Board
Nina D. Hoffman
    Senior Vice President

**Field of daisies, Tennessee**

*Prepared by The Book Division*
William R. Gray
    Vice President and Director
Charles Kogod
    Assistant Director
Barbara A. Payne
    Managing Editor
David Griffin
    Design Director
Elizabeth L. Newhouse
    Director of Travel Publishing

*Guidebook Staff*
Barbara A. Noe
    Editor
Joan Wolbier
    Art Director
Caroline Hickey
    Senior Researcher
Marilyn Gibbons
    Illustrations Editor
Carl Mehler
    Senior Map Editor and Designer

Bob Devine, Jerry Camarillo Dunn, Jr., Sean M. Groom, Alison Kahn, K.M. Kostyal, Mark Miller, Barbara A. Noe, Geoffrey O'Gara, Donald S. Olson, William and Kay Scheller, Jeremy Schmidt, John M. Thompson, Mel White, Marilyn Wood, David Yeadon
    Writers

Margaret Bowen, Linda Hill, Mary Luders
    Text Editors

Kristin Edmonds, Mark Fitzgerald, Sean M. Groom, Mary E. Jennings, Keith R. Moore
    Researchers

Linda McKnight
    Designer

Victoria Garrett Jones
    Copy Editor

Sven M. Dolling, Christine Epperson, Thomas L. Gray, Sean M. Groom, Keith R. Moore, Joseph F. Ochlak
    Map Research
Jehan Aziz
    Map Production Manager
Sven M. Dolling, James Huckenpahler, Mapping Specialists, Ltd., Sean Mohn, Michelle H. Picard
    Map Production
Tibor G. Tóth
    Map Relief

Meredith C. Wilcox
    Illustrations Assistant

Richard S. Wain
    Production Project Manager

Lewis R. Bassford, Lyle Rosbotham
    Production

Peggy J. Candore, Mark Fitzgerald, Dale M. Herring
    Staff Assistants

Mark A. Wentling
    Indexer

Kristina Gibson, Thomas B. Powell III, Martin S. Walz
    Contributors

*Manufacturing and Quality Management*
George V. White, Director
John T. Dunn, Associate Director
Vincent P. Ryan, Manager
Polly P. Tompkins, Executive Assistant

**Cover: Lake Placid, New York**
**Previous pages: Cumberland Falls**
            **State Park, Kentucky**
**Facing page: Cumberland Island, Georgia**

**Mountain biking near Steamboat Springs, Colorado**

National Geographic Guide to

# America's
# HIDDEN
# CORNERS

Prepared by the Book Division
National Geographic Society
Washington, D.C.

# Contents

## Northeast

## South

## Great Lakes and Plains

## South Central

## Mountain and Desert States

## Pacific States

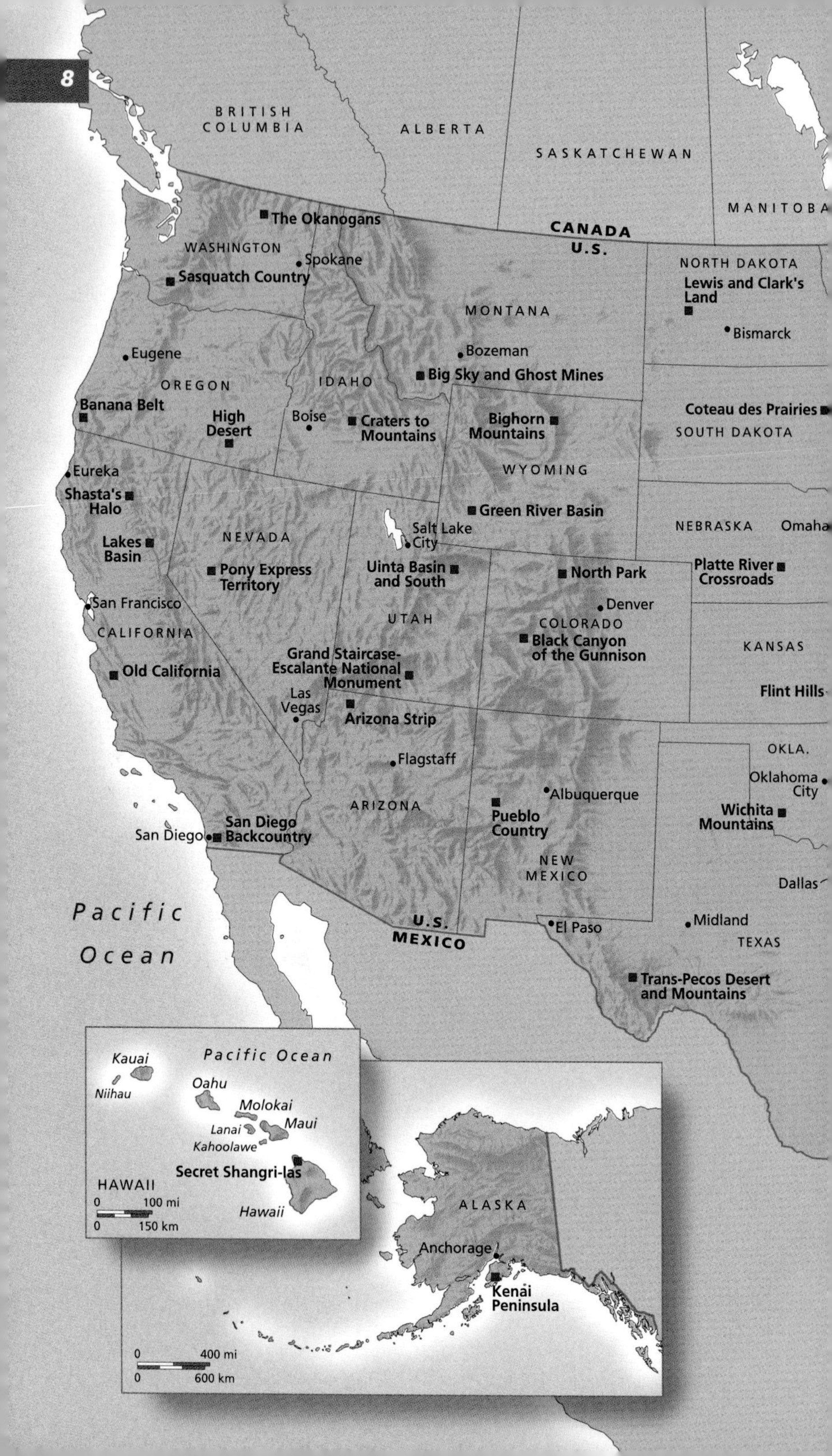

BRITISH
COLUMBIA

ALBERTA

SASKATCHEWAN

MANITOBA

■ The Okanogans

•Spokane

WASHINGTON

CANADA
U.S.

NORTH DAKOTA

■ Sasquatch Country

Lewis and Clark's
Land
■

•Bismarck

•Eugene

MONTANA

•Bozeman

OREGON

IDAHO

■ Big Sky and Ghost Mines

Banana Belt
■

High
Desert
■

Boise
•

■ Craters to
Mountains

Bighorn
Mountains ■

Coteau des Prairies ■

SOUTH DAKOTA

•Eureka

WYOMING

Shasta's
Halo ■

■ Green River Basin

NEBRASKA    Omaha

Lakes
Basin ■

NEVADA

Salt Lake
•City

■ Pony Express
Territory

Uinta Basin
and South ■

■ North Park

Platte River ■
Crossroads

•San Francisco

UTAH

•Denver

CALIFORNIA

COLORADO

KANSAS

Black Canyon
of the Gunnison ■

■ Old California

Grand Staircase-
Escalante National
Monument ■

Las
Vegas

Flint Hills

■ Arizona Strip

•

•Flagstaff

OKLA.

ARIZONA

•Albuquerque

Oklahoma •
City

■ Pueblo
Country

Wichita ■
Mountains

San Diego
Backcountry

NEW
MEXICO

Dallas

San Diego•■

Dallas

Pacific

•El Paso

•Midland

Ocean

U.S.
MEXICO

TEXAS

■ Trans-Pecos Desert
and Mountains

Kauai

Pacific Ocean

Niihau

Oahu

Molokai

Lanai    Maui

Kahoolawe

HAWAII

Secret Shangri-las

0      100 mi

0      150 km

Hawaii

ALASKA

•Anchorage•

Kenai
Peninsula

0      400 mi

0      600 km

ONTARIO

QUEBEC

NEW BRUNSWICK

P.E.I.

NOVA SCOTIA

MAINE

Grand Portage

Mississippi Headwaters

Duluth

Isle Royale National Park

Land of the Moose

Waterville

Land of Hiawatha

Lakes of the Northeast Kingdom

Rockland

Vinalhaven

Burlington

N.H.

New Hampshire's Utopia

MINN.

North Country

WISCONSIN

Central Adirondacks

VT.

Manchester

Grand Monadnock

MICHIGAN

Upper Hudson River Valley

N.Y.

Albany

Hartford

MASS.

Boston

Berkshire Fringes

R.I.

Cuttyhunk Island

Detroit

Along the Housatonic

CONN.

South County

Iowa's Great Lakes

Little Switzerland

Endless Mountains

North Fork Nuances

Galena

Lake Erie Islands

Cleveland

N.J.

New York

Chicago

PA.

Big Valley Amish

Trenton

IOWA

Cedar Rapids

Amish Country

Laurel Highlands

Pine Barrens

ILLINOIS

INDIANA

Columbus

OHIO

MD.

Down Jersey

DEL.

Delaware Marshlands

Northern Loudoun

Chesapeake & Ohio Canal

Topeka

Lincoln Hills

Louisville

WEST VIRGINIA

Almost Heaven

Historic St. Marys

Washington, D.C.

Missouri Vineyards

St. Louis

KENTUCKY

VIRGINIA

Roanoke

MISSOURI

Boone Country

Knoxville

Appalachia

Raleigh

Albemarle Area

Ozark Hills and Hollows

TENNESSEE

NORTH CAROLINA

Cumberland Plateau

ARKANSAS

Memphis

SOUTH CAROLINA

Hot Springs

Little River Canyon

Old Ninety Six

Ouachita Mountains

Hills of Mississippi

Augusta

Birmingham

GEORGIA

East Texas

MISSISSIPPI

ALABAMA

Between Two Rivers

Jackson

Swamp to Sea

LOUISIANA

Tallahassee

Jacksonville

New Orleans

Apalachicola Coast

Marjorie Kinnan Rawlings Country

Atchafalaya and Beyond

FLORIDA

Atlantic Ocean

Gulf of Mexico

0        400 mi

0        600 km

# Discovering America

I remember the time when I thought I knew the United States pretty well. I'd visited most of the key cities, national parks and monuments, famed sights and Disneyesque parks, and in general felt I'd done a thoroughly good job of "seeing" the country. But then, one late summer evening 20 years ago or so my real adventures began while driving home on the interstate between San Francisco and Los Angeles. To the west I spotted a pristine valley, couched in forest-clad hills with small pastures dappled in golden sunlight, a few scattered barns and farmhouses, and a narrow back road winding beside a sinuous, sparkling stream. That unexpected vista was my undoing. My journey home took days rather than hours.

**Ludlams Pond, Pine Barrens, New Jersey**

I soon became addicted to discovering such delights, finding a whole other America—the "real" America—of secluded canyons, secret valleys, unroaded ranges, quiet lakes, cozy hollows, magnificently empty bays and beaches, and hidden historic communities, where the pace of life is gentle and changes come slowly, and where countless generous people always seem willing to share their tales, insights, and even their homes, with an itinerant wanderer.

America is unbelievably rich in hidden corners. Some wonder if we should leave them unsung and untouched. But my experiences suggest that exploring them not only brings a little useful revenue to these often needy places, but also deepens our appreciation of their beauty, history, and intrinsic value—and thereby, hopefully, ensuring their sustainability.

This book is merely an introduction to—a brief sampling of—some of the nation's lesser known nooks and crannies. They are offered only as examples of what awaits the more adventurous traveler. But in the end, of course, the best hidden places are the ones you find—not in books—but entirely by yourself.

As Helen Keller once said, "Life is a daring adventure or nothing." We hope this volume will be the beginning (or extension) of a whole new world of adventures for you. So tread softly in these secret places and allow them to release the secret, silent places within your own spirit. And may you enjoy all your journeys.

DAVID YEADON

# About This Guide

The NATIONAL GEOGRAPHIC GUIDE TO AMERICA'S HIDDEN CORNERS brings you 75 out-of-the-way places selected for their interest and diversity and because they're ideal for weekend getaways or week-long vacations. They range from forests to bird-rich swamplands, from village-dotted valleys to mining ghost towns, from mountaintop aeries to secluded coves. Our regional travel writers know each place intimately, and share historical tidbits, cultural lore, interesting geography, and whatever else makes each corner a special place. All narratives include a Travel Notes section, with major sites keyed to a detailed map, directions, the best seasons to visit, information sources, plus suggested activities, annual festivals, and inns or hotels of special interest. Information about every site has been checked, and to the best of our knowledge is accurate as of press date. However, it is always advisable to call ahead when possible. In addition to the stated days of closure, many sites close on national holidays.

## MAP KEY and ABBREVIATIONS

| | |
|---|---|
| MILITARY RESERVATION | |
| NATIONAL CONSERVATION AREA | N.C.A. |
| NATIONAL HISTORICAL PARK | N.H.P. |
| NATIONAL HISTORICAL PARK & PRESERVE | |
| NATIONAL LAKESHORE | N.L. |
| NATIONAL MONUMENT | N.M., NAT. MON. |
| NATIONAL PARK | N.P., NAT. PARK |
| NATIONAL PRESERVE | |
| NATIONAL RECREATION AREA | N.R.A., NAT. REC. AREA |
| NATIONAL RIVER & RECREATION AREA | |
| NATIONAL SCENIC RIVERWAYS | |
| NAVAL AIR STATION | N.A.S. |
| NAVAL AIR WARFARE CENTER | |
| FOREST RESERVE | |
| NATIONAL FOREST | N.F., NAT. FOR. |
| NATIONAL GRASSLAND | N.G. |
| NATURAL AREA RESERVE | |
| STATE FOREST | S.F. |
| PARK | |
| STATE PARK | S.P. |
| INDIAN RESERVATION | I.R. |
| ELK REFUGE | |
| NATIONAL ANTELOPE REFUGE | |
| NATIONAL WILDLIFE REFUGE | N.W.R. |
| WATERFOWL PRODUCTION AREA | W.P.A. |
| WILD HORSE RANGE | |
| WILDLIFE & FISH REFUGE | |
| WILDLIFE AREA | |
| WILDLIFE MANAGEMENT AREA | W.M.A |

| | |
|---|---|
| Br. | Branch |
| BYW. | Byway |
| Co. | County |
| Cr. | Creek |
| Fk. | Fork |
| Ft. | Fort |
| H.S. | Historic Site |
| H.S.P. | Historical State Park |
| I.-s. | Island-s |
| Mt.-s. | Mount, Mountain-s |
| NAT. BATTLEFIELD | National Battlefield |
| N.B. | National Battlefield |
| N.B.S. | National Battlefield Site |
| N.H.L. | National Historic Landmark |
| N.H.S. | National Historic Site |
| N.R.T. | National Recreation Trail |
| N.S.T. | National Scenic Trail |
| Pk. | Peak |
| R. | River |
| Ra. | Range |
| RD. | Road |
| Res. | Reservoir |
| R.P. | Regional Park |
| S.A.S. | State Archeological Site |
| S.B. | State Beach |
| S.H.P. | State Historical Park |
| S.H.S. | State Historic Site |
| S.R.A. | State Recreation Area |
| S.R.P. | State Resort Park |
| S.S.C. | State Scenic Corridor |

| Desert | Swamp | Glacier |
|---|---|---|

**Boundaries**

| N.W.R. | NAT. FOR. | NAT. PARK |
|---|---|---|

■ Point of Interest   ✪ State Capitol

| | |
|---|---|
| I Dam | ) ( Pass |
| + Elevation | II Falls |

| Interstate Highway | National Border |
|---|---|
| (88) | State Border |
| Trans-Canada Highway | County Border |
| (17) | Continental Divide |
| Principal Canadian Highway | Historic Trail |
| (55) | Recreational Trail |
| U.S. Federal Highway | Railroad |
| (60) | Ferry |
| State Road | Intracoastal Waterway |
| (44) | Canal |
| County, Local, or Other Road | In Use        Abandoned |
| H13 | |

| ● Albuquerque | 200,000 and over |
|---|---|
| ● Wilmington | 20,000 to under 200,000 |
| ● New Castle | under 20,000 |

# Northeast

## MAINE

# Land of the Moose

Not all of America's frontier country lies in Alaska, or in the great roadless spaces of the Rocky Mountains. Much of northern Maine has the look and feel of a place settled yesterday—and in parts, not settled at all. Between Rockwood and The Forks, where the mighty Kennebec River spills out of Moosehead Lake and roils through a logging and sporting empire, the terrain still bears a rugged look. After all, this is territory that belongs to the loon, the bear, and most of all, the lordly moose.

   In the 1780s the Commonwealth of Massachusetts held a lottery of unsettled land in its northernmost province—a wilderness called Maine, which had few inland inhabitants and another quarter-century to go before it would achieve statehood. A Philadelphia banker named William Bingham drew several townships in the lottery and bought out the rest, thus becoming master of two million acres. Half of that land was along the upper reaches of the Kennebec River, west and south of **Moosehead Lake.**
   Lumbermen began clearing Bingham's domain soon after he acquired it. Down came the stands of giant white pine prized for ships' masts during colonial days. Thankfully, the woods grew back fast and, although lumbermen are still at it, great silent (albeit second-growth) forests still cover much of this northwestern part of the state. Rivers once choked with logs being funneled downstream now support another industry—adventure vacations. From early May through mid-October white-water rafting enthusiasts head for a stretch of the upper Kennebec River between The Forks and Moosehead to begin a 12-mile run through secluded forest and a deep,

**Fall foliage in Adirondack Park, New York (see Central Adirondacks, p. 55)**

rock-walled gorge. Seven or eight times each season, dam waters at Flagstaff Lake are released into the Dead River, creating one of the longest stretches of continuous white water in the East—a turbulent, 15-mile stretch of Class IV and V rapids. Several companies offer trips for all levels of experience, as well as activities such as float-tube fishing and "sportyaking" (with inflatable kayaks). And canoeists have many options, including the outstanding, 34-mile Moose River Bow trip outside Jackman, which winds through some of the North Woods' most scenic wilderness. The trip begins and ends at Attean Pond, and includes two portages. There are launching points along the way for paddlers who prefer to avoid the carries, and several businesses offer shuttle service. Primitive campsites are scattered along the route. Less strenuous trips include the Moose River/Long Pond route and portions of the Kennebec River and Moosehead Lake. To the north, the legendary Allagash Wilderness Waterway beckons, although trips here require strenuous portages.

Like its rivers, Maine's forests are appreciated nowadays for more than their commercial value. The burgeoning moose population attracts riflemen (with awfully big freezers back home), as well as outsiders armed with cameras. The Moose River and Moosehead Lake regions are among the Northeast's most popular spots for moose watching. The Moosehead Lake Region Chamber of Commerce provides a "moose sighting" map; and several businesses around the lake offer seasonal "moose cruises" to observe moose and other wildlife, including bears, eagles, peregrine falcons, and ospreys. Some might think the area is downright moose-crazy: Just ask the folks in Greenville, site of the month-long **Moosemainea** festivities that begin each May. Then moose and their young can be seen everywhere—especially in the early morning and at dusk when they come out to feed. Accordingly, drivers should proceed with particular caution at those times. Other Moosemainea events include moose-calling competitions, moose-meat tastings, and a Tour de Moose mountain-bike race.

For hikers, excellent trails lace the region. The venerable Appalachian National Scenic Trail crosses US 201, just north of Caratunk, on the way to its northernmost point at Mount Katahdin in Baxter State Park. In the Moosehead Lake region, a 3.25-mile trail leads to the top of 3,196-foot **Big Squaw Mountain** and panoramic views of Moosehead Lake. Alternatively, an easy 0.5-mile trail begins at the Attean Lake Overlook rest area on US 201, 5 miles south of Jackman; it affords excellent vistas to the south and southwest.

Another prime attraction in these northern woods is found in Solon, on a

## Mount Kineo

Two Indian legends explain the origin of Mount Kineo, the peak that rises from a peninsula thrusting into Moosehead Lake. One tells of a hunter who killed an enormous moose on this spot; the mountain is the animal's shoulders bleaching in the sun. According to the other tale, the mountain was the home of an outcast named Kinneho, who lived here in proud isolation.

**Moose mealtime**

ledge located on the western bank of the Kennebec River—one of the Northeast's best preserved **petroglyph** sites. Drawings incised in rock, the petroglyphs were made by ancestors of Maine's modern Abnaki tribes between 200 and 1,500 years ago. Long before Europeans came this way, the natives were threading their way between present-day Quebec City and the mouth of the Kennebec River along a trail of waterways and portages. A number of items excavated in the area are on display at the **Evergreens Campground and Restaurant,** across the river from the petroglyphs.

In 1819, long after Native Americans staked their ground here, Capt. Samuel Holden and his family paddled and snowshoed north along the Kennebec River to The Forks, then plodded more than 30 miles to become the first white settlers in the Moose River valley. Their two-story frame house, now on the Moose River Golf Course, is one of the valley's oldest structures. Tiny Jackman began to thrive after 1888 when the Canadian Pacific Railroad rolled into town. Today the town remains perched at the threshold of the wilderness. As in railroad days, Jackman is a jumping-off point for hunters, anglers, and backwoods explorers.

Moosehead Lake, heart of this hidden corner and gateway to a wilderness domain stretching to Baxter State Park, the Allagash Wilderness Waterway, and Canada, is the largest lake in New England contained within one state: It's 35 miles long and 10 miles across at its widest point. Much of the shoreline is publicly owned and retains its primitive character; beyond lie miles and miles of unbroken forest and views ranging as far as distant Mount Katahdin. Opposite Rockwood, **Mount Kineo** (see sidebar p. 14) rises dramatically out of the water. Attached to land by way of a peninsula, but most accessible by boat, the sheer-faced flint peak is the haunt of bald eagles and peregrine falcons. Here along the **Indian Trail**

**Sacked out along the Moose River**

hikers can follow in the footsteps of Native Americans who once climbed to the summit to chip flint for weapons and tools.

Before roads were built, steamboats ferried livestock and provisions to camps dotting Moosehead's shoreline, and carried supplies to men building the Canadian Pacific's line between Quebec and New Brunswick. The story of the lake's steamboat era is told at the **Moosehead Marine Museum,** home to the last remaining ship in the fleet, the *Katahdin,* which now chugs out for scenic cruises. The museum is nestled in **Greenville**, an isolated but snug little town that services the area's many sporting lodges and vacation retreats. It's the perfect hub from which to seek adventure in this Land of the Moose.

—*William and Kay Scheller*

# Travel Notes

### Directions

The region is north of Skowhegan and is roughly bounded by US 201 and Maine 6/15. **By car:** From the south, take the Maine Turnpike to Fairfield and US 201 north. **By air:** Folsom's Air Service *(Greenville. 207-695-2821)* offers charter service and wilderness fly-ins from Bangor, Augusta, and Portland. Coleman's Flying Service *(Jackman. 207-668-4436)* also provides fly-in service.

### General Information

The best times to visit this hidden corner are spring through fall. For information, contact the Moosehead Lake Region Chamber of Commerce *(Maine 15, Indian Hill Plaza, P.O. Box 581, Greenville 04441. 207-695-2702)*; Upper Kennebec Valley Chamber of Commerce *(US 201, P.O. Box 491, Bingham 04920. 207-672-4100)*; or the Jackman-Moose River Region Chamber of Commerce *(P.O. Box 368, Jackman 04945. 207-668-4171)*.

### Things to See and Do

**1. Indian petroglyphs** *(Solon. 207-643-2324. Call for directions)* The petroglyphs carved on a ledge on the west bank of the Kennebec River were carved by ancestors of the Abnaki between 200 and 1,500 years ago. Though they lie on private property, they are accessible to visitors. Across the river, the **Evergreens Campground and Restaurant** *(US 201A, Solon. 207-643-2324)* has a small display related to the Abnaki petroglyphs, as well as artifacts and archaeological exhibits.

**2. Moxie Falls** *(Off US 201, 2.5 miles E of The Forks)* A 0.6-mile boardwalk leads to the 90-foot falls, one of New England's largest. Small pools in the Staircase Falls are perfect for a refreshing dip.

**3. Borestone Mountain Wildlife Sanctuary** *(Elliotsville Rd., off Maine 15, 10 miles N of Monson. 207-631-4050 May-Oct., 207-564-7946 year-round. Donation)* This National Audubon Society sanctuary offers natural history and historical exhibits and a nature trail to the summit.

**4. Greenville** *(Chamber of Commerce 207-695-2702)* The downhill ski area at **Big Squaw Mountain Resort** *(Maine 15. 207-695-1000)* provides dramatic views of Moosehead Lake and Mount Katahdin. Chairlift operates during fall foliage season *(Sept.-*

*Oct.)*. From the **Moosehead Marine Museum** *(Main St. 207-695-2716. July–Columbus Day, no cruises Mon. or Fri.; fare for cruises)* visitors can take a cruise on the **Katahdin,** a restored 115-foot lake boat and the last of Moosehead Lake's passenger fleet. The ride provides incomparable views of the lakeshore and surrounding mountains.

**5. Lily Bay State Park** *(Lily Bay Rd., 9 miles N of Greenville. 207-695-2700. May–mid-Oct.; adm. fee)* Get here early to hear the cry of the loons and take an invigorating dip from the sandy beach. Camping is permitted.

**6. Mount Kineo** *(Opposite Rockwood)* Native Americans chipped flint from the mountain's rugged cliffs. Among the hiking paths is the 1-mile **Indian Trail,** which follows the cliff edge to the summit. Shuttles leave from Rockwood *(Kineo Launch Corp. 207-534-8812)*.

### Other Activities

**Aerial tours** Those looking for a bird's-eye view of the wilderness can call Folsom's Air Service *(Greenville. 207-695-2821)* or Currier's Flying Service *(Greenville. 207-695-2778)*.

**Canoeing** Rentals are offered at Sally Mountain Cabins *(Jackman. 207-668-5621 or 800-644-5621)* and Northwoods Outfitters, Inc. *(Main St., Greenville. 207-695-3288)*.

**Cross-country skiing** Contact Birches Resort *(Rockwood. 207-534-7305 or 800-825-9453)* or Moosehead Nordic Ski Center *(Greenville. 207-695-2870)*.

**Kayaking** Cry of the Loon Outdoor Adventures *(Jackman. 207-668-7808)* rents equipment.

**Moose watching** Call Birches Resort *(Rockwood. 207-534-7305 or 800-825-9453)*.

**Mountain biking** For bike rentals contact Birches Resort *(Rockwood. 207-534-7305 or 800-825-9453)* or Northwoods Outfitters, Inc. *(Greenville. 207-965-3288)*.

**White-water rafting** For rentals, contact Northern Outdoors *(The Forks. 207-663-4466 or 800-765-7238)* or Windfall Outdoor Center *(207-668-4818 or 800-683-2009)*.

### Annual Events

**Mid-May–mid-June** Moosemainea *(Greenville. 207-6956-2702)*

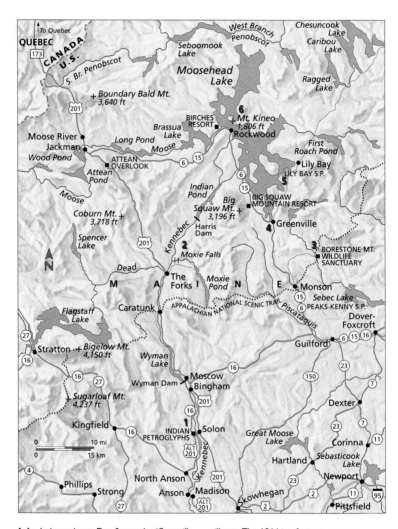

**July** Independence Day fireworks (*Greenville. 207-695-2702*)
**August** Forest Heritage Days (*Greenville. 207-695-2128*)
**September** International Seaplane Fly-in (*Greenville. 207-695-2821*)

## Lodging

**Chesuncook Lake House** (*Chesuncook Village. 207-745-5330*) Fifty miles north of the Moosehead Lake region and accessible only by boat, canoe, plane, or a 5-mile hiking/snowmobile trail, this country inn is at the site of one of the few remaining 19th-century North Woods lumbermen's villages. The 1864 inn features sunny, lakefront rooms, electricity by generator, gas lights, and French cuisine. There are also housekeeping cabins.

**Greenville Inn at Moosehead Lake** (*Norris St., Greenville. 207-695-2206 or 888-695-6000*) Ship carpenters worked 10 years to complete the carved embellishments and paneling in this 1895 lumber baron's mansion. The inn features elegantly appointed rooms, great views of the lake, and a superb dining room.

# Vinalhaven

Thirteen miles out on a fog-prone inlet of the Atlantic called Penobscot Bay lies Vinalhaven, a rugged outrider of the rock-bound coast of Maine. At 5 by 7 miles, Vinalhaven is the largest of the bay's numerous Fox Islands—and a place of elemental beauty. The ocean is its primal force: Nowhere on the island is it possible to leave saltwater far behind. Between the island's cool dark forests of scrub spruce and the granite bulwark of its coast, 1,100 year-round residents live their lives the old Down East way, in partnership with the uncompromising sea.

Vinalhaven is a working island, home to one of the country's largest lobster fleets. Unlike other Maine coastal communities, though, it offers neither cute "in-the-rough" restaurants, nor nightly clambakes on the beach. Vinalhaven has not been veneered for tourists: The people who live and work here year-round love their remote, wind-scourged isle just the way it is, with slightly frayed edges. For the most part they welcome the visitors that the ferry deposits on their doorstep daily, along with a contingent of long-time summer residents. But there are few tourist amenities, and most of the islanders like that just fine.

**Buoys, Vinalhaven**

Yet Vinalhaven has undergone a great number of changes since the first permanent settlers arrived here in the 1760s, shortly after the French and Indian War. At one time it was one of the world's granite-quarrying capitals and home to the state's largest fish-curing plant. Today, lobstering provides the bulk of the island's income, and residents are loathe to pay too much attention to yet another industry—tourism—that might one day leave them high and dry.

Vinalhaven was a somnolent fishing port when Joseph Bodwell and Moses Webster arrived in the mid-1800s and formed Bodwell, Moses &

**Carver's Harbor, Vinalhaven**

Company to quarry the island's granite. Prior to the Civil War, the federal government contracted with the company for stone to reinforce forts along the Atlantic and Gulf coasts. Later, Vinalhaven granite found its way into buildings as far-flung as the flamboyant Old Executive Office Building in Washington, D.C.

The company thrived until 1910, when steel and concrete became popular, and taste in national architecture shifted to less lavish ornamentation. A report from Vinalhaven in the August 1918 *Granite Cutter's Journal* stated "nothing doing and no sign of anything." By World War II, the granite industry was dead. But many legacies of Vinalhaven's glory days of granite remain: Two of the most popular of the abandoned quarries that dot the island are the town-owned **Lawson's** and **Booth Quarries,** the first a favorite of small children because its shallow ledges create a warm pool; the latter, colder, cleaner, and popular with teenagers.

Today, most of Vinalhaven's shops and restaurants are clustered around tiny Carver's Harbor, home to the bulk of the lobster fleet. The artist Robert Indiana has restored the town's most impressive building, the Odd Fellows Hall, for his home and studio. The dock across the street is a delightful spot to sit at daybreak and watch the boats as they slip from their moorings and head out to sea, pursued by flocks of hopeful gulls.

In 1968, with the help of a home-grown fundraising campaign and substantial private donations, islanders purchased 45 acres of pristine wilderness comprising nearly two-thirds of adjacent **Lane Island** (attached to Vinalhaven by a causeway) and donated it to the Nature Conservancy. There are few places that better exemplify Maine's adamantine coast than this preserve of windswept moors, tiny driftwood-strewn beaches, and stark granite cliffs. Trails lead to the ocean where, at low tide, tiny sea creatures scuttle about in shallow pools. In summer, a profusion of rugosa roses perfume the salt air; a bit later in the season, blueberries, blackberries, and huckleberries are ripe for picking. In fall the preserve, which lies athwart the Atlantic flyway, is a popular stopover for numerous species of migrating birds.

Back on Vinalhaven, the summer visage the island presents to visitors is rustic yet engaging. But for islanders who make a living from the sea, a memorial in Grimes Park serves as a solemn testament that life here can be hard and dangerous.                    —*William and Kay Scheller*

# Travel Notes

### Directions
Vinalhaven lies in Penobscot Bay, 13 miles off the Maine coastline. **By ferry:** Maine State Ferry Service *(517A Main St., Rockland 04841. 207-596-2202)* operates daily between Rockland and Vinalhaven. **By car:** If you must bring your car to Vinalhaven, make ferry reservations (they're available up to 30 days in advance). Those without them have to park in line and wait for a ferry that has room. **By air:** There are airports in Portland and Rockland.

**Local lobster catch**

### General Information
The best time to visit is June through September, when services are open and the weather tends to be sunny and warm. For general information contact the Town Office *(P.O. Box 815, Vinalhaven 04863. 207-863-4471)*. The Rockland-Thomaston Chamber of Commerce *(P.O. Box 508, Rockland 04841. 207-596-0376 or 800-562-2529)* has limited information available. For a copy of Vinalhaven's visitor's guide write P.O. Box 546, Vinalhaven 04863. Copies of "The Wind," Vinalhaven's weekly bulletin, are stored in a box on the side of the Old

Fire Hall in the public parking lot at the ferry terminal.

### Things to See and Do
**1. Vinalhaven** *(Town Office 207-863-4471)* All of the town's sights are clustered in the harbor area. At aptly named **Armbrust Hill** *(Off Atlantic Ave.)*, visitors will find a 30-acre abandoned-quarry site, which is now a lovely park. Owned by the town, **Lawson's** *(North Haven Rd.)* and **Booth** *(E. Main St.)* **Quarries** are popular spots for swimming. The craftsmanship of local stonecutters is displayed in the intricately carved headstones in

the **John Carver Cemetery** *(High St.)*. Among the most unusual is the Athearn stone, topped by a bouquet of lilies. Displays of local history can be examined at the **Vinalhaven Historical Society Museum** *(Old Town Hall, High St. 207-863-4410. Mid-June–mid-Sept., and by appt.)*. Forty-five acres of shoreline, tidal pools, beaches, and moors await at **Lane's Island Nature Conservancy Preserve** *(Via Lane Island Bridge. 207-729-5181)*. Although the **Brown's Head Lighthouse** *(NW end of island)* is now automated (and a private residence), visitors are welcome to park in the designated area and enjoy views of North Haven Island and the mainland.

**2. North Haven Island** Call Brown's Boat Yard *(207-867-4621)* for a three-minute ride (no cars) to the island and its century-old summer colony. There are few tourist amenities, but cyclists can visit places such as Pulpit Harbor.

**Changing hues, Penobscot Bay**

### Other Activities

**Berry picking** Starting in late summer, berries are ripe for picking at Booth Quarry, Armbrust Hill, and Lane's Island Nature Conservancy Preserve.

**Biking** Bikes can be rented at the Tidewater Motel *(Main St. 207-863-4618)* in Carver's Harbor, just a half mile from the terminal. From here it's an easy pedal to Lane's Island Nature Conservancy Preserve and several other points of interest.

**Clamming** A license is not required for "messdiggers" who want to harvest for their own consumption. Check at the Town Office *(207-863-4471)* to make sure there's no red tide, a periodic condition in which microorganisms render shellfish inedible.

**Fishing** No license is necessary for ocean fishing, but a Maine license is required for freshwater fishing. Contact the Town Office *(see above)* for more information.

**Hiking** The Vinalhaven Land Trust *(Sands Rd., Skoog Park. 207-863-2543)* is a conservation organization that owns and protects 350 acres on the island, including several preserves with wonderful hiking trails. They'll be glad to provide a map.

### Annual Events

**July** Independence Day Parade and Celebration *(207-863-4471)*

### Lodging

**Payne Homestead at the Moses Webster House** *(Atlantic Ave. 207-863-9963 or 888-863-9963)* Children are welcome at this Victorian inn, the former home of granite baron Moses Webster.

**Tidewater Motel** *(Main St. 207-863-4618)* This motel is built on a bridge overlooking Carver's Harbor; most of the nicely decorated rooms have wonderful views and decks. It's open all year and with advance notice the owners will meet your ferry.

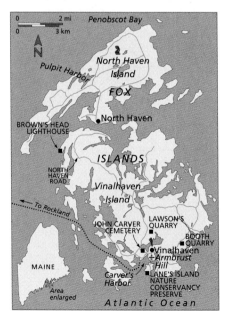

## NEW HAMPSHIRE

# New Hampshire's Utopia

A rolling countryside backed by mountains and stippled with small towns covers this pastoral midsection of New Hampshire. Once pocked by ice age glaciers, the area now glistens with forest-rimmed lakes—the queen of them, bustling Lake Winnipesaukee, lies off to the northeast. But in the quiet of this hidden corner nothing louder than the call of a loon or the whirr of a potter's wheel disturbs the peace.

   In the early 19th century, when waves of revivalism swept across the East, utopian groups set up many communities in central New Hampshire. Later, sculptor Augustus Saint-Gaudens came to the area, and a stream of creative souls followed in his wake; they formed an art colony that lasted from 1885 to 1935. Though these original groups are gone now, potters, glassmakers, and other artisans began settling here in the 1960s to form their own utopias.

**Aerial of New Hampton**

The Shakers were among the religious groups that flocked to this area in the last century. An ardent Quaker splinter group under the leadership of Mother Ann Lee, they spread their communities from Maine to Kentucky. Their celibate ways eventually led to their demise, but their heritage is preserved at the **Canterbury Shaker Village,** one of their former communities. Here visitors can view 25 restored, furnished buildings.

More history awaits just south of Franklin, where one of America's most impassioned orators was born. Daniel Webster (1782-1852), whose voice, energy, and dedication to the Union still resonate in this part of New Hampshire, is memorialized at the **Daniel Webster Birthplace State Historic Site,** a two-room cabin off N.H. 127.

**View from Meeting House Bell Tower, Canterbury Shaker Village**

From Franklin, backroads lead north across hills, over mountains, and through the maple-shaded streets of small towns such as Hill, Bristol, Alexandria, and Hebron. **Newfound Lake,** whose 7-mile length is rimmed by hills, forms a watery centerpiece in the area. Along its western shore, **Wellington State Beach** is mobbed with beachgoers in summer, but you can still find a quiet spot to contemplate the lake's crystal-clear waters, if you hike out to the park's rocky, fir-frilled point. Another popular swimming hole lies just northwest of Hebron, at the **Sculptured Rocks** on the Cockermouth River. In this shady canyon bathers jump from granite overhangs into a series of pothole pools gouged by waterborne stones and sediment during the last ice age.

Along the roadsides here streams flow through pastureland that stretches away to distant mountains. Pressing down from the north are the peaks of the White Mountains. Mount Cardigan, flanked by Firescrew Mountain and South Peak, dominates the western horizon where the sleepy villages of Canaan and Orange lie in a hollow along the Indian River. The road out of Orange leads to **Mount Cardigan,** where the West Ridge Trail winds up to the 3,121-foot summit.

On the western edge of the region stands **Hanover,** home to Dartmouth College and its myriad cultural offerings. North of town awaits a string of small towns, including Lyme, a charmer with its classic church, town green, and old clapboard houses; and Orford, with its remarkable collection of early mansions. South of Hanover, N.H. 12A presses close to the broad Connecticut River—one of the most scenic routes in the state. Along the way stands the **Saint-Gaudens National Historic Site,** summer home to one of the country's most exceptional turn-of-the-century artists, Augustus Saint-Gaudens. The Italianate-influenced gardens and magnificent views to Mount Ascutney attest to the magical landscape that nurtured him—and so many others in New Hampshire's Utopia.

—*Marilyn Wood*

# Travel Notes

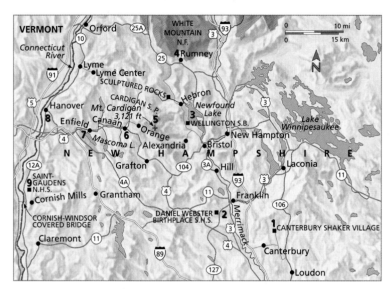

## Directions

This hidden corner is south of the White Mountains between Laconia and Hanover; I-91 and I-93 frame its western and eastern boundaries. **By car:** Take I-91 or I-93 from the north or south. **By plane:** The closest airports are in Manchester, Boston, Mass., and Portland, Me. **By train:** Amtrak operates to White River Junction, Vt.

## General Information

Spring through fall is the best time to visit the area. For information, contact the Hanover Area Chamber of Commerce *(P.O. Box 5105, Hanover 03755. 603-643-3115)*; the Newfound Region Chamber of Commerce *(P.O. Box 454, Bristol 03222. 603-744-2150)* or the Greater Laconia/Weirs Beach Chamber of Commerce *(11 Veterans Sq., Laconia 03246. 603-524-5531)*.

## Things to See and Do

**1. Canterbury Shaker Village** *(Follow signs off I-93 to Shaker Rd., Canterbury. 603-783-9511. May-Oct. daily, April and Nov.-Dec. Sat.-Sun.; adm. fee)* A guided tour of this complex of buildings provides insight into Shaker life.

**2. Daniel Webster Birthplace State Historic Site** *(North Rd., off N.H. 127,*

*Franklin. 603-934-5057. Mid-June–Labor Day Sat.-Sun.; adm. fee)* This two-room cabin contains period furniture, as well as mementos and artifacts relating to the life of Daniel Webster, statesman and orator. Included here is the sign he hung to advertise himself as a lawyer.

**3. Newfound Lake** *(Chamber of Commerce 603-744-2150)* A good place for swimming and picnicking is **Wellington State Beach** *(West Shore Dr., off N.H. 3A, Alexandria. 603-744-2197 in season)*, which features a 0.5-mile-long beach on an unspoiled lake. For birdwatching, shoreline trails along lake and marsh can be found at **Newfound Audubon Center** *(N. Shore Rd., E. Hebron. 603-744-3516. Mem. Day–Labor Day)*. Just northwest of the lake, **Sculptured Rocks** *(Sculptured Rocks Rd., Groton)* is an ancient swimming hole and picnicking spot.

**4. Rumney** On view at the **Mary Baker Eddy Historic Homes** *(58 Stinson Lake Rd. 603-786-9943 May-Oct. Tues.-Sun.; adm. fee)* are two former homes of the remarkable Mary Baker Eddy, who lived in the area in the mid-1860s. Her physical afflictions led her to alternative therapies such as homeopathy and spiritualism, and eventually led her to found the Christian Science Church. One of the houses is perched on the side of a small

**Saint-Gaudens National Historic Site**

mountain in a lovely remote location.

**5. Cardigan State Park** *(Off N.H. 118, Orange. For information, contact Appalachian Mountain Club 603-466-2721)* A scenic road here leads to the western slope of **Mount Cardigan** and a picnicking area with panoramic views. There's hiking and cross-country skiing, too.

**6. Canaan** The displays at the **Canaan Historical Museum** *(Canaan St. 603-523-7364. Mid-June–Sept. Sat., and by appt.; donation)* focus on local history and include Shaker farm and household items, plus games, tools, and historic photographs. There's even some china and the gravestone of the first settler.

**7. Enfield** At the **Enfield Shaker Museum** *(N.H. 4A. 603-632-4346. June–mid-Oct. daily, mid-Oct.–May Sat.-Sun.; adm. fee)* you can see an introductory video and take a self-guided tour of seven buildings. Among the jewels are the great stone dwelling, the largest and most expensive building erected by any Shaker community, and the 1854 cow barn. The site was abandoned by the Shakers in 1923 so it is not as intact as Canterbury, but it occupies a lovely vale between Mascoma Lake and Shaker Mountain. Also on the property is Dana Robes Wood Craftsmen *(603-632-5385)*, where you can watch furniture being made. Across the street stands the **Shrine of Our Lady of La Salette** *(N.H. 4A. 603-632-7087. Mass Sat. evening year-round and Sun. morning in summer)*. This pilgrimage site is maintained by the Missionaries of Our Lady of La Salette.

**8. Hanover** *(Chamber of Commerce 603-643-3115)* Chartered in 1769, **Dartmouth College** *(E. Wheelock St. 603-646-3661)* has a 200-acre main campus surrounded by natural beauty. The Baker Library *(Dartmouth Green)* contains brilliant frescoes by Mexican artist José Clemente Orozco. One of the oldest college art collections in the United

States, the fine **Hood Museum of Art** *(Wheelock St. 603-646-2808. Closed Mon.)* contains nearly 60,000 objects. The strengths of the collection are the European and American art and the arts of Africa, Oceania, and Native America, as well as contemporary art. Next door, the **Hopkins Center** *(Wheelock St. 603-646-2422)* performance hall serves up dance, drama, film, and music.

**9. Saint-Gaudens National Historic Site** *(Saint-Gaudens Rd., Cornish, off N.H. 12A. 603-675-2175. Mem. Day–Oct.; adm. fee)* The home, gardens, and studios of sculptor Augustus Saint-Gaudens feature marvelous mountain views. See his early cameos and portrait reliefs as well as his masterpieces: the Sherman Monument, the Shaw Memorial, and the moving funerary memorial to Clover Adams, wife of Henry Adams. Just down the road awaits the 450-foot-long **Cornish-Windsor Covered Bridge** *(Off N.H. 12A)*. Resting above the Connecticut River and connecting New Hampshire and Vermont, it is New England's longest covered bridge.

### Other Activities

**Canoeing** For canoe rentals on the Connecticut River, call North Star Canoe *(Cornish. 603-542-5802)*.
**Cross-country skiing** Eighteen miles of trails are available at the Eastman Cross-Country Ski Center *(Grantham. 603-863-4500)*.
**Hiking** Cardigan State Park has trails to its 3,121-foot summit. Contact the Appalachian Mountain Club *(603-466-2721)* for information on hiking in the area.
**Skiing** There's downhill skiing at Snowhill at Eastman *(Grantham. 603-863-4241)* and Dartmouth Skiway *(Lyme Center. 603-795-2143)*.

### Annual Events

**August** Cornish Fair *(Fairgrounds, Cornish. 603-542-4622)*

### Lodging

**Chase House Bed & Breakfast Inn** *(N.H. 12A, Cornish. 603-675-5391 or 800-401-9455)* This historic inn offers eight beautifully appointed rooms. The 160-acre spread has extensive lawns and gardens and great views of Mount Ascutney.
**Wyman Farm** *(22 Wyman Rd., Loudon. 603-783-4467)* This well situated farmhouse rests on 55 acres. The three suites are furnished with fine antiques.

# Grand Monadnock

From its solitary 3,165-foot summit in southern New Hampshire, Mount Monadnock, the "one that stands alone," looks out across the whole of New England. Its far-flung vistas have moved such writers as Henry David Thoreau, Mark Twain, and Nathaniel Hawthorne. Around its base cluster small historic villages and towns where artists' colonies flourish and life flows peacefully along in harmony with the inspirational surroundings.

Mount Monadnock has drawn many admirers to its forested slopes and rocky crags. Indeed, it is one of the most frequently climbed mountains in North America. In the 1860s, the long-gone Halfway House tavern-hotel on its southwestern slope was a favorite vacationing spot for Ralph Waldo Emerson and his family. Exalted by the views from atop the mountain, the transcendentalist writer rhapsodized: "See New England underspread/ South from St. Lawrence to the Sound/ From Katskill east to the sea-bound."

Emerson's claims are somewhat exaggerated, but on a clear day you can indeed see all six New England states from this "aerie citadel." The panoramic, 150-mile view takes in the steepled villages, fields, and woods stretching north to New Hampshire's Presidential Range and Mount Washington, southwest to the Berkshires, and west to Vermont's Green Mountains. To fully experience Monadnock's allure, climb the 1.9-mile White Dot Trail in **Mount Monadnock State Park** that leads through sheltered woodlands of mixed hardwoods before it snakes up to the craggy, treeless summit.

**Fall colors, Keene**

**Mount Monadnock and reflection**

Mount Monadnock has several smaller satellites thrusting up around it, including 1,883-foot Little Monadnock. At its base lies aptly named **Rhododendron State Park,** where creamy white blossoms blanket the wooded understory in mid-July. The nearby village of **Fitzwilliam** was settled in 1762 and is still blessed with a neatly fenced town common faced by a steepled church-turned-town hall, several historic federal houses, and an old inn. As with so many New England towns, this one was virtually abandoned after the Civil War, when its citizens migrated to the burgeoning cities.

But the quiet villages of this region have lured writers and artists for the last two centuries. Willa Cather (see sidebar p. 221) used to summer in **Jaffrey,** another quaint 18th-century village on the southern shoulder of Mount Monadnock. At an inn here she wrote much of *My Ántonia* (1918) and *One of Ours* (1922), and per her request, she was buried in the Old Burying Ground behind the town's white-frame Congregational Meeting House.

Along with its artistic past, the area has a long tradition of industrialization. **Harrisville,** a classic mill village, is now a National Historic Landmark. Huddled beside a reed-rimmed pond, its cluster of handsome brick buildings includes the old Harris and Granite Mills, both woolen manufacturers in the mid-19th century. Today, weavers still flock to **Harrisville Designs,** a weaving center and school located in an 1850 brick building beside the Penstock Canal.

The intellectual hub of the area is **Peterborough,** a town of redbrick buildings stretched along the banks of Nubanusit Brook and the Contoocook River. Back in the 19th century, mills lined the waterfront, turning out textiles, piano stools, wrapping paper, and machinery. Today publishing ranks as the major industry, and some 40 special interest magazines are headquartered in the area—from *Cobblestone* to *Byte Magazine.* The venerable *Yankee* magazine is located just up the road in Dublin, a town with stunning lake and mountain views.

Peterborough itself has always nurtured intellectual and artistic pursuits. As long ago as 1833, it established what is believed to be the nation's first free library. And the renowned MacDowell Colony, a retreat for artists, musicians, and writers, stands on the town's northwestern edge, its 32 studios secluded amid 450 wooded acres. It was here that Thornton Wilder penned *Our Town*; some say his characters were inspired by the townsfolk of Peterborough. It's not surprising that he and—so many others—found their muse in this quiet corner of New Hampshire. —*Marilyn Wood*

# Travel Notes

### Directions
This region is located in New Hampshire's southwestern corner between Manchester and Brattleboro, Vt. **By car:** From I-91, exit to Keene; from the Everett Turnpike, exit to Nashua. **By plane:** There are airports in Manchester, N.H., and Boston, Mass.

### General Information
The best seasons are spring through fall, while winter brings skiing. Contact the Monadnock Travel Council *(P.O. Box 358, Keene 03431. 603-355-8155 or 800-432-7864);* or the Greater Peterborough Chamber of Commerce *(P.O. Box 401, Peterborough 03458. 603-924-7234).*

### Things to See and Do
**1. Fitzwilliam** Tucked in a 13-room 1837 house, the **Amos J. Blake House Museum** *(On the Common. 603-585-7742. Mem. Day–Sept. Sat.-Sun., and by appt.)* dis-

plays toys, early farming tools, glass, and pottery. At **Rhododendron State Park** *(Off N.H. 119, 2.5 miles W of Fitzwilliam. 603-532-8862. Adm. fee),* 16 acres of these wild majestic shrubs (some as tall as 20 feet) are on view, along with fine vistas of Mount Monadnock.
**2. Rindge** At the **Cathedral of the Pines** *(75 Cathedral Entrance, off N.H. 119. 603-899-3300. May-Oct.)* visitors find an outdoor place of worship containing the Altar of the Nation, dedicated to American war dead, with Mount Monadnock as a backdrop. The 10-acre roadside site, **Annett State Wayside** *(Cathedral Rd., off N.H. 119. 603-532-8862),* offers picnicking and is adjacent to the undeveloped woodland of Annett State Forest.
**3. Jaffrey** *(Chamber of Commerce 603-532-4549)* This little town is home to the **Jaffrey Center Improvement Society Melville Academy Museum** *(Blackberry Ln. and Thorndike Pond Rd. 603-532-7455. July-Aug. Sat.-Sun., and by appt.),* housed in a coeducational

**Yarn heaven at Harrisville Designs**

secondary school founded in 1843. The museum on the first floor is notable for its Hannah Davis bandboxes. Among the 40 miles of trails at nearby **Mount Monadnock State Park** *(Off Dublin Rd., 4 miles W of Jaffrey. 603-532-8862. Adm. fee)* are several leading to the 3,165-foot summit and views across all six New England states. The park also has camping and cross-country skiing.

**4. Peterborough** *(Chamber of Commerce 603-924-7234)* The cultural hub of the area, this former mill town offers many diversions. The **New England Marionette Opera** *(Main St. 603-924-4333. Adm. fee)* is a rare marionette theater devoted primarily to opera, while the **Peterborough Players** *(Hadley Rd. 603-924-7585. Mid-June–Aug.)* has presented summer stock since 1933. Beautifully crafted New Hampshire furniture is on view at the **Peterborough Historical Society** *(19 Grove St. 603-924-3235. Mon.-Fri., and by appt.; donation)*, along with exhibits tracing regional history. The **Sharon Arts Center** *(7 School St. 603-924-7256)* displays fine arts and crafts—including pottery, textiles, and sculpture. Three miles east of town awaits **Miller State Park** *(Off N.H. 101. 603-924-3672. Adm. fee)*, where visitors can hike or drive to the summit of Pack Monadnock Mountain (2,290 feet). The park offers picnicking, hiking trails, and wonderful views of the Green Mountains. **Wapack National Wildlife Refuge** *(Off N.H. 101 at Miller S.P. 978-443-4661)* features 1,672 acres on North Pack Monadnock Mountain. A wilderness area of bog, rock, and swamp,

it's also good for hawk spotting. Hiking and cross-country skiing are available, too.

**5. Harrisville** *(Historic Harrisville 603-827-3722)* This classic mill village is the nation's only intact 19th-century textile village. **Harrisville Designs** *(Main St. 603-827-3333 or 800-338-9415)* offers week-long weaving workshops. Visit the spinning mill and shop to see the spun yarn and looms.

**6. Hillsborough** *(Chamber of Commerce 603-464-5858)* The **Franklin Pierce Homestead Historic Site** *(N.H. 9 and N.H. 31. 603-478-3165. July-Aug. daily, Mem. Day–June and Labor Day–Columbus Day Sat.-Sun.; adm. fee)* preserves the childhood home of Franklin Pierce. Built in 1804 by his father, Gov. Benjamin Pierce, it reflects the atmosphere during the time the young president grew up here (1820-1828). The nearby 1,445-acre **Fox State Forest** *(Center Rd. 603-464-3453)* features hiking and cross-country ski trails.

### Other Activities
**Biking** For information and tours call Monadnock Bicycle Touring Center *(Harrisville. 603-827-3925)*; for rentals, try Spokes and Slopes *(Peterborough. 603-924-9961)*.
**Hiking** Call the N.H. Division of Forests and Lands *(603-271-2214)*.
**Skiing** You can enjoy day and night alpine skiing and snowboarding at Pat's Peak *(N.H. 114, Henniker. 603-428-3245 or 888-728-7732)*.

### Annual Events
**August** The Cheshire Fair *(Swanzey. 603-357-4740)*
**October** The Pumpkin Festival *(Keene. 603-352-1303)*

### Lodging
**Amos A. Parker House** *(N.H. 119, Fitzwilliam. 603-585-6540)* This elegantly appointed historic house offers two rooms, two suites, and six fireplaces. The owner is a passionate gardener, as proven by the superb grounds.
**Colby Hill Inn** *(The Oaks, Henniker. 603-428-3281 or 800-531-0330)* This 1795 farmhouse boasts an idyllic setting, with beautiful gardens and a weathered barn. There's a restaurant and swimming pool, too.
**Hannah Davis House** *(106 N.H. 119 west, Fitzwilliam. 603-585-3344)* The rooms of this 1820 inn are all beautifully decorated (four have fireplaces).

# VERMONT
# Lakes of the Northeast Kingdom

As if partial possession of magnificent Lake Champlain were enough for any small state, Vermont was not favored with a great many large lakes. But the Green Mountain State does have a "lake district," made all the more alluring by a location thoroughly off the beaten path, way up in the "Northeast Kingdom."

Vermont's own "kingdom" got its magically suggestive name from that most down-to-earth Yankee politician George Aiken, the senator known for spending $17 on his last—successful—campaign. "This is such a beautiful country up here," Aiken boasted in 1949. "It ought to be called the Northeast Kingdom of Vermont." Although the borders of the region are subject to endless around-the-woodstove debate, the general understanding is that the scantily populated, heavily forested Northeast Kingdom comprises Vermont's three northeasternmost counties: Orleans, Caledonia, and Essex. At its heart

**Bird's-eye view of Newport, on Lake Memphremagog**

**Bailey's Country Store**

sprawl the cold, deep lakes named Willoughby, Seymour, and Crystal, along with the southern reaches of great Memphremagog, a lake that extends between steep, verdant shores for nearly 25 miles into Quebec.

The early 19th-century industrial railroad town of **St. Johnsbury** is the southern gateway to the kingdom. St. "J" is an old company town; its eclectic **Fairbanks Museum and Planetarium** and the sumptuous Victorian art gallery at the **St. Johnsbury Athenaeum** were donated by members of the local Fairbanks family. But urban pleasures—even antiquarian ones—are not what this corner of the Green Mountain State is mostly about. A few miles north in **East Burke,** all of the pieces of idealized rural Vermont, late 20th-century style, come together: a challenging, small ski area, **Burke Mountain,** with a summer auto road to the top; cozy inns; and Bailey's Country Store, typical of those latter-day Yankee emporia where you can buy down-home cheddar and a good Bordeaux.

Many Vermonters consider Lake Willoughby the most beautiful body of water in the state, Champlain not excepted. Drive north over a crest on Vt. 5A and there it lies, azure and fjordlike beneath the rugged sentinel brows of Mounts Pisgah and Hor. Lake Willoughby and its shoreline village of Westmore are a rare example of a resort where a lot more was going on a hundred years ago; back then there were even Swiss-style lake steamers, while today a dozen motorboats on a sunny Saturday are what locals call a crowd on this 5-mile-long, 300-foot-deep mountain jewel.

"Look out my back window here—I should put up a scenic vista sign," says the proprietor of the Morgan Country Store, on the north shore of Seymour Lake. So she could. From the hilltop where the rambling general store-cum-post office stands, Seymour stretches 2 miles in one direction, then 3 in another, and a visitor might wonder if the townspeople of Morgan can possibly grow used to so grand a panorama when they come to pick up their mail. Some, of course, pay the lake very close attention: Like Willoughby just to the south (via the wonderfully scenic Vt. 5A), Seymour grows some gargantuan lake trout and landlocked salmon. Above the postmaster's window hangs a painting of a local angler holding a 44-inch, 25-pound laker yielded by Seymour in 1956.

**Newport** is the capital of Vermont's "north coast" on Lake Memphremagog. A compact little city, it has built a striking new marina at the southern tip of the vast lake that straddles an international border. There's a decidedly French flavor to the Newport dock; in summer, many of the sleek sailboats that tie up here are crewed by Quebecers down for a day's outing. Boat liveries make it possible to return the visit (with a stop at shoreside customs)—and the cruise boat *Newport's Princess* offers regular lake tours.

South of Newport, the north shore of **Crystal Lake State Park** sets the standard for freshwater beaches. It's common here to drop into a chair, unfold the Sunday paper—and then forget the news in favor of the view of green hilltops reflected in the waters of a most aptly named lake.

*—William and Kay Scheller*

# Travel Notes

### Directions
Bounded by St. Johnsbury in the south, the Northeast Kingdom extends through mountains and lakes to the Canadian border. **By car:** The area is accessible from St. Johnsbury via I-91. **By air:** The closest major airport is in Burlington, roughly 75 miles west.

### General Information
Summer and fall are the best times to visit the region. For a free copy of the annual "Vermont Traveler's Guidebook," contact the Vermont Chamber of Commerce *(P.O. Box 37, Montpelier 05601. 800-VERMONT).* Information is also available from the Northeast Kingdom Travel and Tourism Association *(P.O. Box 355, Island Pond 05846. 802-723-9800 or 888-884-8001)*; and the Northeast Kingdom Chamber of Commerce *(30 Western Ave., St. Johnsbury 05819. 802-748-3678 or 800-639-6379).*

### Things to See and Do
**1. St. Johnsbury** *(Chamber of Commerce 802-748-3678)* At the **Fairbanks Museum and Planetarium** *(Main and Prospect Sts.*

**Farmland, Lake Memphremagog**

*802-748-2372. Adm. fee)* visitors will find natural history exhibits, ethnographic displays, and a public planetarium, all in a handsome Victorian building. Nearby is the town's 1871 library, the **St. Johnsbury Athenaeum** *(30 Main St.. 802-748-8291. Closed Sun.),* which houses a fine collection of 19th-century paintings.
**2. East Burke** The steep, **Burke Mountain Summit Road** *(Burke Mountain*

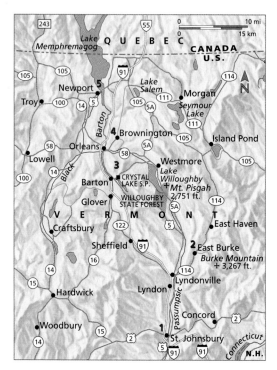

## Other Activities

**Boat rentals** On Lake Memphremagog: Newport Marine Services *(US 5, Newport. 802-334-5911)*. On Lake Willoughby: Bill & Billie's Lodge *(Vt. 5A, Westmore. 802-525-6660)*. On Seymour Lake: Seymour Lake Lodge *(Vt. 111, S of Morgan. 802-895-2752)*. On Crystal Lake: Anglin' Inn B&B *(US 5, S of Barton. 802-525-3904)*.

## Hiking

**Hiking** The Willoughby State Forest South Trail *(St. Johnsbury District Office 802-748-8787)* begins on Vt. 5A near the southern shore of Lake Willoughby, and ascends 1.7 miles to the 2,751-foot summit of Mount Pisgah. Here are spectacular views of the lake below, as well as of Mount Hor, distant Lake Memphremagog, and the mountains of Vermont and Quebec. The nearby North Trail takes a somewhat longer route to the summit and connects with the South Trail.

## Annual Events

**July** Strawberry Festival *(East Burke. 802-748-3678 or 800-639-6379)*

**August** Caledonia County Fair *(Lyndonville. 802-626-5917)*; Orleans County Fair *(Barton. 802-525-3555)*

**September** Festival of Traditional Crafts *(St. Johnsbury. 802-748-2372)*

## Lodging

**Old Cutter Inn** *(Mountain Rd., East Burke. 802-626-5152)* Nestled against Burke Mountain and its ski slopes, this snug inn features the splendid cuisine of its Swiss owner-chef and a heated outdoor pool.

**Wildflower Inn** *(Darling Hill Rd., Lyndonville. 802-626-8310)* Rooms in a restored farmhouse and other structures include a suite with hot tub and kitchenette. Several units have mountain views. Pool, tennis, cross-country skiing and mountain bike trails, and dining.

**Willough Vale Inn** *(Vt. 5A, Westmore. 802-525-4123 or 800-594-9102)* This handsome lodge with a big wraparound porch overlooks Lake Willoughby; inn rooms and lakefront cottages available.

Resort, off Vt. 114) winds to the top of Burke Mountain (used by skiers in winter). The summit affords the Northeast Kingdom's finest panoramic vistas.

**3. Crystal Lake State Park** *(Vt. 16, E of Barton. 802-525-6205. Mem. Day–Labor Day; adm. fee)* One of Vermont's most idyllic swimming and picnicking sites, this park features vistas of the entire lake framed by surrounding mountains.

**4. Brownington** Twenty rooms of the 1836 **Old Stone House Museum** *(28 Old Stone House Rd. 802-754-2022. July-Aug. daily, mid-May–June and Aug.–mid-Oct. Fri.-Tues.; adm. fee)* showcase the collections of the Orleans County Historical Society. Made of granite, the structure once served as a schoolhouse. Views from a nearby park are wonderful.

**5. Newport** Board the reproduction of the stern-wheeler *Newport's Princess* at **Lake Memphremagog Cruises** *(City Dock. 802-334-6617. Mem. Day–mid-Oct.; fare)*. Participants explore the big lake Vermont shares with Quebec; there are brunch, dinner, and sightseeing cruises.

## MASSACHUSETTS

# Berkshire Fringes

In summer the popular towns of the western Berkshires hum with
visitors lured by the Tanglewood Music Festival, the charms of
postcard-pretty Stockbridge, and the mansion-lined streets of staid
Lenox. But along the eastern fringe of these tourist magnets lies a
quiet landscape of enduring beauty, where lush hills and sweeping
river valleys cradle old towns steeped in Yankee forthrightness.

The allure of the Berkshires has drawn people to this area for centuries—
since the Mahican Indians discovered the fine hunting and fishing grounds
around what is now Stockbridge and Great Barrington. Later, pioneers
from the Massachusetts Bay Colony established farming and trading

**Winding country lane, southern Berkshires**

**Jacob's Pillow Dance Festival, Becket**

communities in Sheffield and Stockbridge during the 1730s. Clashes between the Native Americans and European newcomers were common—until matters were settled in favor of the British colonists after the French and Indian War ended in 1763.

In the early 1800s, as native son William Cullen Bryant (see sidebar p. 37) began extolling the beauty of the Berkshires in his poetry, the region was fast losing its bucolic, agrarian character and becoming industrialized. In the 19th century, its thick forests were felled to provide fuel and its rivers dammed for industry. By the end of the century, though, these local industries were eclipsed by better operations elsewhere, and whole villages were abandoned. Still, the Berkshires' appeal never died, and its slow-paced summer resorts began attracting artists and literary figures.

Avant-garde art found its way to this quiet corner in the 1930s, when Ted Shawn began the annual summer **Jacob's Pillow Dance Festival** in **Becket**. Shawn's male dance troupe introduced a bold, muscular style of dance that celebrated images such as toiling sharecroppers and union machinists. Now the oldest dance festival in the nation, it showcases a variety of traditional and contemporary dance including ballet and jazz.

To the south awaits Otis Reservoir, which is edged by a host of smaller lakes and draws summer residents to its idyllic setting. In the 18th century, this area had a few small industries, but was dominated by farms. This quiet character survives in the lovely communities of Otis and East Otis, with their friendly general stores and nostalgic Main Streets. Stroll though them and admire the locally sewn quilts, sample the ice cream, or swap fishing tales with the locals.

Nearby **Chester**, a former mining town clustered along the Westfield River, is notable for its celebrated **Miniature Theatre**. Named for its minimalist sets and small casts, the theater launches a full-scale summer season every year. From Chester, the Skyline Trail leads to the hill town of **Middlefield.** A lovely grouping of white clapboard houses propped atop a ridge surrounded by forest, river, and rock, the village has glorious views west across the rolling Berkshires to 3,491-foot Mount Greylock, the state's highest peak.

Water-powered mills and farming were the lifeblood of the communities that existed in this region in the 18th and 19th centuries. To the north, in **Dalton,** Zenus Crane harnessed the power of the Housatonic River to manufacture paper. Founded in 1801, Crane & Company continues to make fine rag papers and has supplied the federal government with all of its currency paper since first winning the contract in 1879. Crane's Old Stone Mill houses the **Crane Museum of Papermaking,** which is devoted to the history of American papermaking since the Revolution, including exhibits on the paper collar fad of the 1860s.

With its well-watered valleys, sprucedraped mountains, and spring bloom of violet and columbine, the Berkshire landscape inspired William Cullen Bryant to write his greatest poetry. He penned his first major poem, "Thanatopsis," when he was still a teenager, composing it in the upstairs bedroom of the family's clapboard, Dutch-style home, now the **William Cullen Bryant Homestead.** The 21-room house still stands at the end of a maple-lined drive west of Cummington, its rooms filled with family belongings.

About 8 miles south of here, the Westfield River runs through the **Chesterfield Gorge,** a 30-foot-deep cleft cut by glaciers in the last ice age. Its hemlock-darkened rim makes a fine picnic spot, with views of the remains of a 1770s stone bridge.

At the eastern end of Mass. 143, the elegant town of Williamsburg once whirred with all manner of water-powered industries—cotton, woolen goods, shoes, and ironware. In 1874 the factories were destroyed when a dam above town broke. The flooding killed 138 people, and in its aftermath the town lapsed into the somnolence that still characterizes it today.

From here north to the Vermont border the roads are relatively untraveled, weaving through small towns such as Buckland, where local matron Mary Lyon ran a private girl's school in the brick federal-style **Major Joseph Griswold House.** Visitors can view the third-floor schoolroom, where the students' benches are built into the wall. Lyon went on to found Mount Holyoke College in South Hadley in 1837.

---

**Native Son**

Born in Cummington, William Cullen Bryant spent an idyllic boyhood in the Berkshires. He pushed his versifying into the background and practiced law as a young man. But words remained dear to his heart, and from 1829 into the 1870s he served as editor of the *New York Evening Post.* He used his professional position as a platform to spread his liberal ideas, particularly those on antislavery. He frequently returned to his beloved Berkshire streams and hills and, after buying back his parent's home, spent his last years here.

Slicing through Massachusetts, the Connecticut River forms the eastern border of this hidden corner. Nestled in this peaceful region known as the Pioneer Valley, **Deerfield** is famous for a massacre that occurred on a frigid February night in 1704. In a surprise Indian attack led by the French, 49 townspeople were killed, 111 taken captive, and the town buildings left for kindling. The tomahawk-slashed doorway of the Sheldon Homestead is one of the items on view at the **Memorial Hall Museum.** Carefully preserving its colonial heritage, the town is also home to 14 period museums dedicated to furniture, decorative arts, silver, and other crafts.

Today, Deerfield's Main Street is a quiet haven edged by dozens of colonial and federal houses and the playing fields of the Deerfield Academy prep school, founded in 1797. Thankfully, the town shows no trace of the industry that once blighted the surrounding areas. Though this town, and the other villages scattered in this sleepy nook of the Berkshires, may be slighted by the crowds—the verdant hills, thick forests, and fresh air willingly embrace it. —*Marilyn Wood*

# Travel Notes

## Directions

The Berkshire Fringes are located between the Connecticut and the Housatonic Rivers in western Massachusetts. **By car:** The region can be accessed from either the Massachusetts Turnpike (I-90) via the Lee exit, or from I-91 via Mass. 9. **By plane:** The closest airport is in Hartford, Connecticut. **By train:** Amtrak offers service to Springfield.

## General Information

The best time to visit is spring through fall, but winter is enjoyed by skiers. For more information, contact the Berkshire Visitors Bureau *(Berkshire Common, Plaza Level, Pittsfield 01201. 413-443-9186 or 800-237-5747).*

## Things to See and Do

**1. Becket** Exhibits of works by Berkshire artists are displayed in the **Becket Arts Center of the Hill Towns** *(Mass. 8 and Brooker Hill Rd. 413-623-6635. Mid-June–mid-Sept.; donation),* housed in an 1850s Greek Revival building. The best in national and international dance and performance art arrives every summer at **Jacob's Pillow Dance Festival** *(George Carter Rd., off US 20. 413-243-0745. Late June–Aug.; fee).*

**Deerfield snowfall**

**2. Chester** The **Miniature Theatre of Chester** *(Town Hall, Middlefield St. and US 20. 413-354-7770. July–Labor Day)* presents four plays per summer featuring national and international professional actors.

**3. Middlefield** Dramatic bronze figurative sculptures by Andrew DeVries are on view at the **Andrew DeVries River Studio** *(36 E. River Rd. 413-238-7755. July–Sept., and by appt.).* Call ahead if you want to see a casting.

**4. Dalton** Housed in an 1844 mill on the Housatonic River, the **Crane Museum of Papermaking** *(Jct. of Mass. 8 and Mass. 9. 413-684-2600. June–mid-Oct. Mon.-Fri.)* tells the history of fine papermaking through samples and exhibits. Six-hundred-plus acres for hiking, fishing, and picnicking await nearby at **Wahconah Falls State Park** *(Mass. 9, E of Dalton. 413-442-8992).*

**5. William Cullen Bryant Homestead** *(Bryant Rd., off Mass. 112, Cummington. 413-634-2244. Late June–Labor Day Fri.-Sun., Labor Day–Columbus Day Sat.-Sun.; adm. fee)* The boyhood home of the poet and, later, his summer retreat, retains its original 195-acre setting. See 21 rooms with furnishings.

**6. Chesterfield Gorge** *(River Rd. W, off Mass. 143. 413-684-0148. Adm. fee)* A deep granite chasm with potholes cut by the Westfield River and glaciers, this site makes a fine picnic spot among the hemlock and pine stands atop the gorge.

**7. Deerfield** Fourteen museum houses dating from 1720 to 1850 portray social and architectural history at **Historic Deerfield** *(Main St. 413-774-5581. Adm. fee).* Highlights include museum-quality textile and silver

displays in two of the houses. Exhibits at the **Memorial Hall Museum** *(8 Memorial St. 413-774-7476. May-Oct.; adm. fee)* focuses on the Puritan and Native American heritage of the Pocumtuck Valley. Displays include local artifacts and photographs by Francis and Mary Allen.

**8. Shelburne Falls** Cross this town's old trolley bridge, decorated from early spring to late fall in flowers, and look down into the Deerfield River to see the mysterious glacial potholes. In the nearby town of Buckland, the **Major Joseph Griswold House** *(Old Upper St., off Mass. 112. 413-625-2031. July-Aug. by appt.)* contains the classroom where Mary Lyon, founder of Mount Holyoke College, once taught.

### Other Activities
**Cross-country skiing** Canterbury Farm *(1986 Fred Snow Rd., Becket. 413-623-0100)* has trails, instruction, and ski rentals, plus a 1780 farmhouse for lodging. Notchview Reservation *(Mass. 9, Windsor. 413-684-0148)* is state land that offers ski trails.
**Downhill skiing** Skiers can go to Berkshire East *(Mass. 2, Charlemont. 413-339-6617)* and Otis Ridge *(Mass. 23, Otis. 413-269-4444).*
**Hiking** The Appalachian National Scenic Trail *(Appalachian Mountain Club 617-523-0636)* cuts through the area.

### Lodging
**Deerfield Inn** *(81 Old Main St., Deerfield. 413-774-5587 or 800-926-3865)* The inn offers 23 rooms furnished with antique reproductions and a fine restaurant.

# Cuttyhunk Island

Westernmost of the Elizabeth Islands, Cuttyhunk lies lazily in Buzzards Bay, unaffected by the hubbub going on at its chic next-door neighbor—Martha's Vineyard—or back on the southern Massachusetts mainland, just 14 miles away. Vacation homes, old and new, terrace its low slopes, giving it the look of a Mediterranean hill town. In summer the population swells from the year-round average of 30 hardy souls to an impressive 300 or so urban escapees. Any time of year, though, you can find yourself an isolated, rock-ribbed beach here, sit back in the sun, and forget that there is a world beyond this small bit of New England.

A piece of rock and sand only two-and-a-half miles long and three-quarters of a mile wide, Cuttyhunk is, as one observer aptly described, "an experience entirely surrounded by water." The process of getting out to that seabound dot of land is part of the appeal. The island's lifeline to the mainland has long been the small, no-frills passenger ferry, *Alert II*. Folks showing up at the New Bedford city pier to catch it come last on the list of critical items—after all the boxes and bags of island-bound supplies are

**On Cuttyhunk Island**

loaded. Sometimes the passenger cargo is more canine than human, making the one-hour trip out through Buzzards Bay that much more interesting. As the *Alert II* trundles south, the island slowly emerges out of the sea, and the repeat passengers aboard the ferry seem relieved to find it still there.

As the ferry chugs up to the town dock, a bevy of golf carts, the locals' favorite mode of transportation on the island, gathers round. If you're a day visitor, walking will be your sole choice for getting around. But Cutty-hunk's village, beaches, and sumac-covered hills require no marathon undertaking. You can walk them all in a couple of hours. And pockets of unexpected pleasure make the going easy.

From the dock a single road winds up into the village, passing the modest houses of longtime islanders, their new-washed clothes hung out to dry in the sea breezes. Here and there windows sport signs advertising "island crafts," and people toting grocery bags smile as they pass, carrying their day's supplies back from the only serious shopping spot in town, the General Store. Occupying the downstairs of an old clapboard house, the store keeps its own finicky hours, especially in the off-season, but it carries everything from milk to yellow rain slickers.

Down along the Shore Road that slides around the island's southeast side, the rustic Cuttyhunk Fishing Club was founded by prominent New Yorkers after the Civil War. Overlooking Vineyard Sound, it's been recently converted into a B&B.

As the Shore Road passes a tidy cemetery, a path leads off to the windswept cliffs into the island's natural preserves. The only sounds here are the purring of wind through sumac and bayberry and waves racing across the rocky beach below. Meandering footpaths lead through wildflower-strewn hills rising to the island's high point, **Lookout Hill**, where views and a clearing encourage a picnic. From here, the view east takes in the sun-spangled waters of Vineyard Sound and the cliffs of Gay Head poking up from Martha's Vineyard, 7 miles away. Legend has it that in the great days of whaling, wily island men made a good living off this high point. They would keep an eye out for sailing ships headed for New Bedford harbor, then sail out to meet them and pilot them safely into port.

Paths wind down off the hilltop to the island's southern tip, where the Cuttyhunk Lighthouse warns of shallows. This deserted end of the island

### Early Englishmen

Bartholomew Gosnold and his men were only one of several aspiring bands of Englishmen who tried to plant colonies in the New World in the late 16th and early 17th centuries. In 1585-86, Sir Walter Raleigh's doomed Lost Colony took root in what is now North Carolina, but its inhabitants mysteriously disappeared. In 1607 two other bands of hopeful Englishmen arrived at Jamestown. And in what is now Maine, George Popham and his followers settled on the mouth of the Kennebec River but gave up after only one freezing New England winter and returned to the comforts of England.

**Hanging out in a local ice-cream parlor**

actually holds a lot of history. In 1924 the *Wanderer,* the last whaling ship to leave New Bedford, went down nearby in a gale. Rising on an island in the middle of West End Pond stands a stone obelisk, the **Gosnold Monument,** dedicated in 1903 to "Bartholomew Gosnold and his companions, who landed here May 25th, 1602, old style, and built a fort and storehouse, the first English habitation built on this continent." That statement may take a few liberties with history, but Gosnold (see sidebar p. 41) and his small band of Englishmen did explore the area and choose Cuttyhunk as a likely spot for a colony. Though their attempt at colonization lasted less than a month, it marked the historic high point in Cuttyhunk history.

At the island's opposite end, a narrow isthmus leads over to Copicut Neck, and at the south end of the isthmus, summer beachgoers congregate at popular **Church's Beach.** Another popular meeting spot is the small marina at the edge of the village, particularly in late afternoon when a few fishing and lobstering boats dock alongside with their day's catch. The charter boats with

fishermen are heading back about then, too, the sportsmen red faced and happy from a day in the sun. Private pleasure boats, their sails down, also putter into these protected waters for the night, though Cuttyhunk has few facilities—basically just the general store, one restaurant, and a couple of ice-cream and souvenir shops. But that may be what makes it that rarest of East Coast finds, a true hidden corner.

**Cuttyhunk weathervane**

—*K.M. Kostyal*

# Travel Notes

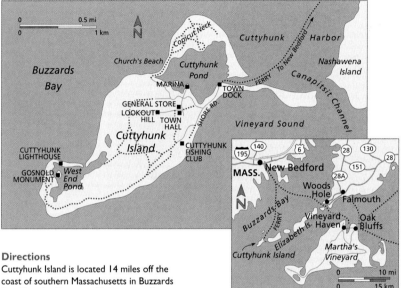

## Directions

Cuttyhunk Island is located 14 miles off the coast of southern Massachusetts in Buzzards Bay. The island is accessible by private boat and sea plane, and by public ferry from New Bedford. **Ferry schedule:** The *Alert II* departs Fisherman's Wharf, Pier 3, New Bedford, every morning and returns in late afternoon from mid-May to mid-October; call the New Bedford Office of Tourism *(see below)* for winter schedules and exact times of departures. Reservations and pre-payment strongly recommended. **By car:** New Bedford is off I-195, about 50 miles from Boston and 35 miles from Providence, R.I. Follow exits for the historic area. The ferry dock is located on Pier 3, behind the city's Waterfront Visitor Center *(Mass. 18)*. **By plane:** Major airports are located in Boston and Providence.

## General Information

Spring through fall are the best seasons to visit. Most accommodations on the island are by the week or month. Though the island has no Visitor Center, visitors can contact the New Bedford Office of Tourism *(Wharfinger Building, Pier 3, New Bedford 02740. 509-979-1745 or 800-508-5353)* for information. Since there are very few phones on the island, it's a good idea to bring a cellular phone.

## Things to See and Do

The entire "town" is only about two blocks long. Just up from the dock, the **Historical Society Museum** *(Mem. Day–Labor Day Tues. and Fri.-Sun.)* features exhibits on island history. Several paths lead to Cuttyhunk's high point, **Lookout Hill,** with wonderful views in all directions. At West End Pond, the **Gosnold Monument** memorializes the first Europeans to land here. **Church's Beach,** north of town, offers protected surf for swimming.

## Other Activities

**Fishing charters** Available from several local sea captains; inquire at the dock, or call the New Bedford Office of Tourism *(800-508-5353)*. **Guided cruise and hike** Departing Woods Hole, Mass., Massachusetts Audubon Society Tours *(Call 508-563-6390 for tour dates. July-Sept.; fare)* offers a day-long cruise through the Elizabeth Islands to Cuttyhunk, with a guided nature hike of the island.

## Lodging

**Cuttyhunk Bed & Breakfast Inn** *(508-993-6490)* The Lombard family runs this casual, comfortable inn located in the village.

# RHODE ISLAND

# South County

Lake pocked and ocean washed, southern Rhode Island stays low to the earth—a flat, intimate landscape that begs exploration and attracts its own colony of artists. You can catch glimpses of history out of the corner of your eye here—shades of Native Americans and colonial celebrities, such as Roger Williams and portraitist Gilbert Stuart. But the present fills most scenes with vitality, what with busy beaches, popular inns, quaint villages, and the hallowed halls of the University of Rhode Island.

## Roger Williams

Initially a Puritan theologian, Roger Williams quickly ran afoul of the Massachusetts Puritan fathers in the early 1600s by claiming that the "forced worship" they insisted upon "stinks in God's nostrils." He also argued that Native Americans should be compensated for their seized lands. After being forced out of Massachusetts in 1636, he and his followers eventually established a settlement they called Providence. Later it became a colony, Rhode Island—a haven for people of all faiths.

Wedged between neighboring Connecticut and the Atlantic, this southern square of Rhode Island is far quieter than the environs of capital city Providence to the north or the state's famous mansion town, Newport, across the waters of Narragansett Bay to the east. As the bay sweeps up the coastline here, it breaches the land, filigreeing the area with marshes, creeks, and narrow rivers. The wetlands give way to state park beaches in the south end, as the bay broadens to meet Rhode Island Sound.

The first white man to recognize the quiet appeal of this coastal landscape was none other than Roger Williams (see sidebar this page), founder of the colony. Warned that he was about to be banished by the Massachusetts Puritans for his blasphemous views, he fled south in 1636 to the lands around Narragansett Bay. In 1637 he established a trading post here, bartering with the Narragansett Indians for beaver furs. He later sold his trading post lands to partner Richard Smith, and today the restored **Smith's Castle** stands on the site, overlooking a lovely stretch of Wickford Harbor. Once a New England saltbox-style clapboard, its style has gone through permutations, but the earliest portions took shape in 1678. That was a couple of years after the Great Swamp Fight wreaked havoc across the area.

The fighting began in 1675, when about a thousand colonial troops gathered on Smith's lands and readied themselves to do battle against the local Indians. Seeing trouble coming, the Indians had taken shelter in the Great

**Enjoying the surf, Narragansett Beach**

Swamp, about a dozen miles to the southwest. In a pitched assault, the colonists massacred them. The swamp, now a marshy woodland, shows no signs of the battle, save a few present-day historical markers. The colonists themselves suffered about 200 casualties, of whom 40 were buried in a mass grave at the edge of Smith's Castle.

A couple of miles away, the lovely village of **Wickford** wraps itself around a small, reedy harbor. Incorporated in 1674, it's now an upscale mecca, with stylish boutiques and alfresco restaurants that attract weekend browsers. The venerable 1707 **Old Narragansett Church** claims the distinction of being the oldest Episcopal Church north of the Mason-Dixon Line.

The atmosphere changes dramatically down the coast in the town of **Narragansett,** once a fashionable Victorian watering hole and now a brawny, condominium-framed beach resort. A few mementos of the elegant past have survived, however: the long, strollable Narragansett Pier and the twin stone Towers, once part of a renowned casino designed by McKim, Mead & White and now a museum to that era. On the edge of town, the 174-acre Canonchet Farm

**Point Judith Lighthouse**

surrounds the **South County Museum,** where a re-created general store, country kitchen, blacksmith shop, and other nostalgic reproductions also recall the past.

As the southern coast opens up onto Rhode Island Sound, its sandy verge

**Fishing fleet, Galilee**

is protected by one state beach after another. At the biggest of these, Scarborough State Beach, you may have to squeeze your blanket in among the weekend crowds, but the breezes and cool ocean waters make it all worthwhile.

Rhode Island's southeastern corner is anchored by the Point Judith Lighthouse. A beacon has stood here since 1810, warning mariners away from the rocky coast. The current sturdy octagonal obelisk, built in the mid-19th century, tops a grassy knoll and is flanked by more recent U.S. Coast Guard buildings. The point has its own quiet charm and long wistful views out to sea. The nearby town of Galilee, with its modest houses and simple seaside flavor, bustles with fishermen and lobstermen and those who come to go charter fishing, eat fresh seafood, or catch the ferry over to Block Island.

Block Island Sound sprawls along the southwestern corner of the state, fronted by the long sandy barrier beaches of Charlestown. On the inland side of the beaches, a series of ponds fill with birdlife during the annual spring and fall migrations down the Atlantic flyway.

Any time of year the area's biggest inland sprawl of water, Worden Pond, makes a serene sunset spot, its shoreline broody with forests and its setting miles from the incessant beat of onshore winds.

It's not a long leap from the pond to the 1,200-acre main campus of the University of Rhode Island. Since 1894, this state institution has been churning out graduates, and its venerable ivy-covered buildings, now joined by more modern facilities, attest to its longevity. It's a good place to learn, as the quiet environs of **Kingston** offer few distractions, save a scattering of fine old roadside inns and historic buildings.

Perhaps the most historic of all the region's buildings is the lovely **Gilbert Stuart Museum**, birthplace of the esteemed colonial American portraitist. At Stuart's birth in 1755, his father was operating a snuff mill here. The small gambrel-roofed building that served as home, and, on its lower level, as mill, still stands beside picturesque Mattatuxet Brook. Stuart's father struggled here financially, finally giving up and moving the family to Newport. As a boy, Gilbert's artistic talent had been apparent, and, while still in his teens, he left to study under the master painters of London. In his long life (1755-1828), he portrayed presidents, statesmen, and military leaders. Reproductions of many of his works now hang on the walls of his simple birthplace.

Aside from celebrating Stuart's early years and accomplishments, the site also sponsors a serious conservation effort to encourage the return of native herring to its stream and pond. In April, when the spring run is on, the fish ladder constructed in the old millrace glistens with silvery herring.

The town of Westerly glistens, too, with stately Victorian houses and a lively and growing arts community. Painters, actors, and musicians flock to the town, particularly in summer, when all kinds of concert and theater series are ongoing. The area's setting is certainly inspiring, from the fountained gardens of Wilcox Park to the white sand beaches and Victorian cottage mansions of nearby Watch Hill. With nostalgia floating in the air, you can get yourself an ice-cream cone, stroll along Little Narragansett Bay, and enjoy the lost art of living gently.                          —*K.M. Kostyal*

# Travel Notes

### Directions
Flanked by eastern Connecticut and Narragansett Bay, this area lies just south of Providence. **By car:** I-95 slices along the western edge of the area, with several exits accessing the area. **By plane:** The closest major airport is located in Providence. **By train:** Amtrak make stops in Westerly and Kingston.

### General Information
Spring and fall are the best times for bird-watching in the area's wetlands, while area beaches make great summer getaways. There are also many summer concert and performing arts series. For general information on the region, contact the South County Tourism Council *(4808 Tower Hill Rd., Wakefield 02879. 401-789-4422 or 800-548-4662).*

**Wickford doorway**

### Things to See and Do
**1. Smith's Castle** *(55 Richard Smith Dr., off US 1, N of Wickford. 401-294-3521. June-Aug. Thurs.-Mon., May and Sept. Fri.-Sun., and by appt.; adm. fee)* Roger Williams established a trading post on this site in 1637; portions of the current structure date from 1678, when Richard Smith, Jr., owned the land. Guided tours interpret 350 years of Rhode Island history.
**2. Wickford** Built in 1707, the **Old**

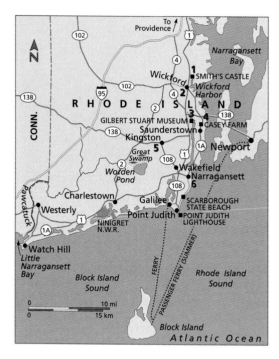

## Other Activities

**Beaches** The area has more than a dozen public beaches; consult the Division of Parks and Recreation (401-222-2632) for openings and fees. Beaches officially open the third week of June, but some open in May.

**Boat tours** Harbor Tours takes passengers for a cruise on the *Southland (departs State Pier, Galilee. 401-783-2954. Fare).*

**Charter fishing** For charter boat operators, call the South County Tourism Council (401-789-4422 or 800-548-4662).

**Concerts** Contact the University of Rhode Island (Fine Arts Center, URI, Kingston. 401-874-2431) for concert information. For Westerly concert and performing arts offerings call Greater Westerly Chamber of Commerce (401-596-7761 or 800-SEA-7636).

**Kayaking and canoeing** For rentals, call Kayak Centre in Wickford (401-295-8190 or 800-SEA-KAYAK).

### Annual Events

**May** Virtu: Westerly Arts Festival (Westerly. 401-596-7761 or 800-SEA-7636)

**June** Narragansett Art Festival (Narragansett. 401-789-7713); Swamp Yankee Days (Charleston. 401-539-0120)

**July** South County Hot Air Balloon Festival (Kingston. 401-789-7713); Wickford Art Festival (Wickford. 401-294-6840); South County Heritage Seafood Festival (Wakefield. 401-783-2801)

**October** Harvest Festival and Apple Pie Contest (Narragansett. 401-783-5400)

**December** Festival of Lights (Wickford and Wakefield. 401-789-4422 or 800-548-4662)

### Lodging

**John Updike House** (19 Pleasant St., Wickford. 401-294-4905) This lovely Georgian house, named for its original 18th-century owner, overlooks its own private beach on Wickford Harbor.

**King's Rose** (1747 Mooresfield Rd., Kingston. 401-783-5222 or 888-230-ROSE) This gracious 1930s house offers well-appointed rooms, a lovely garden, and easy access to many South County attractions.

**Narragansett Church** (Church Lane. 401-294-4357. Open for Sunday services July-Aug.) claims to be the oldest Episcopal Church in the North.

**3. Gilbert Stuart Museum** (815 Gilbert Stuart Rd., off R.I. 1A, near Saunderstown. 401-294-3001. April-Oct. Thurs.-Mon.; adm. fee) The renowned colonial American portraitist was born here in 1755. The family cabin and a gristmill still stand beside scenic Mattatuxet Brook.

**4. Casey Farm** (R.I. 1A, near Saunderstown. 401-295-1030. Tours by appt.) This site on Narragansett Bay has functioned as a working farm since the early 1600s.

**5. Kingston** Fresh produce, seafood, jams, jellies, flowers, and crafts are available every Saturday morning at the **Kingston Farmers Market** (Off R.I. 138, at Keaney Gymnasium Parking Lot, University of Rhode Island. May-Oct. Sat.).

**6. Narragansett** (Visitor Center 401-783-7121) At the **South County Museum** (Canochet Farm, R.I. 1A. 401-783-5400. May-June Wed.-Sun., July-Aug. Wed.-Mon., Sept.-Oct. Wed.-Sun.; adm. fee), thousands of artifacts are displayed in period settings—from a Victorian bedroom to a carriage barn.

# CONNECTICUT
# Along the Housatonic

In this hilly, lake-dotted northwestern corner of Connecticut, Litchfield is the lauded colonial dame, but other equally compelling communities celebrate Yankee hardihood and its simple charms. The area's narrow backroads weave past dark lakes and fast-running rivers and into quiet villages of steepled churches and clapboard houses. Old iron mines stand deserted in the woods, and the era when pioneers wrested a living from the wilderness still wafts along rivers and through the thick northeastern forests.

The Algonquian tread these forests and fished area rivers and lakes long before European settlers arrived. Today only a remnant of the Schaghticoke tribe survive, though their legends and place names still flavor the region. Their small reservation lies along the banks of the Housatonic River, just north of Bulls Bridge, and their heritage is remembered in the stone tools, longhouse, and history exhibits displayed at the **Institute for American**

**Church in misty woods, Litchfield Hills**

**Roadside stand, near Woodbury**

**Indian Studies** in nearby **Washington.** Behind the museum an interpretive woodland trail leads to a reproduction of an Algonquian village, where visitors can duck into a smoke-filled longhouse.

The elegant village of Washington, a country retreat for urbanites since the last century, boasts a vintage green, a classic First Congregational Church (1803), and a fine inn (the Mayflower). Abolitionist and temperance advocate Frederick Gunn founded the private Gunnery School, and he is remembered at the town's **Gunn Memorial Library and Museum.** The library's exceptional ceiling mural was painted by H. Siddons Mowbray, who painted even grander murals in New York City's University Club and Pierpont Morgan Library.

During the American Revolution, this area was caught up in the New England race to industrialize, and the scars from those industries can still be seen. Near Roxbury, off Conn. 67, the **Mine Hill Preserve** lies along the banks of the Shepaug River. As you stroll past the remains of the Roxbury Furnace, you can almost hear the din and clamor here, when men worked and sweated long days to extract and smelt the rich lode of iron ore.

Never spoiled by such struggles, **Lake Waramaug** remains a quiet place to this day, lacking the cheek-by-jowl houses that line other lakes in the area. At the northern end of the lake, you can stand outside the barn at the **Hopkins Vineyard** and look out across the water to gently sloping wooded peaks on the other side—a view whose beauty changes with the seasons.

At the lake's south end, New Preston is a browsable town of antique stores, galleries, and bookshops. In summer, crowds also flock to the lovely town of **Kent** but often overlook its older northern section, known as Flanders. The prolific portrait painter George Laurence Nelson lived here in the early 20th century. Today, his Seven Hearths home, originally a fur-trading post, houses the **Kent Historical Society Museum** and displays his works.

Another famous artist, Eric Sloane, lived in nearby Warren. His passion for early American woodwork is celebrated at the **Sloane-Stanley Museum,** which preserves his collection of mauls, froes, and drawknives. Contemporary local craftsmen share Sloane's passion for working with their hands, and the shops and studios of woodworkers, potters, and glassmakers are scattered along area backroads and small towns.

As you drive through the pretty towns of Sharon, Lakeville, Salisbury, and Canaan, with their stately clapboard houses and taverns facing picturesque greens, you may find it hard to believe that Sharon and Salisbury were once called the arsenals of the Revolution. Their furnaces hissed and glowed and their ironworks turned out much of the cannon and cannonballs used by the patriots during the Revolution. Few vestiges of that early industrial era remain, save an occasional building. In **Lakeville,** the Holley Manufacturing Building survives as a reminder of the Holley Company, which from 1844 to World War II produced legendary Yankee cutlery, including pocket knives.

The thick forests that blanketed this area in the colonial period were felled to fuel that early industrialization. Today some of the forestlands have been replanted, and on dark melancholy days a brooding canopy of trees seems to envelop the winding back roads. On bright days dappled sunlight penetrates their dense foliage with a glow that seems to light the way. To experience the forests close-up, stop at Macedonia Brook State Park, which features a hiking trail along a road the Civilian Conservation Corps built during the Depression; or **Kent Falls State Park,** where hemlocks fringe the top of a 250-foot series of cascades feeding the Housatonic River.

US 7 traces the Housatonic River the length of this hidden corner. Passing through evergreen forests, it pauses at the charming town of West Cornwall, where Main Street rolls downhill across a covered bridge. The shops fronting the block-long town center harbor several surprises,

## Terry Time

In 1814 Eli Terry perfected a shelf clock that revolutionized the clock industry—just one of the industries that made Connecticut famous for its Yankee ingenuity. Made with wooden works, the "Terry" clock sported pillars and a scrolled top. Some 18,000 of these clocks were crafted in the first two years of production. By 1825 Eli's son, Eli Jr., had founded his own clock factory (the town of Terryville was named for him). The **American Clock and Watch Museum** *(100 Maple St., Bristol, 20 miles SE of Litchfield. 860-583-6070. April-Nov.; adm. fee)* preserves many of the clocks produced by the Terrys, as well as the history of Connecticut clock-making.

including Cornwall Bridge Pottery, a Shaker chairmaker, and a wonderful bakery.

Sheltered below **Haystack Mountain** northeast of West Cornwall awaits another classic small town. Norfolk has been drawing summer residents since the 1870s. Prominent businessmen attracted by the rural beauty and cool summers once served as patrons of a summer music colony. Today the town is home to the Yale Summer School of Music and Art; the musical tradition continues each summer and fall at the Norfolk Chamber Music Festival sponsored by the university. Farther to the east, an artistic tradition of a different sort has given unpretentious **Riverton** its own claim to fame. That sturdy Yankee classic, the Hitchcock chair—emblazoned with a bronze stenciling of flowers, fruits, and horns of plenty—was created here in 1826 by Lambert Hitchcock. The factory he established mass-produced chairs of such popularity that all chairs of this style became known as Hitchcock chairs. Ornate and intricately decorated examples of Hitchcock chairs hang from the walls of old Union Church, now the **Hitchcock Museum.** —*Marilyn Wood*

# Travel Notes

## Directions

Along the Housatonic is located in the northwest corner of Connecticut, about 100 miles northeast of New York City. **By car:** From I-84 take US 7/202 to New Milford or from Hartford follow US 44 west. **By plane:** The closest airport is in Hartford. **By train:** Amtrak serves Hartford.

## General Information

Although spring and fall are the best seasons here, summer and winter also offer opportunities. The best source for information is the Litchfield Hills Travel Council *(P.O. Box 968, Litchfield 06759. 860-567-4506).*

## Things to See and Do

**1. Mine Hill Preserve** *(Mine Hill Rd., off Conn. 67 in Roxbury)* Trails along the Shepaug River weave through the site of a 19th-century iron blast furnace.
**2. The Silo** *(44 Upland Rd., New Milford. 860-355-0300. Closed Mon.)* This charming gallery, cooking school, and store is located on the grounds of Hunt Hill Farm.
**3. Washington** This lovely town is home to the **Gunn Memorial Library and Museum** *(Conn. 47 and Wyckeham Rd. 860-868-7756. Thurs.-Sun.).* Housed in a 1781 building and next door to the town library,

the museum displays historic clothing and photographs, and works by artist-naturalist William Hamilton Gibson. Nearby stands the **Institute for American Indian Studies** *(38 Curtis Rd. 860-868-0518. April-Dec. daily, Jan.-March Wed.-Sun.; adm. fee),* one of the few museums that focuses on the history and culture of Native American tribes in the East.
**4. Lakeside** Stroll the sculpture garden and observe sculptor and glassmaker Larry Livolsi and decorative artist Stephanie Kafka at work at the **Lorenz Studio and Gallery** *(226 Old Litchfield Rd. 860-567-4280).*
**5. Lake Waramaug State Park** *(30 Lake Waramaug Rd. 860-868-2592. Adm. fee Mem. Day–Labor Day Sat.-Sun.)* This 95-acre park features a lakeside beach for swimming and picnicking and 77 campsites *(mid-May– Sept.; fee).* Overlooking Lake Waramaug, **Hopkins Vineyard** *(25 Hopkins Rd. 860- 868-7954. May-Dec. daily, Jan.-Feb. Fri.-Sun., March-April Wed.-Sun.)* is a small winery that produces predominantly white wine. A handsome 19th-century barn serves as a wine bar and gift shop.
**6. Kent** Among the sights in this pretty town is the **Sloane-Stanley Museum** *(US 7. 860-927-3849. Mid-May–Oct. Wed.- Sun.; adm. fee).* The collection of early American tools assembled by artist/writer Eric

**Covered bridge, West Cornwall**

Sloane speaks to earlier days when crafts-manship mattered and woodworking was a respected art form. The grounds include a reconstruction of his studio and the remains of the Kent Iron Furnace that operated here from 1826 to 1892. A collection of works by 20th-century artist George Laurence Nelson is displayed in his former home, now the **Kent Historical Society Museum** *(US 7. 860-927-3419. July-Aug. Sat.-Sun.; donation).* The house dates from 1751; furnishings range from Early American to Victorian.

**7. Kent Falls State Park** *(Off US 7, North Kent. 860-927-3238. Parking fee May-Oct. Sat.-Sun.)* A short steep trail here leads to the 250-foot series of waterfalls, which peak in spring. Nearby, **Cornwall Bridge Pottery** *(US 7, 1 mile S of Conn. 4. 860-672-6545)* offers the opportunity to watch potters at work and see what comes out of the wood-fired kiln. The pottery is sold at their store *(860-672-6545. Jan.–mid-March Wed.-Sun., mid-May–Dec. Wed.-Mon.)* on Conn. 128 in West Cornwall. Stretching over 2 miles along the Housatonic River, **Housatonic Meadows State Park** *(US 7, 1 mile N of Cornwall Bridge. 860-672-6772 or 860-927-3238)* features fly-fishing, hiking, camping, cross-country skiing, and picnicking.

**8. Sharon** A collection of furniture, tex-tiles, fashions, tools, and paintings is dis-played in the **Sharon Historical Society** *(18 Main St. 860-364-5688. Mid-June–mid-Oct. Fri.-Sun., mid-Oct.–mid-June Tues.-Fri.),* a 1775 brick colonial house.

**9. Lakeville** Guided living history tours are given at the **Holley House Museum**

and the **Salisbury Cannon Museum** *(15 Millerton Rd. 860-435-2878. Mid-June–early Sept. Wed.-Sun., Tues.-Sat. rest of year, and by appt.; adm. fee).* The 1808 Holley House incorporated a 1768 ironmaster's house. The museum focuses on local history and women's daily lives, and features portraits by folk artists Erastus Salisbury Field and Ammi Phillips.

**10. Haystack Mountain State Park** *(Conn. 272, Norfolk. 860-482-1817)* A 34-foot tower at the mountain's 1,677-foot summit affords great views of the Berkshires, Long Island Sound, and New York State.

**11. Riverton** The **Hitchcock Museum** *(1 Robertsville Rd. 860-379-4826. By appt.)* dis-plays painted furniture and shows how Hitchcock chairs were stenciled and hand-striped. The Hitchcock Company Factory

**Having fun in Kent Falls State Park**

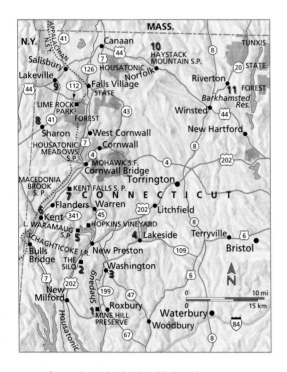

Store is housed in Lambert Hitchcock's original factory building just down the street.

## Other Activities

**Antiquing** Visitors eager to hunt for antiques should try Kent, New Preston, and Salisbury along US 7.

**Auto racing** Lime Rock Park (US 7 and Conn. 112. 860-435-5000 or 800-722-3577. Mid-March–mid-Nov.; adm. fee) is a venue for major sports car races, as well as historic and vintage car races. It's also home to the famous Skip Barber Racing and Driving School.

**Birding** The Sharon Audubon Center (Conn. 4, Sharon. 860-364-0520. Adm. fee for trails) sprawls over 750 acres with 11 miles of trails for ornithological enjoyment. There's also a small museum that features birds, turtles, and snakes and local natural history.

**Boating** You can canoe, raft, or kayak the Housatonic River. For rental and guided trip information, call Clarke Outdoors (West Cornwall. 860-672-6365).

**Fly-fishing** For instruction and guided trip information, call Housatonic Anglers (West Cornwall. 860-672-4457).

**Hiking** You can hike Mohawk or Bear Mountain and in any of several state parks. The Appalachian National Scenic Trail also cuts through the region. For information call the Connecticut Forest and Park Trail Association (860-346-2372); or the Office of State Parks (860-424-3200).

**Skiing** Downhill slopes are available at Mohawk Mountain (Cornwall. 860-672-6100 or 800-895-5222); cross-country skiing can be enjoyed around Lake Waramaug (860-868-2592) and in Macedonia Brook S.P. (860-927-3238).

## Annual Events

**Mid-June–September** Falls Village Music Mountain Chamber Concerts (Falls Village. 860-824-7126)

**Late June–August and October-November** Norfolk Chamber Music Festival (Ellen Battell Stoeckel Estate, Norfolk. 860-542-3000)

**October** Fall Festival (Salisbury. 860-435-2442)

## Lodging

**Cathedral Pines Farm** (Cornwall. 860-672-6747) This 18th-century-style farmhouse offers one room with an outdoor hot tub, llamas, and luscious gardens.

**Manor House, the Inn at Norfolk** (69 Maple Ave., Norfolk. 860-542-5690) Tiffany windows are just one of the features of this handsome 1898 mansion. Some rooms have fireplaces, balconies, and jacuzzis.

**Mayflower Inn** (Conn. 47, Washington. 860-868-9466) This lavish Relais & Châteaux lodge on 30 acres is stylishly furnished throughout with antiques and offers three dining rooms, an outdoor pool, tennis courts, and trails.

**White Hart Inn** (On the green, jct. of US 44 and Conn. 41, Salisbury. 860-435-0030) The inn's splendid wide porch overlooks the town; fine dining plus an atmospheric tap room.

# NEW YORK
# Central Adirondacks

Cold stream-fed lakes framed by bowers of spruce and cedar;
dense, verdant forests; rolling meadows blanketed in wildflowers;
placid blue water dotted with coves and islands; and Gilded Age
estates, known as Great Camps, which would defy the fantasies
of a feudal lord: All are hallmarks of the central section of
New York State's Adirondack Park.

An officially protected area, the park sprawls across one-fifth of New
York's landmass. At 6 million acres, it is larger than the entire state of Massachusetts. This forested realm has long been a mecca for latter-day voyageurs

**Lows Lake, Adirondack Park**

**Adirondack chairs, Great Camp Sagamore**

who seek to tackle a piece or all of the 90-mile **Adirondack Canoe Route**. It also draws vacationers seeking the pleasures of camping and hiking.

Eschewing the heavily trod sections of the park, the focus here is on its central region—defined by a cluster of cerulean lakes including Long, Blue Mountain, Raquette, Big Moose, Newcomb, and the Fulton Chain. The

**Beckoning canoe, Adirondack Park**

lakes remain relatively uncrowded (even on sparkling summer weekends), though this region's charms are subtler than those of the popular lake resorts to the east and north. Not surprisingly, the accommodations here tend to be a bit more rustic.

And yet the area has a long human history—it was once a rich hunting and fishing ground for the Iroquois and Algonquian. Following the American Revolution, Yankee trappers came in search of beaver, fox, and marten. By the mid-1800s, hordes of loggers were harvesting a seemingly limitless amount of timber.

Toward the 19th-century's end the region once referred to

as a "dismal wilderness" was about to be discovered yet again—this time by captains of industry who bought up swaths of pristine lakefront and constructed elaborate "camps." In 1879 railroad heir William West Durant began his refined, Swiss-style **Camp Pine Knot,** which included a rustic, yet luxurious complex of buildings, lawns, footpaths, and a deluxe houseboat. His achievement set the standard for future Adirondack Great Camps, and his use of local building materials served as a model for public buildings in the National Park Service. Another of Durant's achievements was 1,526-acre **Great Camp Sagamore,** built in 1897. This estate was later owned by the Vanderbilt family (from 1901 to 1954) and served as headquarters for the "Gaming Crowd"—including Gary Cooper and Lord Mountbatten. Today, the 27-building complex is open to the public for tours and residential programs, and takes overnight guests.

Between 1885 and 1894 the New York Legislature passed a series of laws and amendments that laid the groundwork for what is now Adirondack Park, a unique mix of public and private lands. A "Blue Line" was drawn to set its borders. Today approximately 43 percent of the land is constitutionally protected as Adirondack Forest Preserve and will be kept forever wild.

The region is a far more democratic place than it was during the time of Durant, the Vanderbilts, and other Great Camp magnificoes. Many of the estates that lined the shores of lakes such as Raquette and Blue Mountain have been chopped up into smaller parcels or converted into boys' and girls' camps, but they still serve as reminders of an age when a family's rural retreat might be measured in the tens of thousands of acres.

## Why "Adirondacks?"

The term "Adirondack Group" was first applied to the mountains of northern New York by geologist Ebenezer Emmons, who conducted a survey in the mid-1800s. The Adirondack, he claimed, were a tribe of Indians who hunted in the area. An Algonquian tribe called the Montagnais did live across the river from what is now the park. Legend has it that the Mohawk scornfully called the Montagnais Adirondack, or "bark eaters," a slur meaning they were such poor hunters they were reduced to peeling the bark off trees in winter to eat the soft layer inside.

**Raquette Lake Navigation Company**'s narrated boat cruises pass by many of the old wilderness *palazzi,* including Camp Pine Knot. Other estates you can see on the boat tour include the Collier publishing family's Bluff Point and the Carnegie family's North Point.

At Blue Mountain Lake, 23 indoor and outdoor exhibit areas at the **Adirondack Museum** focus on how people have worked and played in the Adirondacks over the years. Among the museum's prime attractions are exhibits on "Hotels, Camps, and Clubs" and "Boats and Boating in the Adirondacks 1840-1940." There's also a collection of Adirondack paintings by artists such as Thomas Cole and Winslow Homer. If you're planning to visit Great Camp Sagamore and take a ride aboard the **W.W. Durant,** ask about the Gilded Age Package at the museum's admission counter.

**Blue Mountain Lake** offers plenty of opportunity to soak up mountain views with paddle in hand. Canoeists can glide under W.W. Durant's classic 1891 bridge and among assorted islands. For more of a journey, a narrow outlet veers west, into Eagle Lake, then Utowana Lake. The western shore here was once the site of the Marion River Railroad, which connected Raquette and Blue Mountain Lakes in the 1880s. A steamboat plied summer vacationers from the train stop to the resorts of Blue Mountain Lake. The Adirondack Museum displays the original locomotive and passenger car of what was once the world's shortest railroad.

Today's visitors can still enjoy the traditional Adirondack pastimes— if not quite in robber baron style. The lakes are studded with countless coves and islands for canoeists to explore. A popular canoe route begins at **Old Forge**, at the foot of the Fulton Chain of Lakes, and follows nearly one hundred miles of waterways to the village of Saranac Lake. Another pleasant option is to paddle down the north branch of the Moose River from Rondaxe Lake to Thendara. Boats and canoe rentals are available at liveries at all of the larger lakes.

A popular pursuit here since the 1870s, hiking draws so many enthusiasts that some of the more than 2,000 miles of trails within the park have been worn down to bedrock and mud. But opportunities to get away from it all abound for anyone willing to travel farther off the main roads. New York's Department of Environmental Conservation maintains 27 miles of trails at **Moose River Recreation Area**, the largest block of remote public land in the Adirondacks readily accessible by motor vehicle.

> ### Traveling Light
>
> In her memoir, *Camp Chronicles,* Mildred Phelps Stokes Hooker lists some of the baggage her family brought by train from New York City to an Adirondack camp in the summer of 1883: 25 trunks, 13 small boxes, one boat, one carriage, 2 stoves, one crate of china, a dozen rugs, 17 cots and mattresses, 3 cases of wine, 3 horses, and 2 dogs. No, the family wasn't moving into a summer home. They were going camping, as evidenced by the fact that they also brought 8 canvas tents— one a 14-by-14-foot parlor. They decorated their tents with Japanese fans, needlepoint chairs, and curtains.

More accessible but no less interesting are the trails that begin at Newcomb's **Adirondack Park Visitor Interpretive Center**, which take in a variety of natural formations including a marsh, a glacial erratic, and a beaver dam. A dirt road nearby leads to the partially restored **Camp Santanoni** on the shore of Newcomb Lake. The nearby fire tower at the top of Goodnow Mountain takes in superb views of distant peaks.

Whether you wish to see the magnificent Great Camps, spot beaver and red fox, or hike through lush woodlands of pine, maple, and birch—it's all waiting for you in this untrammeled corner of Adirondack Park.

—*William and Kay Scheller*

# Travel Notes

### Directions

This hidden corner is situated in the central and western sections of Adirondack Park. **By car:** From Albany take I-87 (Adirondack Northway) to North Hudson, drive west on Blue Ridge Rd. to N.Y. 28 N; continue west to Newcomb. From Syracuse or Albany take New York State Thruway to Utica; drive north on N.Y. 12 and N.Y. 28 through Alder Creek to Old Forge. **By plane:** There are major airports at Albany; Burlington, Vermont; and Montreal, Canada. **By train:** Amtrak's *Adirondack* runs along the eastern Blue Line (park boundary), along Lake Champlain.

### General Information

For information, contact Adirondack Regional Tourism Council's Beekmantown Welcome Information Center (*I-87 south, bet. Chazy and Beekmantown, P.O. Box 2149, Plattsburgh 12901. 518-846-8016 or 800-487-6867*); or the Department of Environmental Conservation (*N.Y. 86, P.O. Box 296, Ray Brook 12977. 518-897-1200. Mon.-Fri.*).

### Things to See and Do

**1. Newcomb** Nature trails, multi-image presentations, and exhibits at the **Adirondack Park Visitor Interpretive Center** (*N.Y. 28 N. 518-582-2000*) focus on the Adirondacks. Down a 5-mile dirt road is the partially restored 1892 **Camp Santanoni,** accessible by foot, mountain bike, or horse-drawn carriage.

**2. Blue Mountain Lake** Superb indoor and outdoor exhibits at the **Adirondack Museum** (*N.Y. 30. 518-352-7311. Mem. Day– mid-Oct.; adm. fee*) present an overview of Adirondack life. Among the standouts is the boating exhibit, which displays one of the country's finest collections of inland pleasure craft.

**3. Raquette Lake** Passengers aboard the 60-foot double-deck cruiser *W.W. Durant* (*Raquette Lake Navigation Company 315-354-5532. Mem. Day–June and Labor Day–Oct. weekends, July-Aug. daily; fare*) receive an engaging narrated tour of the lake as they sail past Great Camps, including **Camp Pine Knot** (*Private*). Luncheon, dinner, and Sunday brunch cruises are offered, along with no-meal cruises. At **Bird's Marine** (*N.Y. 28. 315-354-4441. July–Labor Day Mon.-Sat., and by reservation; fare*), members of the Bird family recount the lake's history as they

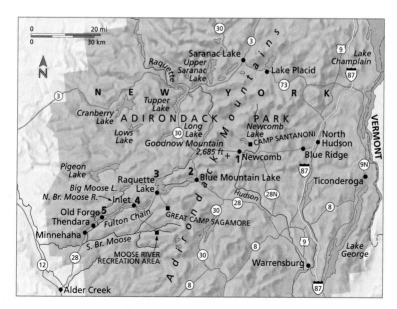

**Master weaver, Great Camp Sagamore**

deliver mail to camps dotting the shore. The boat leaves daily, except Sunday. Also in town is industrialist W.W. Durant's 1897 "rustic" retreat, **Great Camp Sagamore** *(Sagamore Rd. 315-354-5311. Late June–Labor Day daily, Labor Day–Columbus Day weekends; adm. fee)*. Overlooking a private lake, it's open for tours and residential programs, including history, watercolor, and furniture-making *(see Lodging below)*.

**4. Inlet** *(Tourist Information Center 315-357-5501)* A 500-foot boardwalk, **Ferd's Bog** *(Off Uncas Rd. 518-897-1200)* traverses a bog harboring a variety of rare flora, including white-fringed and rose pogonia orchids and pitcher plants. The bog is also home to numerous rarely seen bird species, including black back woodpeckers and olive-sided fly-catchers. The 50,000-acre **Moose River Recreation Area** *(Limekiln Rd., 2 miles S of N.Y. 28. 518-897-1200)* brims with more than 40 miles of roads, 27 miles of trails, and 140 primitive tent sites. The reserve is home to many unusual plants, birds, and butterflies.

**5. Old Forge** This tiny town is the location of the **Arts Center/Old Forge** *(N.Y. 28. 315-369-6411)*, which mounts four major exhibitions a year, including shows on quilts and American watercolors.

### Other Activities

**Boating and canoeing** For tips on renting boats call the Adirondack Regional Tourism Council *(518-846-8016 or 800-487-6867)*. Information on the Adirondack Canoe Route is also available from the council.

**Camping** The state maintains campsites along the undeveloped lakeshores, and on Raquette Lake's Hen and Chicken Islands.

Many sites are listed in the Adirondack council's "Adirondack Region Accommodations & Camping Guide." Request the brochures "Use of New York State's Public Forest Lands" and "Welcome to the Forest Preserve Public Campground" from the Dept. of Environmental Conservation *(518-897-1200)*. A permit is required to camp on state lands for more than three days.

**Fishing** A nonresident 5-day fishing license is available from local sporting good stores and the Department of Environmental Conservation *(N.Y. 86, Ray Brook. 518-897-1200. Mon.-Fri.)*. To find out where fish are biting, call the DEC's Adirondack Fishing Hotline *(518-623-3682)*.

**Hiking** The "Adirondack Great Walks & Day Hikes" brochure published by the Adirondack Regional Tourism Council *(518-846-8016 or 800-487-6867)* is an excellent resource.

**Horseback riding** Contact Adirondack Saddle Tours *(Uncas Rd. and N.Y. 28, Eagle Bay. 315-357-4499. April-Nov.)*.

**Mountain biking** Call the Old Forge Tourist Information Center *(315-369-6983)*; or the Inlet Tourist Information Center *(315-357-5501)*.

**Rafting** Rentals are available from Adirondack River Outfitters *(N.Y. 28, Old Forge. 315-369-3536 or 800-525-RAFT. April-Oct.)*.

**Train rides** The vintage coaches of the Adirondack Scenic Railroad *(N.Y. 28, Thendara. 315-369-6290. May weekends, Mem. Day–mid-June Sat.-Wed., mid-June–mid-Sept. and mid-Oct.–late Oct. daily, mid-Sept.–early Oct. Sat.-Thurs., mid-Sept.–early Oct. daily; fare)* carry passengers north toward wilderness, or south along the Moose River. On the northern route, mountain bikers can detrain and bike back to the station.

### Annual Events

**June** No Octane Regatta for Wooden Boats *(Blue Mountain Lake. 518-352-7311)*
**September** Adirondacks National Exhibition of American Watercolors *(Old Forge. 315-369-6411)*

### Lodging

**Great Camp Sagamore** *(Sagamore Rd., Raquette Lake. 315-354-5311)* Built in 1897 by W.W. Durant, this 27-building complex takes overnight guests as space permits (participants in residential programs get first option). Among the topics of the programs given here are rustic furniture-making, black-smithing, and wilderness watercolors.

# Upper Hudson River Valley

A mosaic of green and brown farmland, this parcel of Hudson River Valley embraces old Dutch farmhouses and grazing horses, bountiful roadside stands and Gilded Age estates. Narrow country roads lead to delightful little villages brimming with architectural gems that preserve the history of inventors, artists, and Presidents. Once the province of great Dutch patroonships, this magical realm was chronicled by Washington Irving in the early 1800s as: "little retired Dutch valleys...here and there embosomed in the great State of New York [where] population, manners, and custom remain fixed." Indeed, little has changed to this day.

Westchester, Putnam, Dutchess, and Columbia Counties march north from Manhattan along the Hudson River's east bank, each one less suburban than the one before, until upper Dutchess and Columbia step forward as true rural counties. Bordered by the glittering Hudson River and by Massachusetts' pastoral hills—and safely north of the auto-choked lower Hudson Valley—this quiet corner seems overlooked, lost to time. But if you

**Montgomery Place, Annandale-on-Hudson**

**Rural patchwork, Columbia County**

take the time to seek out its charms, the past will be unveiled.

Imbued with the 19th century, the riverside estate of **Montgomery Place** recalls an era when the Hudson River aristocracy emulated English gentry in their sweeping green landscapes and handsome estates. Janet Livingston Montgomery, widow of Revolutionary War hero Richard Montgomery, began building this federal-style palace in 1802; it was later transformed by architect Alexander Jackson Davis into the 23-room classical revival mansion standing today. Andrew Jackson Downing originally designed the grounds, which overlook Sawkill Falls and mirror the beauty of a Hudson River painting.

In the nearby town of **Annandale-on-Hudson**, bucolic Bard College showcases the stone Gothic Revival chapel of the Holy Innocents. Fire destroyed the first chapel soon after if was completed in 1857, and today's acoustically improved chapel, completed by 1860, hosts concerts and recitals for the Bard Music Festival, which takes place every summer.

A short distance away, the village of Tivoli presents elegant Victorian mansions in a still-extant planned community. Peter de Labigarre bought riverfront land here in the 1790s for his estate, Tivoli, which no longer stands. His vision of an "ideal" town is reflected in the street names he chose, such as Friendship, Liberty, and Peace—some of which survive today. But de Labigarre's scheme collapsed and Robert R. Livingston bought the entire town in 1807. Several generations of Livingstons rest in the graveyard behind St. Paul's Church on Wood Road. Stop and linger awhile at the antique store, the bookstore, the artist's co-op, or the DePeyster art gallery tucked in a former firehouse on Broadway.

Nearby awaits **Clermont State Historic Site,** a lavish Georgian-style mansion resting on 485 acres, with a glorious garden and views of the Hudson. One of the oldest in the region, the estate belonged to seven successive generations of Livingstons, from 1730 to 1962. Its most distinguished resident was Robert R. Livingston, chancellor of New York state from 1777-1801. He also helped draft the Declaration of Independence, aided negotiations on the Louisiana Purchase, and backed Fulton's steamboat (see sidebar this page). The interior includes a central hall containing portraits of family members.

Less patrician and much more idiosyncratic, **Olana State Historic Site** overlooks a bend in the river painted many times by Frederic Church (1826-1900), the Hudson River landscape artist and owner of this lavish residence. Inspired by his extensive travels in the Middle East, Church meticulously designed this Arabic fantasy and its lush grounds. Fanciful and whimsical, the architectural extravaganza features glazed Mexican and Persian tiles, balconies, arched windows, and a colorful bell tower.

## Not Fulton's Folly

On August 17, 1807, Fulton's folly, as Robert Fulton's steamboat *Clermont* was derisively called by some, set out from the west side of Manhattan for its maiden voyage up the Hudson to Albany. The sidewheeler slowly made its way north. "It was a monster moving up the river defying wind and tide and breathing flames and smoke," wrote one bystander. After 24 hours it arrived at Clermont, home of Robert R. Livingston, 110 miles north of the city. There it docked for the night before pressing on to Albany. In all, the one-way trip from Manhattan was clocked at a then-speedy 32 hours.

In stark contrast to this Shangri-la, the little town of **Hudson** has a gritty air. Settled in 1783 by prominent whaling families from Nantucket and New Bedford, Hudson had 25 registered schooners working in sealing, whaling, and the West Indian trade by 1790. In the mid-1800s, the little town had become the center of Columbia County, a position still held today. Historic 19th-century houses line the main street, with elegant doorways and elaborate cornices testifying to Hudson's earlier wealth. Promenade Hill Park (1795) offers magnificent river views, while expensive antiques and fine art fill store after store. On Harry Howard Avenue, the **American Museum of Firefighting** displays a fine collection of fire engines, buckets, and other memorabilia dating back to 1725.

Turning away from the river, country roads slice through grassy hills and hedge-enclosed meadows. Centuries-old houses, many in the Dutch brick gambrel style, fill the little village of **Claverack,** where it's said Alexander Hamilton tried cases at the old Court House, and Clement Moore penned "'Twas the Night Before Christmas." The Dutch patroon Van Rensselaer built the lovely, rosy-brick Reformed Dutch Church in 1767, complete with an elevated pew and canopy for his family.

One of the Dutch families who made good in this farming county were the Van Burens. Just south of Kinderhook stands Lindenwald, preserved as the **Martin Van Buren National Historic Site.** The retirement home of the eighth President of the United States, the structure was originally built in colonial style, but Van Buren's son had it embellished with gables, dormers, cornices, and an Italianate tower. Van Buren was known as the "red fox" of Kinderhook, a reference to his political wiles that took him to the White House. Born in Kinderhook, where his father ran a tavern on Hudson Street, Van Buren is buried in the Kinderhook Reformed Cemetery on Albany Avenue.

Just up the road from Lindenwald nestles the **Luykas Van Alen House,** fronted by a glassy duck pond. With its pitched roof and parapet gables, this picturesque, redbrick farmhouse is a rare survivor of 18th-century-style Dutch architecture. Inside, exposed posts and beams, wide fireplaces, delft tiles, and sturdy furniture give a feel for early Dutch farm life in the Hudson River Valley.

Before leaving this pretty corner, stop at the **Shaker Museum and Library** in Old Chatham. The Shakers established their first community in the Hudson River Valley in 1776, and from there spread as far as Kentucky and Ohio. Farming, worshiping, building furniture, and inventing such household items as the clothespin, their numbers grew to as many as 17,000 before declining. The Shaker Museum contains a fine collection of Shaker furniture and tools, as well as a blacksmith's shop, nine period rooms, and a schoolroom—all displayed simply and elegantly, a fitting conclusion to this hidden corner of the Upper Hudson River Valley. —*Marilyn Wood*

## Beyond Thomas Cole and Frederic Church

The Hudson River School was a legendary branch of 19th-century American landscape painting. Although the most famous members of this group—Thomas Cole, Frederic Church, and John Kensett—lived and painted by the Hudson River, many of the artists who were considered Hudson River artists did not. One of them was Robert S. Duncanson, an African-American painter who worked most of his life in Cincinnati. Among his most famous paintings is the *Land of the Lotus Eaters* (circa 1861), inspired by Tennyson's poem. It was exhibited in Toronto, Montreal, and London before being acquired for the Royal Collection in Stockholm, where it resides today.

# Travel Notes

### Directions
This hidden corner stretches along the east bank of the Hudson River from northern Dutchess County to northern Columbia County. **By car:** From I-87 take the Rhinecliff Bridge east to N.Y. 9G. **By plane:** The closest major airport is in Albany. **By train:** Amtrak stops in Albany.

### General Information
The best months to visit are April through October. For more information, contact Columbia County Tourism (401 State St., Hudson 12534. 518-828-3375 or 800-724-1846); or Dutchess County Tourism (3 Neptune Rd., Ste. M-17, Poughkeepsie 12601. 914-463-4000 or 800-445-3131).

### Things to See and Do
**1. Annandale-on-Hudson** Wander through the interior rooms and beautifully landscaped grounds of **Montgomery Place** (River Rd. 914-758-5461. April-Oct. Wed.-Mon., Nov.-Dec. Sat.-Sun.; adm. fee), a well-preserved riverside estate. Boasting Hudson River and Catskill Mountain views, the 434-acre estate features fruit trees, and formal herb, rose, and rock gardens.

**2. Clermont State Historic Site** (Off N.Y. 9G, N of Tivoli. 518-537-4240. April-Oct. Tues.-Sun., Oct.–mid-Dec. Sat.-Sun., grounds daily year-round; fee for tour) This white stucco, Georgian-style brick mansion (with 19th-century additions) was the family seat of the Livingstons from 1730 to 1962. Lovely gardens afford great river and mountain views.

**3. Olana State Historic Site** (Off N.Y. 9G, 3 miles S of Hudson. 518-828-0135. April-Oct. Wed.-Sun.; adm. fee. Reservations requested) This flamboyant masterpiece was designed by artist Frederic Church, with help from Calvert Vaux. The site is magnificent, the landscape moving, and the building itself a riot of colored brick, mosaic, tower and turret, designed in

Persian style. The interior is equally brilliant, with a storehouse of Church's paintings and personal collections.

**4. Hudson** (Columbia County Tourism 518-828-3375 or 800-724-1846) Here you'll find the surprising **American Museum of Firefighting** (125 Harry Howard Ave. 518-828-7695), filled with historic firefighting gear.

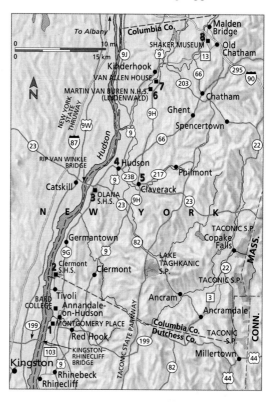

The **Robert Jenkins House** (113 Warren St. 518-828-9764. July-Aug. Sun.-Mon., and by appt.; adm. fee) showcases works by Hudson River artists Henry Ary, Bert Phillips, and Arthur and Ernest Parton, plus memorabilia on the town's interesting whaling industry.

**5. Claverack** At harvest time **Hotalings Farm Market** (N.Y. 9H. 518-851-9864) sells all kinds of apples, raspberries, cherries, pumpkins, gourds, and more.

**6. Martin Van Buren National Historic**

**Olana State Historic Site**

**Site** (N.Y. 9H, 3 miles S of Kinderhook. 518-758-9689. Mid-May–Oct. daily, Nov.–early Dec. Sat-Sun.; adm. fee) This was the home of President Martin Van Buren from 1841 to his death in 1862. French wallpaper panels display a hunting scene in the entrance hall, while political and personal memorabilia, including busts and portraits, are displayed throughout the house. Just up the road, the **Luykas Van Alen House** (N.Y. 9H, 1 mile S of Kinderhook. 518-758-9265. Mem. Day–Labor Day Thurs.-Sun., and by appt.) is a modest 1737 Dutch home that exemplifies the Dutch farmhouses in the region. It consists of two rooms and a garret under a pitched gable.

**7. Shaker Museum and Library** (88 Shaker Museum Rd., Old Chatham. 518-794-9100. Late April–early Nov. Wed.-Mon., early Nov.–mid-Dec. Sat.-Sun.; adm. fee) Eight buildings and 21 galleries display the woodworking, weaving, and basketry skills of different communities of Shakers—from New England to Ohio and Kentucky.

### Other Activities
**Ballooning** See the Hudson River Valley in all its splendor from above. Contact Balloon Meadows (N.Y. 9H, Kinderhook. 518-758-6538).
**Cross-country skiing** Skiers can log some miles at Clermont (518-537-4240) and at Olana (518-828-0135), but there are no rentals at either.
**Fruit picking** Apples, pears, plums, and berries can be picked in season. Try Philip Orchards (N.Y. 9H, Claverack. 518-851-6351); Greig Farm (Pitcher Ln., off US 9, 3 miles N of Red Hook. 914-758-1234); or Montgomery Place Orchards (Montgomery Place, River Rd., Annandale-on-Hudson. 518-758-6338).
**Summer theater** Good summer stock can be enjoyed at the MacHaydn Theater (N.Y. 203, Chatham. 518-392-9292).

### Annual Events
**May** Herb Fair and Plant Sale (Old Chatham. 518-794-9100)
**July** Winterhawk Bluegrass Festival (Ancramdale. 888-946-8495)
**August** Bard Music Festival Rediscoveries Series (Bard College, Annandale-on-Hudson. 914-758-3226)
**September** Columbia County Fair (Fairgrounds, Chatham. 518-828 3375)

### Lodging
**Beekman Arms** (US 9, Rhinebeck. 914-876-7077) This atmospheric old tavern dates from 1766 and offers colonial-style rooms. There's a fine dining room, too.
**Belvedere Mansion** (10 Old Rte. 9, Staatsburg. 914-889-8000) Seven lavishly furnished rooms filled with ormolu, silks, and lace are found in this Greek Revival mansion.

# North Fork Nuances

Jutting out far beyond the edge of New York City's urban sprawl, the North and South Forks of Long Island are like two siblings: one gentle and retiring, the other brash and flamboyant. While the South Fork offers surf-pounded Atlantic shores and a who's-who social scene, the North Fork eddies along through quieter channels, clinging to the small pleasures of windmill-laced landscapes, quiet bays and coves, and historic villages. Its rural demeanor preserves abundant traces of an earlier way of life, when fishermen worked the local waters for oysters, scallops, and clams, and farmers tilled the island's rich soil.

The town of Riverhead marks the splitting point in Long Island's personality. Here, Great Peconic Bay and smaller Flanders Bay wedge in between the island's two forks, separating them like two halves of a pincer. Sound Avenue heads toward the North Fork and away from the neon signs and strip development to the south. Buffeted by Long Island Sound on the north and a series of bays on the south, the narrow North Fork peninsula is green with sod farms, Christmas tree nurseries, orchards, summer fields of strawberries and raspberries, while fall fields are stippled pumpkin orange. At farm stands and flat-bed trucks parked along the roadsides, you can buy the season's freshest offerings.

**Shelter Island sailboats**

Among the string of small villages lining the North Fork, Mattituck and **Cutchogue** are quaint classics, with their weathered old clapboard houses and churches. In contrast, in nearby New Suffolk grand Victorian houses and a cupolaed Victorian schoolhouse line streets leading to Great Peconic Bay. At the turn of the century, the town was a center for oystering and scalloping, as well as being home to the John P. Holland Torpedo Boat Company, developers of the Navy's first modern submarine. Today, such industries are long gone and the town is a quiet place, where you can linger in a waterfront café and enjoy the views across Cutchogue Harbor and south to Robins Island.

As N.Y. 25 proceeds east on the North Fork beyond Cutchogue, you'll

**Hints of autumn, Shelter Island**

notice that this is wine country. In recent decades vintners have discovered that grapevines appreciate the sandy soil and temperate, Bordeaux-like climate of this bay-bathed spit of land. Pioneers in the local wine industry, Alex and Louisa Hargrave, planted the first vines back in 1973, and in the baronial tasting room of the **Hargrave Vineyards,** you can try their fine chardonnay and merlot.

About midway through the North Fork lies its oldest settlement. The town of **Southold** has roots that reach back to 1640, and its Old First Church on Main Street was founded that year (the current federal-style church building dates from 1803). Its adjacent burial ground, one of the oldest on the island, contains the graves of prominent men of the original settlement, including that of John Young, the first pastor.

The old whaling village of **Greenport** still has a salty flavor about it and its waterfront boasts a real seafarer's store, S.T. Preston & Son, where you can browse the marine supplies, nautical objects, and books. At the town docks a ferry shuttles back and forth to **Shelter Island**—a sleepy sprawl of 6,200 acres floating between the North and South Forks. Settled originally in the 17th century by a sugar merchant, the island later served as a refuge for persecuted Quaker leaders George Fox and Mary Dyer. A Quaker cemetery still lies beside the island's Ferry Road. Shelter Island has remained introverted—a genuine retreat with little commerce marring it, splendid sandy bays on its western side, and **Mashomack Nature Preserve** on its eastern side. You can ramble around the island by car, though its scenic terrain is perfect for cyclists.

As the North Fork funnels to its end, **Orient** clings to its tip by the thread of a causeway. From this delightful village of shingled homes, wander the marsh-lined backroads along Hallocks Bay. Then head out to **Orient Beach State Park,** where osprey glide silently down. At this finger of land wedged between marsh and ocean, the North Fork comes to its dramatic, windswept end.                    —*Marilyn Wood*

# Travel Notes

### Directions
The North Fork stretches for 30 miles at the eastern end of Long Island only 90 miles east of New York City. **By car:** Take the LIE (I-495). Continue east on N.Y. 58 to N.Y. 25. **By plane:** There are airports in New York City and Islip. **By train:** The Long Island Rail Road *(718-217-5477)* operates from Penn Station to the North Fork towns, terminating in Greenport.

### General Information
Summer and fall are the best times to visit the North Fork. Information is available from the Long Island Convention & Visitors Bureau *(350 Vanderbilt Pkwy., Suite 103, Hauppauge 11788. 516-951-3440)*; North Fork Promotion Council *(P.O. Box 1865, Southold, NY 11971. 516-298-5757)*; and the Shelter Island Chamber of Commerce *(P.O. Box 598, Shelter Island 11964. 516-749-0399)*.

### Things to See and Do
**1. Cutchogue** The gem of the buildings gracing the town green is the **Old House on the Village Green** *(N.Y. 25 at Case's Lane. 516-734-7122. July-Aug. Sat.-Mon., Mem. Day–June and Sept. Sat.-Sun.; adm. fee)*. The 1649 clapboard house with leaded casement windows was built for wealthy English merchant John Budd. The Wickham Farmhouse (c. 1740) and Old School House (c. 1840) Museum are also on the green.
**2. Southold** This historic town is home to many attractions. A collection of Native American artifacts at the **Southold Indian Museum** *(1080 Bayview Rd. 516-765-5577. July-Aug. Sat.-Sun., Sun. only rest of year)* includes Algonquian pottery and arrowheads dating back 10,000 years, plus tools, jewelry, and toys. The working **Horton Point Lighthouse** *(Lighthouse Rd. 516-765-5500. Tours Mem. Day–Columbus Day; donation)* offers a nautical museum and great views of Long Island Sound. The **Southold Historical Society Museum** *(Main Rd. at Maple Ln. 516-765-5500. July–Labor Day Wed. and Sat.-Sun.)* features a collection of buildings ranging from a 1750s colonial home to a print and blacksmith shop. Stargazing plus other astrology-related events and performances are held at the **Custer Institute** *(Bayview Rd. 516-765-2626. Sat.)*.

**3.** **Greenport** Formerly the Greenport railroad terminal, the **East End Seaport Museum & Marine Foundation** *(Ferry Dock, 3rd St. 516-477-2100. Mid-May–mid-June and mid-Sept.–Nov. Sat.-Sun., mid-June–mid-Sept. Wed.-Sun.)* is a showcase for the area's maritime history and heritage.
**4. Bug Light Lighthouse** *(Long Beach Point bet. East Marion and Orient)* This unique lighthouse was originally built in 1870 and stood until it was destroyed by an arsonist in 1963. What you see today is a reconstruction.
**5. Orient** Four of the six museum buildings at the **Oysterponds Historical Society** *(Village Ln. 516-323-2480. Mem. Day–Labor Day Thurs. and Sat.-Sun., call for times rest of year; adm. fee)* contain collections that range from furniture to maritime paintings and artifacts. The holdings date from the late 17th to the mid-20th century. Behind one of the homes lies a slave cemetery.
**6. Orient Beach State Park** *(Off N.Y. 25. 516-323-2440. Adm. fee Mem. Day–Labor Day)* A wonderful area of marsh, wetland, and bay where osprey, swans, and other

**Tasting room, Hargrave Vineyards**

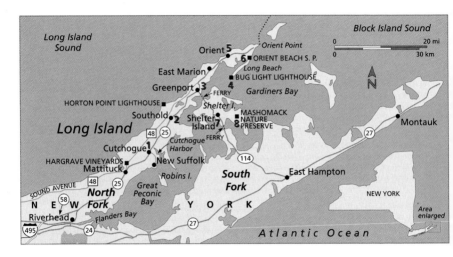

birds gather and turtles, too. Walk to the end of Long Beach for a close-up of the Bug Light Lighthouse. Beach, swimming, bike rentals, and picnic facilities.

**7. Shelter Island** Here at the **Shelter Island Historical Society** *(16 S. Ferry Rd./N.Y. 114. 516-749-0025. Mem. Day–Labor Day Wed. and Fri.-Sun.)* the 1743 Havens House and an adjacent barn contain the furnishings and artifacts of a Shelter Island farm. Nearby, the **Manhasset Chapel Museum** *(24 N. Ferry Rd. 516-749-3429)* houses changing exhibits relating to the island and its history.

**8. Mashomack Nature Preserve** *(Off N.Y. 114. 516-749-1001. Closed Tues.)* This 2,000-plus-acre preserve encompasses about one-third of Shelter Island. It's home to osprey and 75 other species of birds. There are four self-guided walking trails, and guided walks and workshops are sometimes given.

### Other Activities

**Berry picking** Raspberries and strawberries can be picked in season at Wickham Fruit Farm *(N.Y. 25, Cutchogue. 516-734-6441. Mon.-Sat.; fee).* Lathams Farm *(516-323-3701)* in Orient is another possibility, and there are many farms along Sound Avenue.

**Fishing** Flounder, bluefish, cod, striped bass, mackerel, and tuna are all catchable, depending on the season. Numerous charter and open boats operate April through November from Orient's Sea Marina on Main Road *(Prime Time III 516-323-2618; Shinnecock Star 516-728-4563; or SunDowner 516-765-2227).*

**Wine tasting** Visitors can sip wine at Hargrave Vineyards *(Cty. Rd. 48, Cutchogue. 516-734-5158 or 800-734-5158),* as well as about 20 other vineyards along N.Y. 25 and County Rd. 48. For more information call the Long Island Wine Council *(516-369-5887).*

### Annual Events

**August** Long Island Barrel Tasting *(location changes each year. 516-369-5887)* Popular wine festival.

**September** Maritime Festival *(Greenport. 516-477-1383)*

### Lodging

**Annabelle's Hideaway Belle Crest Inn** *(163 N. Ferry Rd., Shelter Island Heights. 516-749-2041)* This historic house is surrounded by pretty gardens. Rooms are comfortable and eclectic; some share baths.

**Bartlett House** *(503 Front St., Greenport. 516-477-0371)* A stately home (1908) with fine architectural detailing, Bartlett House offers ten rooms (some with fireplaces). All are nicely furnished.

**Chequit Inn** *(23 Grand Ave., Shelter Island. 516-749-0018)* At the center of Shelter Island Heights, this inn is its social focal point. Rooms are decked out in country floral and lace. There's a pretty, shaded dining terrace.

**Olde Country Inn** *(11 Stearns Point Rd., Shelter Island. 516-749-1633)* This renovated 1886 Victorian inn has rooms furnished with antiques and reproductions. The fireside dining is cozy in winter.

## PENNSYLVANIA
# Endless Mountains

This high, handsome ledge sweeping across the top of central Pennsylvania once boomed with mining, milling, and railroading might. The best and worst of early 20th-century industrialization marked the landscape, both scarring it with mining and clear-cuts and blessing it with towns boasting the big, imposing houses of new entrepreneurs. The engines of industry have long ceased to roar ferociously here, and, though a few factories still fuel the economy, much of the area lazes along in tranquil small towns, rolling dairy lands, and forested, creek-threaded state parks.

Part of the Appalachian Mountains that run from Quebec to Alabama, the Endless Mountains hump this region in the Piedmont hills. The snaking loops of the Susquehanna River unwind along the region's eastern edge, drained by countless creeks that burrow between hills. In spring and summer, the land greens up in bountiful stretches of farm fields and pastureland, polka-dotted by Holsteins and edged by the forests that filigree hillsides. Fall comes early here, inking the trees with a quick burst of color before the long, gray-brown winter settles in. By November, the hunting clubs—most no more than cabins tucked back on dirt roads—are busy places, peopled by men in Day-Glo caps and vests.

**Morning fog, Endless Mountains**

Any time of year, the country roads are worth meandering, as they loop back and forth, aimlessly zigzagging from one crossroads spot to another. It's hard to imagine that this region of isolated farmhouses once ran rich with the wealth of coal and timber. Believe it or not, railroads and canals once connected this quiet pocket to the markets of the world.

**Victorian house, Towanda**

Today, only weaving, two-laned US 6 connects to the outside. Running east-west through here, it was one of the country's first transcontinental highways and the portion in Pennsylvania still bears the big name Grand Army of the Republic Highway. But as it passes in and out of this area's small towns and hamlets, it becomes simply Main Street.

The first true town it hits in the east, **Towanda** rises on a hillside above the Susquehanna—a sudden apparition of old money and dignified living. Since the early 19th century, it has been the seat of Bradford County. In its early days, it served the settlers scattered on farmsteads across the still wild frontier. Many had come in the wake of Gen. John Sullivan's gruesome 1779 march up the Susquehanna. His 4,000 Continental troops had leveled Indian settlements all along the Upper Susquehanna, "clearing" the land for white settlement. Many of those early white settlers trickled down into the area from New England, attracted by the promise of fertile new land. In fact, the

**Luthers Mills Covered Bridge**

area became disputed ground, claimed by both Pennsylvania and Connecticut. Though Pennsylvania managed to make its claim stick, the Yankee settlers stayed on, and proved their industriousness with prosperous farms. Sawmills, gristmills, and other small waterpowered industries sprang up, fueled by the abundant creeks.

But the region remained remote, its exportable goods having been forced to eke their way overland to other markets. Then in the mid-1800s work began on the North Branch Canal that cuts along Towanda's east side.

Exhibits at the **Bradford County Historical Society Museum** trace the history of the town from frontier times (a re-created log cabin actually stands inside the classical revival building) through the short-lived canal era in the mid-19th century and on into the coal, lumber, and railroading heyday that gave rise to stately Greek Revival and Victorian houses.

An earlier vestige of the past lies about a dozen miles southeast. **French Azilum**, a strangely compelling little settlement, appeared in a horseshoe bend of the Susquehanna at the end of the 18th century. With backing from prominent American financiers, French aristocrats fleeing the revolution in France and the bloody slave uprisings in Haiti had high hopes of turning this 300-acre wilderness into a mecca of European sophistication. There was even talk of Marie Antoinette taking up residence here; Talleyrand and Louis-Philippe (later crowned king of France) did visit. But in a few years, the grand dreams had gone to dust, and the exiled aristocracy had left behind the crude settlement of log huts. Still their impress can be found in the area—in the townships with French names and at French Azilum itself, where a cluster of re-built cabins contains historic exhibits. Also here, the imposing 1836 LaPorte House features period decor, painted ceilings, and a beautiful 1790s piano forté.

Another unexpected little museum stands amid the modest houses in the crossroads of **Rome**. A small white-frame house here, now the **P.P. Bliss Gospel Songwriters Museum,** displays memorabilia and exhibits honoring the popular 19th-century gospel writer. Bliss was born in Pennsylvania and studied briefly at Susquehanna Collegiate Institute in Towanda. In the 1860s he had achieved enough success to move his parents into this modest residence.

During Bliss's childhood, the area was mostly farm country, and it is that

### Stephen Foster

He has been called "the creator of the first distinctly American musical idiom, the singer of the commonplace." He was certainly that, but he wasn't the Southerner that people sometimes take him for. In fact, Stephen Collins Foster was a Pennsylvanian, born in Pittsburgh in 1826. And he wrote his first song here in the Endless Mountains when he was only 14. At the time, he was studying at the respected Athens Academy in Athens, and the song was "The Tioga Waltz," named after Tioga Point on the river south of town. But it was his "Camptown Races," written about the little hamlet that still stands southeast of Towanda, that keeps this area forever alive in song.

again, as the **Valley Stockyards Flea & Farm Market** in **Athens** proves. On Monday afternoons, local people in its indoor amphitheater hear auctioneers rattling off the merits of pigs as big as Volkswagens.

The **Farm Museum,** just outside the picturesque town of **Troy,** takes a lovingly nostalgic look at farming before agriculture became a mechanized big business. Inside the long, barnlike building, exhibits of tools, furniture, and frippery recall the hardships and pleasures of farm life. Next door stands the **Mitchell House.** Built in 1822 and now the oldest house in Troy township, the white-frame Greek Revival functioned for years as a stagecoach stop and gathering place for the county. Behind it, small vegetable, dye, and herb gardens celebrate the many traditional uses of plants.

## Barclay Mountain Ghost Towns

If you look on a map of Bradford County, to the south between Towanda and Troy, there's an open space without a hamlet, just the blue squiggle of Schrader Creek. That's Barclay Mountain, once pocked with the coal mines and towns of the Erie Railroad Company in the 1800s. For decades, miners riddled into the mountain to dig out its bituminous wealth. Hurt badly by the economic depression of the 1880s, the mines limped along for a few years till a heavy snowfall in 1890 brought the operations to a halt. A decade later, timbering interests moved in and stayed until 1925. Today, there's almost nothing in this deserted quarter but recovered forest.

Not far from Troy, **Mount Pisgah State Park** has its own nostalgic appeal, particularly on summer weekends when families flock to its cool, wooded hills and big, inviting lake. Trails lead out from the main facilities and up onto adjoining 2,260-foot Mount Pisgah, which affords views of farmland.

A wilder setting encompasses **Worlds End State Park,** a small preserve set in the southeast corner of the Endless Mountains. Pocketed in a step-sided little canyon cut by the hemlock-shrouded Loyalsock Creek, the park is threaded by woodland trails that climb up—and up—into the surrounding mountains. You can also drive up to the old lakeside, mountaintop Victorian village of Eagles Mere, once a getaway for wealthy Philadelphians and still a worthy stop.

A more dramatic Endless Mountains scenario lies along the region's northwestern edge, where the Grand Canyon of Pennsylvania, **Pine Creek Gorge,** makes a thousand-foot-deep gash in the mountains. In their 50-mile course, canyon and creek twist through a natural area, a state forest (Tioga), and two state parks. Dipping country lanes lead to the two state parks on either side of the gorge—both with plenty of opportunities to enjoy the mountain air and scenic surroundings. On the gorge's west rim, the 368-acre **Colton Point State Park** has picnic areas, an overlook, and 4 miles of hiking paths. From the overlook, the 1-mile Turkey Path Trail weaves down into the gorge. Intrepid fishermen who take on the hike can angle for trout, smallmouth bass, and panfish in the rilling waters of Pine Creek. The east rim's 585-acre **Leonard Harrison**

**State Park** has its own similarly constructed Turkey Path Trail and picnic facilities. In the gorge itself, the newly conceived Pine Creek Trail follows the old Conrail bed from the town of Ansonia south for 19 miles to Rattlesnake Rock. Plans are underway for more segments of the trail to open in coming years.

The gateway town to "Grand Canyon" country is lovely **Wellsboro**, 10 miles away on US 6. Seat of Tioga County, it, too, was settled by New Englanders and has the stately look of a Yankee town, with large houses set back from the street, boulevards lined with maples, and a town green. On Main Street, the **Tioga County Historical Society Museum** has filled the 1820s Robinson House with local furnishings and memorabilia. The museum annex is behind the facade of the 1864 First National Bank, whose founder was one of the Robinson clan. In 1874 the bank and the Robinson family were involved in a robbery that still ranks as one of the greatest events that ever occurred up here in these Endless Mountains          —*K.M. Kostyal*

# Travel Notes

**Directions**
Known as the Endless Mountains, this region lies just below the New York border, with the closest major town being Scranton to the southeast. **By car:** From I-81, head west on US 6. **By plane:** The closest airports are located in Scranton and Williamsport.

**General Information**
The Endless Mountains make a good escape from the spring through the fall, when foliage color can be breathtaking. For more information, contact the Endless Mountains Visitors Bureau *(712 Pa. 6,*

*Tunkhannock 18657. 717-836-5431 or 800-769-8999);* or the Tioga Tourist Promotion Agency *(114 Main St., Wellsboro 16901. 717-724-0635 or 800-332-6718).*

**Things to See and Do**
**1. Leonard Harrison State Park**
*(Pa. 660, W of Wellsboro. 717-724-3061. Visitor Center mid-May–mid-Oct. Sat.-Sun., call for other hours)* Here the Turkey Path Trail descends steeply for a mile to the bottom of Pine Creek Gorge. Splendid overlooks are spread along the west rim.
**2. Colton Point State Park** *(Off US 6,*

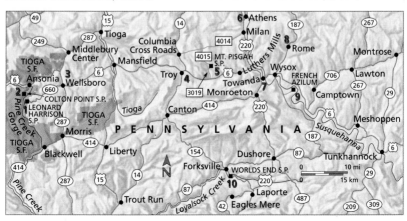

**Bradford Basket Company picnic ware**

S of Ansonia. 717-724-3061. Mon.-Fri.)
Situated at the east rim of Pine Creek
Gorge, the park offers fishing, hiking, and
plenty of picnicking possibilities.

**3. Wellsboro** The **Tioga County Historical Society Museum** *(120 Main St. 717-724-6116. Mon.-Fri.)* features local memorabilia and the facade of the 1860s First National Bank.

**4. Troy** The large barnlike **Farm Museum** *(US 6 and Pa. 14, near Troy. 717-297-3410. Late April–late Oct. Fri.-Mon.; adm. fee)* holds changing exhibits of farm equipment, smithing tools, old clothing, and anything else that recalls life in rural Pennsylvania in the last century. The adjacent 1822 **Mitchell House** is the oldest in Troy. Also in town is the **Bradford Basket Company** *(Pa. 14. 717-297-1020 or 800-231-9972. Tours Mon.-Fri.)*, which is open to visitors and offers a shop *(Mon.-Sat.)*.

**5. Mount Pisgah State Park** *(Pa. 4015, E of Troy. 717-297-2734)* Located at the base of 2,260-foot Mount Pisgah, this park treats summer visitors with a variety of hiking trails and excellent fishing on Stephen Foster Lake.

**6. Athens** The lively auction house at the **Valley Stockyards Flea & Farm Market** *(Pa. 199. 717-888-9333. Auction on Mon. year-round, flea market Mon. April-Oct.)* has been moving pigs, chickens, and other livestock across the blocks since the 1940s. The flea market offers produce, crafts, and antiques.

**7. Towanda** At the **Bradford County Historical Society Museum** *(21 Main St. 717-265-2240. Thurs.-Sat.; donation)*, furnishings, memorabilia, historic photographs, and a log cabin trace the history of the area.

**8. Rome** The **P.P. Bliss Gospel Songwriters Museum** *(Pa. 187. 717-247-7683. Mid-May–late Sept. Wed. and Sat., and by appt.; donation)*, formerly the home of P.P. Bliss, features exhibits on him and other gospel songwriters of the late 19th century.

**9. French Azilum** *(Off Penn. 187, near Wysox, then follow signs. 717-265-3376. June-Aug. Wed.-Sun., May-Oct. Sat.-Sun.; adm. fee)* A few log cabins and a house are all that remain of the attempt by French exiles to establish a town here in the late 18th century.

**10. Worlds End State Park** *(Pa. 154, W of Forksville. 717-924-3287)* The Loyalsock Creek, with its swimming, kayaking, and fishing, is the centerpiece of this 780-acre park.

### Other Activities

**Covered wagon rides** The Mountain Trail Horse Center *(Ansonia. 717-376-5561. Mem. Day–late Oct. Thurs.-Sun.; fee)* offers rides through Pine Creek Canyon.

**Train rides** The Tioga Central Railroad Excursions *(3 miles N of Wellsboro, on Pa. 287. 717-724-0990. Mid-May–late Oct. weekends, call for weekday schedule; fare)* offers locomotive rides.

### Annual Events

**April** Endless Mountains Maple Festival *(Troy. 717-836-5431 or 800-769-8999)*
**June** Heritage Days Festival *(French Azilum. 717-265-3376)*
**August** Towanda Riverfest *(Towanda. 717-265-2696)*
**September** Carriage and Wagon Festival *(Troy. 717-596-2093)*; Fabulous 1890s Weekend *(Mansfield. 717-662-3442)*
**December** Dickens of a Christmas *(Wellsboro. 717-724-1926)*

### Lodging

**Eagles Mere Inn** *(Mary and Sullivan Aves., Eagles Mere. 717-525-3273)* This rambling 1878 Victorian offers a pleasant way to enjoy the latter-day atmosphere of Eagles Mere.

**Four Winds Bed & Breakfast** *(58 West Ave., Wellsboro. 717-724-6141 or 800-368-7963)* Though this elegant Victorian B&B with its tin ceilings and impressive central staircase dates from the 1870s, it offers such modern amenities as a heated outdoor pool.

**Lewis's Bed 'n' Breakfast** *(Church St., East Smithfield. 717-596-3428 or 800-309-0666)* The Lewis's home dates from the early 1800s and has been renovated and redecorated with Victorian furnishings.

# Big Valley Amish

Wedged into a broad ripple in the Allegheny Mountains, central Pennsylvania's silo-dotted Big Valley seems to have cloistered itself from the outside world. That's because this wide, fertile place is peopled by longtime Amish farmers. Happily, the land is unsullied as yet by the commercialism and gawking visitors that plague their more famous brethren to the southeast, around Lancaster. Though some Mennonite farmers and a handful of "English" (as the non-brethren are known) share the valley with them, it is the Amish that set the tone and pace in this place blessedly apart.

Wednesday is definitely the day to take a drive down Pa. 655, the main route through the valley—though you'll have to share the road with the Amish buggies clopping their way to the weekly market in Belleville. Long before there were motor cars, the Amish were here in the broad swatch between Jacks and Stone Mountains. They came in the late 18th century, and they haven't let the machinations of the last two hundred years much disturb their Old Order ways. The silos of their dairy farms rise like sentinels between the folded hills, and the black-hatted menfolk still stand upright behind their plows, guiding draft horses through the fields. Barely touched by the 20th century, the Amish hunkered down here in the Kishacoquillas

**Amish buggy stop**

**Kishacoquillas Valley farmland**

Valley, as it's known on maps, only open up to a wider world on Wednesdays.

Then, the quiet village of **Belleville** becomes quite a mecca, with buggies vying for hitching spaces and the cars of town residents filling the parking lot of the **Belleville Livestock Auction and Flea Market.** Around the market buildings, local farmers set up tables laden with seasonal vegetables, homemade jams, and pickles; beyond them, the flea market folks have the usual offerings of discarded junk, mixed up with a few treasures. In the livestock auction house, long-bearded Amish men confer together, the black brims of their hats nodding as they discuss the price of hay or the relative merits of a heifer in the pens below. At 1 p.m., one of the Glick brothers (they're not Amish but their "pappy" did found the auction house in 1946) will step into the small amphitheater, along with a cow or a sow, and the bidding begins.

When you tire of hoofed stock, stop by the poultry house, where chickens, rabbits, and even emus make an appearance on the auction block. And if the barnyard smells start to wear on you, you can step into the low-slung concrete building where Amish women sell their specialties: crescent-shaped moon pies, rich shoofly pies, and every shape of homemade noodle. Over in the Big Valley Hayloft Restaurant, diners hunker down over hefty plate lunches of dumplings served up with chicken, or pork and sauerkraut—lingering testaments to the Swiss-German heritage of the Amish.

The Amish trace their beginnings to the Anabaptist movement that swept Europe in the 16th century. One group of Anabaptists who hived off to follow the teachings of Menno Simons, a Dutch elder, became known as Mennonites. As disagreements within the Mennonite community flared, another group broke away under the leadership of Jakob Ammann. These became the

Amish, and by 1791, a contingent of them had made their way into this valley, the Kishacoquillas, which took its name from a local Shawnee chief. Mennonites, too, settled here, and still share the land with the Amish. Their **Mennonite Heritage Center,** occupying an old brick building in Belleville, exhibits clothing, tools, and other items. More progressive than the Amish, the Mennonites do not reject with quite such ferocity the "worldly" devices of the 20th century, and their farms prosper with a little help from technology.

Even one of the Amish sects has succumbed to the charm of the automobile, though confining themselves, for their own arcane reasons, only to ones with black bumpers. But most of the brethren are still "buggy Amish," with the colors of their rigs giving some clue to their owners' spiritual leanings. Buggy tops come in white, yellow, and black, and identify which major grouping of Amish their owners belong to. White toppers tend to be the most traditional, even leaving one side of their barns austerely unpainted. Such lifestyle issues—how to dress, how a barn should be built or painted—constantly cause schisms in the community, and more than a dozen different small sects now exist in this one valley.

But all Amish share a common belief in the need to keep themselves apart from the outside world. Their one-room schools (education stops after the eighth grade) interrupt the farm fields that splay out from Back Mountain Road. Dipping and turning along the base of Stone Mountain, the road weaves past farms with hand-lettered signs at the ends of their lanes advertising butter or quilts for sale. If you pull into a farmyard, the owners will happily welcome you into their spare, simple home and show you their wares.

A great sprawl of non-Amish, antique wares can also be found on Wednesdays at the valley's north end, where the **Dairyland Antique Center** plays host to its own market day. In the warm months, a hundred different vendors set up booths in the field surrounding the cavernous building, selling antique furniture, jewelry, tools, and such. Even the neighbors along Pa. 655 get into the act, with roadside tables of produce or discarded "collectibles." And down the road the **Brookmere Farm Vineyards,** quaintly housed in a picturesque old red barn, offers wine tastings.

Admittedly, the winery does seem a little incongruous in this particular area, a hotbed of biblical sobriety. As if to warn all comers against the wages of sin,

**Farm goods, Belleville Livestock Auction and Flea Market**

billboards along Pa. 655 quote scripture at you as you drive back into the world of mammon. The messages seem to sprout from the soil, nurtured by the firm beliefs of the Amish in this big valley.  —*K.M. Kostyal*

# Travel Notes

## Directions

The Big Valley, also called the Kishacoquillas Valley, is located in central Pennsylvania, between Harrisburg and State College. **By car:** From US 322, head south on Pa. 655, which bisects the valley. **By plane:**

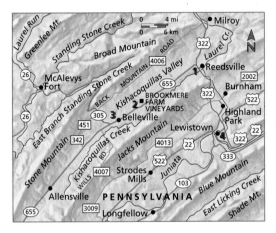

The closest airports are located in State College and Harrisburg. **By train:** Amtrak trains make stops in Lewistown.

## General Information

Spring through fall are the best seasons to visit, when the Wednesday markets are in full swing and roadside produce is readily available. For more information, contact the Juniata-Mifflin Counties Tourist Promotion Agency (*3 W. Monument Sq., Lewistown 17044. 717-248-6713*).

## Things to See and Do

**1. Reedsville** Filled with small antique stalls year-round, the **Dairyland Antique Center** (*US 322 and Pa. 655. 717-667-9093. Wed.-Sun., outdoor flea market April-Nov. Wed.*) is noted for its extensive Wednesday outdoor flea market.

**2. Brookmere Farm Vineyards** (*Pa. 655, bet. Reedsville and Belleville. 717-935-5380*) The small winery offers tastings and a look at its charming vintner's loft, now displaying the works of regional artists and artisans.

**3. Belleville** The lively **Belleville Live-**

stock **Auction and Flea Market** (*Penn St. 717-935-2146. Wed.*) features livestock auctions, fresh produce, and such Amish specialties as pies, dried beans, and homemade egg noodles. A flea market offers assorted new and used oddities, and the Big Valley Hayloft Restaurant (*717-935-5023*) serves traditional Swiss-German fare. Also in town, the **Mennonite Heritage Center** (*Pa. 655 and Walnut St. Wed. and Sat.*) is housed in a former bank building. It holds small exhibits on the history of Mennonites in the valley and extensive genealogical archives.

**4. Lewistown** Birthplace of soldier-statesman Maj. Gen. Frank Ross McCoy, the 1841 **McCoy House Museum** (*17 N. Main St. 717-242-1022. Call for schedule; adm. fee*) displays artifacts related to the general's career and furniture from many generations of McCoys.

## Other Activities

**Farm goods** Amish farms selling quilts and butter are scattered throughout the area, as are small roadside stores selling Amish noodles, dried legumes, and baked goods.

## Annual Events

**August** Belleville Fireman's Festival (*Belleville. 717-248-6713*)
**October** Harvestfest (*Reedsville. 717-248-6713*)

## Lodging

**Hameau Farm** (*Off Pa. 655, about 2 miles N of Belleville. 717-667-3731*) At the center of a working dairy farm, this cozy home offers a chance to experience farm life in the valley.
**Harmon House** (*19 W. Main St., Belleville. 717-935-2291 or 800-299-8849*) Housed in a turn-of-the-century, Greek Revival bank building in the heart of Belleville, this inn blends antiques with new comforts, such as its own small swimming pool. Stays include full breakfasts.

# Laurel Highlands

Pocketed in the Allegheny Mountains, the Laurel Highlands of southwestern Pennsylvania tumble along in wooded ridges and dipping vales cut by fast-flowing creeks. Though the steel towns of the rust belt surround them, a gentle beauty prevails here. Old inns stand beside long-forgotten stagecoach routes, a famous white-water river races beneath lacey hemlocks, and the architecture of Frank Lloyd Wright crowns forested bluffs.

The quiet simplicity of the Laurel Highlands today gives little hint of their storied past. Long before 19th-century industrial barons of nearby Pittsburgh discovered the highlands, others had recognized their worth—particularly as a gateway to the coveted Ohio River Valley in the west. As early as 1754, a regiment of Virginia frontiersmen was dispatched to this area to protect British colonial interests from French encroachment. The commander of the small group was an untested, 22-year-old lieutenant colonel named George Washington. Soon enough he was put to the test—and found up to it. At **Fort Necessity National Battlefield,** you can learn of Washington's bravery: How he launched a surprise attack on the French at a place called **Jumonville Glen;** how he prepared for what he knew would be sure and swift retaliation by hastily constructing a makeshift stockade he called Fort Necessity (the park service has built a reconstruction of it); and how, despite his efforts, he had to surrender to the French forces, who outnumbered him almost two to one. It was the first defeat of Washington's career, and he and nearly all his men were allowed to walk away from the battle. But the whole affair sounded the opening salvo in the French and Indian War.

A year later Washington was back, as an aide to British Maj. Gen. Edward Braddock. Braddock's formal style of fighting proved little good in the wilds of America, and he was mortally wounded in battle. He died near Fort Necessity, and though few of the cars whizzing down US 40 today

## On the Road Again

In 1806, when Congress authorized the first federal highway, the country was young and raw but full of hope. Untold potential lay in the Ohio River Valley, but getting there was a hard trek. This new National Road (now US 40 and US 40A) would pave the way. Beginning in Cumberland, Maryland, the highway paralleled the military road cut by Washington and Braddock during the French and Indian War. By 1818, it had made its way down to Wheeling, West Virginia. By the 1830s, it reached Vandalia, Illinois, where lack of funds stopped it forever. Today, interstates have usurped its stature, but they lack the romance of travel that you can still find along the old National Road.

**Living room terrace, Kentuck Knob**

take time to stop, there is a roadside marker for Braddock's Grave. Near the fort itself, the 1828 **Mount Washington Tavern** details the glory days of the National Road, as US 40 and US 40A (see sidebar p. 81) was designated. Built in the early 1800s, it was the federal government's first foray into road building.

A more elaborate French and Indian War-era fort lies north in the postcard-quaint village of **Ligonier.** In 1758, on the banks of the Loyalhanna, the British built **Fort Ligonier** as their main staging point for a final press on the French. Now a reconstruction of the fort, with living quarters, armory, hospital, and other buildings, gives a sense of what life was like in this isolated post amid an unfriendly wilderness. The fort's museum features a couple of period rooms, colonial artifacts discovered at the site, and a film.

The footprints of past skirmishes rest easy now on these Appalachian Highlands. In the centuries since the war, other, more appealing structures than rustic colonial forts have risen in the once contested quarter—two of them by America's most vaunted architect, Frank Lloyd Wright (see sidebar this page). Cossetted amid poplar, oak, and the wild rhododendron along Bear Run, his **Fallingwater** is, as one critic rhapsodized, "one of the complete masterpieces of twentieth-century art." Designed to jut out over a small waterfall in the creek, the house actually seems to be part of the landscape, growing out of the rock cliff that it rests against.

Wright was in his late sixties in 1936 when Edgar Kaufmann, a Pittsburgh millionaire, asked him to design a country home on the Bear Run land. With its intimate interior, the house forces the eye outside to the natural surroundings. Though Fallingwater immediately won kudos from architectural critics, the structural weaknesses in Wright's design are beginning to show. Now, the cantilevered terraces may be in danger of weakening, and unappealing shorings have been placed under them until a permanent solution can be found. Still, the place has not lost its sublime mystique. It remains Wright's "nature poem to modern man."

Fallingwater is no longer the only Wright house-museum in the area. As of 1996, a lesser known home also opened to the public. Modest but elegant **Kentuck Knob** was designed in 1953 for local ice-cream entrepreneur I.N. Hagan and his wife, Bernadine. They wanted something far simpler than Fallingwater, and, after interviewing *them* as potential clients, Wright agreed. The low-slung, stone hexagon of a house bears all the Wright signatures—an intimate fit with the land, exquisite detailing, and natural materials, this time local stone and tidewater red cypress. You can spend long moments pondering the small details of the place, which the well-informed guides are quick to point out. And when the tours are over, you're free to walk down the knoll from the house to an overlook that takes in the sweeping Youghiogheny River Gorge.

Kentuck Knob's current owner, British

## The Wright Stuff

Born in Wisconsin in 1867, Frank Lloyd Wright began designing buildings in his twenties—and kept at it for almost 70 years. During his career, he designed more than a thousand buildings. Today, only 400 of his American creations still stand, but close to 70 of those have been preserved as museums or tour houses. They span everything from Wright's early prairie-style homes to churches and office buildings. While each is distinctive, all bear that unmistakable Wright artistry. For information on Wright buildings open to the public, contact the Frank Lloyd Wright Building Conservancy (312-663-1786).

Lord Peter Palumbo, collects both architecture and art, and he now uses the wooded grounds around the house to display sculpture by such luminaries as Claes Oldenburg and Ray Smith, whose 960-piece work, "The Red Army," marches across a meadowland. (The grounds also include the greenhouse from Fallingwater, which was moved here and filled with delicate orchids.)

The great gaping gorge that Kentuck Knob overlooks provides more than just visual stimulation. It is one of the main draws in the area, particularly for white-water fans, who flock here to run the "Yough" (pronounced YOCK). About 14 miles of gorge is protected within the 19,000-some acres of **Ohiopyle State Park,** and the rustic little town of Ohiopyle, deep in the gorge, is replete with white-water outfitters, guides, and endless talk of Class IV rapids. The low but wide breach of Ohiopyle Falls roars right through the heart of town, and rafts put in and take out just downstream from them. If you don't like the idea of tussling with white water, the park also has good trout fishing, camping, and about 40 miles of hiking trails, including part of the 70-mile-long **Laurel Highlands Hiking Trail,** which begins in the park. For nature enthusiasts, the Ferncliff Peninsula, just across the river from the town of Ohiopyle, supports a unique biosystem of flora normally found much farther south. For winter sports lovers, the park offers snowmobiling, tobogganing, and cross-country skiing amid silent, hemlock-draped forests.

**Hikers, Laurel Highlands**

The only real city in the area, **Johnstown** is wedged into a perilous bowl between steep-sided hills. In this working town of rust belt vintage, the smokestacks of the steel industry still rise like yesteryear's skyscrapers, and the nostalgic **Johnstown Inclined Plane** still carries cars and people up its 71.9-degree slope (billed as the steepest such vehicular slope in the world). The town is still flavored by the traditions of the Irish, Italian, and Slavic workers who came in the last century to labor in the town mills and mines. But for all its Industrial Revolution success, Johnstown is better remembered for the tragedy that occurred here on May 31, 1889. When heavy rains that fateful spring put pressure on the lake's neglected South Fork Dam, it gave way. "A roar like thunder" shook the area, as 20 million tons of water hurtled down the Conemaugh Valley toward the people trapped in the steep-sided bowl of Johnstown. When the carnage was over, some 2,200 people lay dead.

At the **Johnstown Flood Museum,** an Academy Award-winning film recounts the horror, and outside town the National Park Service maintains a Visitor Center and exhibits at the **Johnstown Flood National Memorial.** Ironically, it was here in this magical countryside that local industrialists such as Andrew Carnegie and Andrew Mellon maintained elaborate vacation cottages overlooking the man-made lake. The Great Johnstown Flood became a symbol of the tragic side of industrial success.

*—K.M. Kostyal*

# Travel Notes

### Directions
Stretching between Pittsburgh and John-stown, the Laurel Highlands lie just above the Pennsylvania-Maryland border. **By car:** I-70/76 cuts east-west through the highlands. Travelers approaching from the south along I-68 can take the Keysers Ridge exit onto US 40 west. **By plane:** The closest major airport is Pittsburgh. **By train:** Amtrak trains serve Johnstown and Greensburg.

### General Information
The highlands are lovely at all times of year; winters can be cold and snowy but make for good skiing. For more information, contact the Laurel Highlands Visitors Bureau *(120 E. Main St., Ligonier 15658. 724-238-5661 or 800-925-7669).*

### Things to See and Do
**1. Fort Necessity National Battlefield** *(US 40, 10 miles SE of Uniontown. 724-329-5512. Adm. fee)* George Washington hastily threw up a small stockaded enclosure here in 1754, as protection against the French and Indian forces in the area. The National Park Service site includes a reconstruction of the stockade, the adjacent 1828 **Mount Washington Tavern,** and nearby **Jumonville**

**Glen** *(5 miles NW of Fort Necessity via US 40 and Collspring Rd. April-Oct.).*
**2. Ohiopyle State Park** *(Pa. 381, 15 miles E of Uniontown. 724-329-8591)* The 19,046-acre park, one of the largest in the state, surrounds the scenic Youghiogheny River Gorge, famous for its white water and its 25-foot Ohiopyle Falls. For nonrafters, the park has hiking trails, fishing, and some unusual plant communities.
**3. Kentuck Knob** *(Off Chalk Hill/Ohiopyle Rd., SE of Uniontown. 724-329-1901. April-Nov. Tues.-Sun.; adm. fee)* This small but elegant country house, designed by Frank Lloyd Wright, fits into a hilltop within sight of the Youghiogheny River Gorge. A meadowland sculpture garden includes Ray Smith's "The Red Army," a 960-piece work.
**4. Fallingwater** *(Pa. 381, N of Ohiopyle. 724-329-8501. Mid-March-Nov. Tues.-Sun., weekends only mid-Nov.–Dec. and first two weeks of March; adm. fee)* One of architect Frank Lloyd Wright's best known designs, Fallingwater is located in a wooded setting above Bear Run. Due to structural problems, its famous terraces are now supported by temporary pilings, but tours of the house are still given, and the famous view of the facade's southwest elevation is unobstructed.

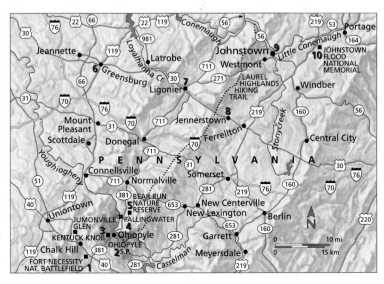

**At Fort Necessity National Battlefield**

**5. Bear Run Nature Reserve** *(Pa. 381, adjacent to Fallingwater. 412-288-2777)* More than 20 miles of hiking trails lace this 5,000-acre woodland preserve owned by the Western Pennsylvania Conservancy.

**6. Greensburg** The **Westmoreland Museum of American Art** *(221 N. Main St. 724-837-1500. Wed.-Sun.; donation)* displays national and regional artwork.

**7. Ligonier** A reconstruction of the French and Indian War-era fort, **Fort Ligonier** *(216 S. Market St. 724-238-9701. April-Oct.; adm. fee)* features officers' quarters, barracks, and an armory. The museum has a good collection of 18th-century portraits.

**8. Jennerstown** One of the oldest summer stock theaters in the area, **Mountain Playhouse** *(Pa. 985. 814-629-9201. Late May–mid-Oct.)* stages comedies and musicals in a converted 1805 gristmill.

**9. Johnstown** *(Convention & Visitors Bureau 814-536-7993 or 800-237-8590)* Exhibits, a 24-foot animated map, historic photos, and an Academy Award-winning film retell the tale of the great 1889 flood at the **Johnstown Flood Museum** *(304 Washington St. 814-539-1889 or 888-222-1889. Adm. fee)*. Also in town, the **Johnstown Inclined Plane** *(711 Edgehill Dr. 814-536-1816. Fare)* carries passengers and vehicles up a 71.9-degree grade to an observation deck, surrounded by a neighborhood of fine old houses.

**10. Johnstown Flood National Memorial** *(US 219, 10 miles NE of Johnstown. 814-495-4643)* Abutments of the ill-fated South Fork Dam are still visible above the empty lake basin. A movie and exhibits at the Visitor Center recount the tragic 1889 flood.

## Annual Events
**February** Winterlude *(Greensburg area. 412-838-4360)*
**April** Pennsylvania Maple Festival *(Meyersdale. 814-634-0213)*
**May** National Road Festival *(Along US 40. 724-329-1560)*
**August** Antique Flea Market *(Somerset. 814-445-6431)*; Laurel Highlands Wine and Food Festival *(Champion. 814-352-7777 or 800-452-2223)*
**September** Ligonier Highland Games *(Ligonier. 412-851-9900)*

## Other Activities
**Covered bridges** Eleven covered bridges are scattered throughout the Laurel Highlands. For information on their locations, consult the Laurel Highlands Visitors Bureau *(724-238-5661 or 800-925-7669)*.
**Hiking** The 70-mile Laurel Highlands Hiking Trail cuts diagonally through the heart of the highlands, beginning in Ohiopyle and ending in Johnstown. There are overnight shelters along the way. Call for a map and reservations *(724-455-3744)*.
**Rafting** The best time to raft on the Youghiogheny is spring through fall. For a list of white-water concessionaires, contact Ohiopyle State Park *(724-329-8591)*.
**Skiing** Several large downhill ski resorts and more than one hundred miles of cross-country trails are scattered throughout the area. For lists and descriptions, contact the Laurel Highlands Visitors Bureau *(724-238-5661 or 800-925-7669)*.
**Summer band concerts** Concerts are held Sunday nights in the Victorian-style bandstand at the center of Ligonier *(724-238-4200)*.
**Train ride** The Laurel Highlands Railroad *(Station on Pa. 819, Scottdale. 724-887-4568. Mem. Day–Oct. weekends; fare)* is a steam-powered train that winds through the countryside, offering good views of the rural scenery.

## Lodging
**Glades Pike Inn** *(Pa. 31, 6 miles W of Somerset. 814-443-4978)* A wraparound porch welcomes guests to this old stagecoach stop, established in 1842. Rooms preserve a 19th-century grace; the inn also operates a winery.
**The Stone House** *(US 40, Chalk Hill. 724-329-8876)* Formerly the Fayette Springs Hotel, this fine old Victorian has stood by the National Road since 1822. Rooms feature period antiques.

# NEW JERSEY
# Pine Barrens

Endless, empty pine and oak forests make the Pine Barrens of central New Jersey seemingly inauspicious. But for those with time to pause and ponder, this strange region, also known as the Pinelands, entices with its rich history and folklore. It offers glimpses of a little explored world of cranberry bogs, ghost villages, old cabins that once housed the reclusive "Piney" people, secretive swimming lakes and cedar swamps, sugar-sand back-woods, and winding rivers ideal for canoeists—and even its own unique monster, the notorious Jersey Devil.

In the hot summer months—when winds cease to move the thick sticky air, when trees, ferns, and grasses droop, and when blackwater ponds and lily-strewn swamps gleam like glass—an eerie silence settles over the Pine Barrens. The sun's rays, occasionally piercing the dark forest gloom, dance on wriggling white sand paths. Amber necklaces of resin, drawn out by the

**Young pilgrims, Batsto Village**

heat, speckle the furrowed pine bark like beads of sweat.

In 1859 the *Atlantic Monthly* described the Pine Barrens as "a region . . . where forests extend in uninterrupted lines over scores of miles, where, in a word, we may enjoy the undiluted essence, the perfect wildness. . ." And fortunately not too much has changed today. This remarkable region, as vast as Grand Canyon National Park, contains over 1.1 million acres of protected lands. Designated an international biosphere reserve by the United Nations, it is underlain by an aquifer whose freshwater reserves are vast enough to cover the state of New Jersey to a depth of 10 feet. It is by far the largest tract of open land between Washington, D.C., and Boston.

And yet the barrens are as elusive in some places as the Sahara Desert—an

**Harvesting Jersey cranberries**

apt comparison as most of the forest grows out of a vast sandy wilderness. Legends abound of pirate hideouts in the swampy interior, smuggling operations up the Mullica River, and moonshine activity during Prohibition. But all such anecdotes pale beside the legend of the Jersey Devil, a creature whose activities seem to be as oddly diverse as those claiming to have seen it (see sidebar p. 89).

And then, of course, there are the stories about the legendary "Pineys" themselves—those reclusive backwoods residents of the barrens who once scratched a living hunting game, harvesting cranberries, and selling pinecones. Most are gone now, but remnants of their rough-hewn cabins can occasionally be found by adventurers who walk the 50-mile-long **Batona Trail** through the wilds that connect the Lebanon, Wharton, and Bass River State Forests.

Canoeists claim similar discoveries on their occasionally arduous journeys through the winding, forest-edged Oswego, Wading, Batsto, and Mullica Rivers.

Ironically, today's wilderness was a hotbed of industrial activity for a century, beginning in the 1760s. Ironmaking settlements flourished using wetland bog iron, charcoal made from the forests, and waterwheel-generated power from the rivers. A wide range of goods were produced from cannonballs for the Revolutionary War to stoves and kettles during more peaceable times. Even in the 1850s, as the iron industry failed, the glass industry emerged briefly, using the sugar-fine white sands that lie here in abundance.

The region's former character comes alive at historic **Batsto Village**, site of what was once the Pinelands' most prominent iron- and glassmaking town. Unlike most other area communities that disappeared, Batsto was restored after the state purchased a major portion of the area in the 1950s. Today the elegant Italianate mansion, the workers' cottages west of the lake, and a score of other exhibits offer a fascinating glimpse of an unusual era in New Jersey history. A nature trail around nearby Batsto Pond also provides an excellent introduction to varied Pinelands inhabitants.

On the northeast side of the barrens, **Double Trouble State Park** contains fascinating traces of a town that began as a sawmill in the mid-1700s and later became a cranberry plantation. The cranberry harvest is a popular event here, but most evocative are the schoolhouse, pickers' cottages, and a restored sawmill.

While most of the old manufacturing industries have long since disappeared from the barrens, cranberry bogs and blueberry fields through the region are active, especially during the harvest season. Although modern methods of cultivation now predominate, the influence of two locals is still felt. "Old Peg-Leg" (aka John Webb) first cultivated cranberries here around 1845; and Joseph White's 1870 book *Cranberry Culture* became the bible for cranberry farmers. Their pioneering efforts have made this one of the highest-yield regions in the nation, a fact celebrated at the popular October Cranberry Festival in Chatsworth, the unofficial capital of the Pine Barrens.

Cranberry cultivation is a relatively benign industry, occupying a tiny fraction of this sprawling wilderness. It's easy to lose all sense of direction here as one wanders off the main highway on those meandering soft-sand tracks that seem at first so enticing and then, as side paths and forks increase, become increasingly mazelike.

Caution here is rewarded by the seductive beauty of the barrens. The quietude of the forest is almost meditational; swimmers delight in the hidden ponds and lakes; canoeists explore the channels of gold-brown "cedar-waters" rippling against lily-edged banks; and birdwatchers flock to the **Edwin B. Forsythe National Wildlife Refuge** to watch the spring and late fall bird migrations. One can wander on cushion-soft pine needle paths and breathe in the resin-laced scents of the forest like the bouquet of a fine wine. Drink in these Pinelands. They're intoxicating.

—*David Yeadon*

## Jersey Devil

New Jersey's most notorious resident is the mischievous and occasionally terrorizing Jersey Devil. Witnesses as diverse as naval hero Commodore Stephen Decatur and Joseph Bonaparte (Napoleon's brother) are reputed to have spotted a strange creature in the Pine Barrens. The "devil" has been variously described as having the face of a horse, the head of a dog, batlike wings, horns, and a serpent's tail. The folklore says that it raids chicken coops, destroys crops, kills animals, and periodically rampages through towns on the fringes of the vast barrens. But the mysterious creature remains elusive in its lair deep in this pine-covered, sandy realm.

# Travel Notes

### Directions

The Pine Barrens rest between Philadelphia and the Atlantic Seaboard. **By car:** Take the New Jersey Turnpike or Garden State Parkway from Newark. The Atlantic City Expressway *(toll)* is the main thoroughfare through the southern barrens. Motorists from the south can also take the Cape May–Lewes Ferry *(800-64-FERRY. Fare)* across Delaware Bay to the Garden State Parkway exit between US 30 and County Rd. 530. **By plane:** The closest major airports are in Philadelphia and Newark. **By train:** The New Jersey Transit System *(215-569-3752)* runs from Philadelphia to Hammonton and Egg Harbor City.

### General Information

Spring and fall are the best seasons, while summer can be hot and humid. The best sources for information are the New Jersey Department of Environmental Protection, Division of Parks and Forestry *(501 E. State St., Trenton 08625. 609-984-0370 or 800-843-6420)*; and the Pinelands Preservation Alliance *(114 Hanover St., Pemberton 08068. 609-894-8000)*.

### Things to See and Do

**1. Wharton State Forest** Perched at the edge of this forest, **Batsto Village** *(Cty. Rd. 542. 609-561-3262. Adm. fee for mansion)* provides a glimpse of 1880s life in a small glass and iron company town. The Batsto Pond Nature Trail winds through a varied Pinelands habitat.

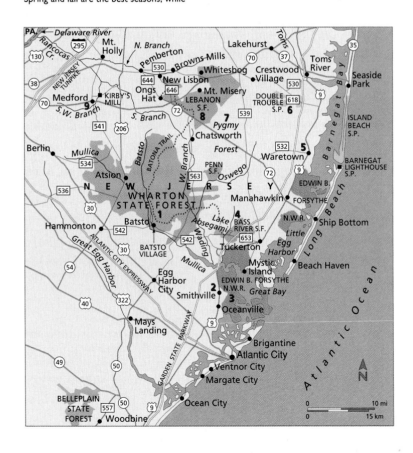

**2. Smithville** Over 35 stores centered around the 1787 Smithville Inn comprise the **Towne of Historic Smithville** *(US 9. 609-652-7777)*, a commercialized re-creation of 18th-century village life and crafts.

**3. Edwin B. Forsythe National Wildlife Refuge** *(Brigantine Division headquarters, Great Creek Rd., off US 9, Oceanville. 609-652-1665. Adm. fee)* An 8-mile wildlife drive and two short nature trails provide opportunities for enjoying nature up close. More than 270 species of birds frequent the refuge.

**4. Bass River State Forest** *(Cty. Rd. 542, off US 9. 609-296-1114. Adm. fee Mem. Day–Labor Day)* Centered around Lake Absegami, this 18,200-acre park features swimming, hiking, camping, boating, and fishing. A half-mile nature walk winds through pine and oak woods and across a small white cedar pond.

**5. Waretown** The **Albert Music Hall** *(125 Wells Mills Rd. 609-971-1593. Open year-round for special and Sat. night performances; fee)* hosts regular Pinelands folk, bluegrass, and country music concerts.

**6. Double Trouble State Park** *(Double Trouble Rd., near the Garden State Pkwy. 732-341-6662)* Remains of a turn-of-the-century company town include a schoolhouse, cranberry sorting house, and pickers' cottages. The park also offers hiking and canoeing.

**7. Pygmy Forest** *(NE of Chatsworth)* The nation's largest pygmy pine forest—with trees barely head high—fills this unique 12,000-acre area.

**8. Lebanon State Forest** *(Jct. of N.J. 70 and N.J. 72. 609-726-1191)* Hiking at Pakim Pond, cabins and campsites, old cranberry farms (such as Historic Whitesbog Village), and special walks and events can be found in this 31,879-acre preserve.

**9. Medford** Displays and demonstrations on local life highlight **Kirby's Mill** *(275 Church Rd. 609-654-0768. June-Aug. Sun.)*, a delightful, restored 1778 gristmill. If time allows, go for a paddle on the South Branch Rancocas Creek, which powers the mill.

**Other Activities**
**Blueberry picking** *(609-292-5068. Ask for the "Guide to Pick Your Own Farms in New Jersey")* Visitors can fill pails from June through August.

**Canoeing and tubing** The season runs from April through October; for rental and guided trip information call the New Jersey Division of Travel & Tourism *(609-292-2470*

Medford street scene

*or 800-JERSEY-7)*.

**Hiking** *(Lebanon State Forest 609-726-1191, Wharton State Forest 609-561-3262, Bass River State Forest 609-296-1114)* Connecting Lebanon, Wharton, and Bass River State Forests, the level, sandy footpath of Batona Trail ambles through dusky pine woods, offering close contact with such native plant life as mountain laurels, inkberries, and sweet pepperbushes.

**Annual Events**
**February** Ocean County Bluegrass Festival *(Albert Music Hall, Waretown. 609-971-1593)*
**May** Pine Barrens Festival *(Waretown. 609-971-1593)*
**June** Whitesbog Blueberry Festival *(Lebanon State Forest. 609-893-4646)*
**October** Batsto Country Living Fair *(Batsto Village. 609-561-3262)*; Jersey Devil Cranberry Company Harvest *(Double Trouble S.P. 732-341-6662)*; Cranberry Harvest Tours *(Lebanon State Forest. 609-893-4646)*; Apple Festival *(Medford. 609-654-0768)*; Chatsworth Cranberry Festival *(Chatsworth. 609-859-9701)*

**Lodging**
**Inn at Sugar Hill** *(5704 Mays Landing-Somers Point Rd., Mays Landing. 609-625-2226)* Perched on a knoll above cozy Great Egg Harbor, this 19th-century inn offers six rooms and an elegant continental breakfast on the veranda.

# Down Jersey

The Delaware Bay arcs against the southern coast of New Jersey, its marshes seeping inland in a slow, steady melding of land and sea. Life here in "Down Jersey" moves more to the tides than to any human rhythm, though the tides of human history have brushed quickly over this place—and moved on. In their wake, they left behind some captivating remnants of a prosperous colonial past, when this coastline supported lively summer resorts, some now no more than ghost villages on stilts; and a clam and oyster industry memorialized in high white mounds of shell.

## Down Jersey's Shipbuilding Legacy

In the small river and bay towns of southern New Jersey, the sea traditionally provided a livelihood for many families. The early colonists used the area's abundant forests of oak and pine to craft fine ship masts and hulls. The shipbuilding industry that began then continued well into the mid-20th century. Towns such as Greenwich and Bridgeton became famous for their tugs, yachts, freighters, fishing smacks, and—above all—oyster schooners. Sadly, the days of those beauties gliding across the Delaware Bay in full sail are gone, but the romance of men, ships, and the sea lingers in this pocket of Down Jersey.

Though the East Coast megalopolis rages at the edge of this place, the shimmering quiet here is far from the rush of malls and freeways. Only empty country lanes angle out toward the Delaware Bay, and motion lies gentle on the mind. Gulls sway in the breezes that push onshore, playing through tall, tassled prairies of phragmite. In the many wildlife management areas along the coastline, stiff-legged egrets keep watch over sun-spangled marshes, and small pleasure boats putter up weaving rivers. In the past, those rivers were thriving corridors of trade that gave rise to towns of promise.

One of these, **Greenwich** (say GREEN-WICH), has kept its colonial heritage largely intact. Along the shady berm of Ye Greate Street stand house after house from the village's long, historic past. It was Quaker John Fenwick who purchased land for the town in 1685. Within a few decades, Quakers from the nearby village of Salem had moved here, as had Calvinists from New England. The latter called the town Greenwich, after the Connecticut village. Today, the architecture of the village reflects its mixed roots. There's a touch of New England saltbox mixed with Middle Atlantic Georgian and Chesapeake telescope. (The telescopes are particularly easy to identify, as each successive wing, added in a straight line, is a little taller than the next, giving them the look of an extended telescope.)

Greenwich's pièce de résistance today is the **Gibbon House,** a dignified

*A.J. Meerwald,* **Delaware Bay**

colonial fronted with Flemish bond brickwork. Downstairs, a parlor, dining room, and kitchen reflect the life of a prominent family from the mid-18th to mid-19th centuries. Upstairs, rooms house collections of local memorabilia. Behind the house stands a low-slung log building, built in the mid-1600s as a granary by the Swedish settlers who first colonized the Delaware Bay and River and moved here from a nearby township.

Across the street stands the **John DuBois Maritime Museum,** whose exhibits trace the long history of boat-building in the area. The new **Cumberland County Prehistorical Museum,** located near the town's funky general store, preserves the heritage of the native peoples who were here centuries before there was a town.

Once there was a town, however, the Calvinists claimed the north end of it, and their graveyard, dating from 1707, still lies near the church they built in 1835. At the south end of town, the 1771 Quaker meetinghouse rises near the banks of the Cohansey River, the waterway that brought the town its early prosperity. A nearby monument marks Greenwich's great moment in history: Taking their cue from their Boston brethren, local townsmen confiscated tea stored by a Tory sympathizer and burned it defiantly on the town square.

Such passions seem far from the serenity of the town or its environs today. If you dogleg down the roads west of town, through whispering stands of phragmite, you'll eventually come to Bayside, with its windbeaten views of cargo ships plowing out of the Delaware River and into the bay. Now virtually uninhabited, Bayside was once known as Caviar, after its bustling industry in sturgeon roe. The sturgeon were fished out long ago, and the town's name was almost lost to history.

A new industry moved into the area a few decades ago, when a nuclear power plant was built upriver at Salem. Its massive white cooling tower now stands like a sentinel near the mouth of the Delaware. Originally,

**Bivalve oystermen**

plans called for the plant to be built along this stretch of coast, and even today, local houses bought by the power company in anticipation of the project still stand in fields, boarded up and forlorn. Perhaps to make amends, the power company has put aside 4,500 acres in the Bayside Tract, to protect coastal wetlands and uplands for wildlife. Migratory birds seem to appreciate these efforts, because great flocks of them—Canada geese, snow geese, and other shore birds—wheel and dabble in the capacious marshlands.

As you drive through this flat, consoling countryside, the whole nuclear age seems the figment of some sci-fi imagination, particularly at a place such as Seabreeze. Languishing at the very edge of the bay, its tiny, 1950s-style beach cottages are mostly deserted now, but the hamlet once had a prosperous hotel and docks for a steamboat that ferried passengers from here to Philadelphia. Today, the ghost village conjures up nostalgic visions of the inner-tube days of beach resorts, before boogie boards and multi-deck vacation homes took over.

The old resort community of Fortescue, farther down the coast of

Delaware Bay, has managed to hold on, its row of modest houses facing into the sea winds and its small public beach well attended by sunbathers in summer and beachcombers in the off-season.

Inland from the town, the road passes through pockets of the pine, oak, and bayberry forest that once greened much of the Atlantic coastal plain. Most of that natural woodland fell long ago, cleared to make room for farm fields that produced bountiful grain and vegetable harvests. Today, the farms of yesteryear have given way to a more urbanized endeavor—wholesale nurseries. Arrow straight rows of young saplings and shrubs now march across fields, replacing the old rows of corn and tomatoes.

But farming was not the only industry here in the past. The shellfish industry kept many communities alive—and still does to a limited extent.

Oystermen reaped a plentiful bounty from planting grounds at the mouth of the Maurice River, and the small road's-end enclave called Bivalve celebrates that past. A packing company continues to operate at the edge of the river here, mounding the shoreline with white shells. But the real draw is the high-masted, 1928 oyster schooner *A.J. Meerwald* docked amid the pleasure boats at Bivalve's marina. One of hundreds of such schooners built along New Jersey's bay shore early in this century, the *Meerwald* had a long career—first in oystering until the bust brought on by a parasite in 1957, then in clamming. Now she takes groups out on the bay for a taste of the old schooner days.

**Horseshoe crabs, Delaware Bay**

Along with the *Meerwald,* Bivalve holds another attraction: an observation tower and a new 2-mile trail, part boardwalk, part path, which threads out into the reclaimed marshlands here. Long ago, farmers diked these marshes to grow salt hay. Now the dikes have been taken down so that the natural life of the wetlands can return. A second 800-foot-long boardwalk also leads into the moody woodland swamps edging the marshes.

Nearby, in the small town of **Port Norris**, the **Delaware Bay Museum** documents the bay's richness—natural, cultural, and historical—in old photographs, artifacts, and exhibits.

Probably the prettiest town in this part of Down Jersey lies upriver. As you drive through the tidy grid of streets that mark 18th-century Mauricetown, you may not see a soul. But its perfectly tended, Greek Revival and gingerbread-style Victorian houses attest to its long, proud history with the river. Thanks to grassroots boosters, the river is now protected as the Maurice Scenic and Recreation River. What used to be a hard-working, waterman's river has reverted to its natural impulses. In fact, the same could be said of the whole wild sweep of Down Jersey.
—*K.M. Kostyal*

# Travel Notes

### Directions
Situated at the southwestern end of New Jersey, the area is within 30 miles of Wilmington, Delaware, and Philadelphia, Pennsylvania. **By car:** From the Delaware Bay Bridge and I-295, take N.J. 49 east. From the Atlantic City Expressway *(toll)* exit south onto N.J. 55 and 47 toward Mauricetown. From the south, travelers can take

the Cape May–Lewes Ferry *(800-64-FERRY. Fare)* across Delaware Bay, then follow US 9 to N.J. 47 north. **By plane:** The closest airports are located in Philadelphia, Atlantic City, and Wilmington.

### General Information
The bird migration down the Atlantic flyway fills area marshlands with birdlife in the spring and fall. Summers can be hot and humid, and winters cold and damp. For information contact the Bridgeton-Cumberland Tourist Association *(50 E. Broad St., Bridgeton 08302. 609-453-2177 or 800-319-3379).*

### Things to See and Do
**1. Greenwich** *(Jct. of Cty. Rd. 623 and Cty. Rd. 607)* The following attractions in this small jewel of a town are located on Ye Greate Street, which isn't numbered. Filled

with period furniture, the **Gibbon House** *(609-455-4055. April-Thanksgiving. Tues.-Sat.; donation)* also offers local memorabilia. The **John DuBois Maritime Museum** *(609-455-1774. April-Thanksgiving Sat.-Sun., and by appt.; donation)* documents the area's history of boat-building, while the **Cumberland County Prehistorical Museum** *(609-455-8141. April-Thanksgiving Wed. and Sat.-Sun.; donation)* spotlights Native American culture.
**2. Port Norris** The small **Delaware Bay Museum** *(1727 Main St. 609-785-2060. April-Oct. weekends, and by appt.; donation)* features historic photographs, artifacts, and exhibits that detail this area's oyster and shipbuilding industries and the natural resources of its wetlands.
**3. Bivalve** After decades of oystering and clamming, the schooner *A.J. Meerwald (Bivalve dock. 609-785-2060. Public sailings sporadically April-Nov., call for schedule; fare)* is now used to educate the public on the history of the watermen who once worked the bay.

### Other Activities
**Birding, hiking, and hunting** For information on these activities in shoreline preserves call 609-339-7915 or 888-MARSHES.
**Scenic drives** The statewide New Jersey Coastal Heritage Trail *(New Jersey Division of Travel and Tourism 609-292-2470 or 800-537-7397)* leads travelers to historic and natural sites from Salem, on Delaware Bay, up the Atlantic coastline to Perth Amboy.

### Annual Events
**June** Delaware Bay Day *(Bivalve, Shellpile, and surrounding hamlets. 609-785-2060)*
**September** Greenwich Craft Faire *(Greenwich. 609-455-4055)*
**November** Greenwich Antique Show *(Greenwich. 609-455-4055)*
**December** Christmas Candlelight House Tour *(Mauricetown. 609-785-1137)*

### Lodging
**Meadow View Bed & Breakfast** *(103 Barth Rd., Port Elizabeth. 609-825-7489)* This Cape Cod home on the banks of the scenic Manumuskin River prides itself on being a birders' paradise.

# DELAWARE

# Delaware Marshlands

In a blizzard of feathers they descend on Bombay Hook National Wildlife Refuge, the thousands of snow geese that come to winter here, far from their Arctic nesting grounds. First they're tiny, white dots that seemingly fill the sunset-washed sky. Band by band they lower until you see their black-tipped wings and pink feet plashing on the marshy waters in a great cacaphonic chatter. Bombay Hook is the heart of Delaware's marshlands, the rich landscape of wetlands, tilled fields, woods, and ponds along the Delaware River and Bay between New Castle and Dover. All kinds of birds—travelers along the Atlantic flyway such as Canada geese and sandpipers, and year-round residents such as great blue herons and egrets—make the region an all-year paradise for casual and serious birders both.

But there's more to the Delaware marshlands than birds. This is a historic land, settled in turn by the Swedes, Dutch, and English, and now

**Canada geese, Bombay Hook National Wildlife Refuge**

punctuated with slumberous, old hamlets whose tidy frame houses overlook once proud ports. In 1651 Dutchman Peter Stuyvesant purchased from Native Americans a parcel of land along a bend in the Delaware River. The subsequent village that prospered became **New Castle**, Delaware's colonial capital. Bypassed by time, its picturesque historic district showcases Stuyvesant's original town common, which is edged by cobbled streets, old frame structures, and antique shops. One of the few surviving buildings from the Dutch period of settlement (1651-1664), the

**Court House, New Castle**

tiny **Dutch House** looks a bit out of place with its sloping pent eaves, but its colonial antiques provide a good understanding of life here centuries ago. The state assembly met at the **Court House** between 1732 and 1777, when the government moved to Dover. Another remnant of the past, the **George Read II House**, dating from 1801, is a federal beauty with 14,000 feet of living space and famous Palladian windows.

Founded in the 18th century as Cantwell's Bridge, wee **Odessa**, too, once flourished, but since has passed into the history books. Where steamers docked in the mid-1800s to load bushels of corn, tobacco, and wheat, and hundreds of people flurried, quiet streets now beckon with lovingly

**Odessa roadside fruit stand**

preserved houses and flower-filled gardens. Harking back to the town's beginnings, several house museums owned and operated by Winterthur portray the differing lifestyles of early residents, from a Quaker family to a wealthy merchant.

The area's other river towns move more intimately with the ebbs and flows of the tidal marshes. Folks residing in such diminutive fishing villages as **Delaware City, Port Penn, Woodland Beach**, and **Leipsic** make their livings from blue crab, shad, and muskrat, just as their forebears have for centuries. Sparkling white trawlers bob from dockside moorings and the colorfully striped buoys of crabbing pots hang from gray, weathered structures like Christmas decorations.

A great way to visit this hinterland is to drive south from New Castle on Del. 9, which more or less rambles beside the Delaware River, skirting boundless carpets of cordgrass and capacious fields of soybeans and corn, crossing tiny bridges where locals toss their lines for crabs and eels. Lying close to navigable waters, old brick mansions—some restored, others not—bespeak of a more prosperous time, when farmers grew wealthy on the rich, heavy soil. Narrow, pockmarked roads wander off to fishing piers, an odd lighthouse or two, and modest beaches—maybe sandy **Woodland Beach** or rocky **Port Mahon.** For a better grasp on the local heritage, you can study the exhibits at the **Port Penn Interpretive Center,** and wander the interpretive trail just north of town that leads out into the marsh's depths.

But for the best understanding of Delaware's marshlands, stay on Del. 9 as far south as **Bombay Hook National Wildlife Refuge,** and stand on the edge of Delaware's largest marsh. You may think you're peering into an inhospitable realm of biting insects, extreme summer heat, and icky muck (which, in essence, you are). But biologists know these wetlands comprise an incredibly rich ecosystem. Indeed, each acre produces about ten tons of organic material, twice the amount of a typical hayfield. Crabs, flounder, oysters, clams, and striped bass all breed in the salt grass. In turn, this fecundity lures all kinds of fishermen—commercial and feathered alike. Taking all this in, you understand why the region's major focus is the marsh . . . for it's the marsh that gives life to the region.

*—Barbara A. Noe*

# Travel Notes

## Directions
This hidden corner along northern Delaware's shore more or less fringes Del. 9 between New Castle and Dover. **By car:** From Wilmington, go south on Del. 9. **By plane:** The closest major airport is in Philadelphia, Pennsylvania. **By train:** Amtrak serves Wilmington.

## General Information
The best times to visit are during the spring and fall migrations. Autumn is particularly lovely, when changing foliage contrasts against the golden marsh grasses. Summer can be humid and buggy, while winter, though cold, brings overwintering birds. For information contact the Delaware State Visitor Center *(406 Federal St., Dover 19901. 302-739-4266).* The Coastal Heritage Greenway, which connects cultural and natural sites along the Delaware coastline, runs through this hidden corner; booklets are available from state park offices and the Delaware State Visitor Center.

## Things to See and Do
**1.** **New Castle** *(New Castle Visitors Bureau 800-758-1550)* Delaware's early capital pre-

serves its colonial atmosphere with lovely old buildings, brick sidewalks, and seasonal festivities. A brochure for the New Castle Heritage Trail, available from local merchants, describes a walking tour of the major historic sites. Among them, don't miss the **George Read II House and Gardens** *(42 The Strand. 302-322-8411. March-Dec. Tues.-Sun., Jan.-Feb. Sat.-Sun.; adm. fee);* the **New Castle Court House Museum** *(211 Delaware St. 302-323-4453. Closed Mon.),* featuring a restored pre-Revolutionary courtroom and small museum; and the **Dutch House** *(32 E. 3rd St. 302-322-2794. March-Dec. Tues.-Sun., Jan.-Feb. Sat.-Sun.; adm. fee).*
**2.** **Delaware City** Nineteenth-century houses line tree-canopied streets in this former Delaware River port on the Chesapeake and Delaware Canal. A ferry regularly departs from the waterfront for **Fort Delaware State Park** *(302-834-7941. Mid-June–Labor Day Wed.-Sun., late April–mid-June and Labor Day–Sept. Sat.-Sun.; fare).* Built on Pea Patch Island to defend the sea approach upriver and used during the Civil War to imprison 33,000 Confederate soldiers and political prisoners, this bastion offers soldiers'

interpreters. A nature trail leads to an overlook of the East Coast's largest heronry.

**3. Port Penn** Historic houses dating as far
back as 1740 fill this typical tidewater town,
which, with its deepwater port, once har-
bored high hopes of becoming the next
Philadelphia. The **Port Penn Interpretive
Center** (Del. 9 at Rte. 2. 302-836-2533. Mem.
Day–Labor Day Wed.-Sun.) has brochures for a
self-guided village walking tour. Also at the
center, exhibits portray area history. A mile
north of town, the **Port Penn Interpretive
Trail** explores the marshlands.

**4. Odessa** With its excellent examples of
Georgian architecture, Odessa's tiny historic
district offers the four **Historic Houses of
Odessa** (302-378-4069. March-Dec. Tues.-
Sun.; adm. fee), owned and operated by Winterthur. Start at the **Brick Hotel Gallery**
(Main and 2nd Sts.) to buy tickets and see the
nation's largest collection of Victorian furniture manufactured by John Henry Belter. Tour
houses include the **Corbit Sharp House**

(Main St.), which portrays Quaker family life
from 1774 to 1818; the 1769 **Wilson
Warner House** (Main St.), built by a wealthy
merchant; and the **Collins Sharp House**
(2nd St.), dating from the 1700s and featuring
hearth cooking demonstrations on Fridays and
Saturdays March through October.

**5. Woodland Beach** Fronting the hamlet
of Woodland Beach, a narrow beach offers a
fishing pier and a quiet, uncrowded place to
fish, stroll, or take in some sun. The surrounding **Woodland Beach Wildlife
Area** (Del. 9. 302-653-2079) features fishing,
crabbing, and a tower for birdwatching.

**6. Bombay Hook National Wildlife
Refuge** (Off Del. 9 on Whitehall Neck Rd.
302-653-6872. Visitor Center closed summer
and winter weekends; adm. fee) Consisting
mostly of tidal saltmarsh and large freshwater ponds, the 15,978-acre refuge harbors
thousands of migrating and wintering ducks
and geese along the Atlantic flyway. A gravel,
12-mile, interpretive auto/bike route loops
the refuge, and several short hiking trails
make birdwatching easy.

**7. Leipsic** Wood-frame houses edge
golden marsh grasses in this typical water-
oriented village. For fresh seafood, locals
flock to **Sambo's Tavern** (283 Front St.
302-674-9724), whose windows oversee the
comings and goings of crab boats.

**8. Port Mahon** A long causeway leads to
an old wharf on Delaware Bay, with fishing
piers still popular among anglers. The mudflats here are a good place to observe the
spring arrival of horseshoe crabs and migrating shorebirds. **Little Creek Wildlife
Area** (Off Del. 9. 302-653-2079), at the
southern tip of Port Mahon, claims to be one
of the nation's best shorebird-watching sites.

## Annual Events
**May** A Day in Old New Castle (302-
322-5774)
**Nov.-Dec.** Yuletide in Odessa (302-378-4069)

## Lodging
**Armitage Inn** (2 The Strand, New Castle. 302-
328-6618) The elegant 1732 inn offers a taste
of the past with canopy beds and fireplaces.
**Cantwell House** (107 High St., Odessa. 302-
378-4179) This charming wood-frame residence serves breakfast in a colonial dining
room or overlooking the garden.
**William Penn Guest House** (206
Delaware St., New Castle. 302-328-7736) The
oldest section of the house dates from 1680.

# MARYLAND
# Chesapeake & Ohio Canal

A lazy, winding course along the Potomac River, the Chesapeake & Ohio Canal is quiet now, the wooded domain of great blue heron and painted turtle, red fox and beaver. But in its heyday some hundred years past, the 184.5-mile-long route between Washington, D.C., and Cumberland, Maryland, resounded with the clipped shouts of canal men guiding low-slung riverboats, with the muffled hoofbeat of mules clopping along its towpath. Named a national historical park in 1971, the Chesapeake & Ohio Canal embraces serene woodlands, breathtaking riverscapes, miles of springtime bluebells, and the rugged Appalachians—a boon for walkers, bicyclists, birders, rock climbers, canoeists...anyone who enjoys nature. Along the way, bits and pieces of the past—crumbling aqueducts, lockhouses, bridges, dams, and a masterful brick tunnel—serve as reminders of the early industrial age.

Beginning in D.C., in the historic heart of trendy, bustling **Georgetown,** the C&O's towpath quickly sweeps you into an endless burrow of trees, with views of the rippling Potomac on one side, and placid canal waters on the other. So close to metropolitan life, silence reigns, punctuated solely by the wind's rustling of maple and sycamore leaves, by songbirds warbling in spring and fall. All is quiet, that is, except on sunny weekends, when flocks of sun-loving locals swarm along the towpath's first few miles, many heading for Great Falls.

Even before the canal came into being, **Great Falls** and its stunning scenery were a popular destination for Washingtonians. Here a boardwalk

## Wash Out

There's a reason why a lush forest flourishes along the canal. It's situated in the Potomac's floodplain, a strip of limestone and calcium-rich land that's nourished with occasional floodings—not the safest place to be in a rainstorm. Just after canal work began in 1828, a flood delayed the schedule. The 1852 flood caused $100,000 worth of canal damage, an 1889 rainstorm forced the canal into a receivership, and the 1924 flood shut the canal down forever. The 1985 flood accrued $20 million in damages, while repairs from the 1996 flood are still underway. So is it worth fixing and refixing this fragment of history? Outdoor lovers think so...every new flood they donate money and volunteer thousands of hours to mend their beloved canal.

**Along the C&O Canal, near Spring Gap, Maryland**

trail jumps across several channels and islands to the middle of the Potomac, where a front row seat of the spectacle awaits: a fury of white water pouring through chutes and over rocks. So near the powerful river, it's easy to understand why a canal bypass was needed. Indeed, six locks dropped canalboats 41 feet in less than one mile. On shore, historic **Great Falls Tavern** was built in 1829 as a lockkeepers house, and later enlarged as a popular hotel. Today it houses a National Park Visitor Center with exhibits on canal history.

Considered one of the nation's most ambitious industrial experiments of its time, the C&O Canal began as the dream of George Washington, who foresaw using the Potomac River to link the rich Ohio River Valley with coastal towns. Though his efforts through his Patowmack Company failed, Washington's concept prevailed with the founding of the Chesapeake & Ohio Canal Company. Or so champions of the ancient canal technology thought. For on July 4, 1828, just as President John Quincy Adams was shoveling the canal's first earth in Washington, D.C. (the greatest moment of his life, he said), a similar ceremony was taking place in Baltimore, Maryland...the christening of the Baltimore & Ohio Railroad. No one knew exactly how the new-fangled steam railway—America's first—would fare. The race was on.

It was soon evident, however, which was the quicker, cheaper mode of transport. Beset by a daunting list of difficulties—financial woes, legal battles, unforeseen geography problems—the canal didn't reach Cumberland until 1850, eight years after the railroad had whizzed on through. Though the canal was itself a major engineering feat, with 74 lift locks built to move canalboats 605 feet above sea level, there was no sense in proceeding on to the Ohio River, as originally planned. In a cruel twist, the canal eventually went into a receivership to the B&O Railroad, serving the farms and businesses of the Potomac Valley until the Flood of 1924 closed it for good.

Beyond Great Falls, the river calms, the droves thin out, and the towpath enters an especially peaceful realm. Surrounded by the Piedmont's gentle hills, where pileated woodpeckers tap on old dead limbs and spotted turtles sun on logs, it's easy to understand why in the 1950s Supreme Court Associate Justice William O. Douglas waged a fierce battle to prevent this from being cemented over as a scenic parkway. Challenging journalists to walk its entire length, Douglas swayed the *Washington Post* to editorialize in favor of the canal's preservation, thereby saving the property. "One who walked the canal its full length could plead that cause with the eloquence of a John Muir," he wrote. And indeed, you can.

Farther upstream, visitors come across one of the canal's many engineering achievements, the Monocacy River Aqueduct, constructed of local quartz sandstone. With its seven arches, the 560-foot structure celebrates the craftsmanship of Irish immigrants. Lacking sophisticated tools or equipment, they and other immigrant groups constructed 11 aqueducts, more than 150 stone culverts, seven dams and many bridges—all masterful in their design and durability.

Historic canal towns line the length of the C&O, probably none so famous as **Harpers Ferry,** West Virginia, perched at the dramatic confluence of the Shenandoah and Potomac Rivers in the shade of the Blue Ridge. Established in 1747 as a ferry crossing and chosen as a national armory site in 1795, the hilly town prospered with the canal's arrival in the 1830s. But it is best known for abolitionist John Brown's unsuccessful raid on its federal arsenal in 1859. During the Civil War, the Union and Confederate armies took turns occupying the river town, and it never recovered economically. Today, restored buildings hold museums, shops, and restaurants, and a spectacular hike up Maryland Heights leads to an unforgettable

### Family Affair

Captains spent nine months a year moving their barges up and down the C&O, often depending on their families to serve as crew members. Wives helped out with the cooking, cleaning, washing, child-rearing, and sewing, while the older kids (from age 6 on) were responsible for the all-important mules, taking care of them on board and driving them on the towpath. The youngest ones spent their days tethered to the cabin roof, safe from any misadventures. The family's cabin measured 12-by-12.5 feet—not a lot of space, considering much of it was reserved for coal, flour, grain, and other cargo. Despite the tight quarters, however, many canallers complained of boredom, long stretches of canal with distractions few and far between.

vista of the river valley. Enchanting **Shepherdstown,** another former canal town 12 miles upstream, is West Virginia's oldest inhabited community, settled in 1727 by Pennsylvania German farmers. **Williamsport,** too, is an old canal town whose historic sections preserve its 19th-century mood.

Any sign of civilization is left behind as the canal enters the dry ridges and valleys of the Appalachians, carpeted in oaks and scattered with prickly pear cactuses. Rugged, rocky, and wild, this landscape describes the isolation experienced by early pioneers long before the canal was pushed through. In the 1750s, the colonial government built a series of forts along the Maryland border to protect frontier settlers from warring French and Indian soldiers. The sole remaining, **Fort Frederick,** evokes a frontier feel along the canal, with muskets crackling and cannons booming on summer weekends.

Such unforgiving mountainous terrain truly challenged canal workers, whose detailed blueprints didn't always take into account harsh local conditions. Their ingenuity shines at **Paw Paw Tunnel,** a 3,118-foot bore through a mountain that took some 3,000 workers nearly 15 years to complete...a pretty price to avoid 6 miles of the loopy Potomac. In the tunnel's spooky blackness, where the only sounds are the drip-drip of water and your smothered foot slaps on the towpath, it's easy to picture canalling days, when lanterns illuminated the way for mules and the walls resounded with the muffled shouts of bargemen demanding the right-of-way (indeed, in such a tight space, who backs up?).

The end of the line is industrial **Cumberland,** where the canal's last lock lies seemingly forgotten beneath an interstate overpass. Looking back, it's clear the canal, created on the cusp of the industrial age, was obsolete from the start. But living on as a nature sanctuary in the heart of a thriving metropolis, where white-tailed deer, beaver, and red fox can roam more freely than even a century ago, it offers perhaps an even greater value than what it originally set out to be. —*Barbara A. Noe*

**Harpers Ferry from Maryland Heights**

# Travel Notes

### Directions
The C&O Canal traces the Potomac River for 184.5 miles between Georgetown in Washington, D.C., and Cumberland, Maryland. Mile markers make it easy to locate points of interest along the way. **By plane:** The nearest airports serve Washington, D.C. **By train:** Amtrak's *Capital Limited* stops at Washington, D.C.; Harpers Ferry, West Virginia; and Cumberland. **By car:** Access points and parking areas are found all along the canal; consult a National Park Service map for details.

*The Georgetown,* **on the C&O Canal**

### General Information
The best times to visit are spring and fall, when the temperature is mild and foliage is blooming or changing color. The canal's busiest sections are from Washington to Seneca (miles 1 to 23) and near Harpers Ferry (around mile 60). The most isolated sections are from Shepherdstown to Dam 4 (miles 70 to 85) and from Hancock to North Branch (miles 125 to 180). For more information, contact the Chesapeake & Ohio Canal National Historical Park Headquarters *(Box 4, Sharpsburg 21782. 301-739-4200).*

### Things to See and Do
**1. Georgetown** *(Mile 2)* Nineteenth-century row houses line the canal front in the heart of Georgetown, which predates the founding of Washington. *The Georgetown (Tickets at Visitor Center, Foundry Mall, 1057 Thomas Jefferson St. 202-653-5190. Mid-April–Oct.; fare)* is a mule-drawn canalboat offering rides; interpretive walks explore the life and times of the once-thriving tidal port.
**2. Great Falls** *(Mile 14. 301-299-3613. Adm. fee)* This boulder-strewn torrent of water on the Potomac is one of the East's most spectacular natural wonders. Bridges and boardwalks lead to an overlook in the middle of the river. On shore, the **Great Falls Tavern** has been reincarnated as a Visitor Center. Living history programs are offered aboard a canalboat that rides through a lift lock.
**3. White's Ferry** *(Mile 35. 301-349-5200)* The *Gen. Jubal A. Early* carries on a 150-year tradition ferrying passengers across the Potomac.
**4. Harpers Ferry National Historical Park,** West Virginia *(Mile 60. 304-535-6298)* A footbridge across the Potomac River leads

to this charming little town filled with restored 19th-century buildings. Interpretive programs and museums feature local subjects.
**5. Shepherdstown,** West Virginia *(Mile 72.8. Visitor Center, 102 N. King St. 304-876-2786)* Shops and restaurants line this quaint village's main street.
**6. Williamsport** *(Mile 99. Visitor Center, 205 W. Potomac St. 301-582-0813)* George Washington once considered Williamsport as a possible location for the nation's capital. Several historic sections retain their 19th-century canal town flair.
**7. Fort Frederick State Park** *(Mile 112. 301-842-2155. Visitor Center May-Sept. daily, Oct.-April Mon.-Fri., grounds open year-round; adm. fee to fort)* Built in 1756 to protect the British colonies' frontier during the French and Indian War, Fort Frederick features a small museum and summer interpretive programs.
**8. Hancock** *(Mile 125. Visitor Center, Main St. 301-678-5463)* Once a frontier trading post, this small river town blossomed after the canal came through in 1839; many canal families wintered in its warehouses. The Visitor Center has a small historical museum.
**9. Paw Paw Tunnel** *(Mile 155)* This engineering marvel was built between 1836 and 1850. Hiking trails, picnic tables, and interpretive walks are offered.
**10. C&O Canal Boat Replica** *(Mile 175. 301-722-3136. June-Aug. Mon.-Fri. and Sun., and by appt.)* The furnished captain's quarters and mule stall aboard this drydocked canal boat vividly portray canal life.
**11. Cumberland** *(Mile 184.5. Visitor Center, Canal St. 301-722-8226. Closed Mon.)* This steepled town flourished in the 19th century thanks to its location on the railroad and canal

lent to poor due to weather, rocks, and tree roots. Bikes can be rented at Fletcher's Boathouse (*4940 Canal Rd., Washington, D.C. 202-244-0461. April-Oct.*) and Swains Lock (*Mile 16, N of Great Falls. 301-299-9006. Mid-March–mid-Nov.*).

**Birdwatching** Birders can walk along the towpath any time of year and spot Carolina chickadee, northern cardinal, or great blue heron. Spring is exceptional, with songbird migrants passing through, and autumn brings the annual hawk migration. Contact park headquarters for information.

**Camping** There are free tent campsites for hikers and bikers along the canal between miles 16 and 180. Sites are first come, first served. Drive-in camping areas are found at McCoys Ferry, Fifteenmile Creek, and Spring Gap, all offered on a first-come, first-served basis.

**Canoeing and boating** The canal is watered between Georgetown and Violettes Lock (the first 22 miles). Canoes can be rented at Fletcher's Boathouse (*see above*) and Swains Lock (*see above*). The park also offers public access boat ramps.

**Fishing** Fishing is allowed on the river and in the canal, subject to Maryland and Washington, D.C., laws. Anglers catch perch, catfish, striped bass, and other freshwater species.

**Hiking** The towpath's 12-foot-wide, level surface makes for excellent hiking along the canal's entire length. There are also trails at Great Falls and Paw Paw Tunnel.

**Horseback riding** Riding is permitted from Swains Lock to Cumberland.

**Ranger programs** Ranger-led walks, talks, and bike rides are offered year-round; contact park headquarters.

### Annual Events
**August** Williamsport Canal Days (*Williamsport. 301-223-7711*)
**September** Canal Apple Days (*Hancock. 301-678-5325*)

### Lodging
**Cohill Manor Bed & Breakfast** (*W of Hancock on Md. 144. 301-678-7573*) Deer, goats, and chickens roam on 11 private acres at this 250-plus-year-old estate.
**Ground Squirrel Holler Bed & Breakfast** (*6736 Sharpsburg Pike, Sharpsburg. 301-432-8288*) At this whimsical, circa-1910, lavender-trimmed house, 13 llamas graze on 5 acres of oak woods and rolling hills. Three guest bedrooms feature pressed tin ceilings and antique headboards.

lines. Housed in the old Western Maryland Station Center, the Visitor Center contains small museums on railroad and canal history.

### Other Activities
**Biking** Biking is permitted along the entire towpath, with conditions varying from excel-

# Historic St. Marys

By day St. Marys County is a lovely place, all golden fields and curvaceous blue rivers, weathered tobacco barns and copses of oak, maple, and pine. But as darkness shrouds the landscape, spirits seem to stir. Perhaps it's because Maryland's oldest settlement took root here in 1634, just 14 years after the Pilgrims stepped ashore at Plymouth Rock. Perhaps it's the lingering tales of the Civil War prisoners who died at Point Lookout—whose restless ghosts, locals insist, inhabit the county's old estates. Or perhaps it's simply the gossamer of predawn mists that hangs on the waterways, eerily lit by hard-driving trawlers.

Footing Maryland's western shore and bounded by the Patuxent and Potomac Rivers, St. Marys County is a 373-square-mile outpost of pastoral calm that embraces an old-fashioned mix of agricultural and tidewater ways of life. Aside from the Patuxent Naval Air Station, which crowds Lexington Park a bit, the county mostly remains the tranquil setting that two ships full of English Protestants and Catholics discovered in 1634.

Escaping Europe's bloody religious wars, these hardy pioneers ended

**Boats hugging shoreline, St. Marys City**

**St. Marys County panorama**

their long ocean journey at what's now **St. Clements Island**. Here, on March 25, 1634, the first Mass in the English New World was held, thereby setting the foundation of a society that, unlike Massachusetts' Pilgrims, would tolerate all religions. You can't reach the flat, low-lying island without your own boat, but you can see it resting just offshore from the **Potomac River Museum**. Exhibits at the museum provide a good understanding of the hopes and dreams of these daring colonists.

On the site of an Indian village purchased by their leader, Gov. Leonard Calvert, the settlers built **St. Marys City**, with up and down views of the St. Marys River. It served as Maryland's colonial capital until 1695, when the legislature moved to Annapolis. The region remained rural through the

**Drying tobacco**

centuries, leaving the colonial foundations undisturbed. That is until the 1960s, when archaeologists set about re-creating the colonial town—now an impressive, 800-acre living history museum. The reconstructed State House of 1676 contains upper and lower chambers, and interpreters occasionally prosecute a "villager" for murder, blasphemy, or simply shooting a turkey on Sunday. Nearby, aboard the *Maryland Dove*— a reproduction of one of the colonists' two ships—the wake of every passing boat makes one wonder how the diminutive vessel made it so far.

An interpretive trail links these sites with Governor Calvert's residence, an English Catholic church, and other frame buildings either reconstructed or in the process of being so. A short drive away, the re-created Godiah Spray Plantation showcases the mainstay of the colonial economy: tobacco.

Over the next century, tobacco helped build gracious manor houses all across St. Marys County. Many still stand at the end of tree-canopied lanes; the best way to see them is from the water, aboard a boat. Others you can drive by, or even spend the night. Among them, **St. Michael's Manor** and the Old Kirk House in Scotland are now B&Bs, and gracious Tudor Hall in Leonardtown, once belonging to the family of Francis Scott Key, houses administrative offices.

But to truly get a taste of the past, stop by **Sotterley Plantation,** a Georgian mansion near Hollywood built about 1710 on a bluff overlooking the Patuxent River. Surrounded by the state's only working 18th-century plantation lands, the mansion—with its long veranda, brick gables, and freshly cut flowers—offers a glimpse of what plantation life must have been like. In 1822, George Plater V, the last in a long line of Platers to own Sotterley, allegedly gambled the estate away in a dice game. On certain nights, some say, he can be heard galloping on horseback up the pebbled path to reclaim his home. Maybe so. But for those who really take ghost stories to heart, **Point Lookout** is the place to be.

Seemingly at the end of the world, the lonely, breeze-whipped point lies where the Potomac flows into Chesapeake Bay. Rough waters just offshore have claimed hundreds of lives—and perhaps it's their ghosts that locals say roam the area. But then there are the thousands of Confederate soldiers who perished at the point's infamous Civil War prison. Conditions were so harsh and cruel that many died delirious—and some say that when a person dies insentient, his confused spirit haunts the earth….Whatever the case, the point offers rustic **Point Lookout State Park,** featuring all kinds of water-based activities.

The long line of anglers flinging their bait from the park's causeway serves as a reminder of the region's intricate ties to the sea. Indeed, the colonists culled oysters, clams, fish, and crabs to sate their appetites. But the seafood industry didn't take off until after the Civil War, when the invention of the steamboat made it possible to ship perishables to distant markets. To this day, watermen head into the open Chesapeake beneath the veil of night, returning with bows full. If you know where to look, you can find some of their catch at seafood joints tucked along the county's corregated shoreline. And look you should, because sitting on a sunny deck watching the trawlers skim by, cracking open crabs, and munching oysters, you can truly appreciate the simplicity and beauty of St. Marys County…a slow-paced world of long ago.
— *Barbara A. Noe*

## County Churches

Silent reminders of a rich religious legacy, a bounty of diminutive churches dot St. Marys County. Among them, **St. Ignatius Catholic Church** (*Off Md. 5 on Villa Rd., St. Inigoes. 301-872-5590*), successor to the first Catholic chapel at St. Marys City, features magnificent stained-glass windows. Founded in 1640, **Historic Christ Church** (*Md. 238 off Md. 234, Chaptico*) was occupied by British soldiers during the War of 1812. Established in the 1650s, **All Faith Episcopal Church** (*Md. 6, Charlotte Hall*) showcases an impressive rose window and slave gallery. Consult the "Visitor's Guide to St. Marys County," available at the Chamber of Commerce (*301-884-5555*).

# Travel Notes

## Directions

St. Marys County is situated south of Washington, D.C., at the southernmost tip of Maryland's western shore. **By car:** From I-495 south of Washington, D.C., take Md. 5 south, the main artery through the county. **By plane:** The closest airports are in Washington, D.C. **By train:** Amtrak serves Washington, D.C.

## General information

Autumn is a fine time to visit, when tobacco hangs in curing barns and the landscape takes on the rich hues of changing foliage. Oyster season is October through December. Summer is often humid and buggy, while winter can be cold and bleak. For tourist information contact the Department of Economic Development (*P.O. Box 653, Leonardtown 20650. 301-475-4411 or 800-327-9023*) or

**Maryland blue crabs**

the St. Marys County Chamber of Commerce Visitor Information Center (*28290 Three Notch Rd./Md. 5, Mechanicsville 20636. 301-884-5555*).

## Things to See and Do

**1. Farmer's Market & Auction** (*S of Hughesville, E side of Md. 5. 301-884-3966. Wed. and Sat.*) A large number of Amish inhabit the northern part of St. Marys County, as evidenced at this biweekly market. Over 150 vendors purvey fresh fruit,

vegetables, chickens, furniture, and more.

**2. St. Clements Island Potomac River Museum** (*Md. 242, off Md. 5, Coltons Point. 301-769-2222. Mid-March–Sept. daily, Oct.–mid-March Wed.–Sun.; adm. fee*) Exhibits focus on the English colonists who landed in 1634 on St. Clements Island and Native American culture before the colonists' arrival. Accessible only by boat, nearby **St. Clements Island** offers hiking trails, exhibit panels, picnic facilities, and a steel cross marking the colonists' landing site; inquire at the museum about an excursion boat.

**3. Leonardtown**  Platted in 1730, this attractive little town was once an important tobacco port. On the courthouse lawn stands the stout, granite **Old Jail Museum** (*301-475-2467. Tues.–Sat.*), housing county artifacts and memorabilia. Across the street, 1750 **Tudor Hall** (*Private*) is a handsome Georgian manor with a hanging staircase.

**4. Piney Point Lighthouse Museum and Park** (*Lighthouse Rd. off Md. 249. 301-769-2222 Museum open April–Oct. weekends, grounds year-round; donation*) The first permanent light on the Potomac River contains artifacts belonging to a U-1105 German submarine. The surrounding park offers a picnic area and boardwalk.

**5. St. Marys City** (*Md. 5, S of Lexington Park. 301-862-0990 or 800-SMC-1634. Wed.–Sun.; adm. fee*) This 800-acre living history museum, complete with costumed interpreters and over 300 important archaeological sites, tells the story of Maryland's first capital (1634-1695). A Visitor Center offers an archaeology exhibit and information on guided walking tours.

**6. Confederate Monument** (*Md. 5, S of Scotland*) An obelisk marks the burial site of more than 3,000 Confederate soldiers imprisoned at Point Lookout during the Civil War.

**7. Point Lookout State Park** (*20 miles S of Lexington Park on Md. 5. 301-872-5688. Visitor Center open daily Mem. Day–Labor Day, weekends April–May and Sept.–Oct.; adm. fee*) Occupying the tip of a peninsula at the confluence of the Chesapeake Bay and the Potomac River, **Point Lookout** is the site of Fort Lincoln, used as a Confederate prison during the Civil War. A small museum in the Visitor Center focuses on the point's role in the Civil War. Activities include

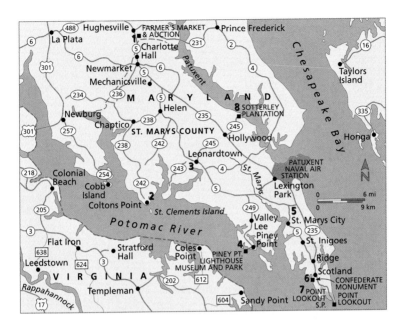

camping, fishing, swimming, and boating. Cruises *(fare)* depart Wednesday to Sunday in summer for historic **Smith Island.**

**8. Sotterley Plantation** *(E of Hollywood on Md. 245/Sotterley Rd. 301-373-2280 or 800-681-0850. House open May-Oct. Tues.-Sun., grounds year-round; adm. fee)* Established about 1710, Sotterley was a colonial port of entry and a thriving tobacco plantation. The 43-acre site includes a manor house, slave quarters, smokehouse, and formal gardens.

### Other Activities

**Biking** Flat, winding lanes and little traffic make the county an ideal place for biking. The Department of Economic Development *(301-475-4411 or 800-327-9023)* has a route map for the area.

**Boating** The area's many marinas include Tall Timbers *(Herring Creek Rd. 301-994-1508)*, Cedar Cove Marina *(Md. 249, Herring Creek, Valley Lee. 301-994-1155)*, and Point Lookout Marina *(16244 Millers Wharf Rd., Ridge. 301-872-5000)*.

**Fishing** Charters chase bluefish, striped bass, sea trout, flounder, white perch, and more in the Chesapeake Bay, Potomac River, and Patuxent River. Contact the Chamber of Commerce *(301-884-5555)* for information.

### Annual Events

**June** St. Marys Crab Festival *(Governmental Center, Leonardtown. 301-475-9023)*

**July** Tidewater Archaeology Dig *(Historic St. Marys City. 301-862-0990)*

**October** Blessing of the Fleet *(Potomac River Museum. 301-769-2222)*; St. Marys County Oyster Festival *(County Fairgrounds, Md. 5, 2 miles S of Leonardtown. 301-863-5015)*

### Lodging

**Bards Field of Trinity Manor** *(End of Pratt Rd., Ridge. 301-872-5989)* Featuring typical tidewater architecture, this lovingly refurbished house was built in 1798 on Rawley Bay, a prime birdwatching spot.

**St. Michael's Manor** *(Md. 5, Scotland. 301-872-4025. Closed Jan.)* Built about 1805 with bricks allegedly brought from England, this handsome manor house overlooks a vineyard and Long Neck Creek.

### Tidewater Dining

**Courtney's Restaurant** *(End of Wynne Rd., Ridge. 301-872-4403)* and **Scheible's Crab Pot Restaurant** *(Wynne Rd., Ridge. 301-872-5185. May-Oct.)* These small, watermen-owned seafood joints feature oysters, crabcakes, and other local specialties.

**Evans Seafood** *(Md. 249, St. George Island. 301-994-2299. Closed Mon.)* Crabs, crabcakes, and oysters are served on a sunny deck overlooking the Potomac River.

# The South

## VIRGINIA

# Northern Loudoun

Silent as a still life, the old Waterford Mill stands on the South Fork Catoctin Creek, an icon awaiting artists and others seeking a link to a simpler past. Inside, worn, creaky floorboards and bulky, russet gears speak of an era when grinding wheat and corn sustained the surrounding village. Beauty and function entwined, the mill is emblematic of the northern realm of Virginia's Loudoun County, picture-perfect farm country sprinkled with centuries-old villages, rolling green hills, fieldstone fences, and grazing thoroughbreds.

To enjoy northern Loudoun's charms is to experience unexpected plea-sure, as its hidden beauty lies less than an hour northwest of the nation's capital. Somehow this bulge of land—bordered on the west by the fabled Blue Ridge, on the north and east by the Potomac River, and on the south by Va. 7—has escaped the developer's plough, although change is in the air.

For now, a pastoral idyll and nostalgic elegance graces the land, the legacy of a long and full history beginning in the early 1700s. Back then, Germans, Quakers, and Scots worked small, tidy farms, while migrant planters from Tidewater Virginia grew tobacco on larger estates. They all shopped and gossiped and attended religious services in a scattering of country towns, most of which have little changed with the years. The largest of them is **Leesburg,** established in 1758 as a trading center, and whose historic core hides behind the region's only suburban clutter. Late Georgian and federal dwellings, now housing restaurants, antique shops, and B&Bs, cluster around a stately, old brick courthouse shaded by elms and guarded by a copper Confederate soldier. It's said James and Dolley Madison sought refuge here during the War of 1812 (stashing official

**Cumberland Island, Georgia (see Swamp to Sea, p. 141)**

**Loudoun County landscape**

copies of the Declaration of Independence and the Constitution somewhere nearby), and Gen. Robert E. Lee stopped over on his way to Antietam during the Civil War.

Sinuous country lanes lead to other historic villages, slicing through rolling farmland and wooded hills and glens scented sweetly of blackberry brambles, fresh-cut grass, and clover. Along the way, you may pass a horse farm (indicative of the county's esteemed horse culture), winery, pick-your-own flower farm, tucked-away B&B, or elaborate country estate. Not far from Leesburg, Purcellville brims with gracious Victorian houses built when the railroad came through in 1874. Wealthy Washingtonians once escaped the summer heat in the little community of Round Hill, and their elaborately detailed Victorians still line shady streets. In contrast, old stone houses (even the pig sties are stone!) dot nearby Hillsboro, a 19th-century mill town. And in the county's topmost corner, the stone dwellings of German-settled **Lovettsville** sit European-style, close to the street.

Of all Loudoun's villages, however, the most quintessential is the little town of **Waterford.** Amos Janney, a Quaker from Pennsylvania, built a mill here in 1741, and others of that faith soon followed. Known for their tolerance, the Quakers attracted an eclectic community, including a number of freed blacks. Seemingly not much has happened since then—growth stopped in the early 1800s, and the village remains almost unbelievably untouched by modern commerce, with impeccably maintained dwellings lining empty, tree-canopied streets.

A different memory of the past lingers at **Morven Park,** a 1,200-acre horse farm on Leesburg's environs. Two governors—Thomas Swann of Maryland and Westmoreland Davis of Virginia—reposed and entertained in the 1781 Greek Revival mansion, adorned with Flemish tapestries,

Renaissance furniture, and art nouveau. A long sweeping lawn, boxwood gardens, and a mile-long allée richly portray the good life, a vision further elucidated by an extensive carriage collection and the nation's only fox-hound museum, both on site.

While Loudoun exudes a peaceful calm, it wasn't always so. During the Civil War, its proximity to the North made it a prime crossroads for armies marching north and south. The abolitionist Quakers's opposition to the county's southern stand resulted in cruel confrontations between neighbor and neighbor, brother and brother. Many of the Civil War's cavalry battles erupted in Loudoun, including one along present-day US 15. The nation's second smallest national cemetery, just north of Leesburg, commemorates the 1861 Battle of Ball's Bluff.

Just as the Civil War ravaged the landscape, so suburban sprawl threatens it again. Eastern Loudoun County has already succumbed to strip malls, housing developments, and an international airport, and unprecedented growth is expected in the western realm. For now, however, this hidden corner remains lost in the past, a place of songbirds and red-tailed hawks, where farmers till the soil season in, season out, an artist's dream come true. —*Barbara A. Noe*

# Travel Notes

### Directions
This hidden corner is located less than an hour northwest of Washington, D.C., in the northern pocket of Loudoun County. **By car:** To reach Leesburg from Washington, head west on I-66, Va. 267, and the Dulles Greenway. **By airplane:** The nearest airports serve Washington, D.C. **By train:** Amtrak serves Washington, D.C.

### General Information
Spring brings festoons of flowers, humid summer features lush, green hillsides, and crisp autumn days showcase richly hued foliage. While winter can be cold and dreary, a full slate of year-round activities makes a visit worthwhile any time. The best information source is the Loudoun Tourism Council *(108-D South St. S.E., Leesburg 20175. 703-771-2170 or 800-752-6118)*.

### Things to See and Do
**1. Leesburg** *(Loudoun Tourism Council, see above)* Antique shops, restaurants, and B&Bs occupy 18th- and 19th-century structures in this charming old town. A walking tour booklet and historical exhibits await at the **Loudoun**

**Museum** *(16 Loudoun St. S.W. 703-777-7427. Adm. fee).* Just west of town, **Morven Park** *(Old Waterford Rd. 703-777-2414. April-*

**Potter at Waterford Homes Tour & Crafts Exhibit**

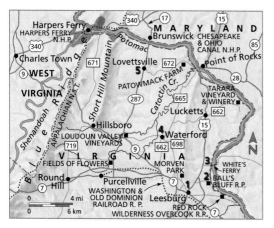

**Hiking** The famed Appalachian National Scenic Trail *(304-535-6331)* rides the crest of the Blue Ridge, on the county's western edge. A nature trail at Red Rock Wilderness Overlook Regional Park *(43098 Edwards Ferry Rd, Leesburg. 703-779-9372)* winds through woodlands to a Potomac overlook.

**Washington & Old Dominion Railroad Regional Park** *(703-729-0596)* A 45-mile paved trail running from Arlington to Purcellville, the W&OD leads bicyclists, walkers, and runners through rolling Virginia countryside.

**Wine tasting** Among several wineries open for tours and tastings are Loudoun Valley Vineyards *(Va. 9, NW of Leesburg. 540-882-3375. April-Dec. Wed.-Sun., Jan.-March Sat.-Sun.)*, and Tarara Vineyard and Winery *(Cty. Rd. 662. 703-771-7100. March-Dec. daily, Jan.-Feb. Sat.-Sun.)*.

### Annual Events
**Spring and fall** Steeplechase events take place throughout the county; contact the tourism council *(800-752-6118)* for a schedule. **June** Potomac Celtic Festival *(703-771-2170)* **October** Waterford Homes Tour & Crafts Exhibit *(540-882-3085)*; Leesburg Hauntings Tour *(703-777-7427)* **December** Leesburg Historic Homes Tour *(703-777-7427)*

### Lodging
The Loudoun County Bed & Breakfast Guild at www.vabb.com provides a comprehensive listing of places to stay.

**Buckskin Manor** *(13452 Harpers Ferry Rd., near Hillsboro. 540-668-7056 or 888-668-7056)* Snuggled against the Blue Ridge, this rustic structure was built in the 1750s as a tavern. **Catoctin House Inn** *(36959 Charles Town Pike, Hillsboro. 540-668-6725 or 800-348-9599)* Quakers built the oldest part of this stone dwelling around 1780. Feather beds and huge fireplaces make for a cozy stay. **Laurel Brigade Inn** *(20 W. Market St., Leesburg. 703-777-1010)* Eight guest rooms with period decor highlight this 1759 colonial inn. **Milltown Farms Inn** *(14163 Milltown Rd., Waterford. 540-882-4470 or 888-747-3942)* This 1765 log-and-stone house on 300 acres offers period antiques, feather beds, fireplaces, and sunsets over the Blue Ridge.

Oct. Tues.-Sun., Nov. weekends; adm. fee), an expansive horse farm, offers tours of its stately Greek Revival house, foxhound museum, carriage museum, and boxwood gardens.

**2. Ball's Bluff Regional Park and National Cemetery** *(3 miles N of Leesburg off US 15 Bypass, on Ball's Bluff Rd. 703-779-9372)* Together with the triumph at the First Battle of Manassas, the Confederate victory won on this site on October 21, 1861, deflated the North's hope for a quick end to the war. An interpretive trail visits the battle grounds and a small national cemetery.

**3. White's Ferry** *(N of Leesburg, at end of Cty. Rd. 655. 301-349-5200. Fare)* The only ferry still crossing the Potomac between Cumberland and Georgetown, it has operated since the 1820s.

**4. Waterford** *(Waterford Foundation 540-882-3018)* Nearly every structure in this picturesque village dates from the 19th century. Walking tours are offered in spring and fall.

**5. Lovettsville** Originally a German settlement, this village has the **Lovettsville Historical Society Museum** *(4 E. Pennsylvania Ave. 540-822-5499. May-Dec., and by appt.)*, containing town artifacts.

### Other Activities
**Antiquing** Leesburg and its surrounds host numerous antique shops.

**Farm visits** Several farms offer tours, including the organic Patowmack Farm *(42461 Lovettsville Rd., Lovettsville. 540-822-9017. Mid-July–Thanksgiving Thurs.-Sun., and by appt.)*; and Fields of Flowers *(37879 Allder School Rd., Purcellville. 540-338-7231. Mid-April–Oct. Wed.-Sun.)*, a cut-your-own flower farm.

# Appalachia

Known as the "rooftop of Virginia," this land of high peaks harbors alpine mountain balds, dense forests of red spruce, and vibrant blooms of purple rhododendron. Hardy, independent Scotch-Irish first settled this quiet, fog-shrouded region, much of which today is protected from development as the Mount Rogers National Recreation Area and adjacent state parks. Noteworthy for its solitude and beauty, the region has a strong lure for outdoorsmen. In addition, within this hidden corner's scattered small towns and peaceful scenery you can still find the Appalachian crafts and music of the early settlers, their legacy passed on to a dedicated community of artists.

Main Street, **Abingdon,** perched on the region's western edge, was once the rugged Wilderness Road leading pioneers to the Cumberland Gap and into Kentucky. Daniel Boone came here to survey the road. After spending a sleepless night protecting his dogs from preying wolves, he named the area Wolf Hills. Today, evening lights warm brick houses and specialty shops along paved streets, welcoming visitors to a cultural oasis. Among the town's numerous art venues is the **Barter Theatre,** founded during the Great Depression by Robert Porterfield, an aspiring actor in New York City. Reflecting on the abundance of food and lack of theater in his native southwestern Virginia, Porterfield opened the doors of his theater declaring,

**Pioneer cabin at Grayson Highlands State Park**

"With vegetables you cannot sell, you can buy a good laugh." At the end of its first season, the theater cleared $4.35 and two barrels of jelly, while the cast collectively gained more than 300 pounds. Although a Virginia ham no longer gets you in the door—in the 1960s Lady Bird Johnson bartered her way in with a tree—the Barter's players still perform.

Just down the street, an artists' cooperative has transformed an old railroad station into the **Arts Depot.** Here you can wander into artists' studios, watch a weaver's shuttle clatter through the loom, or breathe in the damp smell of clay being worked on a potter's wheel—all the while listening to artists expound on their inspirations and techniques.

The depot once served the Virginia-Carolina Railroad, which was

**Galax fiddlers**

dubbed the Virginia Creeper either for the woody, high-climbing vine common to the area, or for the train's slow progress through the mountains. While the train stopped running in 1977, its route, a rails-to-trails conversion, still brings the peripatetic to town. Following the course of a Native American footpath, the Virginia Creeper Trail winds some 33 miles from Abingdon through farmland and forest, crossing nearly a hundred trestle bridges above creeks and rivers, to the slopes of Whitetop Mountain. Here, bikers gather courage to speed downhill while day hikers pause to sample a wild blackberry or two.

The Virginia Creeper Trail is just one of a plethora of paths beckoning hikers, bikers, and horseback riders to explore the **Mount Rogers National Recreation Area,** part of the national forest bearing Thomas Jefferson's name. Jefferson wrote, "Of all the exercises, walking is the best," and the Mount Rogers area and adjacent **Grayson Highlands State Park** offer some of the best hiking opportunities in the region. A network of local trails intersects with the Appalachian National Scenic Trail, the grande dame of eastern hiking trails, along the slopes of Virginia's two highest peaks: Whitetop Mountain (5,520 feet) and Mount Rogers (5,729 feet). On clear days, mountain gaps frame breathtaking vistas of overlapping hills—but at higher elevations the moist environment often fogs in the view. At these times, it's better to appreciate up-close the surrounding forest, sprinkled with red spruce and fir. Summer hikers along the mile-long Rhododendron Trail, which begins in the state park, are greeted with late-blooming spring wildflowers, honeysuckle, and showy Catawba rhododendron. Entering the recreation area, the path crosses open windswept terrain reminiscent along Wilburn Ridge of a rocky creek bed. Connect with a 3-mile stretch of the Appalachian Trail and a 1.25-mile spur to reach the top of Mount Rogers.

The ridges and gaps along these trails bear the names of such men as hunter and trapper Wilburn Waters, who sought to make a home in this rugged land. You can imagine their hardscrabble mountain lives as you sit in a mud-chinked log cabin or wander among the outbuildings at the park's homestead. In addition to growing and making their basic necessities, these folks produced all their own amenities and entertainment.

**Main Street, Abingdon**

Some 20 miles east of the park, in **Independence,** an old courthouse serves as a cultural center, displaying and selling such Appalachian crafts as pottery, quilts, hand-made dulcimers, and wooden toys. Here the Scotch-Irish heritage of the settlers comes alive when fiddle players and storytellers gather for ceildhs (KAY-lees)—Celtic jam secessions. As the stories are spun and the fiddle strains lost among the hills you may find yourself relaxing into a slower pace of life, and perhaps even envying those who have made this corner home.                    —*Sean M. Groom*

# Travel Notes

### Directions
Located in southwestern Virginia, Appalachia falls within a rough semicircle north of the Tennessee and North Carolina borders formed by I-81 and I-77. **By car:** I-81 leads south from Roanoke and north from Knoxville, Tennessee. **By plane:** Roanoke and Blountville, Tennessee, have the nearest airports.

### General Information:
Spring through fall are the best seasons to visit the area. For more information contact the Mount Rogers National Recreation Area Headquarters *(3714 Va. 16, Marion 24354. 540-783-5196 or 800-628-7202);* Abingdon Convention & Visitors Bureau *(335 Cummings St., Abingdon 24210. 540-676-2282 or 800-435-3440);* or Independence Tourist Information Center *(107 E. Main St., Independence 24348. 540-773-3711).*

### Things to See and Do
**1. Abingdon** *(Abingdon Convention & Visitors Bureau, see above)* Many Hollywood stars have cut their teeth at the historic **Barter Theatre** *(W. Main St. 540-628-3991. Adm. fee).* The **Arts Depot** *(314 Depot Sq. 540-*

*628-9091. Thurs.-Sat., and by appt.)* houses several studios and serves as a gallery for local and regional artists. An affiliate of the Virginia State Museum of Fine Arts, the **William King Regional Arts Center** *(415 Academy Dr. 540-628-5005. Tues.-Sun.; donation)* presents rotating exhibits. Some of the best meals in the area can be found at the **Starving Artist Cafe** *(134 Wall St. 540-628-8445. Closed Sun., lunch only Mon.)* and the **Hardware Company Restaurant** *(260 W. Main St. 540-628-1111).*
**2. Mount Rogers National Recreation Area** *(Headquarters 540-783-5196 or 800-628-7202)* Part of the Jefferson National Forest, the recreation area comprises 120,000 acres braided with 400 miles of trails, including 150 miles of horse trails. Hikers are drawn by the famous Appalachian National Scenic Trail and increasing numbers of mountain bikers are attracted to the area's other paths. Call for the location of seasonal information centers.
**3. Grayson Highlands State Park** *(Grayson Highlands Ln., off US 58, Mouth of Wilson. 540-579-7092. Adm. fee)* In sight of the state's two highest peaks, the park provides picturesque alpine scenery and trails

for both equestrians and hikers. It adjoins Mount Rogers National Recreation Area.

**4. Independence** *(Tourist Information Center 540-773-3711)* The **Historic 1908 Courthouse** contains an information center and serves as the county's arts and cultural heart. Inside, the **Treasury** is a gallery of Appalachian arts and crafts, including pottery, quilts, dulcimers, and jewelry. In the **Vault Museum,** artifacts from an early 1900s homestead tell of life in the surrounding rugged hills. The Scotch-Irish heritage of the pioneering settlers comes to life three times a year during the Courthouse Ceildhs. Just down the street from the courthouse, the **Pear Tree** *(122 W. Main St. 540-773-2030. Thurs.-Sat., and by*

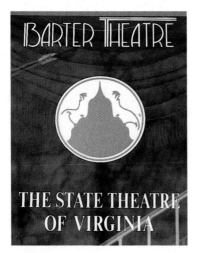

**Barter Theatre, Abingdon**

*appt.)* offers regional fine arts and crafts.
**5. Galax** *(Visitor Center 540-236-2184)* bills itself as the World Capital of Old Time Mountain Music. Armed with bows and fiddles, bluegrass and folk musicians have descended on the town each August since 1935 for the Old Fiddlers Convention. Also of interest, the **Rooftop of Virginia Community Action Program** *(206 N. Main St. 540-236-7131. Mon.-Sat.)* has converted an old church into a showroom of Appalachian crafts.
**6. Shot Tower Historical State Park** *(US 52, near Austinville. 540-699-6778. April-Nov. daily, tours Mem. Day–Labor Day Sat.-Sun.; adm. fee)* Around 1807 this 75-foot-tall tower was constructed above a 75-foot hole to make lead shot for muskets. Molten lead, poured through a sieve at the top of the tower, fell 150 feet into a large kettle of water where it cooled. The shot tower is located at Milepost 25.2 of the **New River Trail State Park** *(540-699-6778)* and serves as the headquarters of this 57-mile-long rails-to-trails park that will eventually connect Galax and Pulaski. Much of the trail runs along the New River, one of the oldest rivers on the continent.

**Annual Events**
**August** Virginia Highlands Festival *(Abingdon. 540-676-2282 or 800-435-3440)*; Old Fiddlers Convention *(Galax. 540-236-2184)*

**Lodging**
**Martha Washington Inn** *(150 W. Main St., Abingdon. 540-628-3161 or 800-555-8000)* A historic 1834 building across from the Barter Theatre, this has served as a private home, women's college, Civil War hospital, and inn.

# WEST VIRGINIA
# Almost Heaven

Embracing a swath of the Monongahela National Forest along the eastern border of West Virginia, the region from Seneca Rocks to Lewisburg is a special place to outdoorspeople both resident and visiting. Poet William Blake wrote, "Great things are done where man and mountain meet," and recreationists in West Virginia must agree. If you seek big cities, bright lights, and cosmopolitan pursuits, you had best travel elsewhere.

**Rock climber, Seneca Rocks**

Here, the dramatic landscape is the attraction, the lights are celestial, and the cacophony of great rivers provide the background music. Mountains rise in rows across the horizon, each riven by tiny clear streams. Cascading down hollows and valleys, the creeks rasp the mountainsides, building to swift, strong currents along the valley floors and feeding the five major river systems draining this area. Trout fishermen and white-water enthusiasts look for challenge here, while those seeking more relaxed adventure find quieter stretches for lazy summer afternoon floats.

Laced with more than a thousand miles of dirt roads, paths, and trails, Monongahela beckons hikers, bikers, and naturalists to explore its hills and hollows. Those who have made their homes here take their cues from the land. As the state moniker declares, they are mountaineers; as rugged and

**Blueberries**

unpretentious as the hills and as friendly as the valleys stretched out between them. A town may be only a pair of buildings at the intersection of two roads in the shadow of a hollow. The general store survives here as naturally and comfortably as the deer that overrun the hills. Beyond the twin gas pumps and store-length front porch, customers enter a screen door and wander aisles of wide-plank flooring. Conversation flows freely, and the social time is savored as necessities are purchased.

Protruding 900 feet above the North Fork South Branch of the Potomac River in the heart of this rugged landscape, the knife-edge ridge of Seneca Rocks cleaves the sky. The rock face's seemingly paper-thin peak rises so dramatically from the valley floor that even casual passersby stop and gawk. Legend holds that the Seneca princess Snow Bird chose a husband from among her many suitors by declaring she would marry the man who could follow her up the cliff face to the top. Today, both beginning and experienced rock climbers trace her footsteps at the **Spruce Knob-Seneca Rocks National Recreation Area.** Those not inclined to scale the cliffs can watch the action from the Front Porch Restaurant of Harpers Old Country Store. Or walk across the street and take the 1.3-mile trail up Seneca Rocks to an observation platform just below the summit. In addition to a bird's-eye view of the valley below, the recreation area's other namesake, Spruce Knob, is visible to the southwest.

The state's highest point at 4,861 feet, Spruce Knob is a stark outpost

**Yew Mountains, Monongahela National Forest**

that rewards hearty hikers with stunning views of endless ridges to the east (there is also a road to the top), while American kestrels can often be seen soaring in the valley below. Buffeted by high winds and severe weather conditions along the rocky peak, the Whispering Spruce Trail to the observation tower leads through a forest of stunted, people-size trees. Known as one-sided whispering spruce, or flagpole spruce, these trees are nature's weather vane—branches grow away from the prevailing winds on the tree's eastern side. The lower branches hug the rocky ground, often growing more than 10 feet from the trunk, while the highest branches are little more than stubs of needles. Spruce Mountain's west side is designated the Seneca Creek Backcountry Area, a natural playground for hikers and mountain bikers where some 70 miles of trails and roads weave through mature hardwood forests, mountain meadows, and steep creeks. You're likely to spot owls, beaver, deer, and maybe black bears.

While determined adventurers can spend weeks exploring this national forest without exhausting all its possibilities, the unspoiled wilderness region you visit in this corner is a 20th-century creation. The post-Civil War railroad boom allowed the harvesting of West Virginia's forests as if locusts had passed over the land; the damage led to the establishment of the Monongahela National Forest in 1915 for reforestation.

A slice of West Virginia logging history and culture is preserved at the former company town-turned-state park at **Cass.** Here the gear-driven Shay steam locomotives of the logging railroad still huff and puff their way up the steep grades of Bald Knob with a throaty roar, belching steam at the leisurely pace of 6 miles per hour. But the timber loads have since been exchanged for loads of children, railroad buffs, and the just plain curious who line the open windows, peering at startled deer, vibrant sugar maples in autumn, and the powerful locomotive, as the train nearly doubles back on itself negotiating the tight turns to the observation area at 4,842 feet. With grades up to 11 percent, the track requires brakemen on each car to control the descent. Strike up a conversation with these old-timers and learn a wealth of information about the railroad and the logging industry. In town, the small, white-frame houses have been restored as lodgings. Walking the raised

### Rails to Trails

Across the road from the Cass Scenic Railroad State Park depot, the northern terminus of the **Greenbrier River Trail** (Contact Watoga S.P. 304-799-4087) serves as a gateway to the countryside for cyclists, hikers, and equestrians. Stretching 77 miles to Caldwell, the old riverside railroad bed of hard-packed gravel explores a gradually changing landscape, from tightly packed, crumpled mountains to rolling terrain with open valleys. The trail crosses 35 bridges and passes through 2 tunnels; its highlight is probably the 511-foot long Sharps Tunnel (Mile 65.7), which emerges onto a 229-foot-long open span 30 feet above the Greenbrier River. Food and camping are available at numerous trail access points.

**Cass Scenic Railroad**

wooden sidewalks along the quiet main street, it's tough to imagine that a scant 80 years ago this was a rough-and-tumble boomtown of 2,000 souls.

During the Civil War, this border region seesawed between Northern and Southern control. One little-remembered battle occurred in November 1863, when Union troops clashed with Confederate forces in **Lewisburg.** Today this is a cozy town of 3,600 nestled among the rolling hills of the Greenbrier River Valley just outside the southern boundary of the national forest. Lewisburg's historic center radiates a charm that reflects the best features of rural and town life. A lively mix of old-monied professionals, young urban escapees, farmers, and loggers meet along Washington Street, where warm, redbrick storefronts have been reincarnated as galleries, craft shops, and specialty stores. While hearty country cooking characterizes the fare throughout the region, this town is justly proud of its gourmet food. Travelers and farmers converge after church for Sunday brunch at the **General Lewis Inn,** where elegant houses line the streets. Or you can join a leisurely paced walking tour of the 18th- and 19th-century structures and battle sites to glimpse an earlier life west of the Blue Ridge. The cafés and coffee shops along the way will recharge your batteries for your next adventure in West Virginia's accessible wilderness.           —*Sean M. Groom*

# Travel Notes

## Directions

This area comprises the southern three-quarters of Monongahela National Forest and the Greenbrier Valley south of the forest to Lewisburg. **By car:** Drive west on I-64 from Lexington, Va., to Lewisburg. US 220 and W. Va. 28 go south from Cumberland, Md., to the national forest. **By plane:** Charleston has the nearest major airport. **By train:** Amtrak stops at White Sulphur Springs.

## General Information

There are activities year-round, though winter weather can make higher roads treacherous. The best sources of information are the West Virginia Division of Tourism *(2101 Washington St. E., P.O. Box 50312, Charleston 25305. 304-558-2746 or 800-225-5982);* and the Monongahela National Forest *(Headquarters, 200 Sycamore St., Elkins 26241. 304-636-1800).*

## Things to See and Do

**1. Lewisburg** *(Visitor Center 304-645-1000 or 800-833-2068)* The cultural and social heart of the area contains 18th- and 19th-century structures, now housing shops, inns, and restaurants.

**2. Droop** A boardwalk loops through a wonderland of rock features at **Beartown State Park** *(2 miles E of US 219. 304-653-4254).* Three miles north, **Droop Mountain Battlefield State Park** *(US 219. 304-653-4254)* preserves West Virginia's largest Civil War battlefield.

**3. Cranberry Glades Botanical Area** *(FR 102 off W. Va. 39/55. 304-653-4826)* The four bogs in this area display plant and animal life most commonly found in the northern U.S. and Canada.

**4. Cass Scenic Railroad State Park** *(W.Va. 66, Cass. 304-456-4300. Late May–*

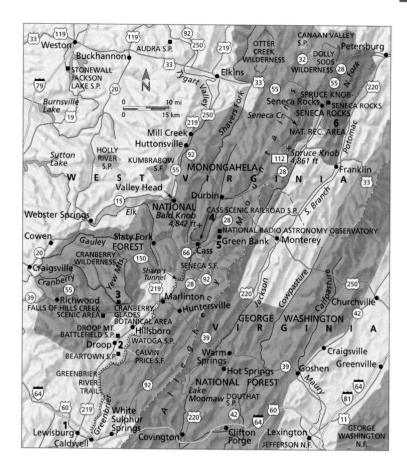

Aug. daily, Sept.–early Nov. Fri.-Sun.) This park's restored logging railroad (fare) offers trips to the state's second highest peak. The houses of the former company town have been restored as lodgings.

**5. Green Bank** Tours of the **National Radio Astronomy Observatory** (W.Va. 28/92. 304-456-2011. Mid-June–Labor Day daily, Mem. Day–mid-June and Labor Day–Oct. Sat.-Sun.) will in 1999 include the world's largest fully steerable radio telescope. A few miles south, the **Green Bank Country Store** (W.Va. 28/92. 304-456-4410. Closed Sun.) has everything from roast beef sandwiches to antique pistols.

**6. Spruce Knob–Seneca Rocks National Recreation Area** (US 33/W.Va. 55. 304-567-2827. Visitor Center April-Oct. daily, Nov.-March weekends) Jutting 900 feet into the sky, the sandstone palisades are especially popular among hikers and rock climbers. The Visitor Center features an 1860s homestead.

**Other Activities**

**Canoeing and rafting** Contact West Virginia Professional River Outfitters (304-345-1588) for guidance.

**Rock climbing** Seneca Rocks Climbing School (Seneca Rocks. 304-567-2600 or 800-548-0108. April-Oct.) offers climbing instruction and guiding at Seneca Rocks.

**Lodging**

**Carriage House Inn** (W. Va. 39, Huntersville 304-799-6706) A cozy B&B with two gift shops filled with terrific West Virginia crafts.

**General Lewis Inn** (301 E. Washington St., Lewisburg. 304-645-2600) A wide veranda welcomes guests to antique-filled rooms.

# NORTH CAROLINA

# Albemarle Area

The Albemarle is a watery place tucked up in the northeast corner of the state. Quiet rivers run through it, and bays and sounds scallop the coastline from the Virginia border to the Pamlico River. The bottom half of the Albemarle covers a large peninsula bracketed by the Albemarle and Pamlico Sounds and laced with swampy lakes and forest, blackwater canals, and brackish marshes. It is a world of contrasts, at once wild and cultivated.

Bobcats, black bears, deer, alligators, and countless birds roam pristine wildlife refuges. State parks offer prime hiking, boating, and fishing. On the fringes of the wild are sprawling farms and country junctions, historic towns and antebellum plantations, Civil War landmarks, antiques—and superb barbecue.

For many, this quiet backwater is an invisible landscape, the last fast leg of the trek to the beaches of the Outer Banks. A more discreet beauty, the Albemarle demands time, revealing itself not in spectacle but in moments: the hoot of an owl here, a fish jumping there—maybe a wave from a porch, a handmade quilt drying on the line, or children playing by a row of shotgun-style sharecroppers' shacks.

The seasons of the Albemarle, too, are subtle, except summer, which is anything but—all earthy and hot and wet and green, when things grow with tropical unrestraint. In fall the air clears and cools, gold splashes the green, and the ripe cotton dapples the fields like snow. When winter settles, brief and still, so return the tundra swans and snow geese back to Lake Mattamuskeet. Spring comes early with a show of wildflowers and acres abloom with daffodils, peonies, gladiolus, and tulips on Terra Ceia's Dutch bulb farms.

Eons ago a more prolific ocean covered the East Carolina coast. When it receded during the last ice age, it left behind a large, sediment-rich coastal

## Edenton Tea Party

In the days before the Revolutionary War, Edenton was a small, prosperous seaport—one that didn't sit on the sidelines in the fight for liberty. Less than a year after Boston's famous "tea party" in 1773, a group of Edenton ladies drew up and signed a resolution to boycott the pernicious custom of tea-drinking. They also vowed to wear no more English-made clothing until British taxes were abolished. This group of North Carolinians made the history books for launching one of the first known, purely political actions by women in the Colonies. The site of the Edenton Tea Party is marked in town by a colonial teapot mounted on a Revolutionary War cannon.

**Bald cypress, Albemarle Sound**

plain that the centuries again transformed into a swamp so dense and uninviting that settlers dubbed it the "dismal swamp." Though three centuries of logging, draining, and canal-digging have substantially shrunk the swamp, the land remains characteristically well-watered.

Take, for instance, the rampant oval-shaped lakes and pocosins you see around here, so distinctive they call them the "Carolina Bays." Pocosins (from the Algonquian word for "swamp on a hill") are actually peat bogs that lie higher than the land around them, holding huge amounts of water in their spongy soil and acting as landlocked drainage basins. They support dense thickets of evergreen shrubs and trees—lovely bay trees, pond pine, loblolly pine, bald cypress. In fact, the Albemarle boasts the largest pocosin system in the world. You can stand right in the middle of it at Phelps Lake at **Pettigrew State Park.** The state's second largest natural lake after Mattamuskeet, its unusually acidic waters have the remarkable ability to preserve wood by limiting the growth of organisms that cause wood to decay. From its shallow waters archaeologists have dredged dugout canoes and other ancient artifacts left behind by early Native Americans, whose history around these parts dates back some 11,000 years.

European history, too, runs as thick as sorghum here. French Protestants from Virginia settled first near the Pamlico River in the 1690s. By 1705, North Carolina had established its premier town and port of entry at **Bath,** a hideout of the nefarious Blackbeard. Today when you walk the streets of Bath's well-restored historic district, you get the sense that things haven't changed all that much around here, including Sunday service at St. Thomas Episcopal Church, the state's oldest (1734).

Time, too, seems to have bypassed the prosperous colonial port of **Edenton,** North Carolina's first capital, incorporated in 1722. With a wide main boulevard that dead-ends at the cypress-studded bay and streets shaded by ancient magnolia and pecan trees, the town proudly preserves its architectural legacy, which pre-dates the American Revolution. Speaking of which, another significant colonial "tea party" happened right here in 1774 (see sidebar p. 126).

**Tundra swan, Mattamuskeet N.W.R.**

In the early 1700s, planters began staking their claims on the Albemarle. They drained the swampland, planted such crops as rice, corn, and wheat, and built an economy based on slave labor. **Hope Plantation,** erected in 1803 by Governor and U.S. Senator David Stone, lets you glimpse the lavish lifestyle of this bookish planter-politician and his family, while secluded **Somerset Place State Historic Site** near Creswell provides a rare window on the workings of the plantation system itself, including slavery, in the context of the times. The main house was built in the 1830s by Josiah Collins III. Home to more than 300 enslaved people, this is one of the largest and best-preserved plantations in the South.

The Civil War brought an end to the Albemarle's plantations. After the war, planters carved up their lands and rented plots to sharecroppers, many of them former slaves, who now farmed fields of tobacco and cotton and lived in rows of tiny, identical shacks. You see them still around the countryside and on the edges of some towns.

The war also left many towns in ruins. Among the survivors was the port of **Washington,** named in 1776 for the future President and referred to as the original Washington. Attacked and burned by Union troops in 1864, the town escaped total destruction by fire. Down by the river, across from

**Patches of farmland, Albemarle**

the new **North Carolina Estuarium,** you can still see cannonballs embedded in the facades of two of the city's antebellum clapboard houses. Just another Albemarle moment, frozen in time.

You cannot hurry the Albemarle. Its rhythms are measured and subtle, as ancient as the tides or the cypress swamp or the annual migrations of snowbirds. Its pace mesmerizes—probably something to do with the predominant horizontals: Flat land parceled into broad fields of soybean and tobacco, cotton and corn. The sweep of horizon beyond a blue bay. The steady course of a boat tracing a river's far shore. The plentiful waters—flowing or stagnant, wide or pooled, blue or tannin-black, brackish or fresh. Above it all, hawks and turkey vultures languidly circling and soaring on thermals and great V's of geese pointing high across a hazy sky.

Change comes, but slowly. You'll still see folks picking crabs and culling shrimp, making and repairing their own nets or crab and eel pots, building boats, crafting decoys, and hand-harvesting tobacco. They still come home for family reunions and old-fashioned pig-pickin's. And on Sundays, they mostly go to church, and you may hear, if you listen, the sound of sweet singing or an ecstatic gospel choir. These, too, are Albemarle moments, which come to those who wait.                                       *—Alison Kahn*

# Travel Notes

## Directions

The Albemarle Area is located east of Greenville. **By car:** The main routes from the west are US 64 or US 264; from the north, take US 13; from the south, take I-95 to US 64 or US 264. **By plane:** The closest airports are Raleigh-Durham and Norfolk, Va., with limited service to Greenville. **By train:** Amtrak services Rocky Mount.

## General Information

Summers here are sticky hot; if you can't stand the heat, visit in spring or fall. The best source for information is the North Carolina Travel & Tourism Division *(301 N. Wilmington St., Raleigh 27601. 919-733-4171 or 800-VISIT NC).*

## Things to See and Do

**1. Edenton** *(Historic Edenton Visitor Center, 108 N. Broad St. 252-482-2637. April-Oct. daily, Nov.-March Tues.-Sun.; fee for walking tours)* For history and charm this town has few rivals, and it is best seen on foot. An early 1900s school building now houses the **Chowan Arts Council Gallery** *(200 E. Church St. 252-482-8005),* which showcases

and sells regional arts and crafts.

**2. Hope Plantation** *(N.C. 308, 4 miles W of Windsor. 252-794-3140. Closed Christmas–New Year's Day; adm. fee)* preserves the 1803 mansion, outbuildings, and gardens. Also of interest on the grounds is the 1763 **King-Bazemore House,** with its gambrel roof.

**3. Washington** *(Chamber of Commerce, 102 Stewart Pkwy. 252-946-9168 or 800-999-3857)* This eclectic port's historic district dates from the late 1700s; explore on a self-guided walking tour. The **North Carolina Estuarium** *(223 E. Water St. 252-948-0000. Closed Mon.; adm. fee)* interprets the Albemarle-Pamlico estuarine system through interactive and multimedia exhibits.

**4. Goose Creek State Park** *(10 miles E of Washington on US 264 to N.C. 1334 for 2.5 miles. 252-923-2191)* Some 1,500 acres preserve swamp forest, pocosins, marshes, and beaches for hiking, canoeing, and swimming.

**5. Bath** *(Historic Bath Visitor Center, 207 Carteret St./N.C. 92. 252-923-3971. April-Oct. daily, Nov.-March Tues.-Sun.)* North Carolina's first town features a National Register historic district; walking tour brochures are available from the Visitor Center.

**6. Belhaven** (Chamber of Commerce 252-943-3770) This quiet port of call's unique **Belhaven Memorial Museum** (201 E. Main St. 252-943-6817. Closed Wed.) displays bride and groom fleas, farm equipment, and more.

**7. Swanquarter National Wildlife Refuge** (Off US 264. 252-926-4021. No facilities) This is the heart of Hyde County's commercial fishing industry.

**8. Mattamuskeet National Wildlife Refuge** (N of US 264, off N.C. 94. 252-926-4021. Visitor Center open Mon.-Fri.) offers prime birdwatching, hiking, and boating. Don't miss the view from the tower at **Lake Mattamuskeet Lodge** (252-926-1422. Closed Mon.), built in 1915 as the world's largest pumping station and converted to a hunting lodge by the CCC.

**9. Pettigrew State Park** (7 miles S of Creswell off US 64. 252-797-4475) offers virgin forest, cypress swamp, marshlands, pocosins, and **Phelps Lake** for hiking, biking, fishing, boating, and swimming.

**10. Somerset Place State Historic Site** (2572 Lake Shore Rd. off US 64. 252-797-4560. April-Oct. daily, Nov.-March Tues.-Sun.) This antebellum plantation offers tours of the main house, outbuildings, and a reconstructed slave cabin, as well as special programs.

**11. Pocosin Lakes National Wildlife Refuge** (3255 Shore Dr. 252-797-4431) shelters characteristic pocosin fauna and flora.

### Other Activities

**Biking** For a free guide to bicycling highways in the Albemarle Area, call the Division of Bicycle and Pedestrian Transportation (919-733-2804).

**Canoeing** Albemarle Region Canoe Trails (pick up maps at 412 W. Queen St., Edenton. 252-482-7437) offers a growing network of self-guided trails across 10 counties.

### Annual Events

**March** Historic Edenton Antique Show and Sale (Edenton. 252-482-7800)

**April** Terra Ceia Dutch Festival (Terra Ceia. 252-943-2018)

**September** Indian Heritage Week (Pettigrew S.P. 252-797-4475)

**December** Swan Days Festival (Swanquarter. 252-925-5201) The snowbirds' annual return is celebrated with birdwatching, field dog demonstrations, crafts, and kayaking.

### Lodging

**Lords Proprietors' Inn** (300 N. Broad St., Edenton. 252-482-3641) This unique in-town complex includes 20 guest rooms in three distinctive historic houses, country breakfasts, four-course dinners (Tues.-Sat.), afternoon tea, and cordials.

**Pamlico House Bed & Breakfast** (400 E. Main St., Washington. 252-946-7184 or 800-948-8507) Listed on the National Register of Historic Places, this inviting inn began life as a church rectory.

**River Forest Manor** (738 E. Main St., Belhaven. 252-943-2151 or 800-346-2151) Join the list of celebrities who've stayed at this antique-filled, riverside 1899 mansion, famed for its daily smorgasbord.

# SOUTH CAROLINA
# Old Ninety Six

They call it the Old Ninety Six District, a carry-over from frontier
times. Subtle in beauty and quirky in character, this mostly flat
and forested western Piedmont is an in-between place, north of
the Low Country's sand hills and south of the rolling uplands,
neither coastal plain nor upcountry.

Here, deep woods and occasional dairy farms and small cattle ranches conceal the shimmering lakes of the Savannah River. Lakeside state parks and Sumter National Forest provide shady trails through pine woods, tranquil waters for canoeing and fishing, and sandy beaches, while back roads lead through history-steeped towns and rustic hamlets. You might catch a show at a turn-of-the-century opera house, or a meal at a Mennonite restaurant, or visit a Revolutionary War battle site. (Antique mavens beware: These are prime hunting grounds.) Beyond the mix of forest, lakes, and villages, though, the soul of this place emerges through the palpable presence of the past—and the people.

You can see it at any of the local lunch counters; it starts on this side of noon, swelling to a steady stream by the high hour. The waitress deftly buses booths and tables as fast as they fill up,

**Burt Stark Mansion, Abbeville**

bantering with the customers, asking "tea, or sweet tea?" Toward the back,
a chalkboard lists the daily specials, served up cafeteria-style. Can't beat the
price, really, for a home-cooked, rib-sticking, Southern plate lunch. Sound
like a scene from a 1950s movie? Well, that's how life is in Abbeville—and
McCormick, and Edgefield, and Due West, and Ninety Six, and the other

**Resident potter, Old Edgefield Pottery**

time-worn towns around the Old Ninety Six. Decidedly off the tourist path, it operates on its own time dictated by church and custom, and never mind the inconvenience. They roll up the sidewalks on Sundays—and by 8 p.m. every night. And "business" hours are strictly laissez-faire. These small towns, too, with their old but extant frontier facades, main streets, town squares, and old-fashioned ways, preserve a continuum between past and present that keeps life on a more human scale.

You can't know this place if you follow the main road or stay in your car. Stick to the county and forest roads, even the unpaved roads. There you'll find its textures—in places like Godfrey's Market in Hodges, stocked with cracklins, hash, hoop cheese, and binfuls of country hams, and a vintage lunch counter. Or in the gas station selling jars of pig's feet, pig's knuckles, pickled eggs, pork rinds, and peanuts. Poverty, too, is part of the picture, and pool halls, barbecue joints, has-been towns, countless peeling churches, and eye-blink places called Catfish Peninsula, Hester Bottoms, and Promised Land. In the Old Ninety Six, you encounter the past—imperfect, in the rough, with pieces missing and broken, visible testaments to the real passage of time. And that's part of its charm.

The Old Ninety Six, a regional district, takes its name from a strategic fork in the Cherokee path that was located some 96 miles south of the Cherokee capital, Keowee. The name, it seems, stuck to anything subsequently built on that spot—a trading post; a fortified frontier town; and a British fort, affectionately called "Old Ninety Six," where in 1775 the Revolutionary War's first land battle south of New England took place. After statehood, South Carolina was carved into districts and Ninety Six became this district's seat of government. Today at **Ninety Six National Historic Site** a winding trail and subtle imprints on the silent land—star-shaped earthworks, sunken roads, two reconstructions—are all that remain.

The Civil War also came here. In 1860 **Abbeville** hosted the first public vote on secession. Less than five years later, on May 2, 1865, Jefferson Davis held the last Confederate war council here in the elegant **Burt Stark Mansion.** Cotton mills and the railroads revved the region's economy enough to put Abbeville's exquisite 1908 **Opera House** on the New York-Atlanta circuit. (You can still see a live performance here on most weekends.) It was also enough to grow the town of **Greenwood,** now a bustling commercial center and the home of **Park Seed Company,** where you can stroll through acres of gardens.

While freight trains still roll past the flat-fronted blocks lining **McCormick**'s 19th-century main street, the legacy of the town's gold-rush days lies *beneath* the streets, in nearly 5 miles of tunnels dug by various mining interests. Neighboring Edgefield County's reputation as a pottery-making center—a tradition maintained at **Old Edgefield Pottery** (see sidebar this page)—is rivaled only by its remarkable record of having produced (so far) 10 governors and 5 lieutenant governors, including J. Strom Thurmond.

At the heart of all this lies the **Long Cane District** of **Sumter National Forest,** a great, green swath of loblolly pine and hardwood bottoms. The Savannah River Scenic Highway (S.C. 28, S.C. 81, and S.C. 187) threads through the dense forest roughly parallel to the river, a pleasant enough drive, though the only views you get are trees and more trees. But the woods offer a soothing reprieve, with plenty of room (about 120,000 acres) for solitary hiking, paddling, fishing, or watching wild turkey, water-fowl, deer, and other denizens of this forest.

Along its western boundary, the forest suddenly, gratefully, gives way to two wide, impounded lakes of the Savannah River, **J. Strom Thurmond Lake** (also known by its old name, Clarks Hill) and Richard B. Russell Lake—part of the chain of dammed lakes that form a hidden inland coast along the South Carolina-Georgia border. Looking at the pristine, island-studded lakes banked with red Piedmont clay, it's easy to forget that the U.S. Army Corps of Engineers, not nature, created these beauties as part of an enormous hydroelectric and flood-control project begun in 1946.

While the Corps manages its own recreational areas, among them **Clarks Hill Park** and **J. Strom Thurmond Dam** and **Visitor Information Center,** you'll also find strung along this frontier of forest and lakes four delightful state parks and recreation areas—**Baker Creek, Hickory Knob, Hamilton Branch,** and **Calhoun Falls**—each with its own personality and perks. (Except for the latter, they all overlook J. Strom Thurmond Lake, the U.S. Army Corps of Engineers' largest project east of the Mississippi.) The fish are jumping, the water's fine, and the view's not half bad. What more can you ask for?

—*Alison Kahn*

## Stoneware Tradition

As far back as 2500 B.C., people were making pots out of Edgefield County's thick, rich clay. They're among the oldest pots found in North America. By the 19th century the Edgefield stoneware tradition combined Chinese technology, English methodology, and African slave labor and design. Just after 1800, small potteries began producing basic pioneer utensils; by 1850, five factories employed 35 potters, including slaves, who created imaginative "face vessels" and other whimsical pieces, along with the typical storage jars, jugs, pitchers, and bowls. The most famous, and prolific, of these craftsmen was Dave, a literate slave who would sign, date, and occasionally inscribe his ware with simple verses about such topics as food, shoes, or religion.

# Travel Notes

## Directions
Old Ninety Six lies just north of Augusta, Georgia. **By car:** From Augusta, take Ga./S.C. 28 north; from Columbia, take US 378 west; from Greenville, take S.C. 20 south. **By plane:** The closest airport is in Columbia. **By train:** Amtrak serves Greenville and Columbia.

## General Information
Summer's humid heat is fine for some, but the best seasons are spring and fall. Pick up maps for Abbeville, Edgefield, McCormick, and Greenwood Counties. The best source of information is the Old 96 District Tourism Commission *(1041/2 Public Sq., P.O. Box 448, Laurens 29360. 864-984-2233 or 800-849-9633).*

## Things to See and Do
**1. Abbeville** *(Chamber of Commerce, 107 Court Sq. 864-459-4600. Self-guided walking tour brochure of historic district available)* Doubly honored as the birthplace and deathbed of the Confederacy, the town's historic district includes the 1908 **Abbeville Opera House** *(100 Court Sq. 864-459-2157)* and the 1830s **Burt Stark Mansion** *(400 N. Main St. 864-459-4297. May-Aug. Tues.-Sat., Sept.-April Fri.-Sat., and by appt.; adm. fee),* an antique-

filled house-museum.
**2. Due West** In the center of this historic town, Erskine College's **Bowie Arts Center** *(Bonner St. 864-379-8867. Mon.-Sat. and first Sun. of month)* exhibits fine art, Edward S. Curtis photographs, and a collection of music boxes. **Geralds of Due West** *(206 Main St. 864-379-2357 or 800-854-0087)* boasts the South's largest selection of square-dance apparel.
**3. Greenwood** *(Chamber of Commerce 864-223-8431)* This bustling mill town is home to **Park Seed Company** *(1 Park Ave., about 5 miles N off S.C. 254. 864-223-8555 or 800-845-3369),* the world's largest, family-owned mail-order seed company, with 10 acres of show and test gardens, greenhouses, and a gift shop. Visit the goats and other critters at 75-acre **Emerald Farm** *(Emerald Farm Rd., off E. Cambridge Ave. 864-223-9747. Closed Sun.),* famous for its goats'-milk soap, gift and natural foods shops, and herb garden. The **Greenwood Museum** *(106 Main St. 864-229-7093. Wed.-Sat.; adm. fee)* showcases the area's history, art, and culture.
**4. Ninety Six** *(Welcome Center 864-543-4820)* **Ninety Six National Historic Site** *(2 miles S on S.C. 248. 864-543-4068)* marks the locale of a former stockaded town and British fort, and the state's first Revolutionary War battle, with exhibits and a self-guided trail.
**5. Edgefield** *(Chamber of Commerce, Calhoun St., Johnston. 803-275-0010)* The whole town is listed on the National Register of Historic Places; take a self-guided or guided walking or driving tour of nearby landmarks. Stop and see the resident potter at work at **Old Edgefield Pottery** *(230 Simkins St. 803-637-2060. Tues.-Sat.; donation),* plus displays of historic pieces. The **National Wild Turkey Federation Museum** *(S on US 25. 803-637-3106. Mon.-Fri.; scheduled to open Aug. 1998)* presents exhibits on the bird and the sport.
**6. Clarks Hill** At **J. Strom Thurmond Dam** and **Visitor Information Center** *(US 221/S.C. 28. 864-333-1147 or*

**Park Seed Company's black-eyed Susans**

*800-533-3478 ext. 1147),* view the first dam on the Savannah River and exhibits on the project and recreation opportunities; power plant tours available. East up the road, **Clarks Hill Park** *(US 221/S.C. 28)* offers a sheltered, red-cliffed shore for walking or swimming *(fee).*
**7. Plum Branch** Set on a picturesque peninsula in Thurmond Lake, 731-acre **Hamilton Branch State Park** *(US 221/S.C. 28, 12 miles S of McCormick. 864-333-2223)* offers excellent fishing, plus boating, lakefront camping, and a picnic area.
**8. McCormick** *(Chamber of Commerce 864-465-2835)* In the heart of this old rail stop and antique center, **McCormick Arts Council at the Keturah** *(MACK) (115 Main St. 864-465-3216. Mon.-Fri.; fee for performances)* presents exhibits, plus concerts, plays, and other performances. Nearby, on J. Strom Thurmond Lake, 1,305-acre **Baker Creek State Park** *(US 378. 864-443-2457)* offers swimming, boating, fishing, camping, pedal boats, mountain biking, and a nature trail, while an 18-hole championship golf course, tennis courts, a pool, and more await at deluxe, 1,091-acre **Hickory Knob State Resort Park** *(7 miles W off US 378. 864-391-2450 or 800-491-1764. Use fees).*
**9. Calhoun Falls** On the shores of lovely Russell Lake, **Calhoun Falls State Recreation Area** *(1 mile N of town on S.C. 81. 864-447-8267)* promises great boating, fishing, swimming *(fee),* camping, and nature trails—but no falls.

### Other Activities
**Sumter National Forest** *(Long Cane District office, 810 Buncombe St., Edgefield. 803-637-5396)* This national forest offers a variety of day- and extended-use recreational opportunities, including canoeing, hiking, mountain biking, and horseback riding, fishing, and camping.

### Annual Events
**May** River Oaks Rodeo *(Nation Rd., off US 25, Hodges. 864-456-2728)* Livestock events, ladies' barrel races, and concerts are featured.
**June** South Carolina Festival of Flowers *(Greenwood. 864-223-8431)* Includes garden tours, arts and crafts, horticulture shows, music and sports events, and a flotilla on Lake Greenwood.
**October** Battle of Long Cane *(Troy. 864-465-3216)* Reenactments of the 1780 battle, living-history camps, horse-and-wagon tours, lectures, an auction, and a barbecue.

### Lodging
**Belmont Inn** *(106 Pickens St., Abbeville. 864-459-9625 or 888-251-2000)* A reincarnation of the legendary 1903 Eureka Hotel, this creaky, comfortable, National Register hotel on the town square offers continental breakfast, a cozy lounge, and a fine restaurant.
**Fannie Kate's Country Inn and Restaurant** *(127 S. Main St., McCormick. 864-465-0061)* Built in 1882 as the McCormick Temperance Hotel, the inn offers seven charming suites with ceiling fans and private baths, regional dishes, and spirits.
**Hickory Knob State Resort Park** *(US 378, McCormick. 864-391-2450 or 800-491-1764)* Stay in the woods on Thurmond Lake in a lodge room, a cabin, or the circa 1770 Guillebeau House, a restored, original French Huguenot house.

# GEORGIA
# Between Two Rivers

In west-central Georgia on the Alabama border, the Flint and Chattahoochee Rivers bound a mostly rural place that reaches north to Pine Mountain and south to Plains—each a home to Presidents Franklin D. Roosevelt and Jimmy Carter. The land between these rivers is a dichotomy: its upper half red-earthed and rolling Piedmont, its lower half level and sandy-soiled coastal plain. Spend some time in this diverse area and you'll find antebellum mansions, the Civil War's most infamous prison, Georgia's "little Grand Canyon," a living history village, and botanical gardens. The only thing you may run out of is time.

In Georgia, all rivers form within the state—such as the swift running Flint—or along its borders—such as the slow and sultry Chattahoochee, Georgia's longest river, which marks the state's lower boundary with Alabama. In Georgia, too, land and rivers are sliced by a fall line cutting a ragged diagonal from Augusta to Columbus. Along a line of falls and rapids, rivers drop abruptly from the upland to the lowland and a narrow belt of tawny sand hills meets a band of hills of red Georgia clay. Exactly here lies the divide between the coastal plain and the Piedmont. It is not a subtle line. The lowland is of the Deep South. On the sunbaked flats, amid broad fields of peanuts, cotton, corn, and soybeans, longleaf pine forest predominates, sprinkled with hammocks of beech, magnolia, and other hardwoods. Where swamps intrude, you find cypress and Spanish moss. In contrast, the cooler and greener Piedmont, which climbs up into the Appalachian foothills, feels like a mountain place. Especially on **Pine Mountain**, which is actually a series of hard-rock ridges. Hardwoods prevail, as do cattle farms, peach orchards, and cultivated timberland. At the fall

## Land of Pasaquan

In 1957, Eddie Owens Martin returned from New York City to rural Marion County to begin building a 4-acre spiritual compound out of painted concrete, carved wood, and hammered aluminum. Inspired by dreams, hallucinatory visions, and ancient civilizations and cultures, he filled his "Land of Pasaquan" with serpentine walls, totem poles, pagodas, altars, and shrines, all covered with symbols painted in wild colors. Martin's self-contained world evolved into a cosmology, with himself as its sole devotee. You can still tour the compound of one of America's foremost outsider artists—but call first *(from Buena Vista, N on Ga. 41, W on Ga. 137, to Cty. Rd. 78. 912-649-9444. Sat.-Sun.; adm. fee).*

**Chattahoochee River enveloped in mist**

line, rivers become unnavigable. Early pioneers and traders bound upriver were forced to detour around these cascades or to settle. The falls also provided a source of power for mills and factories.

Columbus, for instance, situated on the falls of the Chattahoochee, grew from a frontier trading center into an industrial boomtown by the 1840s. Old lumber, grist, and textile mills still line the island-studded Chattahoochee, now traced by the Riverwalk park. The once prolific Columbus Iron Works now houses the Convention and Trade Center—an example of how the city has successfully married preservation and development. At the heart of the historic district, containing the original city, **Heritage Corner** preserves the home of "Doc" Pemberton, inventor of a medicinal cordial purported to be the original formula for Coca-Cola. The city also boasts the opulent 1871 Springer Opera House, Georgia's state theater, and the South Commons sports complex, site of the 1996 Olympic softball competition. Here, too, stand the **Columbus Museum,** the **Coca-Cola Space Science Center,** and the **Woodruff Museum of Civil War Naval History.** Nearby at **Fort Benning,** the **National Infantry Museum** showcases shiny accoutrements of battle.

South of the fall line a potent memorial to war's grim realities is softened only by the peaceful setting. Dedicated to all American prisoners of war, the **Andersonville National Historic Site** consists of the national cemetery, a museum, and the site of the Civil War's most hellish prison camp, where nearly 13,000 Union soldiers died. Today you see the remains of trenches, escape tunnels, hospital sites, and fort earthworks. The prison supply center has been restored as rustic **Andersonville Civil War Village.**

Site of three Confederate hospitals during the war, **Americus** rebuilt itself in Victorian style. Today, the city's eclectic architectural legacy includes

**Providence Canyon**

**International Village.** This cluster of simple dwellings exemplifies those built around the world by Habitat for Humanity International, a non-profit ecumenical housing ministry headquartered here. Its most famous supporter is a neighbor from **Plains,** former President Jimmy Carter. In 1980, the 39th President came home to this lowland farm community, the epicenter of Georgia's peanut industry. The town has been understatedly spit-and-polished and turned into a preservation district. At its hub, the **Jimmy Carter National Historic Site** consists of Plains High School, now a Visitor Center; the depot that served as his first campaign headquarters; Carter's boyhood home; and the Carters' current residence (*private*).

On the other side of the fall line, on Pine Mountain's wooded north slope, Franklin Delano Roosevelt built himself a second home near Warm Springs, where he took treatments for his polio. The **Little White House State Historic Site** preserves FDR's clapboard cottage as it looked on April 12, 1945, the day he died of a massive stroke while sitting for a portrait. That haunting, unfinished portrait is still here, along with a host of Rooseveltiana at the adjacent museum. Nearby **Franklin D. Roosevelt State Park** was a hands-on labor of love by FDR himself. The New Deal's Civilian Conservation Corps built the mountaintop highway, an inn, two lakes, a stone bridge, a pool, camps, cabins, trails, and a boathouse, as well as Roosevelt's favorite picnic spot at Dowdell's Knob. The **Pine Mountain Trail** system offers nearly 40 miles of hiking and horse trails.

The forest here comes by its unusual mix of longleaf pine and dry hardwoods thanks to the Flint River, which cuts into the mountain's eastern slopes, bearing the seeds of more northerly flora. In the midst of it all sprawls 14,000-acre **Callaway Gardens,** a man-made wonderland of flower, vegetable, and herb gardens; and woodlands. It is also home to the nation's largest glass-enclosed tropical butterfly conservatory. There are other parks, too, sequestered in this land between the rivers: swampy **Florence Marina** on the Chattahoochee's Walter F. George Reservoir (also known as Lake Eufaula); and **Providence Canyon,** reminiscent of the desert Southwest with its varicolored walls, pinnacles, and spires.

And there are other towns. Mostly small, uncelebrated places, full of character and real life: Buena Vista is a hot and dusty place, its main square lined with has-been businesses and a few old men and new immigrants seated in the shade of faded shop awnings. Or Lumpkin, its own 19th-century square a well-preserved, sentimental journey featuring Dr. Hatchett's Drug Store Museum & Soda Fountain and the family-run Singer Hardware Company. Here you can walk back in time at the living history village of **Westville.** Then there's **Woodland,** where the retired county extension agent will personally guide you through his **Old South Farm Museum.** It's all about tradition, he'll tell you, and life on this good land between the rivers.                                        —*Alison Kahn*

# Travel Notes

### Directions
This region is located between the Chatta-hoochee and Flint Rivers in west-central Georgia. **By car:** From Atlanta drive south on I-85. **By plane:** The closest airports are in Columbus and Atlanta. **By train:** Amtrak has service to Atlanta.

### General Information
Enjoyable anytime of year, this area's prime seasons are spring and fall. For tourism information contact the Georgia Visitor Center *(1751 Williams Rd., Columbus 31904. 706-648-7455).*

### Things to See and Do
**1. Columbus** *(Visitor Center 706-322-1613 or 800-999-1613)* This river town's highlights include the **Columbus Museum** *(1251 Wynnton Rd. 706-649-0713. Closed Mon.),* **Coca-Cola Space Science Center** *(701 Front Ave. 706-649-1470. Closed Mon.),* the **Woodruff Museum of Civil War Naval History** *(202 4th St. 706-327-9798. Closed Mon.),* and a tour of **Heritage Corner** *(Historic Columbus Foundation Headquarters, 700 Broadway. 706-322-0756. Adm. fee).* African-

American landmarks are highlighted on the self-guided **Black Heritage Trail** (available from Historic Columbus headquarters).
**2. Fort Benning** One of the world's largest infantry training center's **National Infantry Museum** *(Bldg. 396, Baltzell Ave. 706-545-2958)* features military and small arms.
**3. Westville** *(0.5 mile S of Lumpkin on Martin Luther King Jr. Dr. 912-838-6310 or 888-733-1850. Closed Mon.; adm. fee)* A living history village re-creates regional life and culture through 1850.
**4. Providence Canyon State Park** *(7 miles W of Lumpkin on Ga. 39C. 912-838-6202. Parking fee)* Georgia's "little Grand

**Land of Pasaquan**

**10. Franklin D. Roosevelt State Park** *(Ga. 190, 5 miles E of US 27. 706-663-4858 or 800-864-7275. Parking fee)* offers 10,000 acres of forest, rocky outcrops, lakes, panoramic views, and the **Pine Mountain Trail** system.

**11. Little White House State Historic Site** *(.25 mile S of Warm Springs on Ga. 85. 706-655-5870. Adm. fee)* FDR's second home, near where he took treatment for polio, is preserved.

**12. Woodland** Numerous items are displayed at the **Old South Farm Museum** *(Ga. 41. 706-674-2894. Closed Sun.; adm. fee).*

**13. Sprewell Bluff State Park** *(10 miles W of Thomaston off Ga. 74. 706-646-6026. Parking fee)* This 1,400-acre park on the Flint River is a good spot for hiking, fishing, canoeing, or picnicking.

**Other Activities**

**Canoeing** The Flint River Outdoor Center *(4429 Woodland Rd./Ga. 36, Thomaston. 706-647-2633. Mem. Day–Labor Day daily, April–Mem. Day and Labor Day–Oct. weekends; fee. Reservations required)* offers guided canoe and raft trips, canoe rentals, and more.

**Horseback riding** The Original City Slickers Riding Stables *(F.D.R. State Park, Pine Mountain. 706-628-4533. Fee)* guides trail rides.

**Annual Events**

**April** Riverfest *(Columbus. 706-323-7979)*
**September** Plains Peanut Festival *(Plains. 912-824-5445)*
**October** Andersonville Historic Fair *(Andersonville. 912-924-2558)*
**November** Steeplechase at Callaway Gardens *(706-324-6252)*

**Lodging**

**Callaway Gardens** *(US 27, Pine Mountain. 706-663-2281 or 800-225-5292)* Stay in the inn, a country cottage, or a luxury villa at this beautiful 14,000-acre resort.
**The Gates House** *(737 Broadway, Columbus. 706-324-6464 or 800-891-3187)* An elegant 1880 inn in the historic district with sumptuous rooms and fresh-baked breakfast breads.
**Windsor Hotel** *(125 W. Lamar St., Americus. 912-924-1555 or 888-297-9569)* Built in 1892, this turreted Victorian features 53 guest rooms and round tower suites.

Canyon" offers overlooks, hiking trails, and an interpretive center.

**5. Florence Marina State Park** *(16 miles W of Lumpkin on Ga. 39C. 912-838-6870. Parking fee)* On Walter F. George Reservoir, this park offers a deep-water marina, a pool, and an interpretive center.

**6. Plains** *(Welcome Center 912-824-7477)* This presidential hometown features the **Jimmy Carter National Historic Site** *(Visitor Center in Plains High School, 300 N. Bond St, off US 280. 912-824-4104)* and a preservation district.

**7. Americus** *(Americus-Sumter Tourism Council 912-924-2646 or 888-924-2646)* Acclaimed for its downtown restoration, the city's main attractions are its historic district and **Habitat for Humanity International** *(322 W. Lamar St. 912-924-6935. Tours Mon.-Fri.).*

**8. Andersonville National Historic Site** *(10 miles NE of Americus on Ga. 49. 912-924-0343)* This memorial park contains a national cemetery and Confederate prison grounds, plus a museum. **Andersonville Civil War Village** *(Welcome Center, 114 Church St. 912-924-2558)* has a museum and pioneer farm.

**9. Pine Mountain** *(Tourism Assn. 706-663-4000 or 800-441-3502)* Along with antiques, **Callaway Gardens** *(US 27. 706-663-2281 or 800-225-5292. Adm. fee)* is here, featuring the Cecil B. Day Butterfly Center and a 2,500-acre horticultural display garden.

# Swamp to Sea

There are few wild places left where you can find true solitude. Two of them—the Okefenokee Swamp and Cumberland Island—happen to lie in southeasternmost Georgia. Mention Okefenokee and you probably think swamp, right? Actually, it's more, and less, than a swamp, lying more than hundred feet above sea level and harboring waters that flow and circulate. Sure, this vast bog contains great, dark swaths of primordial cypress swamp and alligator-infested bayous (as many as 12,000 live in the Okefenokee). But you might be surprised to discover its lighter side: lakes filled with floating islands and flooded prairies and acres of open pinelands. Just 40 miles east, Georgia's largest and southernmost barrier island is a subtropical jungle of maritime forest fringed by wide dunes and white-sand beaches, where wild horses, deer, and armadillos roam amid the ruins of crumbling mansions. Both island and swamp have their stories to tell.

Linked by the St. Marys River, the two are separated by a tranquil backwater of small towns steeped in history and local culture, and inviting state parks where you can canoe, hike, fish, or just watch the birds go by.

A strange thing happens in the **Okefenokee,** this swamp that is not quite a swamp. Near sunrise, when the air is sufficiently wet and the temperature just right, a spectral fog forms over the Okefenokee's canals and bayous, slowly gathering and building above the water until it consumes these arteries, curtaining the swamp's mysteries of the night. Behind the shroud of mist, things unseen stir. It is the magic hour.

One of the country's largest landlocked wetlands, this 438,000-acre swamp is laced with slow-moving, tannin-stained waters that form two

## Okefenokee Queen

Perhaps the Okefenokee's most colorful pioneer was the legendary "Miss Lydia" Smith Stone Crews. Born in 1864, she stood over 6 feet tall and weighed about 200 pounds. Even with only a few days of formal education, she maintained, "A man ain't living that can out figger me." Few could outwork her, either. Strong as well as shrewd, she hauled cypress cross ties on her shoulders and rode herd on 600 cattle. Lydia became a wealthy landowner and married one of the many men she oversaw. After he died, she married another hired hand, whom she called "Doll Baby." She was 63, he 21. Miss Lydia died in 1938. You can't miss her grave in **High Bluff Cemetery** (*Off US 82, Waycross*).

**Okefenokee Swamp alligator**

rivers: The Suwannee River, the Okefenokee's main drain, flows southwest into the Gulf of Mexico, while the **St. Marys River** drains southeast into the Atlantic Ocean. The whole bog, some 7,000 years old, is cupped inside a giant, saucer-shaped depression created by a retreating ancient sea. Over time this bowl filled with layer upon layer of peat, forming a boggy bed that today measures as thick as 15 feet.

It is the Mother Earth of the swamp, this peat, the stuff of its continual regeneration and re-creation. Basically, the peat produces methane gas. When the gas builds up, the earth burps, sending to the lake surface a "blowup" of peat. This floating island becomes a bed for colonies of herbs, then shrubs, and eventually trees. Wet-loving cypress and bay send anchoring roots deep into the swamp's sandy floor, creating a "house." Walk on this peat mat and you may feel it give with your footfalls. Stomp on it and you may see the bushes quiver. That is why Native Americans called this place *okefenokee*, "land of the trembling earth."

**Ruins of Thomas Carnegie's Dungeness, Cumberland Island**

For more than 4,000 years, Indians lived in the Okefenokee. The Seminole were the last to leave, finally driven out in the late 1830s. Pioneer "swampers" followed, scratching out a primitive existence here by hunting, farming, turpentining, raising bees and livestock, making cane syrup—and moonshine. You can get a glimpse of how they lived at historic **Chesser Island Homestead** near Folkston and at **Obediah's Okefenok** near Waycross.

Next came the loggers. In 1891 the Suwannee Canal Company built a 11.5-mile-long canal into the swamp's east side, hoping to drain the land for logging and farming. But the company went bankrupt and sold out to Hebard Cypress Company in 1901. Hebard subsequently constructed a logging railroad in the western swamp. By 1927 nearly 500 million board feet of timber had been removed.

Today, most of the swamp's fragile 438,000 acres are protected within the **Okefenokee National Wildlife Refuge.** Three main entrances reveal the Okefenokee's many faces—and phases: lakes, prairie, islands, forest. Fire and drought are the checks that keep the forest from taking over, ensuring the cyclical restoration of wet prairie. At the east entrance, you can canoe through these serene and open prairies, the habitat of Florida sandhill cranes and other marsh birds and waders.

**Oak tree skeletons, Cumberland Island**

The Okefenokee shows its dark side at the more remote west entrance, **Stephen C. Foster State Park.** Here bayous wend through classic cypress swamp hung with streamers of Spanish moss. Between the trees, golden silk spiders wait for prey in their great yellow orbs. At the north entrance, **Okefenokee Swamp Park** reveals more of the swamp's marvels with interpretive exhibits, trails, and tours.

When the St. Marys River leaves the swamp, it meanders eastward along the state line through scrub country to land's end, where it empties into Cumberland Sound near historic **St. Marys.** An Indian village once stood on this same spot along the river's north bank. Founded by the British in 1787, this storied old port has aged well, preserving its heritage in a handsome historic district. In an old movie theater, the **St. Marys Submarine Museum** reflects the influence of nearby Kings Bay Naval Submarine Base, the Atlantic home of the Trident nuclear sub. Far prettier is its neighbor, **Crooked River State Park,** which offers another view of the rich estuarine system that feeds Cumberland Sound. A marsh-fringed channel through which the Intracoastal Waterway passes, this calm tidewater is separated from the sea by an 18-mile-long barrier of shifting sands: **Cumberland Island**. It's the salt marsh you see first, not the island, as you ferry from St. Marys to Cumberland on the *Cumberland Queen*. When the island's west shore finally appears in the distance, it is the tall, green cordgrass that marks it, waving above the thick mud, tidal creeks, and sheltered inlets.

Disembark at Dungeness Dock near the little **Ice House Museum** or just up the coast at Sea Camp. From either landfall, you must travel on foot, whether by trail or along the north-south Main Road, which itself is barely more than a wide, unpaved trail that tunnels through the trees. You step quickly from the light and airy marsh into the dimmer world of a maritime forest dominated by live oak. The trees' twisted limbs over-arch in a dense canopy that resembles a tangled mass of upside-down roots draped in Spanish moss and covered with resurrection fern. (During dry spells, the fern's fronds curl and gray as if dead; with the first rain it resurrects lush and green.) Thick and sinewy muscadine vines wrap trunks and limbs and dangle in the understory of fan-shaped saw palmettoes.

The forest's gray-green palette is flecked with the vivid plumage of painted buntings, pileated woodpeckers, cardinals, and summer tanagers. Muted as a sound studio, the forest's palpable silence is broken only by birdsong, peeping tree frogs, and the rustling of animals in the brush. Nine-banded armadillos snuffle in the leaf litter. White-tailed deer also inhabit these woods, as do raccoons, wild horses, feral pigs, and birds of prey. Alligators prefer the island's freshwater lakes, ponds, and sloughs.

Where the forest suddenly gives way to lines of dunes and then open beach, it is a relief to reemerge into the light. Seventeen miles of powdery sands and shimmering ocean offer solitary walking and shelling, empty except perhaps for a few grazing horses or migrating shorebirds or butterflies. Come early in the morning and you'll find tracks left by night visitors—maybe, if it's summer and you're lucky, those of a loggerhead turtle come to nest.

Humans, too, have left their marks in the sand here. Native Americans inhabited the island as early as 2000 B.C. In the mid-1500s the Spanish arrived, followed two centuries later by the British. Cumberland's plantation era began with Revolutionary War hero and landowner Gen. Nathanael

## Wild Cumberland

You'll find a bounty of wildlife at Cumberland Island, but the prolific white-tailed deer is its only native mammal. The bobcat was reintroduced to the island by the National Park Service to keep the herds down. It is thought that, in the 1560s, the Spanish introduced hogs and horses that subsequently made themselves quite at home. Pigs released after the plantation era joined the population of feral hogs. As for the island's famed wild horses, the Carnegies tried unsuccessfully to remove them to prevent interbreeding with their thoroughbreds. Today, most of the 200 or so hybrid horses that roam the island descend from the Carnegies' freed stock, including their short-legged polo ponies.

Greene, whose widow built a four-story home here in 1802, which she called Dungeness. At one time more than half the island was covered in rows of fine Sea Island cotton; hence, much of the forest you see today is "new" growth. Then, after the Civil War, the plantations were abandoned. The Settlement was built at the north end for freed slaves who stayed to work.

In 1881 Thomas Carnegie and his wife, Lucy Coleman, of Pittsburgh bought up most of the island and built a new and grander **Dungeness mansion** on the foundations of the original. They carved an elite resort village out of the subtropical jungle. Today, at the center of the historic district, this second Dungeness stands in ruins, slowly reclaimed by the jungly forest—a sad relic of the Gilded Age and its excesses.

Three mansions of interest were built as wedding gifts for the Carnegie children: Stafford (*private*), **Plum Orchard** (*Closed except for special tours*), and, if you're feeling flush, you can stay as a guest at the **Greyfield Inn**, a Gatsbyesque inn still owned by descendants of the Carnegie family. On a private compound overlooking the marsh where wild horses graze quietly and huge, old live oaks spread limbs to the ground, Greyfield presents Cumberland on a silver platter. But the magic is all Cumberland's. And that, money can't buy. —*Alison Kahn*

# Travel Notes

### Directions
Swamp to Sea is located in southeastern Georgia. **By car:** Take I-95 to Ga. 40; drive west to Okefenokee or east to St. Marys for the 45-minute ferry ride (*no cars or bikes allowed*) to Cumberland Island (*departs St. Marys Visitor Center, 106 St. Marys Rd., St. Marys. For ferry reservations, up to 6 months in advance, call 912-882-4335. April-Sept. daily, Oct.-March Thurs.-Mon.; fare*). **By plane:** The closest airports are in Jacksonville, Florida, and Savannah. **By train:** Amtrak offers service to Jacksonville and Savannah.

### General Information
Enjoy the perfect climate and peak bloom during bug-free March and April; the next best season is late October to early December. The best source of information is the Colonial Coast Regional Tourism Office (*P.O. Box 786, Brunswick 31520. 912-262-2341 or 800-422-6278*).

### Things to See and Do
**1. Okefenokee National Wildlife Refuge** The 396,000-acre refuge has three entrances: The **East Entrance** at **Suwan-** nee **Canal Recreation Area** (*8 miles SW of Folkston via Ga. 23/121. 912-496-7156 or 800-SWAMP 96. Adm. fee*) features a Visitor Center, scenic drive, boardwalk trail, and 50-foot observation tower, **Chesser Island Homestead,** hiking and canoe trails, as well as guided (*fee*) and self-guided boat tours, and fishing. The **West Entrance** at 80-acre **Stephen C. Foster State Park** (*Ga. 177, 18 miles NE of Fargo. 912-637-5274. Adm. fee*) offers a museum, boardwalk trail, fishing, cottages, and guided (*fee*) and self-guided boat tours. The **North Entrance** at

**Welcoming rockers, Greyfield Inn**

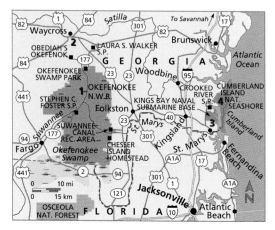

containing the ruins of **Dungeness mansion** and other buildings. Walking is the main mode of transportation. Ask the Visitor Center about guided tours, including **Plum Orchard Mansion** *(First Sun. each month).*

## Other Activities
**Canoeing** Suwannee Canal Recreation *(Okefenokee N.W.R. 912-496-7156 or 800-SWAMP 96)* offers tours and equipment rental, plus wilderness overnight canoe trips. Local outfitters offer canoe, kayak, and charterboat fishing excursions on the **St. Marys River** *(Call Colonial Coast Regional Tourism Office 912-262-2341).*

privately operated **Okefenokee Swamp Park** *(Ga. 177, 8 miles S of Waycross. 912-283-0583. Adm. fee)* includes animal habitats, a nature center, a wildlife observatory, a boardwalk trail, an observation tower, an amphitheater, and tram and boat tours *(fees).* All three locales offer interpretive and special programs.

**2. Waycross** *(Tourism Bureau 912-283-3742)* This 19th-century railroad crossroads offers **Laura S. Walker State Park** *(Ga. 177, 9 miles SE of Waycross. 912-287-4900).* Named after the pioneering conservationist, this 631-acre lakeside recreational park offers a pool, a golf course, a nature trail, plus boating, fishing, camping, and rustic cabins. **Obediah's Okefenok** *(Swamp Rd., 8.5 miles S of Waycross. 912-287-0090. Adm. fee)* features an 1870s homestead, with exhibits, demonstrations, and trails.

**3. St. Marys** *(Welcome Center 912-882-4000 or 800-868-8687)* Gateway to Cumberland Island, this delightful old port has a National Register historic district. Also of interest, **St. Marys Submarine Museum** *(108 St. Marys St. W. 912-882-ASUB. Closed Mon.; adm. fee)* displays a working periscope, models, and artifacts. At 500-acre **Crooked River State Park** *(7 miles N on Ga. 40 Spur. 912-882-5256),* enjoy fishing, boating, a nature trail, pool, cottages, camping, plus nearby ruins of a 19th-century sugar mill.

**4. Cumberland Island National Seashore** *(Visitor Center, 106 St. Marys Rd., St. Marys. 912-882-4335. Note: Number of visitors restricted to 300 per day)* Daytrippers can explore the park's trails, beaches, **Ice House Museum,** and historic district,

## Annual Events
**April** Woodbine Crawfish Festival *(Woodbine. 912-576-3211)* Three tons of crawfish, continuous entertainment, more than 150 artists and craftspeople, clogging, square dancing, a parade, and a carnival are featured; National Wildlife Weekend *(Okefenokee N.W.R. 912-496-7836)* A juried wildlife art show, a guided bird walk and swamp boat tour, a snake show, and music celebrate wildlife. **September** Labor Day Catfish Festival *(Kingsland. 912-729-5999 or 800-433-0225)* A parade, tournaments, and more. **October** Rock Shrimp Festival *(St. Marys. 912-882-4000 or 800-868-8687)* Enjoy live entertainment, arts and crafts, and tons of shrimp; Okefenokee Festival *(Folkston and Okefenokee N.W.R. 912-496-2536)* Arts and crafts, a parade, entertainment, a golf tournament, a "Tour de Swamp" bike ride, an open house at Chesser Island Homestead, and much more.

## Lodging
**Greyfield Inn** *(Cumberland Island. Ferry service included from Fernandina Beach, Fla. 904-261-6408)* This 1901 Carnegie mansion pampers in elegant, turn-of-the-century style. It offers 11 rooms, two cottages, excellent meals, cocktail hors d'oeuvres, a bar, bikes, a private beach, and naturalist-led tours. **Spencer House Inn** *(200 Osborne St., St. Marys. 912-882-1872)* This homey 1872 inn in the heart of St. Marys offers 14 distinctive rooms with private baths, a buffet breakfast, picnic lunch on request—even an elevator.

# FLORIDA
# Marjorie Kinnan Rawlings Country

If you've read *The Yearling* by Pulitzer Prize-winning author Marjorie Kinnan Rawlings, you'll have a picture of this "half-wild, backwoods country" in north-central Florida. Right in Gainesville's backyard, but seemingly a world away from anywhere, you can still find remnants of the old Florida frontier.

This was the home of Indians and "crackers"—whip-cracking cowboys who drove cattle herds here until the early 1930s. The intermittent forest, or hammock, is laced with marshes, rivers, and slow creeks lined with fish camps and moss-draped cypress. The lakes still promise bass and bream and catfish. Between the waters, you'll find has-been railroad junctions as well as comeback towns, the kinds of places where you can browse for antiques or order up a plate of fried frog's legs or gator tail. You can still lose yourself in the "Big Scrub," soak in the forest's warm springs, or canoe down a quiet run. Oh, yes, and if you make your way to Cross Creek, you'll still find Rawlings's homestead standing in the old citrus grove.

"You hear the cranes come in Sunday night?" It was the talk at the old

**Lochloosa Lake**

**Marjorie Kinnan Rawlings's house, near Cross Creek**

Evinston (population about 175) country store and post office. When the sandhill cranes arrive at 2 a.m., no one sleeps. These big birds descend en masse, hundreds of them, flapping and squawking. The annual arrival of the cranes in mid-November is a harbinger of the season, a harvest ritual as traditional as the town's communal Thanksgiving feast in the park. And when the cranes leave the first week in March, their departure marks another turn of season.

"I do not know how anyone can live without some small place of enchantment to turn to," wrote Rawlings. "Enchantment lies in different things for each of us." For her, it was the grove and farmhouse near Cross Creek between **Orange** and **Lochloosa Lakes,** preserved as the **Marjorie Kinnan Rawlings State Historic Site.** You can tour the rambling, old cracker-style house where she settled in 1928. It's a window on the life of this complex and independent woman, who seems only to have left temporarily. Each tour is limited to ten people, but if you must wait, there's always the lovely park and trails through the shady hammock.

The rail stop of **Micanopy** was Rawlings's big city. In the mid-1700s the Seminole established a village here called Cuscowilla. (Micanopy was one of its principal chiefs.) In 1821 a trading post was built, bringing settlers and, later, farmers and planters. The town was incorporated in 1880. Now the whole place is a National Register historic district, headquartered at the **Micanopy Historical Society Museum.**

Pressed by a jungly forest and a low ceiling of live-oak limbs and hanging Spanish moss, Florida's oldest inland town seems to have drawn a curtain on the outside world. The whole hamlet wears a patina of age: lichened stone, weathered wood, worn brick. Vines grow on vines, and some side streets remain unpaved. Traditional Florida bungalows stand beside log-built houses and verandaed Victorians. Micanopy's main street, Cholokka Boulevard, was built along an ancient Indian trading path. You'll still see frontier-style, hand-hewn cypress posts holding corrugated tin awnings, but the old trading post's tiny "downtown" has gone to antiques. Rawlings found enchantment, too, in the fastness of the "Big Scrub" that is **Ocala National Forest,** a semitropical tract of live oaks, cabbage palms, and scrubby sand pines (it's the world's largest sand pine forest) and clear, spring-fed pools—**Salt Springs, Juniper Springs**—whose waters gush at a constant 72°F.

The trees unexpectedly give way to grasslands at **Paynes Prairie State Preserve.** "Darkness to light" was how naturalist William Bartram in 1774 described the "great Alachua Savannah," once home to prehistoric peoples and Seminole and Spanish cattle ranchers. Unlike the Midwest's dry prairies, this preserve lies in a great basin that formed as the land sank into the terrain's underlying limestone foundation. Lakes and ponds lie at the center, surrounded by wet prairie and marshlands, and uplands beyond. Natural cycles of flooding and fire ensure the grasslands' regeneration.

Look around and you'll see marsh birds and alligators. Venture into the prairie's heart and you'll find bison, as well as scrub cattle and wild horses descended from Spanish stock. If you happen to see the sandhill cranes, well, you can likely count the days till Thanksgiving—or spring. Or just call it a moment of enchantment.     *—Alison Kahn*

# Travel Notes

### Directions
This area is located in north-central Florida, south of Gainesville. **By car:** Take I-75, US 301, or US 441. **By plane:** The closest airports are in Jacksonville and Orlando, with regional service to Gainesville. **By train:** Amtrak serves Waldo, Ocala, and Jacksonville.

### General Information
This area offers year-round attractions and a subtropical climate best enjoyed in spring and fall. You'll need maps for Alachua and Marion Counties; once here, stay off US 441 and US 301. For information contact the Alachua County Visitors & Convention Bureau *(30 E. University Ave., Gainesville 32601. 352-374-5231)*; or the Ocala/Marion County Chamber of Commerce *(110 E. Silver Springs Blvd., Ocala 34470. 352-629-8051)*.

### Things to See and Do
**1. Micanopy** *(Town Hall 352-466-3121)* Florida's oldest inland town is an antique and arts center; the **Micanopy Historical Society Museum** *(Thrasher Warehouse, 607 Cholokka Blvd. 352-466-3200. Fri.-Sun.; donation)* tells the whole long story. Walk through the extensive historic district on a self-guided tour *(brochure available at museum)*. Nearby **Paynes Prairie State Preserve** *(Main entrance 1 mile N on US 441. 352-466-3397. Adm. fee)* contains 21,000 acres of wet prairie marsh, pine flatwoods,

**Silhouette of a sandhill crane**

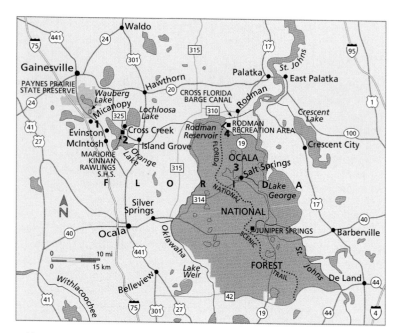

and hammocks. Wildlife includes wild horses, scrub cattle, alligators, and migratory birds. The Visitor Center (352-466-4100) presents exhibits and a good introductory film; ask here about seasonal ranger-led walks.

**2. Marjorie Kinnan Rawlings State Historic Site** (Cty. Rd. 325, off US 301, near Cross Creek. 352-466-3672. Grounds open year-round, house Oct.-July Thurs.-Sun.; adm. fee) The restored homestead of the author of The Yearling includes her farmhouse, outbuildings, personal effects, and citrus grove.

**3. Ocala National Forest** (Visitor Center, Fla. 40, E of Silver Springs. 352-625-7470) Known as the "Big Scrub," this semitropical forest sprawls over marshes, swamps, prairies, hardwood forests, and hammocks, as well as lakes, rivers, and numerous springs. Within lies **Salt Springs Recreation Area** (Visitor Center, Fla. 19 N of Cty. Rd. 314. 352-685-3070), featuring a large swimming spring and bathhouse (fee), plus nature and hiking trails, and a campground. At the head of Salt Springs Run, which flows into Lake George, **Salt Springs Run Marina and Landing** (25711 N.E. 134th Pl., Salt Springs. 352-685-2255) offers fishing, boating, and snorkeling, as well as rentals and guide service. Fifteen miles south, historic **Juniper Springs Recreation Area** (Fla. 40. 352-625-3147) features a swimming freshwater spring and

bathhouse (fee), snorkeling (fee), nature and hiking trails, and excellent canoeing (rentals 352-625-2808) down 7-mile Juniper Creek.

**4. Rodman Recreation Area** (Fla. 19, S of Palatka. 352-236-2464) This section of the new Cross Florida Greenway offers fishing, canoeing, hiking, picnicking, and primitive camping, with access to the beautiful Oklawaha River.

## Other Activities

**Canoeing and fishing** The area's rivers, lakes, and ponds offer great opportunities for both paddling and fishing. Bass is the favored catch in **Orange**, Wauberg, and **Lochloosa Lakes**. Call general information numbers for guides, outfitters, and fish camps.

## Annual Events

**October** 1890 Festival (McIntosh. 352-591-4038)
**November** Micanopy Fall Harvest Festival (352-466-7026)

## Lodging

**Herlong Mansion** (402 N.E. Cholokka Blvd., Micanopy. 352-466-3322 or 800-HER-LONG) This columned and verandaed red-brick house dates from circa 1845. Large rooms and magnificent woodwork set off the antiques.

# Apalachicola Coast

Beach, anyone? Dreaming of a wide strand plastered with greased
bodies? Perhaps an ocean view from your time-share condo? A
boardwalk for watching the local "wildlife?" Warning: This place is
not for you. Florida's last undeveloped coast lies below Tallahassee,
where the panhandle bends south. Together, Apalachicola National
Forest and a swath of swampy marshes form a sort of no-man's
land separating it from roads more traveled. The beaches here are
lined with dunes rather than hotels, the barrier islands are wild
and deserted, and the only boardwalks you'll see are nature trails.
You won't find strips, either, just the odd fishing village or town.
What do you do for fun around here? For starters, come on down
and see how many different ways you can eat oysters.

    On the side of the road near **Apalachicola**'s waterfront stands a little
box with a hand-painted sign reading:
GOD IS LOVE / DOG CAFE / FREE EATS / ALWAYS OPEN
The proprietor keeps it filled with dry pellets so no dog will go hungry.
That's Apalach for you.
    It seems that everyone here comes from somewhere else. (Everyone, that

**Anhinga at Edward Ball Wakulla Springs State Park**

**St. Joseph Bay**

is, except the watermen, who are the only ones you won't meet at the **Gibson** for Friday happy hour.) They say that everyone who comes here has a story. They come to visit, to get away—and they never leave. Life is good at the edge, they'll tell you, easier. Don't worry, be happy. Heck, even be late, the place runs on island time.

Water is the key element here. There's the Apalachicola River, which forms where the Flint and Chattahoochee Rivers meet at Lake Seminole and flows south into shallow Apalachicola Bay. One of the nation's richest estuaries, it is the heart of a great web of rivers, creeks, bays, bayous, marshes, beaches, and barrier islands that makes up **Apalachicola National Estuarine Research Reserve,** at 193,758 acres the largest in the country. The diversity of life here is astounding: more than 180 species of fish, at least 300 kinds of birds, some 1,300 different plants, plus impressive numbers of mammals, reptiles, and amphibians. Beyond the bays and the barrier islands lies the great, blue Gulf of Mexico.

**St. George Island treasures**

These rich waters lured the first native peoples some 12,000 years ago. Centuries later came Spanish explorers and missionaries, who left the coast its legacy of sainted names. During the

1800s, the river was a major highway for steamboats hauling cotton from Columbus, Georgia, to Apalachicola, the Gulf's third largest port. From here, sailing vessels carried the baled cotton off to mills and factories around the world. After the Civil War and the arrival of the railroad, the seafood industry replaced King Cotton as the cash crop. Along the waterfront where the old cotton warehouses once stood, you find seafood plants, shrimp boats, and oyster skiffs. For local color without the frills, run across the bridge to the salty, century-old fishing village of Eastpoint.

Nature is the real draw along this bend in the coast, though. At its western end near magnificent Cape San Blas lies **St. Joseph Peninsula State Park**, surrounded on three sides by water. To the east sprawl **St. Marks National Wildlife Refuge** and **Edward Ball Wakulla Springs State Park**, where you can float above one of the world's deepest springs in a glass bottom boat. In between lie unspoiled barrier-island preserves. You have only to cross a bridge to reach **Dr. Julian G. Bruce St. George Island State Park**, a breathtaking expanse of dunes, powdery sands, and blue Gulf, for solitary walking and shelling. To get to the others—Little St. George, Dog Island, St. Vincent—you must catch a boat. At **St. Vincent National Wildlife Refuge** you may get a glimpse of the island's huge sambar deer.

River. Bay, gulf, and islands. Really, that's all there is to it. But come soon. There's talk of development and who knows how long the last, best coast can resist the tide. —*Alison Kahn*

# Travel Notes

### Directions
The Apalachicola Coast lies southwest of Tallahassee. **By car:** Take US 319 south from Tallahassee then US 98 southwest along the coast. **By plane:** The closest airports are in Tallahassee and Panama City. **By train:** Amtrak offers service to Tallahassee.

### General Information
Summer is the most popular season here, but spring and fall are far more pleasant. The best source for information is the Apalachicola Bay Chamber of Commerce *(99 Market St., Apalachicola 32320. 850-653-9419).*

### Things to See and Do
**1. St. Joseph Peninsula State Park** *(Off US 98, near Cape San Blas. 850-227-1327. Adm. fee)* A renowned birding site, this 2,516-acre park also offers miles of dune-lined beach, forest, nature and wilderness trails, fishing, boating, interpretive programs, furnished cabins, and camping.
**2. St. Vincent National Wildlife**

**Refuge** *(St. Vincent Island. Access by boat only. 904-653-8808. For charter boats call Apalachicola Bay Chamber of Commerce at 850-653-9419)* This diverse island preserve contains 14 miles of empty beaches with 80 miles of sand roads, plus sambar deer, red wolf, and sea turtles. No camping, except during annual refuge hunts.
**3. Apalachicola** *(Apalachicola Bay Chamber of Commerce 850-653-9419)* This revitalized port offers history, galleries, shops, and good eating. Take the self-guided tour *(map available at Chamber)* of the historic district where the **John Gorrie State Museum** *(46 6th St. 850-653-9347. Closed Tues.-Wed.; adm. fee)* commemorates the inventor of man-made ice, refrigeration, and air conditioning. **St. Vincent National Wildlife Refuge Visitor Center** *(Harbor Master Bldg., 479 Market St. 850-653-8808. Closed weekends)* contains displays on the island's natural history, while **Apalachicola National Estuarine Research Reserve** *(261 7th St. 850-653-8063. Closed weekends)*

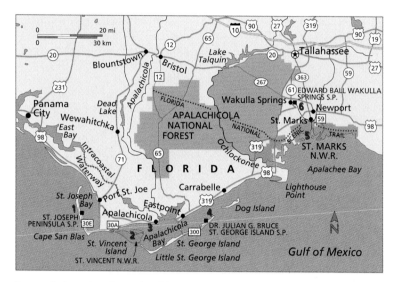

features display tanks and a reptile exhibit, plus a film. Don't miss a sail on the 63-foot *Governor Stone (Reservations through Apalachicola Maritime Museum, 268 Water St. 850-653-8708. Schedule varies; fare),* a restored 1877 Gulf Coast schooner.

**4. Dr. Julian G. Bruce St. George Island State Park** *(St. George Island. 850-927-2111. Adm. fee)* The park offers a magnificent Gulf beach, marshlands, hiking, fishing, and camping.

**5. St. Marks National Wildlife Refuge** *(Off US 98, S of Newport. 850-925-6121. Adm. fee)* This 66,000-acre preserve contains everything from salt marsh to upland pine forest. Highlights include Visitor Center exhibits, a wildlife drive, an 1831 lighthouse, hiking trails, fishing, canoeing, waterfowl, and migrating butterflies in late October.

**6. Edward Ball Wakulla Springs State Park** *(Fla. 267 and Fla. 61. 850-224-5950. Adm. fee)* Centerpiece of this large park is its freshwater spring, one of the world's largest and deepest. Highlights include alligators, waterfowl, glass bottom boat tours *(fee),* riverboat cruises *(fare),* swimming, nature trails, and historic **Wakulla Lodge** *(850-224-5950).*

## Other Activities
**Estuary tours** Eco Ventures *(Apalachicola. 850-653-2593. Fare)* offers wetland cruises aboard a certified, 32-passenger flatboat.
**Fishing** Several outfitters offer fly-fishing, light tackle, and deep-sea fishing trips. For information, call the Apalachicola Bay Chamber of Commerce *(850-653-9419).*

**Island tours** Explore by powerboat, kayak, or canoe the coast's barrier islands and estuary with an informed guide from Jeannie's Journeys *(Apalachicola. 850-927-3259. March-Dec.; fee).* Special trips include shelling, snorkeling, scalloping, and camping, plus children's activities; also equipment rentals.

## Annual Events
**March** St. George Island Charity Chili Cookoff *(St. George Island. 850-927-9810)*
**May** Apalachicola Historic Tour of Homes *(850-653-9419)* Some 24 private homes, buildings, and churches are showcased.
**June** Carrabelle Waterfront Festival *(850-697-2585)* This event features arts and crafts, music, food, and a gumbo-cooking contest.
**November** Florida Seafood Festival *(Apalachicola. 850-653-9419)* One of the state's oldest and largest maritime events, it features three days of music, food, oyster-eating, some 100 arts and crafts booths, a parade, a ball, and the blessing of the fleet.

## Lodging
**Coombs House Inn** *(80 6th St., Apalachicola. 850-653-9199)* This lavishly appointed bed-and-breakfast combines a 1905 Victorian mansion and adjunct cottage.
**Gibson Inn** *(51 Avenue C, Apalachicola. 850-653-2191)* This handsomely restored inn, circa 1907, recalls a fine, wooden ship. It offers 31 charming rooms, verandas, a good restaurant, and the bar for Friday happy hour.

# ALABAMA
# Little River Canyon

Sweet home Alabama. You probably picture broad, baked fields and moss-slung bayous, right? Well, you're in for a surprise. The state's northeast corner is a sylvan and rolling place, bracketed by two parallel mountains, more Appalachia than Deep South. Here, forested ridges conceal a wonderland of pure waters, primordial rock, and a spectacular river gorge. Whatever your recreational pleasure—from a scenic drive to a trail ride to a challenging white-water run—the parks here offer it. There's culture, too, in these hills. Scattered throughout are old mill towns, arty hamlets, and rustic hollows offering such diversions as small museums, antiques and folk crafts, and an enormous trade market.

It is a good thing to encounter **Lookout Mountain** in the fog. Thick fog, viscous fog. Fog so thick you can't even see the guy ahead of you. It's good because when it lifts, the clarity approaches the sublime. On a fall day when the chill air has chased the haze and turned hardwoods burnish the hills, objects in the landscape—cows, fences, barns, fields—assume distinction. At sunset, a broad wash of color sweeps over the long, light-flecked valley and sharpens the edge where the next ridge cuts the sky.

**View from Lookout Mountain**

**DeSoto Falls at DeSoto State Park**

Lookout Mountain. Sand Mountain. They call them mountains, but they're more like mesas. Part of the thickly layered Cumberland Plateau that angles into Alabama from the northeast, these rocky uplands form part of the extreme southwestern end of the Appalachian Mountains, which stretch all the way north to Maine, some 2,000 miles away. You can easily forget you're on top of one of these ridges, so broad and flat are their crowns. The only reference points are the occasional valley view or a shift in road pitch.

This backcountry brims with mystery and lore. Splintered, hand-lettered signs point down empty roads to countless hidden country churches of obscure Christian sects, and here and there a log cabin stands abandoned in a hollow strangled by kudzu vines. Talk to the oldtimers and they may tell you stories of snake handling, and moonshining, and local intrigue.

For sheer beauty, Lookout Mountain is unsurpassed. This plateau, about 100 miles long and sandstone-capped, once formed the floor of an ancient sea. That legacy is preserved in the fossilized layers of sedimentary rock. Early residents, the Cherokee and Creek Indians left their imprint on the mountain. So, too, did the Spanish under Hernando de Soto, who passed through the place around 1540, and later, Confederate and Union troops who skirmished here during the Civil War. Modern-day explorers can travel the length of the mountain along **Lookout Mountain Parkway**, the serendipitous high road to history, local culture, mountain towns, and all manner of collectibles. Of course, the scenery's not bad, either.

**Little River Canyon National Preserve**, sprawled over some 14,000 glorious mountaintop acres, protects a precious remnant of Alabama's dwindled wilderness. At its heart gapes **Little River Canyon**, one of the deepest gorges east of the Mississippi, carved by the famously pure and wild and scenic **Little River—**which descends 700 feet in its 16-mile-long run. **Canyon Rim Drive** leads you 22 miles along the west rim on a spectacular roller-coaster ride hundreds of feet above the boulder-strewn riverbed, with awesome vistas of the striated escarpment. Where the canyon's slab rock falls away, cascades form—Little River Falls, DeSoto Falls, Grace's High Falls—more or less dramatic depending on the season. The river leaves the mountain, quietly, at **Canyon Mouth Park,** an intimate place where you can hike close to the glassy water, tinted green by the limestone bedrock. This is one of the best swimming holes around.

The preserve's crown jewel, though, is **DeSoto State Park.** Occupying about 2,500 acres within the preserve in partnership with the federal government, the park's original stone lodge and rustic log cabins still stand, built to last by the Civilian Conservation Corps in the mid-1930s.

DeSoto is a sheltering place, a comfort zone of tranquil pools, clear streams, and tumbling falls; marvelous outcrops and rock ledges; masses of wildflowers; and a myriad of birds. Everywhere lie the deep and restful upland woods, transformed each spring into a riot of blooming mountain laurel, azaleas, and rhododendron—the kind of place for a contemplative hike or a few hours of solitary fishing.

Over to the west on Sand Mountain it's a different story. Broader and more open, this high, flat plateau seems to go on forever. Its economic base is agriculture, established by Welsh settlers who came to scratch out meager livings here; their descendants still farm the rocky soil, mainly such row crops as cotton, corn, soybeans, and potatoes. Produce stands line the roads, and beyond, long views stretch across fields and pastures.

Getting lost on Sand Mountain is de rigueur. The place is a maze of farm roads identified only by number, and each field, each crossroads, looks much like the last —or the next. These byways lead through tiny farm villages, where they still hold community suppers and school bands practice outside by the playing field. And there's a Baptist church behind every other tree.

Sand Mountain has its natural gems, too. If you really want to get away, lush and primitive **Buck's Pocket State Park** lies mostly at the bottom of a creek-fed, 400-foot-deep mountain gorge, surrounded by steep, forested slopes and massive sandstone blocks. Where does the name come from? A Cherokee legend tells of a large buck trapped by the Indians on a high ledge here. The buck, rather than be taken alive, jumped to its death on the rocks below.

Buried beneath the mountain are **Sequoyah Caverns,** famous for their magical deep pools that mirror the cave's fantastic, fossil-filled formations, some of which bear evidence of visits by early frontiersmen. The caves were named after Sequoyah, the creator of the Cherokee alphabet.

## Socks to You

Ever wonder where your socks were made? Chances are, they come from **Fort Payne.** (Locals say that on any given morning, one person in eight pulls on a pair of Fort Payne-made socks.) The so-called "Sock Capital of the World" produces more socks, more than a million dozen per week, than anywhere else. Not surprising since the industry employs more than half the city's work force. The original men's cushion-foot sock, athletic socks, textured ladies' socks, little girls' lacy socks (sorry, no men's dress socks), they're all made and branded in more than a hundred mills here, not counting the private "home" mills still in operation, a holdover from the early cottage industry.

Sequoyah resided near the present city of **Fort Payne**, established in the late 1800s around a stockade built to hold captive Cherokee prior to their forced exodus on what became known as the Trail of Tears. Fort Payne's valley setting gives view to the red-brown hills and pits mined from the flank of Lookout Mountain. For a little city, it suffers big-time traffic jams, what with three shift changes at the hosiery mills (see sidebar p. 157), 16 railroad crossings, and at least 12 freight trains chugging through each day. Have patience for two stops: the **Depot Museum** commemorates local history, while the **Alabama Fan Club and Museum** honors the hometown boys in the band.

Up on the brow of the mountain, quaint **Mentone** (named for a French resort town of that name) came into its own as a fashionable mountain retreat in the 1880s and '90s. Barely more than a crossroads, this arty enclave has more than its share of galleries, crafts, antiques, festivals, and some good eating.

Tucked in Wills Valley, sleepy Collinsville is the place to be on a Saturday when as many as 30,000 vendors and bargain hunters converge for **Collinsville Trade Day**, an open-air institution since 1950—and a definite cultural event. Rain or shine, the wooded slope fills at daybreak with booths and bodies. Come and browse, or join in the friendly haggling. That's just plain how folks are, here in the Alabama mountains.

*—Alison Kahn*

# Travel Notes

**Rhododendron blossoms**

### Directions
Located east of Huntsville, this region is centered around Lookout and Sand Mountains. **By car:** From Huntsville, go east on US 72/Ala. 2, then east on Ala. 35 or Ala. 40. From Birmingham, take I-59 north. **By plane:** The closest airports are in Birmingham; Chattanooga, Tennessee; and Atlanta, Georgia. **By train:** Amtrak services Birmingham and Atlanta.

### General Information
Prime times to visit are during fall foliage *(mid-Oct.–early Nov.)* and the spring bloom *(mid-May)*. Summers can be quite steamy. Get helpful information from the Alabama Bureau of Tourism and Travel *(401 Adams Ave., Suite 126, Montgomery 36103. 334-242-4169 or 800-ALABAMA)*; or the DeKalb County Tourism Association *(P.O. Box 681165, Fort Payne 35968. 205-845-3957)*.

### Things to See and Do
**1. Little River Canyon National**

**Preserve** *(Via Ala. 35, SE of I-59. 205-845-9605)* The centerpiece of this splendid preserve, which also offers fishing, climbing, and white-water paddling (for the experienced only), is **Little River Canyon**, scenically approached via **Canyon Rim Drive** (Ala. 176). Near its north end, **DeSoto State Park** *(Via Cty. Rd. 89. 205-845-0051)* offers a nature center, swimming, tennis, hiking, fishing, and camping. Great day-hiking and swimming may also be found at **Canyon Mouth Park** *(Ala. 273 N of Leesburg)*.

**2. Mentone** *(DeKalb County Tourist Assn. 205-845-3957)* This funky little town's main street features **Log Cabin Craft Village** *(Ala. 117)*; the **Log Cabin Restaurant and Deli** *(Ala. 117. 205-634-4560)* in a 19th-century trading post; and a lineup of antique shops. **Mentone Brow Park** *(Off Ala. 117)* affords wonderful views.

**3. Sequoyah Caverns** *(NW of Valley Head, off US 11 or via I-59. 205-635-0024. March-Nov. daily, Dec.-Feb. weekends; adm. fee)* Famous for their "looking-glass lakes," the caverns' valley setting is home to deer, bison, pot-bellied pigs, and more.

**4. Fort Payne** *(Tourist Association 205-845-3957)* This bustling mill town's historic sites include the 1889 **Landmarks Opera House** *(510 Gault Ave. N. By appt. through Tourist Assn.)* and the 1891 depot, home of the **Depot Museum** *(5th St. N. 205-845-5714. Closed Tues., Thurs., Sat.)*; while the **Alabama Fan Club and Museum** *(101 Glenn Blvd. S.W. 205-845-1646. Adm. fee)* showcases the music group.

**5. Buck's Pocket State Park** *(393 Cty. Rd. 174, Grove Oak. 205-659-2000)* offers spectacular bluffs, dense forest, hiking, boating, fishing, and creekside camping on the canyon floor.

## Other Activities

**Collinsville Trade Day** *(US 11 S. 205-524-2536)* The action begins each Saturday at daybreak, ending around 2:30 p.m.

**Horseback riding** The 1,000-acre Shady Grove Dude Ranch *(3 miles E of Mentone off Cty. Rd. 165. 205-634-4344)* offers trail rides.

**Scenic drive** The 100-mile-long Lookout Mountain Parkway (Cty. Rd. 89) between

Gadsden and Chattanooga, Tennessee, leads to delightful towns, galleries, antique and craft shops, inns, and restaurants.

## Annual Events

**May** Rhododendron Festival *(Mentone. 205-845-3957 or 888-340-3381)*

**July** Artist's Guild Art Show *(205-634-4245)*

**August** World's Longest Outdoor Yard Sale *(Lookout Mountain Pkwy. bet. Gadsden and Chattanooga, Tenn., and continuing N on US 127 to Covington, Ky. 205-549-0351 or 205-845-3957)* A 450-mile-long sale.

**October** Mentone Colorfest *(205-845-3957 or 888-340-3381)* Storytelling, craft demonstrations, and country music.

## Lodging

**DeSoto State Park Lodge** *(Off Lookout Mountain Pkwy./Cty. Rd. 89, Fort Payne. 205-845-5380 or 800-568-8840)* Hidden in the woods are chalets, rustic cabins, simple motel rooms, and a historic stone lodge.

**Mentone Springs Hotel** *(Ala. 117, Mentone. 205-634-4040 or 800-404-0100)* This colorful old Victorian inn, built in 1884 as a health spa, offers vintage guest rooms, full breakfasts, lawn croquet, an exercise room, and a restaurant.

# MISSISSIPPI
# Hills of Mississippi

The hills of Mississippi may at first seem a geographical oxymoron, like the beaches of West Virginia or the deserts of Minnesota. But they're real, all right—as real as the flat cotton fields that outsiders usually imagine when they think of the Magnolia State. In the extreme northeast rise the Tennessee River Hills, honest-to-goodness highlands that represent the southwesternmost extension of the Appalachian Mountains. Occupying a broad belt through north-central Mississippi are, appropriately enough, the North Central Hills, a red-dirt landscape covered in mixed pine-hardwood forest, dissected by rivers and creeks.

## Celebrating a Slug

Each July, Corinth's Slugburger Festival commemorates a longtime favorite dish with varied activities including, of course, mass consumption of the honoree. Fear not, though: A slugburger isn't really made from...you know. Instead, it's a burger made with ground beef and a cheaper filler (like soy flour) and fried. No one's sure where the name came from; perhaps a slugburger was considered a counterfeit hamburger, just as a slug is a phony coin. For more information, call the Corinth Tourism Council *(601-287-5269 or 800-748-9048)*. If you can't make it to the festival, slugburgers are served at local diners year-round.

It was these rolling hills that inspired one of the great writers of our time, the Nobel Prize-winning novelist who transformed his homeland into fictional Yoknapatawpha County: "William Faulkner, sole owner & proprietor," he wrote on a map of his imaginary dominion. Faulkner's characters—black and white, rich and poor, good-hearted and horrifyingly corrupt—probed the darkest corners of the human condition, and their stories resonate not just with southerners or Americans, but with readers around the world.

Speaking of global influence, it's impossible to visit northeastern Mississippi and not think of Elvis Presley, who, if he didn't invent rock and roll, at least gave it a serious shove onto the center stage of the entertainment world. The King was born in Tupelo, a small town that continues to attract fans eager to see the place that nurtured him. But it's not simply literature and music that make the Mississippi hills a fascinating place: The **Natchez Trace Parkway,** one of the country's finest and most historic scenic drives, cuts across this part of the state, and venerable antebellum houses provide a glimpse back to the days of the Old South.

**Autumn at Faulkner's Rowan Oak**

Just as Lafayette County became Yoknapatawpha in William Faulkner's novels, the fictional county seat of Jefferson was based on **Oxford**, where the writer grew up and spent most of his life. (In the words of one historian, Faulkner "left Mississippi reluctantly and only when he needed money.") In 1930 he bought a Greek Revival-style house that had been built in the 1840s; he named it **Rowan Oak,** and over the years he renovated and enlarged it into a comfortable place to live and work. Today Rowan Oak and its grounds look much as they did when Faulkner died in 1962, with personal items displayed as he left them: no gift shop or audiovisual shows here, just the peaceful spirit of an authentic and unique genius.

Not that Faulkner's life was always quiet. He was known to take a drink or two at times, and locals tell many tales (some undoubtedly embellished) of his reactions to visitors who invaded his privacy and interrupted his work. But Faulkner was no recluse; he liked to walk around Oxford's downtown square and swap stories with friends. The square is still an attractive and historic spot, with several 19th-century buildings and the white-columned Lafayette County Courthouse, an 1872 replacement for one burned by Union troops in 1864.

Faulkner's invented county of Yoknapatawpha seems a very odd name, until you notice some of the places on the real map: Oktibbeha, Tombigbee, Yalobusha, Tallahatchie, Pontotoc, Toccopola. They're reminders of the first inhabitants of what is now northern and central Mississippi, the Chickasaw and Choctaw. (Andrew Jackson helped negotiate the treaties that forced Native Americans out of the region in the early 19th century; white Mississippians were so grateful that they named their new state capital for him.)

**Canoeing at Tishomingo State Park**

The name of **Tishomingo State Park** pays homage to Chief Tishomingo, famed leader of the Chickasaw. Set in the Tennessee River Hills, almost on the Alabama state line, Tishomingo is unique among Mississippi's state parks in its rugged, rocky terrain. Here limestone, shale, and sandstone bluffs overlook pretty Bear Creek. Thirteen miles of fine nature trails traverse this appealing landscape, through a woodland of pine, oak, hickory, sweet gum, dogwood, tulip tree, sassafras, and, along the creek, bald cypress, river birch, and water tupelo.

Winding southwest from the park, the **Natchez Trace Parkway** offers a relaxing alternative to standard highways. Commercial traffic is banned, and a low speed limit means there's time to enjoy the roadside landscape of farms and forest. Administered by the National Park Service, the parkway runs more than 400 miles from Natchez, Mississippi, to Nashville, Tennessee, the majority in Mississippi. The route is rich in history, with parts that were originally Indian paths, and before that, probably just game trails. In the early 1800s riverboatmen used the trace (a French word meaning track or trail) to return on foot to the Ohio River region after taking flatboats down to Natchez or New Orleans.

Nature trails, historic sites, and interpretive displays are scattered all along the Natchez Trace. In northeastern Mississippi you can visit Indian burial mounds, a tiny Civil War cemetery, or the site of a Chickasaw village. The Black Belt Overlook, south of Tupelo, is located on a strip of rich, dark soil that was once an important cotton-growing region. But the parkway's most evocative spots are where you can walk along portions of the original trace. Worn into the earth by Native Americans, explorers, pioneers, outlaws, and mail riders, with trees forming an arching canopy overhead, the old trace is like a tunnel leading travelers back, for a few minutes at least, into America's exuberant and expansive youth.

**Tupelo,** with a population of about 31,000, is the largest city in northeastern Mississippi. Its fame is disproportionate to its size, though, for it was here that rock-and-roll icon Elvis Presley was born in 1935, in a tiny frame house his father built with materials purchased for $180. That humble home is now part of the **Elvis Presley Center,** where fans can visit a small museum and a memorial chapel. For the rest of the city's history, head to the **Tupelo Museum,** one of those folksy, unpretentious, wonderfully eclectic museums found in so many small American towns. A dinosaur fossil, Indian artifacts, and antique vehicles are just a sampling of the items on display; at the other end of the time scale, the museum's space hangar exhibits a spacesuit that went to the moon and the hatch cover from Apollo 14.

South of Tupelo, **Aberdeen** and **Columbus** are known for their restored antebellum and Victorian houses. Some are now bed-and-breakfast inns, while others are open limited times for tours. **The Magnolias,** an 1850 Greek Revival mansion, retains the original front-yard trees that gave the house its name. The Columbus Welcome Center is located in the 1878 Victorian house that was the birthplace of Tennessee Williams, creator of such classic dramas as *The Glass Menagerie* and *A Streetcar Named Desire.*

The grandest of the region's antebellum houses—and one of the most famous in the South—is **Waverly Plantation Mansion.** Named after a 1814 novel by Sir Walter Scott, Waverly was completed in 1852 by George Hampton Young, a cotton king who raised ten children and owned more than 1,000 slaves. Its four floors total more than 8,000 square feet, and the stairs and balconies surrounding its grand central rotunda are edged with 718 mahogany spindles. Its present beautiful state of restoration is all the more impressive considering it stood abandoned and empty from 1913 to 1962.                          —*Mel White*

## On the Elvis Trail

True fans of rock-and-roller Elvis Presley won't be satisfied with simply visiting the museum, chapel, and home at Tupelo's Elvis Presley Center. The local Visitors Bureau (*399 E. Main St., Tupelo. 601-841-6521 or 800-533-0611*) can provide directions for a 4-mile **Elvis Presley Driving Tour** past the King's elementary school, his junior high (where he made an "A" in music), his church, the hardware store where he bought his first guitar, and the Tupelo Fairgrounds where he performed in 1956 and 1957. The Presleys moved to Memphis when Elvis was in the eighth grade. Some years later his singing caught the ear of legendary record producer Sam Phillips, and before long this poor boy from Mississippi was making chart-topping records and headlines around the world.

# Travel Notes

## Directions

The Hills of Mississippi occupy the north-eastern corner of the state, bounded by Oxford, Columbus, and the Alabama and Tennessee state lines. **By car:** From Memphis, Tennessee, take US 78 southeast; from Jackson follow I-55 or the Natchez Trace Parkway north. **By plane:** Major airlines serve Memphis, just an hour or so from Oxford. **By train:** Amtrak's *City of New Orleans* stops in Memphis.

## General Information

The area can be visited year-round; outdoor activities are more pleasant in spring and fall. For information contact the Mississippi Division of Tourism Development *(P.O. Box 1705, Ocean Springs 39566. 800-927-6378).*

## Things to See and Do

**1. Oxford** *(Oxford Tourism Council 601-234-4680 or 800-758-9177)* South of town stands **Rowan Oak** *(Old Taylor Rd. 601-234-3284. Closed Mon.),* the 1840s home of Nobel Prize-winning novelist William Faulkner, preserved largely as it was at his death in 1962. Back in town is one of the most famous bookstores in the South, **Square Books** *(160 Courthouse Sq. 601-236-2262).* Highlights at the **University Museums** *(University Ave. and 5th St. 601-232-7073. Closed*

**Eastern redbud amid waterfall spray, Tishomingo State Park**

*Mon.)* include Greek and Roman antiquities, 19th-century scientific instruments, and southern folk art.

**2. Corinth** *(Tourism Council 601-287-5269 or 800-748-9048)* A reconstruction at the site of an October 1862 battle where Confederate forces tried and failed to take Corinth, **Battery Robinett** *(W. Linden St. 601-287-5269 or 800-748-9048)* is where two vital rail lines met—2,000 soldiers died. The restored 1857 **Curlee House** *(301 Childs St. 601-287-9501. Closed Wed.-Thurs.; adm. fee)* served as headquarters for three Civil War generals. An adjoining **Civil War Information Center** offers a short video on battles in and around Corinth.

**3. Tishomingo State Park** *(Off Miss. 25 2 miles E of Tishomingo. 601-438-6914. Adm. fee)* Mississippi's prettiest state park claims nature trails winding alongside Bear Creek and through rocky valleys.

**4. Brices Cross Roads National Battlefield Site** *(6 miles W of Baldwyn on Miss. 370. 601-680-4025)* An important Civil War battle was fought here on June 10, 1864.

**5. Tupelo** *(Visitors Bureau 601-841-6521 or 800-533-0611)* The **Elvis Presley Center** *(306 Elvis Presley Dr. 601-841-1245. Adm. fee)* includes the house where Presley was born, a small museum, and a memorial chapel. Nearby the **Tupelo Museum** *(W. Main St. in Ballard Park. 601-841-6438. Closed Mon.; adm. fee)* holds a large collection ranging from Indian artifacts to NASA space equipment.

**6. Aberdeen** *(Visitors Bureau 601-369-9440 or 800-634-3538)* **The Magnolias** *(732 W. Commerce St. 601-369-7956 or 800-634-3558. Mon.-Fri.)* is an 1850 mansion with a well-designed, three-level mahogany double staircase.

**7. Waverly Plantation Mansion** *(Follow signs from US 45 to Miss. 50, about 5 miles NW of Columbus. 601-494-1399. Adm. fee)* One of the most imposing antebellum mansions in the South, this plantation has been beautifully restored.

**8. Noxubee National Wildlife Refuge** *(Off Oktoc Rd. S of Starkville. 601-323-5548)* offers excellent year-round wildlife viewing.

## Other Activities

**Scenic Drive** The 400-mile Natchez Trace Parkway *(Visitor Center, Milepost 266 on pkwy.,*

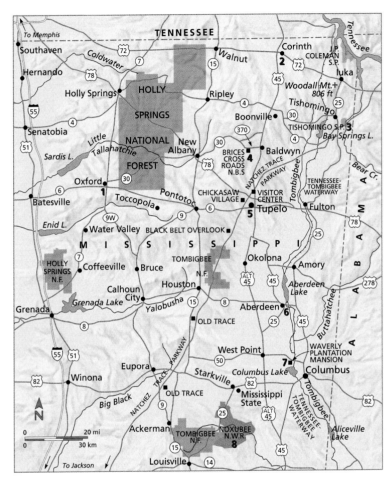

To Memphis

TENNESSEE

Southaven | Coldwater | 72 | Walnut | Corinth | J.P. COLEMAN S.P. | Tennessee
Hernando | 78 | 7 | 15 | 2 | 72 | Iuka
Holly Springs | HOLLY | Ripley | 45 | Woodall Mt.+ 806 ft | Tishomingo | 25
55 | SPRINGS | 4 | Boonville | 30
Senatobia | 4 | NATIONAL | New Albany | 370 | TISHOMINGO S.P. 3 | Bay Springs L.
51 | Sardis L. | Little Tallahatchie | 30 | BRICES CROSS ROADS N.B.S 4 | Baldwyn | 4
FOREST | 78 | PARKWAY | NATCHEZ TRACE | TENNESSEE-TOMBIGBEE WATERWAY | Bear Cr.
Oxford | 30 | Pontotoc | CHICKASAW VILLAGE ■ | VISITOR CENTER | Tupelo | Fulton
Batesville | Toccopola | 9 | 6 | 5 | Tombigbee | 78
Enid L. | 9W | Water Valley | BLACK BELT OVERLOOK ■ | 25
M I S S I S S I P P I
7 | TOMBIGBEE | Okolona | Amory | 278
HOLLY SPRINGS N.F. | Coffeeville | Bruce | N.F. | ALT 45 | 45 | Aberdeen Lake
Calhoun City | Houston | 8 | Aberdeen 6
Grenada | Grenada Lake | Yalobusha | 15 | 25 | 45 | Buttahatchee | A L A B A M A
8
OLD TRACE
55 | 51 | West Point | WAVERLY PLANTATION MANSION
Eupora | PARKWAY | 50 | Columbus Lake | 7 ■ | Columbus
82 | Winona | Starkville | 82 | TENNESSEE-TOMBIGBEE WATERWAY | 82
Big Black | OLD TRACE | Mississippi State | ALT 45
N | Ackerman | TOMBIGBEE N.F. | NOXUBEE N.W.R. 8 | Aliceville Lake
0  20 mi | 15 | 45
0  30 km | Louisville | 14
To Jackson

just N of Tupelo. 601-680-4025 or 800-305-7417) winds through pastoral landscapes and forests from Natchez, Mississippi, to Nashville, Tennessee.

## Annual Events

**April** Aberdeen Pilgrimage (601-369-9440 or 800-634-3538); Columbus Pilgrimage (601-329-1191 or 800-327-2686); Double Decker Arts Festival (Oxford. 601-234-4680 or 800-758-9177)

**May** Gum Tree Arts Festival (Tupelo. 601-841-6521 or 800-533-0611)

**June** Oleput Festival (Tupelo. 601-841-6521 or 800-533-0611) This Mardi Gras-style event features music, arts and crafts, and food (Oleput is Tupelo backwards).

**July** Faulkner and Yoknapatawpha Confer-ence (Oxford. 601-232-7282) Faulkner's works are studied at this annual symposium.

## Lodging

Oxford offers several B&Bs, including **Puddin Place** (1008 University Ave. 601-234-1250), a Victorian with a big back porch.

**Generals' Quarters** (924 Fillmore St., Corinth. 601-286-3325) This 1871 house in the downtown historic district offers period antiques and a full breakfast.

**Huckleberry Inn** (500 N. Hickory St., Aberdeen. 601-369-7294) A 1908 house with hand-painted murals, in the historic district.

**Mockingbird Inn** (305 N. Gloster St., Tupelo. 601-841-0286) Across from Elvis's school, this inn's seven rooms are each decorated to represent a different place and era.

# TENNESSEE

# Cumberland Plateau

Not quite Appalachia. Certainly not Nashville. This east-central section of Tennessee, which includes the upper Cumberland Plateau, is not so easily defined. A land of contrasts, it embraces rugged, forested ridges and rolling valleys, vertiginous gorges and hummocky pastures, all generously laced with clear streams and tumbling falls, and set off by a big, blue lake. Its byways wind up and over the ancient folded land, through pristine parks, time-forgotten towns, and two historic experimental communities. Travel slowly through these storied hills—you'll encounter craftspeople and Mennonite farmers, old-fashioned general stores, the state's largest cave, even some wineries.

## Historic Rugby

In Victorian England, landed gentry bequeathed all to their firstborn son, leaving those younger to pursue an acceptable profession or "starve like gentlemen." In 1880 British author and social reformer Thomas Hughes founded a colony on the Cumberland Plateau where these second sons, and anyone else, could toil honorably in a cooperative, class-free, Christian society. In its decade of existence, Rugby's residents raised more than 75 buildings, organized arts groups, and even made wine. Tour a few of the remaining buildings, plus the café, craft shops, inn, and **Visitor Center** (Tenn. 52, E of Allardt. 423-628-2441. Adm. fee). Then visit Tennessee's oldest winery at nearby **Highland Manor Winery** (US 127. 931-879-9519. April-Dec. daily, Jan-March Mon.-Sat.).

"It never changes around here," he said mostly to himself, never turning from the lake and hills blackened by ominous clouds and coming night. The man had grown up in a nearby hollow. But he'd left years ago and lived in Nashville now—had a nice car, a good life. Hadn't been back for a while, and was on his way to his 30th high school reunion in Smithville when something made him pull over right here on the bridge above the Caney Fork at **Center Hill Lake.** Something about the hills. And the rock. And the water.

Hills. Rock. Water. The basic stuff of the Cumberland Plateau. A few details flesh out the picture: a "crooked" road, a slender stone arch, roiling ridges stretching to the horizon, and streamers of morning mist rising from the valleys. The seasons set the palette, with spring's exuberant rhododendron bloom, the verdant lushness of the summer forest, autumn's brilliant tapestry of nursery rows patterning the hills and valleys, and winter's spare silence.

**Autumn mist over Fall Creek Falls, Fall Creek Falls State Resort Park**

Then there are the people of the plateau, no less essential, such as the blind basketmaker whose gnarled but nimble fingers bear the knowledge of generations, passed down like an old fiddle tune. The pharmacist who offers advice on a cold remedy ("My wife and I like this one"); the Mennonites of **Muddy Pond;** the after-church crowd at Campbell's Restaurant, in Pikeville, for Sunday dinner; even the anonymous zealot who posts hand-printed signs warning, "Jesus is coming. R-U ready?"—all are concerned for your soul here, in one of the "buckles" of the Bible Belt.

Part of the long Appalachian Plateau chain, the Cumberland is one of the largest timbered plateaus in the country. This 2,000-foot-tall tabletop formation stands a thousand feet above the surrounding valley, bisecting Tennessee from the Kentucky border at Cumberland Gap to north-central Alabama. Its flat tablelands belie its essential ruggedness, the result of violent forces that uplifted the ancient sea floor, tilting and folding the soft sedimentary rock. This faulting and folding, over time, helped form the various valleys, such as the wide and scenic Sequatchie.

The Cumberland Plateau proved a formidable barrier to westward expansion. Early settlers had to detour around it through the Cumberland Gap, many then traveling down to this area along an old Native American trail. Settlement was sparse, in part because the pioneers found the sandy soil unfit for farming, except in the Sequatchie. In 1838 the government forcibly evacuated the Cherokee along the what became known as the Trail of Tears, making the way for more newcomers to settle here. Today, you'll see many small farms, and since the 1880s, the nursery industry has transformed the landscape around McMinnville with more than 400 nurseries and growers within 30 miles of town, offering everything from mulch to lilies.

The plateau remains sparsely populated. Although there are no major cities, you will find a diversity of towns rich in history and culture. In **Crossville,** for instance, Franklin D. Roosevelt's administration launched an experimental community in 1933 called the **Cumberland Homesteads Project.** The "showplace of the New Deal," it was one of 102 subsistence communities created around the country. The government purchased land to build homesteads for 250 poor mountain families, establishing shops, mills, mines, and other small-business ventures. None proved profitable, and the project ended in 1945. Today the more than 200 stone cottages, plus the school, churches, and the octagonal water tower—now the **Historic Homesteads Tower Museum**—remain as a monument to the dreams of the New Deal. So does **Cumberland Mountain State Park,** created within the community for the homesteaders, which includes a massive stone dam built by the Civilian Conservation Corps in the late 1930s.

These impoverished hills nurtured a rich crafts tradition, born of utility and revived as a precious cultural legacy. While the town of **Woodbury** doesn't look much like an arts center, it's actually the heart of Tennessee's white-oak basket- and chairmaking traditions. From the early 1800s until World War II, most everyone around here used to craft these items to swap for groceries, lamp oil, and other commodities, or to sell to peddlers to take to the cities. The **Arts Center of Cannon County** has a small exhibit area, but the *real* way to see the work around here is to visit the local craftspeople in their homes.

There's a small but vital arts scene percolating in nearby **Cookeville,** home of the Tennessee Technological University, where you'll find art exhibits and events, theater, cafés, and a great bookstore. The university's satellite branch in **Smithville,** the **Joe L. Evins Appalachian Center for Crafts,** has a wonderful sales gallery of traditional crafts as well as contemporary art and jewelry made by faculty, students, and artisans from across Appalachia.

**Center Hill Lake**

**White-oak chair, Joe L. Evins
Appalachian Center for Crafts**

Much of the area remains a pre-serve of stunning parks and natural areas, including **Burgess Falls** and **Fall Creek Falls,** where you can look down on the clouds hanging over the valley. The main falls of the latter plummets 256 feet—higher than Niagara. Rock Island harbors Great Falls Dam, the headwaters for stunning Center Hill Lake. Tucked at the foot of steep, wooded bluffs, this deep and clear lake at the confluence of the Caney Fork and the Collins River was created by the U.S. Army Corps of Engineers for flood control, hydroelectric power, and pure recreation, whether on the water or along the 415 miles of shoreline. If it's caves you want, head about 30 miles south to where Cumberland Caverns hides the state's largest cave system.

When it comes time to leave, find yourself a bluff with a view—and take solace in the fact that some things never change.　　*—Alison Kahn*

# Travel Notes

### Directions
The Cumberland Plateau lies north of Chattanooga and about halfway between Nashville and Knoxville. **By car:** From the east or west, take I-40; from Chattanooga, follow US 127. **By plane:** The closest airports are located in these three cities.

### General Information
Each season here has its virtues, but the loveliest are spring and fall. The best source of information is the Upper Cumberland Tourism Association (*34 N. Jefferson Ave., P.O. Box 2411, Cookeville 38502. 931-520-1088 or 800-868-7237*).

### Things to See and Do
**1. Cookeville** (*Chamber of Commerce 931-526-2211 or 800-264-5541*) The area's cultural center is home to the **Cookeville Depot Museum** (*116 W. Broad St. 931-528-8570. Tues.-Sat.*), exhibiting railroad memorabilia and an old caboose in a 1909 depot.

**2. Burgess Falls State Natural Area** (*8 miles S of Cookeville off Tenn. 135. 931-432-5312*) The centerpiece of this 155-acre preserve is beautiful Burgess Falls. Hike around Burgess Falls Lake then view the old dam.

**3. Muddy Pond** (*Off Tenn. 164 bet. Monterey and Crawford, or off Tenn. 62 W of Clarkrange*) This rural Mennonite community welcomes visitors to its sorghum mills, general stores, leather shop, and bakery.

**4. Crossville** (*Chamber of Commerce 931-484-8444 or 800-987-7772*) This bustling town hosts the acclaimed **Cumberland County Playhouse** (*Holiday Dr. W. 931-484-5000. Closed mid-Dec.–Jan.; adm. fee*). Sample the house wines and take a tour at **Stonehaus Center Winery** (*2444 Genesis Rd. 931-484-WINE*). **Historic Homesteads Tower Museum** (*4 miles S on US 127. 931-456-9663. March–mid-Dec.; adm. fee*) displays artifacts, photographs, and documents from the historic **Cumberland Homesteads Project.** Nearby 1,535-acre **Cumberland**

**Bluegrass fiddler**

**Mountain State Park** *(4 miles S on US 127. 931-484-6138)* contains a dam, lodge, pool, and many other recreational facilities, plus a restaurant and cabins.

**5. Fall Creek Falls State Resort Park** *(11 miles E of Spencer and 18 miles W of Pikeville via Tenn. 111 or Tenn. 30. 423-881-3297)* This magnificent park features the highest falls east of the Rockies, plus a nature center, swinging bridges, lodging, and more.

**6. Woodbury** The **Arts Center of Cannon County** *(1424 John Bragg Hwy. 615-*

*563-2787. Closed Sun.)* spotlights regional arts and crafts. Visit local craft artists at their homes (request a directory from center).

**7. Smithville** *(Chamber of Commerce 615-597-4163)* On the outskirts of town, **Joe L. Evins Appalachian Center for Crafts** *(Off Tenn. 56 at 1560 Craft Center Dr. 615-597-6801 or 931-372-3051)* exhibits and sells crafts, contemporary art, and jewelry.

**8. Center Hill Lake** *(Information Center, 158 Resource La., Lancaster. 931-858-3125)* This 18,000-acre lake offers nine recreation areas, eight marinas, and three state parks, with good exhibits at the Information Center. Fishing, swimming, boating, and waterskiing.

**9. Silver Point** On Center Hill Lake's north shore, **Silver Point Gallery** *(Tenn. 56 S. 931-858-3269)* features arts and crafts by local and national artists. **Edgar Evins State Rustic Park** *(7 miles SW of Silver Point off Tenn. 96 and Tenn. 141. 931-858-2114 or 800-250-8619)* contains 6,000 lakeside acres, nature trails, boating, cabins, and camping.

## Other Activities

**Canoeing** Contact the Upper Cumberland Tourism Association *(931-520-1088 or 800-868-7237)* for outfitters.

**Horseback riding** Fall Creek Falls State Resort Park Stables *(423-881-3628 or 423-881-3297)* conducts trail rides.

**Scenic drives** The Trail of Tears State Scenic Route more or less follows the 1838 Cherokee exodus; call 615-532-0001 or 800-867-2757 for a tour map.

## Annual Events

**May** Festival of British & Appalachian Culture *(Rugby. 423-628-2441)*

**July** Smithville Jamboree & Crafts Festival *(615-597-8500)*

**August** White Oak Country Crafts Fair *(Woodbury. 615-563-2787 or 800-235-9073)*

## Lodging

**Garden Inn** *(Monterey. 931-839-1400 or 888-263-1444)* This custom inn offers elegant rooms, gourmet breakfasts, and a patio. **Historic Falcon Manor** *(2645 Faulkner Springs Rd., McMinnville. 931-668-4444)* The owners of this opulently restored 1896 Victorian inn lavish guests with antique-filled rooms and a full breakfast.

# KENTUCKY

# Boone Country

Few places in America have a history so influenced by a single person as this corner of Kentucky. Here Daniel Boone and others proficient with an ax cut a road through the Cumberland Gap in 1775, creating the precursor of the Wilderness Road. This, with its resulting settlements, became the overture to the westward movement, America's longest-running historical pageant. What lured Boone here was a wooded wilderness teeming with game and a settler's paradise of fertile lands, prime timber, and strong-running rivers. The 18th-century landscapes of that day, along with pioneer towns, survive as monuments to an era as dramatic as any in the country's past.

Until the very eve of the Revolutionary War, the Appalachian Mountains were the boundary that the British, as rulers of the emerging colony, set for westward expansion. For centuries, however, Native American tribes had followed a little-known bison trail through a thousand-foot-deep V-shaped notch in the Allegheny Mountains, near where Virginia wedges between

**Stone archway, Daniel Boone National Forest**

**Cumberland Gap**

Kentucky and Tennessee. This western exit from Virginia's Great Valley was part of the Warriors' Path from the Potomac River to the Ohio River Valley, and remained their secret until 1750, when British surveyor Thomas Walker located the "gap" and named it in honor of the Duke of Cumberland.

In 1769, Boone and five companions set out from North Carolina on a two-year hunting trip to the Shawnee's ancient homeland and most important hunting ground. One of the party had been to this region via the Ohio River and had heard of the mountain passage. Boone's party found the hunter's trace, a slot through the seemingly impenetrable wall of Cumberland Mountain—Cumberland Gap. Though the meadows beyond were the hunting grounds of the Shawnee, they were, prophetically, already thick with English timothy, a non-native bluegrass seeded from hay used to cushion goods shipped from England and carried west by trappers. Bison and deer relished the invader, spreading it so widely that the region would eventually be nicknamed the Bluegrass.

Boone's party, interested exclusively in deer skins, killed over two thousand deer in the first seven months alone. Not only were they poaching on the Shawnee's ancient homeland, they took only the skins, leaving the venison to rot. Angry, the Indians confronted Boone and his men, confiscated their deer skins, and ordered them out of Kentucky. Boone's attempt to return to Kentucky, in 1773, was thwarted by an Indian attack, and it was James Harrod who founded the first permanent English settlement here, Harrodsburg, in 1774. The following year, Boone and a party of some 30 axmen left what is now Kingsport, Tennessee, to clear a road into Kentucky for settlement via the hunter's trace, later called the Wilderness Road.

US 25E roughly traces Boone's path through the **Cumberland Gap**, centerpiece of the **Cumberland Gap National Historical Park**, 20,000-plus acres that straddle the legendary trail. A half-hour drive leads to the 3.5-mile Chadwell Gap Trail. Follow this to an isolated plateau where the log and split-rail homesteads of the **Hensley Settlement** commemorate a successful early-century bid for backwoods self-sufficiency.

You can still see (and walk) a short stretch of Boone's original route, preserved in **Levi Jackson Wilderness Road State Park** south of London, which also holds a pioneer burial ground and **McHargue's Mill**. Then peek inside the restored log buildings of the **Mountain Life Museum**, where you'll find affecting artifacts of early-day homesteading.

Shawnee and Cherokee hunters, Daniel Boone, and the early settlers all traveled through **Pineville**, located at the Pine Mountain gap. A Wilderness Road tollgate was erected here in 1797 in what became known first as Cumberland Ford.

Boone's legend so pervades this region it's a wonder anyone remembered to commemorate Dr. Thomas Walker, a physician and surveyor who arrived 19 years before Boone and built Kentucky's first pioneer house near **Barbourville**. A copy of his log cabin at the **Dr. Thomas Walker State Historic Site** is a humble memorial to that turbulent time, when a walk to fetch creek water carried the threat of Indian ambush.

The Wilderness Road turned west north of **Corbin**, a pleasant old lumber and tobacco town that stands on farmland granted in 1798 to Boone's associate, Alex McClardy. West of town, the Cumberland Plateau ends in the hills, lakes, streams, and rocky gorges of the **Daniel Boone National Forest**, which stretches from just south of the Ohio state line to northern Tennessee, and the 116,000-acre **Big South Fork National River and Recreation Area.** Here the Cumberland River cuts a deep valley through wooded hills, where there's little to suggest that anyone at all followed Boone through the gap. Hike a trail, ride a horse, or float a raft down the Cumberland River through this foyer of the frontier, and you have surrounding you the Shawnee paradise that drew thousands west into the "great unknown." Nearby in **Cumberland Falls State Resort Park**, the Cumberland River plunges nearly 70 feet into a rocky chasm in a 40-yard-wide cascade. Its perpetual mist is pierced periodically by a full moon in a ghostly arc known as a "moonbow"—a phenomenon believed to occur elsewhere only on South Africa's Zambezi River.    —*Mark Miller*

---

### Daniel Boone, Man and Myth

Hunter, farmer, surveyor, trailblazer, town-builder, state legislator, and father of nine, Daniel Boone was by age 50 America's preeminent frontiersman. Legend, however, obscured a modest life of ups and downs. Unjustly accused of treason during the Revolutionary War and robbed of $20,000 entrusted to him by investors, he spent most of his life in debt. But while business ventures failed, his reputation drew admirers wherever he went. He died in 1820, nearing his 86th birthday in Missouri, holding his daughters' hands.

# Travel Notes

## Directions

Boone Country flanks a scenic 30-mile stretch of I-75 between Corbin and Jellico, Tennessee. **By car:** I-75 links Cincinnati, Ohio, and Knoxville, Tennessee, with most of the miles in between designated a Scenic Byway. **By plane:** The closest major airports are in Lexington and Knoxville.

## General Information

Spring and fall are the most comfortable seasons as summers are hot and humid and winters bring rain and some snow. The best source of information is Kentucky's Department of Travel Development Visitors Information Service *(500 Mero St., Frankfort 40602. 800-225-8747. Ask for the "Kentucky Trails Guide").*

## Things to See and Do

**1. Cumberland Gap National Historical Park** *(Visitor Center, US 25 E, Middlesboro. 606-248-2817)* The park is threaded by scenic trails, one of the most popular leading to Pinnacle Overlook and a panoramic view of three states. Tours depart from the Visitor Center for the **Hensley Settlement** *(Late May–late Aug.; adm. fee),* on Brush Mountain.

**2. Pineville** *(Bell County Chamber of Commerce 606-248-1075)* Located at Pine Mountain gap, this community is home to the art deco **Bell Theatre** *(W. Kentucky Ave. 606-337-1319).* Not wholly bucolic, **Pine Mountain State Resort Park** *(S of Pineville off US*

**Kayaker on Big South Fork Cumberland**

*25 E. 606-337-3066. Closed Christmas–New Year's Day)* offers miniature (April-Oct.; fee) and regular golf *(fee)*—but the park's lodge overlooks forest and mountains, with leafy trails. A nature preserve protects a sandstone shelter once inhabited by prehistoric people.

**3. Barbourville** *(Knox County Chamber of Commerce 606-546-4300)* The **Knox Historical Museum** *(196 Daniel Boone Dr. 606-546-4300. June-Aug. Mon., Wed., Fri.; Sept.-May Wed.)* presents a fine collection of pioneer artifacts that poignantly evoke the daunting peril and hardship facing early-day homesteaders. Don't be shy about asking park attendants to open the copy of Walker's log cabin at the **Dr. Thomas Walker State Historic Site** *(Ky. 459, 5 miles SW of town. 606-546-4400),* atop a hill overlooking the Cumberland River.

**4. Kentucky Communities Crafts Village** *(US 25 E, 11 miles S of Corbin. 606-546-3152. April-Dec. Mon.-Fri.)* Artisans sell wares out of log cabins and demonstrate the handcraft skills that were once part of daily frontier life.

**5. Levi Jackson Wilderness Road State Park** *(998 Levi Jackson Mill Rd., London. 606-878-8000)* This popular campsite for Wilderness Road travelers offers swimming and hiking for solitude-seekers as well as mini-golf *(fee)* and playgrounds. Also of interest are the **Mountain Life Museum** *(April-Oct.; adm. fee)* and the working **McHargue's Mill** *(Mem. Day–Labor Day),* surrounded by millstones.

**6. Corbin** In 1940 self-styled "Kentucky colonel" Harland Sanders introduced his pressure-fried chicken flavored with a secret mix of herbs and spices. Neither his menu nor the original dining room of the goateed innovator's flagship eatery, preserved as the **Colonel Harland Sanders' Cafe & Museum** *(US 25. 606-528-2163),* has changed much since.

**7. Cumberland Falls State Resort Park** *(20 miles SW of Corbin on Ky. 90. 606-528-4121)* You cannot find a prettier place in Kentucky to camp, hike, swim, fish, or picnic. Chances of seeing a "moonbow" are best when the full moon is low, but in summers you can board a boat and take the **Cumberland Falls Rainbow Mist Ride** *(606-528-7238 or 800-541-7238. Mid-June–Labor Day Sat.-Sun.; fare)* to view the falls up close.

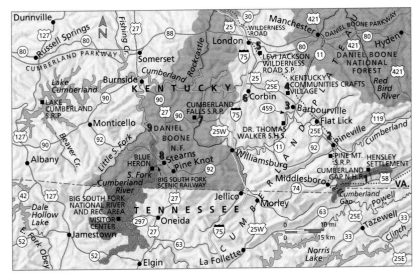

**8. Stearns** (*McCreary County Chamber of Commerce 606-376-5004*) The narrated, 11-mile round-trip from Stearns to Blue Heron and back on the **Big South Fork Scenic Railway** (*21 Main St. 606-376-5330 or 800-462-5664. Mid-April–early Nov. Wed.-Sun.; fare*) follows the Cumberland River's South Fork past old mining towns.

**9. Daniel Boone National Forest** (*Stearns Ranger District 606-376-5323, London Ranger District 606-864-4163*) Kentucky's biggest federal forest claims most of "Boone Country" west of Corbin, where timberlands surround the shoreline of Laurel River Lake. A most primitive area popular among backcountry enthusiasts, the **Big South Fork National River and Recreation Area** (*Visitor Center, Ky. 92 W of US 27, Stearns. 606-376-5073 or 931-879-3625. Visitor Center open daily mid-May–mid-Oct., weekends rest of year*) holds natural arches, lofty rock spires, plunging chasms, and white-water rapids. Visit the **Blue Heron Mining Community** (*End of Ky. 742. 606-376-3787*), a ghost mining town where audio stations, exhibits, and interpretive signs tell its story.

### Other Activities

**Canoeing and white-water rafting** The North Fork Cumberland River and the Big South Fork Cumberland River offer canoeing and white-water rafting mid-March through October; contact Sheltowee Trace Outfitters (*Ky. 90, Whitley City. 606-528-RAFT or 800-541-RAFT*).

**Horseback riding** Available at Cumberland Falls State Resort Park (*606-528-4121 or 800-325-0063*); contact local Chambers of Commerce for other locations.

### Annual Events

**May** Mountain Laurel Festival (*Pine Mt. S.R.P., Pineville. 606-546-4300 or 606-337-3066*)

**June** Lake Laurel Horse Show (*Corbin. 606-528-6390 or 800-528-7123*)

**September** World Chicken Festival (*London. 606-878-6900 or 800-348-0095*) Live entertainment, arts and crafts, and food booths all have an emphasis on chicken; Great American Dulcimer Convention (*Pine Mountain S.R.P. 606-337-3066*)

**October** Daniel Boone Festival (*Barbourville. 606-546-4300*)

### Lodging

**Cumberland Falls State Resort Park** (*7351 Ky. 90. 800-325-0063*) Within the Daniel Boone National Forest, this rustic complex includes historic, 52-room DuPont Lodge, nearby Woodland Rooms (duplexes), and coveted cottages.

**The Marcum-Porter House** (*Ky. 1651, Stearns. 606-376-2242. April-Oct.*) It's best to call for directions to this bed-and-breakfast inn, one of the original (1902) Stearns Coal and Lumber Company houses. Run by the third generation of owners, its five bedrooms offer a taste of early-century, small-town Kentucky life.

# Great Lakes and Plains

## MICHIGAN

# Land of Hiawatha

Far from any track, beaten or not, the north shore of Michigan's Upper Peninsula is a land of two characters: the shining, icy lake on one hand and the deep, sheltering forest on the other. This is the land of Henry Wadsworth Longfellow's Hiawatha, offering miles of lakeshore cliffs, sand beaches, harbor towns, lighthouses, woodlands, marshes, hidden lakes, and waterfalls—and everywhere, scattered relics from the days of iron mining and logging.

When Longfellow wrote his famous lines—"By the shores of Gitche Gumee, By the shining Big-Sea-Water"—he was describing the wild Michigan shore of Lake Superior, where Hiawatha lived with his grandmother Nokomis in her wigwam: "Dark behind it rose the forest, Rose the black and gloomy pine trees...."

It was then, and remains today, a sprawling territory where tea-colored rivers creep out from the shady depths of woodlands and swamps to meet the clear blue waters of the great lake. From Negaunee, near the iron port of Marquette, to Whitefish Point, it is a land of few roads, abundant wild shoreline, and vast forests. The woods are not as dark as they were in Hiawatha's day, because the tall pines were hauled off to lumber mills, and broadleaf species now dominate. But the thickets are as tangled as ever, and the sense of wildness is tangible.

The lake is always near, sometimes a bit too abruptly. You emerge from the sheltering trees on the edge of a wind-torn cliff. At its base, massive waves pound the rocks, exploding upward in thunderous bursts. Superior, which holds a tenth of the world's freshwater, looks like the ocean. With a temperature of 46° to 48°F even in summer, and churned by fast-moving

**Itasca State Park (see Mississippi Headwaters, p. 207)**

**Grand Sable Banks, Pictured Rocks National Lakeshore**

weather, it is viewed by some mariners as more dangerous than the ocean. Of many wrecks, one of the most famous was the *Edmund Fitzgerald*, a bulk carrier loaded with iron ore. The ship broke apart in a November gale and sank within 17 miles of Whitefish Point. All 29 crewmen died.

A hundred years ago, iron and copper mining dominated the economy and generated vast fortunes. The first discoveries were made west of Marquette in 1845. For some years, smelting was done locally, in crude but effective blast furnaces, and a surviving example, **Bay Furnace**, stands just west of **Munising**. Burning charcoal from beech and maple trees, it reached internal temperatures of 2600° to 3000°F, enough to melt iron from the ore. Iron flowed from the furnace

**Lower Falls of Tahquamenon River, Tahquamenon Falls State Park**

into shallow depressions dug in the sand and lined up like suckling pigs—hence the name "pig iron."

Throughout the region you encounter relics of former plunder: huge pine stumps, the foundations of vanished towns, roads overgrown by the forest. Yet considering the huge impact of logging and mining, it's amazing to see how the land has recovered. The forest does heal old wounds.

**Pictured Rocks National Lakeshore** is named for its colorful, eroded sandstone cliffs, but it also has sand beaches, good walking trails, several waterfalls, and historic sites. Forest trails take you into a green world speckled by light filtering through a shimmering canopy of leaves. The trail to Chapel Rock, a 9-mile loop, is such a path, leading to some weirdly eroded rocks, a strip of sand beach, and high cliffs sliced by the lake to form caves and deep slots. North winds drive powerful 6-foot waves against those cliffs.

At **Grand Sable Banks** dunes stand 300 feet above the lake. Here, logs were launched down a wooden chute to the lake, where they were formed into rafts and hauled to mills. The chute had to be kept wet to avoid igniting from the friction.

Of the giant white and red pines, no virgin stands remain, but in some places you can get a hint of former grandeur. Near **Au Sable Light Station**, for example, you see mostly coniferous forest and swamp vegetation. Sandy ridges as tall as 100 feet begin a half mile inland and are forested, for the most part, with northern hardwood species (sugar maple, white and yellow birch, beech, ash, basswood, and elm).

The national lakeshore ends at **Grand Marais**, a picturesque harbor that was settled in the 1860s by fishermen and loggers. Around the turn of the century, it was a lumber boomtown, until the mills closed. Today Grand Marais is a quiet place where you can visit the harbor, watch for threatened piping plovers nesting on the sand beach, or enjoy a dinner of planked whitefish.

The shore drops south at **Whitefish Point**, which annually welcomes migratory birds as they come and go across the lake. At **Tahquamenon Falls State Park**, the Tahquamenon River pitches over several waterfalls. Its waters are tinted the color of tea by tannin from trees upstream. Somewhere along here—"By the rushing Taquamenaw"—Hiawatha built his birch-bark canoe and floated down the path of the setting sun.

—*Jeremy Schmidt*

### King Iron

In 1844, William Burt discovered iron ore deposits in the Marquette Range. The find turned out to have a value exceeding the combined yields of California's famous gold (955 million dollars) and Michigan's lumber (4.4 billion dollars) and copper (9.6 billion dollars). So far, iron from Upper Michigan has earned 48 billion dollars. Rudyard Kipling was right when he wrote:

*Gold is for the mistress—*
*silver for the maid.*
*Copper for the craftsman*
*cunning in his trade.*
*'Good!' cried the Baron,*
*sitting in his hall,*
*'But Iron—Cold Iron—*
*is master of them all.'*

# Travel Notes

## Directions

The area extends from west of Marquette to Whitefish Point. **By car:** Take I-75 north across the Mackinac Bridge; drive west on US 2 and north on Mich. 77. **By plane:** The nearest airport is in Marquette.

## General Information

Summer and fall are best for visits; winter also has recreational opportunities. Contact the Upper Peninsula Travel and Recreation Association (P.O. Box 400, Iron Mountain 49801. 906-774-5480 or 800-562-7134).

## Things to See and Do

**1. Negaunee** Exhibits and an interpretive trail at the **Michigan Iron Industry Museum** (73 Forge Rd. 906-475-7857. May-Oct.) tell the story of the Upper Peninsula's iron industry.

**2. Bay Furnace** (Mich. 28, 5 miles W of Munising. 906-387-3700) You can see a blast furnace once used for smelting.

**3. Munising** (Visitor Information Center, jct. of Mich. 28 and Cty. Rd. H58. 906-387-3700) Just offshore is the **Grand Island National Recreation Area,** offering a bus tour (906-387-4845. Mid-June–mid-Oct.; fare), camping, hiking, and biking. Ferries (906-387-3503. Mem. Day–mid-Oct.; fare) run from Grand Island Landing.

**4. Pictured Rocks National Lakeshore** (Grand Sable Visitor Center, Cty. Rd. H58 W of Grand Marais. 906-494-2660. Mid-May–mid-Oct.) You can hike, camp, and sightsee. Visit the **Au Sable Light Station** and climb 300-foot-high dunes at **Grand Sable Banks.**

**5. Grand Marais** (Chamber of Commerce 906-494-2447) Take in the sights of the picturesque harbor and watch piping plovers.

**6. Seney National Wildlife Refuge** (Off Mich. 77 bet. Seney and Germfask. 906-586-9851. Visitor Center and auto tour mid-May–mid-Oct.) Visitors can take a 7-mile auto tour, or go hiking, canoeing, or biking.

**7. Tahquamenon Falls State Park** (12 miles W of Paradise on Mich. 123. 906-492-3415. Adm. fee) The Upper and Lower Falls are the main attractions. You can also hike, fish, canoe, camp, and view wildlife.

**8. Whitefish Point** The **Great Lakes Shipwreck Museum** (110 Whitefish Pt. Rd. 906-635-1742. Mid-May–mid-Oct.; adm. fee) includes a light tower and shipwreck artifacts, such as the recovered bell from the Edmund Fitzgerald. In spring and fall, migratory birds are abundant at **Whitefish Point Bird Observatory** (Whitefish Pt. Rd. 906-492-3596). The Owl's Roost gift shop (mid-April–mid-Oct.) has an interpretive area.

## Annual Events

**July** Pioneer Days. (Negaunee. 906-486-4841)
**August** Blueberry Festival (Paradise. 906-492-3927)

## Lodging

**Pinewood Lodge** (12 miles W of Munising on Mich. 28. 906-892-8300) The modern but rustic log lodge on the Lake Superior shore has eight guest rooms on three levels and a great-room with views of the lake.

# Isle Royale National Park

The rocky shores and dark forests of Isle Royale rise from the cold waters of Lake Superior. A protected slice of the wild north, the island is complete with interior lakes, high rocky ridges, and shadowed bogs. The haunting cries of loons echo through the dusk, at times mingled with the howling of wolves and the slap of beaver tails. Native Americans, fur trappers, miners, fishermen, and loggers have come and gone, and wilderness has largely covered their tracks. Not for casual visitors, Isle Royale demands at least a few days, and in return it offers gentle rewards.

According to legends, Isle Royale was a phantom, drifting like a ghost ship in the icy mists of Lake Superior. Early maps reflected the confusion, showing not just one but several islands scattered around a vast lake whose shape seemed to change with every survey. Even with today's reliable maps, there is something ephemeral about this wonderful island.

Or rather, islands. More than 200 islands, including some that are very small, seem to shift according to changes in the light, wind, mist, or angle of view. When you are paddling a canoe across the mirror-smooth surface of a hidden bay, your sense of scale can easily be disrupted. What first looks like a peninsula resolves itself into a long island. The apparently lofty

**Canoeists on Moskey Basin**

headland turns out to be a rock ledge barely 8 feet high. And notwithstanding its landless horizons and occasional pounding surf, the oceanic expanse surrounding the island is a lake with water as fresh as a glacial stream.

Add wolves, moose, the northern lights, ghostly shipwrecks, prehistoric copper mines, and the haunting cries of loons. Hide everything behind shifting banks of mist, and you begin to understand the mystique.

Ten major shipwrecks lie scattered around the island perimeter, and a shiveringly uncomfortable number of them occurred in late fall. On the night of December 6, 1906, for example, the 32 crewmen and 12 passengers aboard the *Monarch* must have been terrified when their ship smashed against rocks near Blake Point. They managed to get ashore where they huddled for three days until discovered by the Passage Island Lighthouse keeper. Others were not so lucky (see sidebar this page).

The island is long and narrow, roughly 45 by 9 miles, a corrugated landscape of parallel ridges and valleys. Its high point is 1,394-foot Mount Desor, and its low point, naturally, is the lake, at 600 feet.

Isle Royale is an enchanting place for visitors with canoes or sea kayaks. The complex shoreline invites exploration, while for those willing to portage, several routes traverse the island through interior lakes. Most visitors come to hike. Distances are not great, and though trails can be rough, the relief is never extreme. From the shore at Daisy Farm to the Mount Ojibway lookout on Greenstone Ridge, the distance is only 1.7 miles and about 500 vertical feet, but the summit offers splendid views. The forest—primarily birch, aspen, sugar maple, balsam fir, and white spruce—is lovely and varied. Hiking trails scramble over high rocky slabs, then slip through wetlands dense with alder, cowslip, skunk cabbage, pitcher plant, and horsetail. If you sit quietly on the wooden, elevated wetland trails, you're likely to see moose and beavers. You can practically feel the presence of wolves, but seeing one is rare.

Other animals that would seem suited to the island—bears, porcupines, and skunks—are missing. The mammal checklist claims only 11 species, with 5 more uncertain. For a national park, visitors are also relatively sparse: Fewer than 20,000 come here each year.

In early summer, you might regret the presence of mosquitoes and black flies, but you'll certainly enjoy the birds. Bald eagles are common. Pileated woodpeckers, the size of crows, hammer big rectangular holes in dead

### Message in a Bottle

"I am the last one alive," read the note, "freezing and starving on Isle Royale. I just wanted to have Mom and Dad know my fate." Discovered in a bottle, the forlorn message was written by Alice Bettridge, assistant steward of the *Kamloops,* a Canadian freighter. The ship disappeared in December 1927, and the only clue to its fate or its whereabouts was the poignant farewell note of a young woman thinking about her parents. The ship's location remained a mystery for 50 years. Then, in 1977, divers located the wreck in 200 feet of water off the island's north shore.

trees. Mother mergansers cruise the lakes with flotillas of hatchlings. Kingfishers dive like feathered jewels after minnows.

People have visited the island for a long time, as evidenced by more than 1,500 prehistoric copper-mining pits, some of them 4,500 years old. Copper artifacts include fishhooks, beads, projectile points, and awls. In the 1800s, European miners attacked the rock with steam-powered tools and explosives, but they found limited economic success. The relics of loggers and fishermen—buildings, diggings, and roads—can still be found, but most are vanishing into the mossy forest. One exception is the **Edisen Fishery**, which has been preserved to honor pioneer fishing families and to demonstrate historic commercial net fishing. Nearby, the old **Rock Harbor Lighthouse** has been restored.

On a trail between Lake Richie and Moskey Basin

You can see exhibits inside the base describing lighthouse history, and it's a picturesque place to visit. So is the Rock of Ages Light, at the island's west end; its original 2nd-Order lens is the gleaming centerpiece of the information center at Windigo.

You don't have to walk long miles to experience Isle Royale. A slow circuit of **Scoville Point** yields a good feel for the place—smooth glaciated rock at the tip, greenstone pebbles on the beach, Indian copper pits, forests, lichens, and surf. Spend some time on the **Greenstone Ridge Trail,** which follows the elevated backbone of the island. Its exposed rock and wind-battered trees give the feel of an alpine area.

On a quiet evening, the sky dissolves into pastels, then fades to a soft grey. The calming water doubles everything: Clouds, dark conifers, and basalt cliffs melt into the water, while the lake seems filled with sky. The island seems to lose substance, as if ready to sail off into the sunset.

—*Jeremy Schmidt*

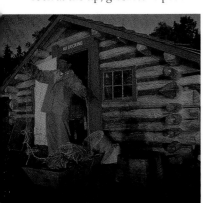

**Edisen Fishery**

# Travel Notes

## Directions

Isle Royale is in the northwest corner of Lake Superior, between Michigan's Upper Peninsula and Minnesota's northeast shoreline. **By boat:** Boat service to the island is from Houghton, Mich. *(906-482-0984)*; Copper Harbor, Mich. *(906-289-4437)*; and Grand Portage, Minn. *(715-392-2100)*. **By plane:** The nearest airports are in Houghton; Duluth, Minn.; and Thunder Bay, Ontario.

## General Information

The island can be visited from April through October *(full services mid-June–Labor Day; user fee)*. Most visitors come in July and August, when temperatures during the day are 65°-75°F; nights are cool (40°F). Expect to see black flies and mosquitoes in June. You may experience windy conditions in September. Isle Royale has no public telephones. Potable water is available at Rock Harbor and Windigo. Contact Isle Royale National Park *(Mainland Headquarters, 800 E. Lakeshore Dr., Houghton 49931. 906-482-0984)*.

## Things to See and Do

**1. Rock Harbor Information Center** *(Near the Copper Harbor Ferry's arrival point)* From here, take the **Scoville Point Trail,** a 2-mile loop trail with interpretive plaques that describe the history of the area and the natural scene.

**2. Raspberry Island** *(Access via boat rental or scenic cruise from Rock Harbor)* Follow a 1-mile nature trail through a bog and see insectivorous plants along the way.

**3. Rock Harbor Lighthouse** *(Near the Houghton Ferry's arrival point)* Dating from the mid-19th century, this restored lighthouse includes a museum with interesting exhibits on shipping and fishing. At the adjacent **Edisen Fishery** *(W of Mott Island, access by boat only)*, historic buildings have been restored and are managed as an interpretive site.

**4. Windigo Information Center** *(Near arrival point for Grand Portage Ferry)* A ranger leads the one-hour **Windigo Nature Walk.** You can also follow the **Windigo Nature Trail,** a quarter-mile loop with a side trip to a fenced enclosure showing how the forest would look if moose did not feed here, or hike the **Greenstone Ridge Trail,** which runs the length of the island.

## Other Activities

**Backpacking** The 165-mile trail system leads to 36 campgrounds, some of which offer three-sided screened shelters. Off-trail hiking is not recommended. A topographic hiking map is available *(800-678-6925)*.

**Boating** Boaters should have Great Lakes Chart No. 14976 *(800-678-6925 to order)*. Special regulations apply for island waters; check with park headquarters. For canoe and motorboat rentals, contact National Park Concessions *(906-337-4993)*.

**Fishing** Contact National Park Concessions *(906-337-4993)* for charters. A Michigan fishing license is required for Lake Superior; no license is needed for inland waters, but Michigan regulations apply.

## Lodging

**Rock Harbor Lodge** *(906-337-4993 in summer, 502-773-2191 in winter)* Managed by National Park Concessions, the lodge provides 60 rooms on the American plan (meals included). The restaurant is open to all.

## OHIO

# Lake Erie Islands

The magic of an archipelago is that each island can be a world unto itself. The Lake Erie Islands, spaced like skipping stones north of Ohio's Marblehead Peninsula, give visitors a different look at each landfall, from vineyards to bird sanctuaries to a party scene that rivals the Florida Keys. An ecological miracle, Lake Erie now teems with fish and birds only a few decades after pollution threatened to turn it into a watery tomb. Whether you come to cast a line in walleye waters, walk in the woods looking for warblers, or wassail at a winery, the sight and sound of the lake is never far, and always alluring.

Dropping a marker over the side of a boat into Lake Erie's pale green water, a middle school science teacher from Columbus looks longingly at Rattlesnake Island, a quarter mile away. "Someday," he says dreamily, "I'd like to get a little piece and retire there, just disappear onto an island." A colorful pheasant marches out from the woods above the limestone cliffs,

**Fog-enshrouded Put-in-Bay**

and shafts of sunlight on the lake catch a flicker of an escaping perch. Who wouldn't want to escape here? Rattlesnake Island is not for sale, but dreams are free when you're out on the lake.

Not long ago, a visibility marker dropped into the water would have become invisible almost immediately. That was the time, in the 1960s, when the lake was choked by algae, and Ohio's Cuyahoga River was so polluted with toxic chemicals that it caught fire. Since then, clean water laws have stanched the worst pollution sources, and an accidentally introduced exotic species, the zebra mussel, has helped filter the water. Although there are lingering problems, Lake Erie is again producing more fish than all of the other Great Lakes combined. That means healthier water and better fishing for the hundreds of sport-fishing boats that cruise Lake Erie.

The five large islands in the Lake Erie group are mounted along an underwater ridge running north to south between Canada and the U.S. The northern islands—Pelee (part of Canada), North Bass, and Middle Bass—primarily grow grapes, a crop that benefits from the lake's moderating effect on temperature. The two big islands closest to the Ohio shore—South Bass and Kelleys—are the main destinations of visitors. You'd need your own sailboat or powerboat to get to smaller (and often private) islands like Rattlesnake, but there is regular ferry service to South Bass and Kelleys.

The ferries run most frequently from Port Clinton and Catawba to **Put-in-Bay,** a snug harbor on **South Bass Island.** Visitors bring their cars on the ferry or rent bicycles and golf carts to tour the island, unless they get waylaid by the strip of shops and bars by the marina. That's a big draw for the thousands of party-ready visitors who pour off the ferry daily in July and August. The more sober-minded folks may raise their eyes to a granite spire east of the harbor: **Perry's Victory and International Peace Memorial.** This Doric column rises 352 feet to honor Commodore Oliver Hazard Perry's bold conquest of a British fleet on Lake Erie during the War of 1812; there is no better way to see the lay of these islands than to ride the elevator to the top.

From there, you can see the other islands to the north: **Middle Bass** (home of the historic **Lonz Winery**), North Bass, and the distant Pelee Island. On a clear day, look to the west for West Sister Island, a federally protected refuge for nesting egrets and herons. Then look east, to Kelleys Island.

## F. T. Stone Laboratory

Gibraltar Island, just offshore from Put-in-Bay, is small but tall: Oliver Hazard Perry put lookouts atop its bluffs to watch for British ships during the War of 1812. These days, the F. T. Stone Laboratory, a branch of the Ohio Sea Grant run by Ohio State University, hosts students and researchers who want to learn about the lake. The scientists are too busy to guide island tours, but on several evenings from mid-June to mid-August they ferry curious visitors over for fascinating talks about the science of the lake. Ask the Chamber of Commerce at Put-in-Bay (419-285-2832) for a schedule. You can also call the laboratory for information (419-285-2341).

You won't find the big parties on **Kelleys Island,** and its historic winery is now a haunting ruin in the woods. What you find instead is a small, peaceful community with abundant birdlife, unique coastal habitat, and glacial grooves.

More than any of the other islands, Kelleys offers dramatic evidence of the past. Chute-like glacial grooves in its rocks were left more than 10,000 years ago by retreating Ice Age glaciers. And at Inscription Rock, Native Americans carved pictographs into limestone centuries ago. Later inhabitants, including the brothers Kelley—Datus and Irad—cut timber, quarried limestone, and built mansions, one of which still stands across Lake Shore Drive from Inscription Rock.

Quarrying activities have employed Lake Erie islanders for more than a century; unfortunately, they have also destroyed rare glacial scars on the island's north end. **Kelleys Island State Park** now protects the largest groove, which is a polished limestone rich with fossils. Nearby, along the shoreline, is a rugged alvar, rare habitat where you can find unusual plants such as the northern bog violet.

Such delicate environments are carefully watched by scientists at the F. T. Stone Laboratory (see sidebar p. 186), who know how little it takes to unsettle the healthy balance of the lake. The water has cleared up, they say, but the bottom of Lake Erie is still mired by runoff from the farms along the Ohio shore-

**Perry's Victory and International Peace Memorial**

line. The scientists know that exotic species, often brought in inadvertently by ships, can be helpful (zebra mussels) or hurtful (sea lampreys). A burgeoning population of cormorants is crowding the herons, while sturgeon and whitefish are making a comeback.

If you stroll into the restaurants and bars along Lakeshore Drive on Kelleys Island and listen carefully to what's being said, you might guess that fish grow faster in beer than they do in water. Anglers who come here favor smallmouth bass, walleye, and yellow perch, often fishing aboard charter boats from Kelleys Island, Put-in-Bay, and coastal towns such as Port Clinton and Sandusky.

Lake weather can be treacherous, transforming suddenly from placid and smooth to stormy 12-foot waves that "beat a small boat to death," as one fishing guide put it. But on a sunny fall day, sails fill and fishing poles bend, and island hoppers happily lose themselves in the very different worlds of the Lake Erie Islands. —*Geoffrey O'Gara*

# Travel Notes

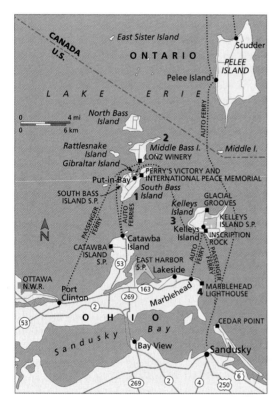

## Things to See and Do

**1. South Bass Island** Take the elevator to the top of **Perry's Victory and International Peace Memorial** (*E of Put-in-Bay. 419-285-2184. Late April–late Oct., and by appt.; elevator fee*). Plaques describe Commodore Perry's decisive victory in the War of 1812. In the island's southwest corner is **South Bass Island State Park** (*Catawba Ave. 419-797-4530*), featuring a small boat launch, a fish-cleaning hut, and campsites.

**2. Middle Bass Island** The restaurant at the **Lonz Winery** (*419-285-5411. Mid-May–late-Sept.; tour fee*) has a view of the lake.

**3. Kelleys Island** Datus Kelley built the three-story **Kelley Mansion** (*Lake Shore Dr. and Addison St. 419-746-2273. May-Oct.; tour fee*) for his son Addison during the Civil War years; the present owners rent rooms. At **Kelleys Island State Park** (*N end of Division St. 419-797-4530. May-Oct.*) you can view glacial grooves. The park includes a small boat launch, a beach, and several hiking trails.

**4. Marblehead Lighthouse** (*Lighthouse Dr. off Ohio 163, Marblehead. Tour information 419-798-9777. Grounds open year-round, tours by appt.*) This is the oldest operating lighthouse on the Great Lakes.

## Other Activities

**Birdwatching** The best birdwatching is in spring and fall. Lake Erie Wing Watch (*419-734-4386 or 800-441-1271*) has a checklist, maps, and activities.

## Annual Events

**May** Nest With the Birds (*Kelleys Island Audubon Society 419-746-2258*)

**July** Islandfest (*Kelleys Island Chamber of Commerce 419-746-2360*)

**August** Sail and Power Boat Yachting Regatta (*Put-in-Bay Chamber of Commerce 419-285-2832*)

**September** Historical Weekend (*Put-in-Bay Chamber of Commerce 419-285-2832*)

## Directions

The islands are north of Sandusky and Port Clinton. **By car:** From Toledo, go east on Ohio 2 and 163 to Port Clinton; from Cleveland, go west on I-90, Ohio 2, and US 6 to Sandusky. You can catch ferries in both cities. **By plane:** Griffing's Island Airlines (*419-734-3149*) flies from Port Clinton to South Bass, Middle Bass, North Bass, and Kelleys Islands.

## General Information

Summer is the busiest time, but spring and fall are good for fishing and birdwatching. Contact Kelleys Island Chamber of Commerce (*P.O. Box 783, Kelleys Island 43438. 419-746-2360*); Put-in-Bay Chamber of Commerce (*250 Delaware Ave., Put-in-Bay 43456. 419-285-2832*); and Ottawa County Visitors Bureau (*109 Madison St., Port Clinton 43452. 419-734-4386 or 800-441-1271*).

# Amish Country

The sight of a bearded Amish farmer plowing his field behind a team of Belgians nourishes an American hunger for a simpler, rural past. In the hill country of central Ohio, the Amish have opened their communities, and sometimes their homes, to curious travelers. Along windy country roads and in friendly towns like Charm, Berlin, and Sugarcreek, the Amish offer simple meals, hand-crafted furniture, beautiful quilts, and a glimpse of a lifestyle that is not so simple as it may at first seem.

On a damp fall morning you are walking along a road in Holmes County, and it's so still you can hear cows munching hay in the adjacent field. Then the quiet is shattered by the sound of an approaching vehicle. Invisible at first in the lingering mist, then clattering into view, black and swift and noisy, is an Amish horse and buggy. Once you get used to the slower pace and lower volume of this country, the clip-clop of a horse and the creaking wheels of a buggy seem a terrific racket.

Of course, automobiles use these roads, too, and some of the houses and motels have telephones and televisions. Sightseers motor past the colorful autumn foliage and take out their credit cards in the many shops that sell cheeses and rocking chairs and hand-sewn quilts. But it is the Amish people who define the character of the area. And they, like the people gawking at them from car windows, sense the irony: By attempting to live simply and apart from the modern world, they have become a modern tourist attraction.

## Good Manners

How do the Amish feel about being treated as a tourist attraction? They don't exactly understand all of the attention, says one former Amish man. Visitors generally know that the Amish do not want cameras thrust in front of their children or their buggies, but they are unsure how approachable the Amish are. Mary Beachy, an Amish woman who sometimes guides tourists, says that the Amish are "receptive" to visitors and are not ignorant of the modern world. "We try to live a plain and simple life in all godliness and honesty." A friendly greeting is timeless, and there is no mistaking the freely given waves and smiles of Amish children walking beside the road.

The Amish and the Mennonites, who also live in the area, began as 16th-century church reformers in Europe. They were known as Anabaptists for their insistence that baptism should occur after an adult confession of faith. The Amish evolved to preserve biblical discipline among membership, while the Mennonites grew to become more accepting of modern amenities. At the **Mennonite Information Center** outside of Berlin, the story of the Anabaptists' struggles against state churches is told in a dramatic mural by artist Heinz Gaugel. The Amish, who originated in Switzerland, and the Mennonites, who came from the Netherlands, sailed to the New World in the late 17th and early 18th centuries, along with other persecuted sects seeking religious freedom.

The fertile soil of Ohio has attracted the largest concentration of Amish in the U.S., as well as a recent stream of secular visitors curious about the Amish way of life. That way of life, they soon discover, is not as simple as beards and bonnets and black buggies. While the Amish continue to eschew autos and electricity, the conservative "Schwartzentruber" light their homes with kerosene lamps and cook on wood stoves; the newer Amish orders allow some technology in their lives. Most Amish children are taught in small country schools having only eight grades; Mennonite children are encouraged to further their education.

The Amish are nonconformist, but not unworldly. Strike up a conversation with an Amish man at a livestock auction and you'll find a savvy businessman who knows the value of horseflesh. The auctions, with adjacent flea markets, are held each weekday in a different town: Sugarcreek Monday, Farmerstown Tuesday, Mount Hope Wednesday, Kidron Thursday, and Sugarcreek again on Friday, when horses are sold. There is enough buggy traffic to wear a pronounced groove in the pavement on country roads, and blacksmithing is an important occupation. Walk around towns such as Sugarcreek, and you may notice a busy, gossipy crowd in the blacksmith shop next to a very quiet used-car lot.

The blacksmith in Sugarcreek runs a bed-and-breakfast on his Amish farm, where visitors read by kerosene lamp and eat a bountiful breakfast. Amish country holds a number of such guest houses, varying from **Down on the Farm B&B** to the **Charm Countryview Inn.**

With a good map, you can find your way around: Follow Ohio 39 between I-71 and I-77 and you'll pass through the heart of Amish country. Cautious driving is not

**Buggy ride on a country road**

just a kindness to the numerous buggies on the roads; it also allows lingering looks at the well-groomed countryside.

There are plenty of stores in towns such as Berlin (accent on the first syllable) and Walnut Creek, but you may need a guide, good directions, or lots of wandering time to discover the small bakery and craft shops located along the back roads. Good luck if you try to dicker: The Amish may live unadorned lives, but they know the value of their work.

**Amish quilt**

A visit to Amish country is not really about finding bargains. What visitors find is a sense of welcome and a peace more easily felt than described. "I don't really know how to say this," said one businessman over breakfast at a Charm B&B, "but we feel closer to God up here."

—*Geoffrey O'Gara*

# Travel Notes

### Directions
Amish country is centered around Ohio 39 in Holmes County. **By car:** From Cleveland or Akron, drive south on I-77. South of Canton, go west on US 62; or take the interstate farther south to New Philadelphia, and go west on Ohio 39. From Columbus, drive north on I-71, and take Ohio 97 and 3 east to Loudonville; or simply follow US 62 to Millersburg. **By plane:** Cleveland and Columbus have the closest major airports.

### General Information
Fall is the most beautiful season to tour the Amish country. The woods put on a colorful display, especially in western Holmes County. The best source of information is the Holmes County Chamber of Commerce *(5798 Cty. Rd. 77, Millersburg 44654. 330-674-3975)*. Also contact the Wayne County Convention & Visitors Bureau *(428 W. Liberty St., Wooster 44691. 330-264-1800 or 800-362-6474)*.

### Things to See and Do
**1. Mennonite Information Center**
*(5798 Cty. Rd. 77 off Ohio 39, N of Berlin. 330-893-3192. Mon.-Sat.; adm. fee)* The cyclorama

mural and a guide's talk introduce you to Amish and Mennonite history and beliefs. Because the differences between the two groups are simplified here, you might ask an Amish person or a Mennonite for additional perspective. The Information Center has a good bookstore. From the center, you can take a **Buggy Trail Tour** *(Mon.-Sat.; fee. Reservations required)*. A three-hour, backroad bus tour stops at cottage industries; a five-hour tour includes a meal in an Amish home and perhaps a buggy ride.

**2. Schrock's Amish Farm & Home**
*(Ohio 39, 1 mile E of Berlin. 330-893-3232. April-Oct. Mon.-Sat.; adm. fee)* This Amish home and farm offers buggy rides *(fee)*, a slide presentation, and year-round craft shops that include quilts, oak furniture, and a Christmas store.

**3. Yoder's Amish Home** *(6050 Ohio 515. 330-893-2541. Mid-April–Oct. Mon.-Sat.; adm. fee)* Some locals quibble that the Yoder family is not practicing Amish, but at the family's friendly farm you can tour a typical Amish home, take buggy rides, buy handmade items, and visit barnyard animals in a pleasant farm setting.

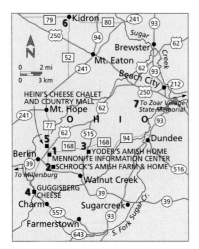

## Other Activities

**Sampling local crafts** Several places have handmade quilts on view or for sale. Try the Helping Hands Quilt Shop and Museum *(Main St., Berlin. 330-893-2233. Mon.-Sat.)*, Land of Canaan Quilts *(3340 Ohio 39, 1 mile W of Ohio 515, Walnut Creek. 330-893-3028. Mon.-Sat.)*, and Schwartzentruber Bakery & Quilts *(7977 Twp. Rd. 654, near Millersburg. Mon.-Sat., bakery Thurs. and Sat.)*. You can find handmade furniture at Country Furniture *(4329 Cty. Rd. 168 off Ohio 39 near Berlin)* and Ole Mill Furniture *(4422 Ohio 557 in Charm. 330-893-2823)*.

**Touring** Country Coach, Inc. *(4949 Walnut St., Walnut Creek. 330-893-3636 or 800-619-7795. April-Nov. Mon.-Sat.; fee)* offers two-hour bus tours that include stops at Amish bakeries and craft shops. Buses leave from the Carlisle Village Inn, Walnut Creek.

## Lodging

**Charm Countryview Inn** *(Ohio 557, 2 miles E of Charm. 330-893-3003)* From this hillside inn you get a pretty country view, electricity, a bountiful breakfast, and other comforts. Owner Paul Miller was raised Amish but is now Mennonite.

**Down on the Farm Bed & Breakfast** *(3836 Ohio 93, N of Sugarcreek. 330-852-8400 or 330-852-4283)* This working Amish farm has a patio view of fields and buildings. It uses kerosene lamps and offers friendly visits with the Schlabach family.

**4. Guggisberg Cheese** *(5060 Ohio 557, N of Charm. 330-893-2500. Watch cheese making Mon.-Fri. mornings)* They claim to have invented "baby Swiss" cheese, and who wants to argue while touring and sampling? Early in the morning, you'll sometimes find Amish buggies delivering milk.

**5. Heini's Cheese Chalet and Country Mall** *(6005 Cty. Rd. 77, NE of Berlin. 330-893-2131. Mon.-Sat.)* This Amish food emporium lets you sample cheeses, and you can still browse for souvenirs and clothes.

**6. Kidron** Once an old-fashioned general store, **Lehman's** *(1 Lehman Circle. 330-857-5757. Mon.-Sat.)* has become big and famous for its huge assortment of old-fashioned country gear. It sells non-electric appliances, tools, and kitchenware. Among them are hand-cranked clothes ringers and a french-fry cutter. The store claims the largest selection of wood cookstoves. And buggies are *still* hitched in front.

**7. Zoar Village State Memorial** *(Ohio 212, E of I-77. 330-874-3011. Mem. Day–Labor Day Wed.-Sun., April–Mem. Day and Labor Day–Oct. daily; adm. fee)* This one-time commune of German Separatists (their society ended in 1898) lies north of the Amish country, but anyone with an interest in the many religious dissidents who built communities on the American frontier might want to visit here. Early in the 19th century, this group pooled their labor, land, and assets, and became a success. At one point they helped construct the Ohio-Erie Canal. Twenty-six restored buildings make up the museum complex. Ten are open to the public.

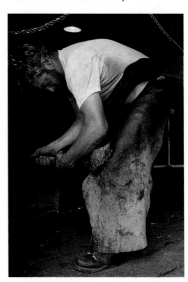

**Amish blacksmith**

## INDIANA

# Lincoln Hills

Credited by history for shaping the character of Abraham Lincoln, southern Indiana's rumpled woodlands above the Ohio River retain an ambience of the frontier isolation that he knew. Antique hamlets like Corydon, Dale, Sulphur, Uniontown, Derby, and Troy seem more connected to the past than to the future, as do the humble farmsteads found in the forests and meadows of the surrounding hills. People come here to canoe, camp, hike, explore the region's limestone caverns, and experience the slower, quieter ways of America's younger days.

**Inspecting Marengo Cave, Marengo**

Though his humble youth offered a useful political image, Abraham Lincoln was unsentimental about the hardscrabble Indiana frontier where he grew up. He cherished the memory of his mother, Nancy Hanks Lincoln, who died when he was nine, yet he never introduced his father and step-mother to his wife and children. What it was about this scenic, wooded hill country that made Lincoln ambivalent about his origins is not apparent at the 200-acre **Lincoln Boyhood National Memorial** in Lincoln City. The re-created early 19th-century farm makes a quietly awesome memorial to his remarkable journey 518 miles east to the White House.

Just outside of Gentryville, the home of a Lincoln friend is preserved at the **Colonel William Jones State Historic Site.** Jones employed young Lincoln in his store, as did merchant James Gentry, for whom the town is named. It was Gentry who sent Lincoln down the Ohio River on a flatboat loaded with goods bound for the Mississippi and New Orleans.

Subsistence was no mean achievement in the early 1800s, when the Indiana Territory was America's western fringe. Settlers like Lincoln's father often had to chop a road to their homesteads. As the Lincolns cleared farmland, starched-collar politicos moved the territorial capital in 1813 from Vincennes to **Corydon**, where the state constitution was first drafted in 1816. Despite streets so steep that horses slipped on them, the leafy burg, founded in 1808 by hero William Henry Harrison, served as the first state capital from 1816 to 1825.

It takes about an hour to explore the **Corydon Capitol State Historic Site** on **Old Capitol Square**, the centerpiece of which is the **Old Capitol Building.** Completed in 1816 with hand-cut timbers and the state's signature limestone, it set state coffers back $3,000. The old federal-style statehouse is filled with authentic furniture and decorations from the period when lawmakers and the state supreme court convened here. Across the street in the Governor's Headquarters, antiques illustrate three styles of domestic design in vogue between 1820 and 1880. Indiana's third chief executive lived and worked here beginning in 1822. The **Corydon National Historic District** is filled with fine old buildings, including what's now called the **Posey House Museum**, finished in 1817 and notable for splendid federal-style architecture and relics from its unusual past. (The bachelor son of Indiana's second territorial governor raised 14 orphaned children here.)

## Lincoln and Education

"I was raised to farm work," Abraham Lincoln wrote in a brief sketch of his life in 1860. When he was seven years old, he and his parents came to the wilds of Indiana—"with many bears and other wild animals still in the woods"— and found that there was "absolutely nothing to excite ambition for education." School was held mostly in the winter months, when farm-work was less pressing. Abraham Lincoln's total schooling amounted to less than a year, but he was a good reader, having been introduced to books at an early age. About his education he later wrote that "he regrets his want of education and does what he can to supply the want."

**Saint Meinrad Archabbey**

Hoosiers supported Lincoln's bid for the presidency and fought for the Union when the Civil War broke out. Bloodshed crossed into Indiana once, on July 9, 1863, when Confederate raiders led by Gen. John Morgan defeated Corydon Home Guard troops, then withdrew. Interpretive markers at the **Battle of Corydon Memorial Park** south of town commemorate the skirmish in which 4 defenders and 11 Confederates died. Duck into the bucolic **Harrison-Crawford State Forest** southwest of Corydon, and you'll find idyllic riverside picnic spots along the Ohio and its Blue River tributary; the Blue also is popular for camping and canoeing.

Pastoral peace prevails throughout most of the Lincoln Hills, particularly along Ind. 62, a scenic ramble between Corydon and quaint little Dale. This ambience was not lost on the Swiss Catholic monks who founded **Saint Meinrad Archabbey,** a Benedictine monastery and theology school established in 1854 in **Saint Meinrad.** To build their church, completed in 1907, they quarried local sandstone, piling it atop walls 3 feet thick to raise steeples 168 feet high. Road cuts along Ind. 62 reveal the stone they chiseled; elsewhere you'll knife through Indiana's trademark limestone, laid down 350 million years ago when this region was the floor of an inland sea.

In northern Indiana, glaciers shaped the landscape; here their runoff sculptured the tilted topography. Percolating into the region's limestone foundation, the water created myriad cave systems. Native Americans mined the area and found shelter in the **Wyandotte Caves,** whose unusual formations include a massive accretion dubbed an "underground mountain." Spelunkers have charted over 8 miles of passages in this labyrinthine refuge and are

**Candlemaker, Squire Boone Village**

making new discoveries almost daily.

As you roam narrow back roads, you'll see vestiges of pioneer life: humble farmsteads notched into woodsy hills and tilted meadows with the zigzag embroidery of split-rail fences corralling pigs and cattle.

You wouldn't guess that early logging kept this country in a bad crewcut until the Depression era. Reforestation efforts have restored the landscapes, particularly in the 196,000-acre **Hoosier National Forest**, which stretches north from the river for some 75 miles. Go exploring between Alton and Cannelton, and you'll find stretches of the river little changed from what young Abe Lincoln saw as he crossed with his family into the "wild region" of the Hoosier State.

—*Mark Miller*

# Travel Notes

### Directions
The Lincoln Hills lie in southern Indiana generally between I-64 and the Ohio River, roughly bounded on the west by US 231. **By car:** Ind. 62 between Corydon and Dale is a scenic alternative to I-64 and points south. **By train:** Amtrak trains stop at Cincinnati, Ohio, and Indianapolis. **By plane:** The closest major airport is in Louisville, Kentucky.

### General Information
The most comfortable traveling weather is in spring and autumn; summer usually is hot and humid, and winter brings snow and ice. The best information sources are the Indiana Tourism Division *(1 N. Capitol St., Indianapolis 46204. 800-289-6646)* and the Perry County Chamber of Commerce *(P.O. Box 82, Tell City 47586. 812-547-2385 or 888-343-6262).*

### Things to See and Do
**1. Corydon** The **Corydon Capitol State Historic Site** *(202 E. Walnut St. 812-738-4890. Mid-March–mid-Dec. Tues.-Sun., call for winter hours)* includes the first state capitol, where the senate met from 1816 to 1825. The historic residence of the second territo-

rial governor's son, now the **Posey House Museum** *(225 Oak St. 812-738-6921. May–mid-Oct. Thurs.-Sun.; donation)* exhibits furnishings and artifacts from 1816 to the 1870s.
**2. Battle of Corydon Memorial Park** *(S of Corydon off Ind. 135. 812-738-8236)* This 5-acre patch of woods and meadowland has flowers everywhere, especially in spring. Interpretive markers recount the Home Guard's challenge to invading Confederates.
**3. Squire Boone Caverns & Village** *(10 miles S of Corydon off Ind. 135. Mem. Day–Labor Day. 812-732-4381. Adm. fee)* In 1790 Daniel Boone's brother Squire eluded Indians in this fairyland of subterranean streams and waterfalls. Later, Squire supposedly asked to be buried in the caverns: A 2-mile trail to his grave starts from the re-created pioneer "village."
**4. Harrison-Crawford State Forest** *(10 miles E of Corydon on Ind. 62)* Ideally, you'd bring a canoe and let the Blue River carry you to the Ohio. Equestrians and hikers follow trails through the preserve's 25,000 acres.
**5. Wyandotte Caves State Recreation Area** *(7315 S. Wyandotte Cave Rd. off Ind. 62. 812-738-2782. Mem. Day–Labor Day daily,*

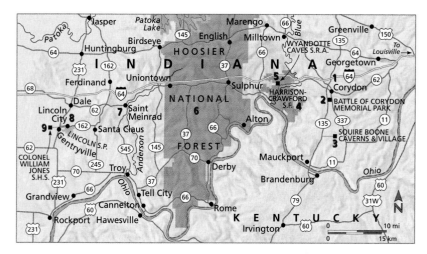

*Tues.-Sun. rest of year; fee for tours)* The two-hour Big Wyandotte Cave tour climbs long stairways; the guided 0.5-mile Little Wyandotte Cave tour is less strenuous. Wear a jacket or sweater for both. Day-long tours offer real spelunking, which means some crawling, with flashlights.

**6. Hoosier National Forest** *(Headquarters, 248 15th St., Tell City. 812-547-7051)* The forest offers hiking, camping, day walks, picnicking, boating, fishing, hunting, and overlooks of the curving Ohio River.

**7. Saint Meinrad** The history of the **Saint Meinrad Archabbey** *(Ind. 62. 812-357-6585 or 800-581-6905. Tours March-Nov. Sat.; donation),* which includes a monastery retreat center, theology school, and publishing house, is as interesting as the architecture. Resident monks lead Saturday tours.

**8. Lincoln City** Though the **Lincoln Living Historical Farm** *(Mid-April–Sept.),* part of the **Lincoln Boyhood National Memorial** *(Ind. 162. 812-937-4541. Adm. fee),* is a re-creation, the future president grew up here, giving the site an aura of destiny. Nancy Hanks Lincoln's grave is near the Visitor Center. Across the road lies the 1,700-acre **Lincoln State Park** *(812-937-4710 or 800-264-4223. Mem. Day–Labor Day daily, March–Mem. Day and Labor Day–Oct. weekends; adm. fee),* where Abe's sister Sarah is buried in the cemetery of the Pigeon Creek Baptist Church. The Lincolns had worshiped at a previous church on the site. A **"Young Abe Lincoln Outdoor Drama"** plays from mid-June to mid-August in the Lincoln Amphitheater *(800-264-4223. Adm. fee).*

**9. Colonel William Jones State Historic Site** *(1 mile W of Gentryville on Boone St. 812-937-2802. Mid-March–mid-Dec. Wed.-Sun; donation)* Period furnishings in the restored house of Lincoln's friend suggest the pride of pioneers who not only prevailed but prospered on Indiana's wild edge.

**Other Activities**
**Canoeing** Cave Country Canoes *(125 Main St., Milltown. 812-365-2705)* offers nonguided rentals for the nearby Blue River.

**Annual Events**
**February** Lincoln Day Celebration *(Lincoln City. 812-937-4541)*
**May** Old Capitol Traditional Music Festival *(Corydon. 812-738-2137)*
**July** Old Settlers Day *(Old Capitol Square, Corydon. 812-738-4890);* Harrison County Fair *(Corydon. 812-738-2137)*
**August** Schweizer Fest *(Tell City. 812-547-3378)*
**October** Hoosier Heritage Fall Tour *(throughout Perry County; call Chamber of Commerce for locations. 812-547-2385);* Alton Fall Festival *(Alton riverfront. 812-739-4426);* Primitive Corn Shredding Festival *(.25 mile N of Ferdinand via Ind. 162. 812-367-1206)*

**Lodging**
**Kintner House Inn** *(101 S. Capitol St., Corydon. 812-738-2020)* Situated in Corydon's historic downtown area near the old capitol, this 15-room, 3-floor brick Victorian dates from the 1870s and features antique furnishings.

# ILLINOIS

# Galena

Tucked away in the northwest corner of Illinois, Galena is one of those secret, special places that snags the heart and captures the imagination. The mists rising from the Galena River, floating up the town's tree-shrouded hills, and gently swirling around 150-year-old brick mansions and white church steeples seem to hold this remarkable river town in a dreamy, time-blurred spell. The town that time forgot is an unforgettable experience for visitors today.

**Galena Generals**

Galena boasts more Civil War generals—nine, including Ulysses S. Grant—than any other town in the United States. The infantry volunteers from Galena served in the 45th Illinois Regiment, known as the "Lead Mine Regiment." What accounts for the high number of Galenians who became generals for their service in the Civil War? As Commander of the Union Army, Grant played a part; so did one of his politically influential friends, Representative Elihu Washburne, a powerful senior Republican in the U.S. Congress.

Entering Main Street, on Galena's south side, visitors must pass through a pair of giant green floodgates. Although they are not closed very often, they serve as a reminder that the Galena River is a force to be reckoned with.

You wouldn't think so, watching its smooth green waters glide slowly past the town, on the other side of a high-banked levee. In Galena's glory years, which lasted from the 1820s until just before the Civil War, the river was a wide, busy artery to the Mississippi, 4 miles away. The town grew up along the humid floodplain of its namesake waterway and for decades was one of the busiest ports on the Upper Mississippi. As many as 15 steamboats a day once docked beside the warehouses on now dry Water Street.

The area was so rich in lead ore that the U.S. government decreed it a Federal Lead Mine District in 1807, and by 1826 the lead boom that would make Galena one of the country's most prosperous and rapidly growing cities was under way. What had been a small settlement was given an official name: Galena—the Latin word for "lead."

Six miles north of town, visitors can learn more about the soft, silver-blue metal by descending into the underground tunnels at **Vinegar Hill Historic Lead Mine & Museum,** one of the area's oldest mines.

Time melts away as you pass through Galena's floodgates and enter Main Street, a long, sweeping curve lined with blocks of stately brick buildings,

**Galena's 19th-century architecture**

most dating from 1840 to 1860. Eighty-five percent of Galena's buildings are listed on the National Register of Historic Places, making it one of the most architecturally significant towns in America. The oldest residence in the city—the simple, limestone **Dowling House**—was built around 1826 when Galena was already a boisterous frontier mining town.

Between 1845 and 1860 Galena hit its peak of expansion. The city climbed from Main Street up steep west-side hills laddered by a series of stairways and spread over to the east side of the river. Rose- and apricot-colored Galena bricks were used to construct dozens of mansions and public buildings in a flurry of revivalist styles. The largest building in Galena when it opened in 1855, the Italianate **DeSoto House Hotel** has been the scene of several historic events. Abraham Lincoln spoke from its second-floor balcony, and Ulysses S. Grant used the hotel as his presidential campaign headquarters. The monumental Renaissance Revival **U.S. Customs House/Post Office** opened in 1857 and is still in operation.

The traffic and bustle of Main Street is muted as you climb one block up to Bench Street, dominated by the evocative Georgian spire of the First Presbyterian Church, built in 1838. Of the eight city churches located on or near Bench Street, the most famous is the Romanesque Revival **First United Methodist Church**, where Galena resident U. S. Grant worshiped.

**Fanciful porch, Galena**

Looking at the photos and exhibits in the **Galena/Jo Daviess County History Museum,** you'll notice that Galena in its glory years was largely devoid of the luxuriant trees that shade it today. Lead smelter workers hacked down the forest and as the city grew, its hillsides were clear-cut to make way for houses. By the 1830s soil erosion from the denuded hillsides was already causing the river to silt up.

**U.S. postman making rounds, Galena**

After the Civil War, Galena's most famous citizen lived on the east side of the river, where his house, now the **Ulysses S. Grant Home State Historic Site,** draws visitors year-round. The Commander of the Union Army was presented with this handsome brick Italianate villa in 1865; three years later, while he was living here, he received the news that he had been elected 18th President of the United States. His statue is the focal point in **Grant Park,** which overlooks the Galena River.

In the years following the war, Galena's short-term boom turned to a long-term bust. The market for lead was dead, the river was unnavigable, and railroads had taken the place of steamboats. By 1865 Galena's population had dropped from 14,000 to 7,000. Like Rip Van Winkle, the town went to sleep and didn't reawaken for a hundred years.

Hidden away in its misty river valley, Galena has understandably become the historic urban showcase of Jo Daviess County. To the south, in neighboring Carroll County, nature lovers can explore the more rugged grandeur of the Mississippi River at **Mississippi Palisades State Park.** The park's 15 miles of hiking trails, winding up from the bottomlands of the great river to the towering limestone bluffs above, traverse a variety of habitats: tallgrass prairies, glowing-white stands of paper birch trees, and dense hardwood forests studded with an abundance of spring and wood-land flowers.　　　　　　　　　　　　　　　　*—Donald S. Olson*

# Travel Notes

### Directions
Galena is located in Jo Daviess County in the northwest corner of Illinois, close to the borders of Wisconsin and Iowa. **By car:** From Chicago drive northwest on I-90 to US 20 west; the trip takes about three hours. From Dubuque, Iowa, cross the Mississippi River and follow US 20 east for 15 miles. **By plane:** The closest airports are in Dubuque; Chicago; and Madison, Wisconsin.

### General Information
Spring, summer, and fall are the best seasons to visit, but nearby ski slopes and Galena's festive Christmas lights attract winter visitors as well. Avoid weekends during the peak summer tourist season. The best source of information is the Galena/Jo Daviess County Convention and Visitors Bureau *(720 Park Ave., Galena 61036. 815-777-3557 or 800-747-9377).*

### Things to See and Do
**1. Dowling House** *(220 Diagonal St. 815-777-1250. Mem. Day–Oct. daily, weekends rest of year; adm. fee)* Galena's oldest house features a collection of primitive paintings and Galena pottery.
**2. First United Methodist Church** *(125 S. Bench St. 815-777-0192)* Ulysses S. Grant attended services here, and the pew his family occupied is marked with a flag.
**3. Old Market House State Historic Site** *(123 N. Commerce St. 815-777-2570)*

Exhibitions and events are held year-round in this 1845 Greek Revival building.
**4. Galena/Jo Daviess County History Museum** *(211 S. Bench St. 815-777-9129. Adm. fee)* An audiovisual show, photographs, paintings, artifacts, and special exhibits in this 1858 Italianate mansion chronicle Galena's interesting boom-to-bust history.

**Iron-ore railway cars**

**5. U.S. Customs House/Post Office** *(110 Green St. 815-777-0225)* The construction of this handsome limestone edifice was supervised by Ely S. Parker, a Seneca Indian who later served in the Civil War as a major general under Ulysses S. Grant.

**6. Grant Park** *(E bank of the Galena River)* This lovely hilltop park has a statue of the town's most famous citizen, a memorial to Civil War heroes, and a charming turn-of-the-century pavilion.

**7. Ulysses S. Grant Home State Historic Site** *(500 Bouthillier St. 815-777-3310)* Costumed interpreters guide visitors through Grant's Galena home, painstakingly restored and filled with many of his family's original furnishings.

**8. Belvedere Mansion** *(1008 Park Ave. 815-777-0747. Mem. Day–Oct.; adm. fee)* Built in 1857 for a steamship captain, this large mansion is furnished with an odd mixture of formal Victorian pieces, memorabilia from Liberace's estate, and the green drapes from the movie *Gone With the Wind.*

**9. Vinegar Hill Historic Lead Mine & Museum** *(8885 N. Three Pines Rd., 6 miles N of Galena off Ill. 84. 815-777-0855. June-Aug. daily, May and Sept.-Oct. weekends; adm. fee)* Hard hats are provided on the guided tours of this underground mine, where the lead ore that fueled Galena's 19th-century boom years was extracted as early as 1821.

**10. Mississippi Palisades State Park** *(About 20 miles S of Galena on US 84. 815-273-2731)* Grand vistas of the Mississippi River and an impressive assortment of plants and wildlife are found along the rugged blufftop hiking trails in this 2,500-acre park near the confluence of the Mississippi and Apple Rivers.

## Other Activities

**Cross-country skiing** If you like Nordic skiing, try the Eagle Ridge Inn & Resort *(444 Eagle Ridge Dr., East Galena. 815-777-2444 or 800-892-2269).*

**Downhill skiing** Skiers can take to the slopes at Chestnut Mountain Resort *(8 miles N of Galena off US 20. 815-777-1320 or 800-397-1320, ski conditions 800-798-0098).*

**Trolley tours** One of the best ways to enjoy the historic, hilly ambience of Galena is to take the narrated one- or two-hour

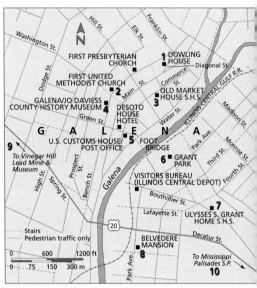

Galena Trolley Tour *(314 S. Main St. 815-777-1248. Fare).*

## Annual Events

**June** Annual June Tour of Historic Homes *(Galena. 815-777-9129);* Stagecoach Trail Festival *(Scales Mound, Apple River, Warren, Nora, and Lena. 800-747-9377)*

**August** Annual Civil War Encampment *(Grant Park, Galena. 815-777-3310)*

**October** Galena Country Fair *(Grant Park, Galena. 815-777-1048)*

**December** Country Christmas *(downtown Galena. 815-777-0203);* Night of the Luminary *(Galena riverfront. 815-777-0203)*

## Lodging

**DeSoto House Hotel** *(230 S. Main St., Galena. 815-777-0090 or 800-343-6562)* A downtown landmark since 1855, the hotel offers 55 luxurious rooms and boasts a past roster of famous guests, including Abraham Lincoln and Theodore Roosevelt. Restored in the late 1980s, it has restaurants, lounges, and an impressive curved staircase for dramatic entrances and exits.

**DeZoya House** *(1203 3rd St., Galena. 815-777-1203)* Quiet country elegance reigns in this beautiful 1830 federal-style mansion located on two acres adjoining forested Davis Creek. The main house has four bedrooms with private baths; the adjacent cottage, built in 1835, is perfect for a romantic getaway.

# WISCONSIN

# North Country

Glaciers shaped Wisconsin's Vilas County, creating what locals call the "North Country," a land of abundant water and forest served by pleasant backwoods towns and hidden lakeside resorts. It offers woodland trails for walking and bicycling, an extensive backcountry road system, abandoned farms, logging relics, and chains of interconnected waterways. Fishing has always been popular—for walleye, panfish, and the local monster-fish, muskie.

The North Country begins where the highways end, where the four-laners narrow to two, and shoulders disappear beneath an overhanging canopy of forest. Lakes glint through the trees. Dark creeks slide quietly beneath giant hemlocks. Your foot eases on the accelerator, and the coil of tension starts to unwind. A tiny lane, carpeted in pine needles and maple leaves, leaves the highway behind and makes its way to a small lake. The water is still and mirror-smooth. Mist creeps from the bogs and makes ghost fingers along the shore. As you launch your canoe, a loon cries mournfully while frogs clutch autumn reeds.

The spell of the North Country would exist without roads, but the roads

**Lakeside, Eagle River Chain of Lakes, Vilas County**

**Fishing for muskie**

are important, if only for the memories and traditions they evoke. Describing Vilas County K, part of which is a designated Rustic Road, local author George Vukelich wrote: "It winds unstressed through coniferous and hardwood forests, past lakes that knew my father's wooden boats and his wooden Pikie Minnows, Bass-Orenos, and River Runts…. You travel through a seam in time…a byway to the Old Wisconsin where the past is present and, hopefully, where the present is the future."

The past—and present—has a lot to do with fishing. Since the turn of the century, vacationers have come here for walleye, northern pike, bass, panfish, and above all, the mighty muskie—the virtually inescapable muskie. The North Country apparently has an unwritten and rarely broken law that no bar, restaurant, or shop can operate without a trophy muskie on the wall.

Muskie fishing becomes a passion, pursued by North-Woods Ahabs questing after the freshwater equivalent of Moby Dick. While walleye fishermen dangle minnows and sip hot coffee, the muskie chasers are in constant motion, hurling foot-long lures and dreaming of the world record 70-pounder. Days of endless casting and retrieving can pass without feeling the powerful surge of a muskie taking the bait. "But when it does," says a muskie old-timer, drawing a deep breath, "when it does…."

Visitors of 50 years ago would be baffled to know that these days, people come to the North Country for activities besides fishing. Of course, fishing remains important, but bicycling, birdwatching, hiking, camping, skiing, snowmobiling, and boating all have their places.

Much of the area is state and national forestland, crisscrossed by a huge network of backcountry roads and trails. Some trails are paved, others are gravel or dirt, and many are mere tracks suited for adventurers. A good example of the more civilized sort is the **Bearskin State Trail,** 18 miles of abandoned railway grade—ideal for bicycling.

Water trails include the Eagle River Chain of Lakes, a series of 29 lakes with 148 miles of shoreline and not a single portage to interrupt cruising motorboats. It's common for people to travel by boat to cabins, golf courses, restaurants, and shopping areas in town. Cottages by the lakes range from true cabins to lakeside mansions with elaborate boathouses dating back to the time of wooden speedboats, Prohibition, and gangsters.

Yes, gangsters. At Little Bohemia Restaurant *(closed Feb.-March)* in Manitowish Waters, you can see the aftermath of a shoot-out on April 22, 1934, between John Dillinger and FBI agents. Shattered windows and bullet-holed walls were left unrepaired in what was once the lodge of the Little Bohemia Resort. Display cases show some of the things abandoned by the fleeing gang: clothing, shaving kits, and tubes of Burma Shave (but no tommy guns).

If you want to go further back in time, try the **Sylvania Wilderness.** Most of its 36 lakes can be reached only by canoe or foot, as in the old days of timber cruisers and fur trappers. No motors disturb the natural sounds. You have gotten beyond the reach of even the smallest roads.

*—Jeremy Schmidt*

# Travel Notes

### Directions
The center of this area is Vilas County, on Wisconsin's northern border. **By car:** US 51 and US 45 are the main routes from southern Wisconsin. From Minneapolis, Minn., US 8 is the most direct route. Milwaukee is a five-hour drive. **By plane:** The nearest airports are in Rhinelander and Wausau.

### General Information
Summer and fall are the best times to visit; winter is popular for snowmobiling and cross-country skiing. A good information source is the Vilas County Advertising *(330 Court St., P.O. Box 369-Courthouse, Eagle River 54521. 715-479-3649 or 800-236-3649).*

### Things to See and Do
**1. Northern Highland-American Legion State Forest** *(Headquarters, 8770 Cty. Rd. J, Woodruff. 715-356-5211)* The 200,000-acre forest offers campsites, boat ramps, trails, swimming beaches, and more than 900 lakes.
**2. Sylvania Wilderness & Recreation Area,** Michigan *(Cty. Rd. 535 off US 2, in the Ottawa N.F. of Michigan. 906-358-4551. Mid-*

*May–Sept.; adm. fee)* Canoe and hiking trails connect 36 wilderness lakes. Access is from the north only, via Watersmeet.
**3. Boat Houses of Vilas County** *(Eagle River Chain of Lakes. 715-479-8575 or 800-359-6315)* A self-guided water tour visits numerous historic boathouses.
**4. Fallison Lake Interpretive Trail** *(Off Cty. Rd. N, W of Sayner. 715-385-2727)* This traipse through the forest and bogs around Fallison Lake is one of the several nature trails maintained in the area.
**5. Cathedral Point** *(DNR Trout Lake Forestry Headquarters, 4125 Cty. Rd. M. 715-385-2727)* A stand of old-growth pines shades a walk-in picnic area overlooking the lake.
**6. Lac du Flambeau** Dedicated to Ojibwa culture, the **George W. Brown, Jr., Ojibwe Museum and Cultural Center** *(603 Peace Pipe Rd.. 715-588-3333. May-Oct. Mon.-Sat., in winter Tues.-Thurs.; adm. fee)* exhibits canoes, traditional arts and crafts, and living history presentations. Next door enjoy tribal dances and costumes at the **Indian Bowl Powwows** *(July-Aug. Tues. p.m.; fee).*
**7. Bearskin State Trail** *(From Minocqua S to Cty. Rd. K. 715-385-2727. Trail fee)* An

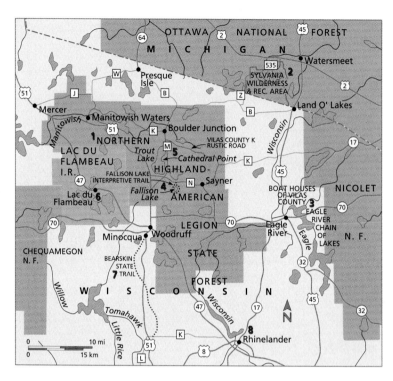

abandoned railway grade winds 18 miles through forests and along lakes.

**8. Rhinelander** The **Rhinelander Logging Museum** *(Oneida Ave. in Pioneer Park. 715-362-7464 or 800-236-4386. Mid-May–Labor Day)*

**Vilas County signposts**

remembers the logging era with artifacts, tools, a blacksmith shop, and more.

### Other Activities

**Guided fishing** Eagle River Area Guides *(715-479-8804)* keeps a listing of local guides. The muskie are biting from late May to late November.

**Winery tour** Check out cranberry wine-making techniques (and sample the results) at Three Lakes Winery *(off Wis. 45, Three Lakes. 715-546-3080 or 800-546-5434)*.

### Annual Events

**July** Bear River Powwow *(off Indian Village Rd., Lac du Flambeau. 715-588-3346)*
**August** Muskie Jamboree *(Boulder Junction. 715-385-2400)*
**September** Cranberry bog tours *(Manitowish Waters 715-543-8488)*

### Lodging

**Brennan Manor B&B** *(1079 Everett Rd., Eagle River. 715-479-7353)* Resembling a German hunting lodge, this lakeshore inn has cathedral ceilings and a three-story fireplace.

# MINNESOTA
# Mississippi Headwaters

Where a shallow stream flows from a forest-rimmed lake in northern Minnesota, the Mississippi River begins its long journey. The headwaters region is a landscape of lakes, marshes, and forests, filled with wildlife and outdoor opportunities. It offers old-growth forest, hidden bogs, canoeing rivers, bicycle trails, lakeside cabins, Paul Bunyan legends, a glimpse of logging history, and the chance to stride across the mighty Mississippi.

Minnesota is one-tenth water. But the landscape around Bemidji and Park Rapids looks a great deal wetter than that. Lakes are everywhere. Roads wind around their shores. Loons float on calm waters, their long mournful calls sounding the anthem of the north. Great blue herons wade in the marshes, among dome-shaped houses of beavers. Shallow bays are thick with wild rice, which is still harvested each fall by Ojibwa using the old techniques—bending the stalks over canoes, and knocking the grains free with sticks.

In 1832 Indian agent Henry Schoolcraft was guided by Ozawindeb to

**Fall foliage at Itasca State Park**

**Canoeing at Lake Itasca State Park**

the outlet of a narrow lake that he declared the true source of the Mississippi River. He coined the name Itasca, from the Latin *veritas caput*, or "true head." The Ojibwa called the lake "Omushkos," or Elk Lake. They knew it well and understood that the waters flowed downhill from this point, but they felt no need to distinguish one regional stream from all others as the official, authorized headwaters (see sidebar p. 209).

Source of the great river, the headwaters region also gave rise to the powerful legend of Paul Bunyan, who is said to have been born in Bemidji. King of the loggers, he was as tall as the trees he cut. On his first birthday, his father gave him a blue ox named Babe. Together, they grew to giant stature and changed the shape of the north. Never mind what geologists say on the matter: The popular legend tells us that the Mississippi River resulted from an accident. Paul and Babe started it when their big water-tank wagon sprang a leak. And area lakes, of course, are just Babe's hoofprints.

Paul Bunyan's trees were primarily red pine and eastern white pine. They made excellent lumber for the building of houses, barns, and churches throughout the Midwest and out across the treeless plains. In the loggers' wake, there grew up a new forest of aspen, maple, birch, oak, and other broadleaf species. This second-growth forest

**Paul Bunyan statue near Itasca State Park**

is different from the original but still deemed beautiful by visitors who flock to lakeshore resorts and family cabins. The resorts started as fishing camps. Around the turn of the century, vacationers from around the Midwest would hop northbound trains to go rusticating in the woods.

Today's experience is similar but less rustic. Resorts have gone modern, with not only flush toilets but also microwaves, satellite dishes, and even Internet connections. And while fishing is still important, visitors now come for a variety of reasons: bicycling, canoeing, hiking, skiing, snowmobiling, or enjoying the forest in its seasonal glory. Spring is wildflower season: trillium, bloodroot, bellwort, showy lady's slipper. Summer is green piled upon green, and in fall, the mixed hardwoods—maple, oak, basswood, birch, and aspen—explode with color.

There's no better place for exploring than **Itasca State Park.** Established in 1891, the park protects the source of the Mississippi and preserves a tract of pre-Bunyan woodland. Wilderness Drive winds for 11 miles beneath great pines that have never felt the woodsman's ax. Here you'll find Itasca's largest white pine, 112 feet tall, and Minnesota's largest red pine, 120 feet tall. White pine logs make up the Old Timer's Cabin, which stands on the lakeshore near Itasca's historic **Douglas Lodge.** Using wind-toppled trees, the Civilian Conservation Corps built the cabin in 1934. Only a few trees were needed: Four logs make an entire wall.

Of course the most famous place in the park is the outlet of Lake Itasca, where a shallow stream of clear water slides out from beneath wild rice to become the great Mississippi, America's central waterway. At this point, children hop easily across the river on stepping-stones. Standing here, you can almost feel the connection with the Gulf of Mexico, more than 1,400 feet lower and 2,350 river miles away.

## The True Headwaters?

How was it decided that this particular area of the Mississippi's huge basin held the true headwaters of the mighty river? The Ohio River has greater volume. The Missouri River is longer and falls from a higher elevation. Yet those rivers are considered tributaries. Lake Itasca is not even the highest point in its own drainage system. Several streams flow into the lake, but Henry Schoolcraft thought them too small to qualify as rivers. In the end, no hard rules can be used to settle the matter. With Lake Itasca, 150 years of tradition carry as much weight as anything else.

You can follow its course along the **Great River Road,** a marked series of highways and back roads that stay close to the river. It flows first to the northeast, winding through a landscape of forests and farms, and gradually gathers strength from tributary streams. Canoeists enjoy floating along this stretch of the river, where the water is pure, and even a child can toss a stone from one side to the other.

More opportunities for wandering can be found at the **Tamarac National Wildlife Refuge,** where trails lead through a variety of habitats managed specifically for waterfowl and other wildlife, and at the

110,000-acre **Paul Bunyan State Forest.** Stripped of salable timber in the early 1900s, the forest was abandoned by loggers after 1920 and eventually turned over to the state and county in lieu of tax payments by various owners. Severe forest fires between 1913 and 1926 did further damage, preventing regrowth of the great pines and encouraging today's aspen-dominated forest. It sounds like a sad tale of sylvan waste until you enter that leafy world and see its many beauties. A network of roads and trails connect small ponds, campgrounds, and hidden crannies.

Minnesota is famous—perhaps notorious—for its hard winter and the cheerful way local residents cope with it. Snowmobiling and cross-country skiing are big items on the snowy agenda, but there's probably no better symbol for winter cheer than ice fishing at the annual eelpout festival. For several days each February, the frozen surface of **Leech Lake** hums with life. Several thousand people arrive and set up a village of ice-fishing shacks, including some that are two and three stories high. People fish for the unlovely and not-much-wanted eelpout, or burbot, and call this northern Mardi Gras the highlight of the year. The event is typically Minnesotan, with people making the most of what they have.

*—Jeremy Schmidt*

# Travel Notes

**Directions**

Bemidji, Park Rapids, and Walker are at the center of the headwaters area, with forests and lakes extending in all directions. **By car:** Major highways to the headwaters are US 2 from Duluth, and US 71 via US 10 from Minneapolis. **By plane:** The nearest airports are at Bemidji and Duluth.

**General Information**

Settled weather and fewer insects make July and August the most popular time for a visit. Autumn colors draw people in September and early October, and winter activities are increasingly popular. Contact the Park Rapids Area Chamber of Commerce *(P.O. Box 249, Park Rapids 56470. 218-732-4111 or 800-247-0054)*; or the Bemidji Area Chamber of Commerce *(300 Bemidji Ave., Bemidji 56601. 218-751-3540 or 800-458-2223).*

**Things to See and Do**

**1. Itasca State Park** *(Off US 71 N of Park Rapids. Headquarters 218-266-2100, reservations 800-246-2267. Adm. fee)* Surrounding the Mississippi headwaters, Itasca offers boating, fishing, hiking, biking, camping, and extensive visitor services.

**2. Lake Bemidji State Park** *(3401 State Park Rd., Bemidji. 218-755-3843. Adm. fee)*

**Minnesota wild lupine**

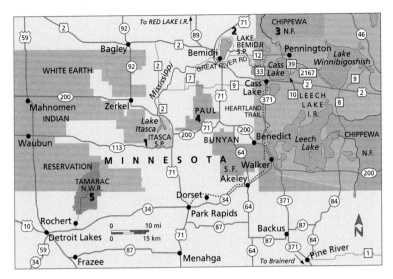

On Lake Bemidji, this park has camping, fishing, hiking, biking and cross-country skiing trails, and an unusual boardwalk suspended over a native bog.

**3. Chippewa National Forest** (Headquarters, Rte. 3, Cass Lake. 218-335-8600) The forest includes several interesting sites, including the Lost Forty, 144 acres of old-growth pine, and Camp Rabideau, with historic buildings and an interpretive center (Mem. Day–Labor Day).

**4. Paul Bunyan State Forest** (Park Rapids Area Forest Supervisor, 607 W. First St., Park Rapids. 218-732-3309) Mostly woodland with some lakes and numerous wetlands, the forest has many trails and back roads good for mountain biking, cross-country skiing, walking, and driving.

**5. Tamarac National Wildlife Refuge** (Rochert. 218-847-2641. Refuge open year-round, Visitor Center May-Sept.) The refuge is home to many species; it offers a driving tour, hiking, and cross-country skiing.

### Other Activities

**Canoeing** The state has 23 designated canoe routes (612-296-6157 or 888-MIN-NDNR). The Crow Wing River Canoe Route begins near Akeley on the 11th Crow Wing Lake and runs 115 miles to the Mississippi River near Brainerd. Easy paddling on the Shell and Crow Wing Rivers and public campsites allow for multiday family trips.

**Great River Road** (Information and brochure, Mississippi River Pkwy. Commission 612-449-2560) Specially marked back roads and highways follow the Mississippi's course.

**Hiking** The 50-mile Heartland Trail (Park Rapids to Cass Lake. 800-247-0054), 28 miles of which are paved, follows an abandoned railroad grade.

**Powwows** Attend a powwow at Red Lake (218-679-3341) or Leech Lake (218-335-8200) Reservations during the summer.

**Winter sports** Hundreds of miles of groomed snowmobile trails go as far as Canada and Duluth; ice fishing and cross-country skiing also keep people outdoors. Check with the local Chambers of Commerce.

### Annual Events

**February** Eelpout Festival (Leech Lake. 218-547-1751 or 800-833-1118); Minnesota Finlandia Ski Marathon (Bemidji. 800-458-2223); **July** Water Carnival (Bemidji. 800-458-2223); Headwaters Rodeo (Park Rapids. 800-247-0054)

**August** A Taste of Dorset outdoor food festival (Dorset. 800-247-0054)

**September** Headwaters Hundred Bike Ride/Race (Park Rapids. 800-247-0054)

### Lodging

**Douglas Lodge** (Itasca S.P. 218-266-2122) On a breezy, pine-covered knob at the south end of Lake Itasca, this log lodge was built nearly a century ago. In addition to guest rooms in the main building, the lodge offers separate cabins, motel units, and a ten-room log clubhouse that rents as a unit.

# IOWA
# Little Switzerland

For anyone who assumes Iowa is lacking in dramatic scenery, the awesome spectacle of the Mississippi River flowing past the towering bluffs of Allamakee and Clayton Counties, in the state's northeast corner, can be a mind-altering experience. Less hilly but equally captivating are the neighboring counties of Winneshiek and Fayette, where country roads dip and wind through a rolling landscape of forest and farmland, sparkling rivers, and 19th-century towns that preserve Iowa's immigrant heritage. In this lushly scenic pocket of rural America, known as Little Switzerland for its lovely landscapes, visitors find not only natural wonders but also historical and cultural treasures.

The bluff-top observation platform about 500 feet above the Mississippi River at **Pikes Peak State Park** is a good place to survey the natural wonders of what the Ojibwa Indians called the Messipi, or "great river." This portion of the "Upper Miss," dotted with forested islands and lined with massive limestone cliffs, is part of the 200,000-acre **Upper Mississippi River National Wildlife and Fish Refuge.** Wild turkeys, bald eagles, cormorants, deer, black bears, bobcats, and river otters are among the animals that have been sighted here.

**Sheep at the Farm Park in Decorah**

Farther south along the river, at **Guttenberg,** is **Lock and Dam No. 10.** An observation platform lets visitors watch barge and boat traffic navigate around a giant dam completed in 1936.

McGregor, Guttenberg, and the other small river towns are fairly recent additions to a landscape inhabited at least 2,500 years ago by a mysterious culture known as the Mound Builders. At **Effigy Mounds National Monument** nearly 200 sacred burial mounds, some shaped like bears and birds, are preserved along an interpretive trail system that climbs through densely wooded grounds overlooking the river.

**Mississippi River from Pikes Peak State Park**

North of Effigy Mounds, **Yellow River State Forest** spreads a leafy canopy of native trees—sugar maple, red and burr oak, white ash, black walnut, and white pine—over some 9,000 spectacular riverside acres.

A strong ethnic influence is noticeable in several small towns west of the Mississippi. **Decorah**, nestled among the hills and limestone palisades of the Upper Iowa River, retains much of its Norwegian heritage. The saga of settlement unfolds as you walk through the **Vesterheim Norwegian-American Museum.** Its collections include reconstructed rooms typical of Norwegian and American homes of the mid-19th century, as well as festive costumes, home furnishings, and arts and crafts that the immigrants brought with them or made in their new Vesterheim, or "western home."

Antonín Dvořák, the famous Czech composer, had already written the "New World Symphony" when he arrived in Czech-settled **Spillville** in 1893. The house where he spent the summer is now the **Bily Clock Museum.** Visitors who come to see the Dvořák exhibit are equally fascinated by the museum's incredible collection of wooden clocks. The Bily brothers, two local farmers, designed and hand carved these ingenious timepieces from native and imported woods during the long Iowa winters.

In 1840, before there were towns in Winneshiek County, **Fort Atkinson** was established in the Iowa Territory's 40-mile-wide Neutral Ground. A reconstructed stockade surrounds the grounds of this former federal mili-

**At the Bily Clock Museum**

tary post, built to contain and protect the Winnebago Indians. In 1848 the Winnebago were forced west again by the U.S. government, and the fort was abandoned in 1849. A few miles away, on a gravel road in the softly rolling farmland near Festina, is **St. Anthony of Padua Chapel**, better known as "the world's smallest church." Built in 1885, the tiny, impeccably maintained structure measures a mere 14 by 20 feet and contains four pews.

If you drive south into Fayette County, you can see **Montauk**, one of Iowa's grandest mansions. The elegant Italianate house, which contains most of its original furnishings, was constructed in 1874 for William Larrabee, an Iowa state senator who later served as governor. It is a gem among Little Switzerland's many treasures.

*—Donald S. Olson*

# Travel Notes

### Directions

Winneshiek, Allamakee, Fayette, and Clayton Counties are in Iowa's northeast corner. **By car:** From Minneapolis and St. Paul, Minnesota, you can travel along the Mississippi River by taking the Great River Rd. (US 61) south to Minn. 26/Iowa 26 and following County Rd. X52 to Iowa 364. From Waterloo, take the scenic route: Iowa 281 to Iowa 150 to US 52. From Dubuque, take US 52 west and north. **By plane:** The nearest airports are in Dubuque and Waterloo/Cedar Falls, Iowa, and in Minneapolis/St. Paul and Rochester, Minnesota.

### General Information

Spring, summer, and fall are the best times to visit. For information contact the Allamakee County Economic Development & Tourism Commission *(12 E. Main St., Waukon 52172. 319-568-2624 or 800-824-1424)*; the Winneshiek County Tourism Council/Decorah Area Chamber of Commerce *(111 Winnebago St., Decorah 52101. 319-382-3990 or 800-463-4692)*; Clayton County Development Group *(132 S. Main St., P.O. Box 778, Elkader 52043. 319-245-2201 or 800-488-7572)*; or Fayette

County Visitor Center *(P.O. Box 528, Fayette 52142. 800-798-4447)*.

### Things to See and Do

**1. Guttenberg** An observation platform on the banks of the Mississippi River lets visitors watch barges and boats navigate through **Lock and Dam No. 10** *(Lock & Dam Ln. 319-252-1261)*, a giant dam completed in 1936.

**2. Pikes Peak State Park** *(Iowa 340, 2 miles S of McGregor. 319-873-2341)* An observation platform provides great river views.

**3. Effigy Mounds National Monument** *(Iowa 76, 3 miles N of Marquette. 319-873-3491. Adm. fee April-Oct.)* See mysterious mounds built by early Native Americans and enjoy spectacular views on 11 miles of walking trails.

**4. Upper Mississippi River National Wildlife and Fish Refuge** *(McGregor Dist. Office 319-873-3423)* This 200,000-acre wildlife refuge is home to 292 species of birds, 57 species of mammals, 45 species of amphibians and reptiles, and 113 species of fish.

**5. Yellow River State Forest** *(E of Iowa 76 on Cty. Rd. B25. Headquarters 319-586-2254)* Located along spectacular bluffs of the

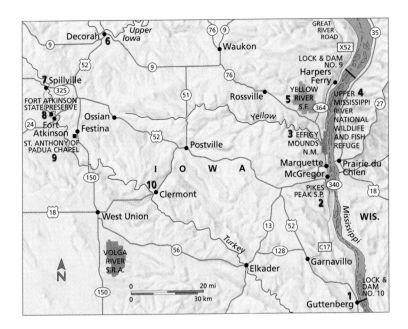

Mississippi River, this forest encompasses timbered hills and valleys with trout streams, primitive campgrounds, and hiking trails.

**6. Decorah** *(Chamber of Commerce 319-382-3990 or 800-463-4692)* One of Decorah's finest homes is now the **Porter House Museum** *(401 W. Broadway. 319-382-8465. Mem. Day–Labor Day weekends; adm. fee).* This 1867 Italianate villa contains the butterfly and rock collections of its last owner. The **Vesterheim Norwegian-American Museum** *(502 W. Water St. 319-382-9681. Adm. fee)* is the nation's largest museum dedicated to a single immigrant group. Its superb indoor exhibits and historic buildings introduce visitors to life in Norway and guide them through the history of Norwegian settlement in America. Set in a massive barn complex, **Farm Park** *(Luther College, 730 College Dr. 319-382-5947. May-Oct.; adm. fee)* works to protect endangered farm animals. North of Decorah is **Seed Savers Heritage Farm** *(3076 N. Winn Rd. 319-382-5990).* Endangered varieties of vegetables, apples, and grapes are cultivated in the gardens and orchards of this "living agricultural history museum."

**7. Spillville** At the **Bily Clock Museum** *(323 Main St. 319-562-3569. April-Oct. daily, March-Nov. weekends, call for additional hours; adm. fee)* an intriguing collection of hand-carved wooden clocks are displayed in a building that served as the summer home of Czech composer Antonín Dvořák in 1893.

**8. Fort Atkinson State Preserve** *(Off Iowa 24, Ft. Atkinson. 319-425-4161. Museum open Mem. Day–Sept. weekends, fort open year-round)* A small museum is housed in the former barracks of this fort, established in 1840.

**9. St. Anthony of Padua Chapel** *(1110 Little Church Rd., near Festina)* Called "the world's smallest church," this tiny gem dating from 1885 sits beside the Turkey River.

**10. Clermont** A stately brick mansion built in 1874, **Montauk** *(26223 Harding Rd. 319-423-7173. Mem. Day–Oct.; adm. fee)* was the home of Iowa's 12th governor.

**Annual Events**
**May** Syttende Mai/May 17 *(Vesterheim Norwegian-American Museum, Decorah. 319-382-9681)* Celebration of Constitution Day in Norway is centered around children.
**June** Back Home on the Farm *(Vesterheim Norwegian-American Museum, see above)*
**July** Nordic Fest *(Decorah. 319-382-9010 or 800-382-FEST)*
**September** Fort Atkinson Rendezvous *(Fort Atkinson. 319-425-4161)*
**October** Scandinavian Food Fest *(Vesterheim Norwegian-American Museum, see above)*
**December** Norwegian Christmas *(Vesterheim Norwegian-American Museum, see above)*

# Iowa's Great Lakes

Cupped and sparkling like jewels in the palm of the northern plains, Iowa's Great Lakes have a magical allure that brings people back year after year. When West Okoboji Lake glows sapphire-blue and a perch tugs at the line, or Spirit Lake burns ruby-red as the crickets scratch out their twilight melody, even first-time visitors to north-central Iowa can feel a powerful sense of nostalgia.

Large freshwater lakes are about the last things people expect to find in Iowa. But just below the Minnesota border, in rural Dickinson County, an enticing chain of lakes offers prime fishing and a splashing bounty of recreational opportunities.

The lakes and the surrounding landscape of forested ridges and shallow depressions were carved out by a brief, final surge of ice that fingered its way down from the north between 12,500 and 14,000 years ago. Known collectively as Iowa's Great Lakes, the chain includes, most prominently, Spirit Lake, which covers some 5,684 acres and is the largest natural body of water in Iowa; and West Okoboji Lake, at 136 feet the state's deepest. Less known are the surrounding watershed's dozen or so smaller lakes,

**Spirit Lake**

including the interconnected trio of Upper Gar, Minnewashta, and Lower Gar. Smaller still, but equally important as wildlife habitats, are the area's many sloughs, ponds, and marshes, remnants of a much larger wetland ecosystem that has disappeared under the plow.

The most beautiful body of water is West Okoboji Lake, whose deep, clear, spring-fed waters shimmer intensely and offer up a steady stream of fresh breezes on even the hottest summer days. Sandy beaches, marinas, leafy parks, and small lakeside towns that cater to the seasonal flow of visitors are clustered along its shores and those of East Okoboji Lake.

**Arnolds Park,** a summer resort town wedged in between West Okoboji, East Okoboji, and Upper Gar Lakes, has for generations been the site of the

most popular gathering place for summertime fun at the lakes. At **Arnolds Park Amusement Park** there are no gigantic "theme" rides. Instead, you will find a refreshingly old-fashioned assortment of kid-pleasers, including a famous and recently renovated 1927 roller coaster called "The Legend."

The exhibits at the **Iowa Great Lakes Maritime Museum,** adjacent to the park, document the long history of the lakes as a recreation area. By the early part of the 20th century, grand hotels had been built, a fleet of steamboats plied the waters, and a large pavilion at Arnolds Park hosted events for up to a thousand people. When the last steamboat, the *Queen,* was dismantled in 1973

**Abbie Gardner Cabin Historic Site**

after 89 years of service, residents raised funds to build the **Queen II,** a diesel-powered reproduction launched in 1986.

The **Abbie Gardner Cabin Historic Site,** a few blocks from the amusement park, was the scene of a violent confrontation between the first white settlers and a band of Dakota Indians in March 1857. One of the few survivors of what came to be known as the Spirit Lake Massacre, in which 33 settlers were killed, was 13-year-old Abbie Gardner. She returned to Arnolds Park in 1891 and operated the cabin as one of Iowa's first tourist attractions.

West Okoboji Lake attracts water sports enthusiasts of all kinds. Anglers from throughout the Midwest come for freshwater perch, blue gill, crappie, small and largemouth bass, walleye, and northern pike. City Beach in Arnolds Park is a popular swimming spot, but if you want something more restful, head to **Gull Point State Park,** on a peninsula in West Okoboji. Its beach is a perfect place for a leisurely swim, and the adjacent Barney Peterson Nature Trail provides a self-guided introduction to the area's flora and fauna.

Spirit Lake, separated from East Okoboji Lake by a narrow isthmus, is less commercially oriented than West Okoboji. One of the best places to enjoy its solitude is **Mini-Wakan State Park,** reached by a causeway on the lake's northern shore. Water lilies float on small ponds near the park, and the fishing pier is a favorite spot for contemplative anglers.

Other areas of quiet natural beauty are hidden away among the orderly fields of corn and soybeans west of Spirit Lake. At the **Kettleson Hogsback State Wildlife Management Area,** public hiking trails weave through a mosaic of wetlands, open-field uplands, and a high, forested "hogsback" ridge separating two small lakes. Giant Canada geese are frequently seen here; at the nearby **Kettleson Waterfowl Production Area,** reintroduced trumpeter swans may be spotted floating serenely in a portion of their original habitat.

**Cayler Prairie State Botanical Preserve** offers a rare glimpse of the lush tallgrass prairie that covered much of Iowa when the lakes' first summer visitors arrived in 1884. Purple coneflowers, golden alexanders, downy gentians, pasqueflowers, Indiangrass, larkspur, and dotted blazing-stars bloom from April through October. Dragonflies stitch the air; monarch butterflies float from flower to flower; and a chorus of bobolinks, red-winged blackbirds, and meadowlarks sing the song of the old prairie.

—*Donald S. Olson*

# Travel Notes

### Directions
Iowa's Great Lakes are in north-central Dickinson County, just south of the Minnesota border. **By car:** From Minneapolis, Minnesota, take US 169 south, drive southwest on Minn. 60, and follow US 71 south to Iowa 9, which heads west to Spirit Lake. From Sioux Falls, South Dakota, head east on S. Dak. 42 to Iowa 9. From Des Moines take I-35 N to US 18 and head west to US 71 north. **By plane:** The closest airports are in Des Moines, Sioux City, and Sioux Falls; Minneapolis/St. Paul; and Omaha, Nebraska.

### General Information
Summer is the best season to visit Iowa's Great Lakes, but year-round recreational opportunities abound. The best source of information is the Okoboji Tourism Committee (*P.O. Box 215, Okoboji 51355. 712-332-2209 or 888-656-2654*).

### Things to See and Do
**1. Arnolds Park** (*Chamber of Commerce 712-332-2107*) You can see the sole surviving structure of the Spirit Lake Massacre at the **Abbie Gardner Cabin Historic Site** (*Monument Dr. 712-332-7248. Mem. Day–late Sept.*). The lakeside grounds of this 1856 cabin include an interpretive center, pioneer cemetery, and an obelisk memorializing the event. The **Iowa Great Lakes Maritime Museum** (*Queen's Ct. and Lake St. 712-332-5159. Mem. Day–Labor Day, call for schedule rest of year*) documents the lakes' recreational history through an extensive photographic exhibit and artifacts ranging from hand-built wooden boats to bathing suits. Narrated 18-mile cruises of West Okoboji Lake are offered on the **Queen II** (*712-332-5159. Fare*). The oldest amusement park west of the Mississippi, the **Arnolds Park Amusement Park** (*37 Lake St. 712-332-2183 or 800-599-6995. Mem. Day–Labor Day; adm. fee*) has been drawing summer crowds for more than a hundred years.

**2. Okoboji** Permanent and traveling exhibits are on display at the **Lakes Art Center** (*US 71. 712-332-7013*). Films, concerts, and recitals are regular features.

**3. Gull Point State Park** (*Off Iowa 86, 1500 Harpen St. 712-337-3211*) Here you'll find a good beach, a 1930s-era lodge, picnic facilities, and an adjacent nature trail.

### 4. Cayler Prairie State Botanical Preserve (Cty. Rd. M38/170th Ave. bet. Cty. Rd. A22/190th St. and Iowa 9) This
160-acre natural prairie is a pristine example of what most of Iowa once looked like.

### 5. Kettleson Hogsback State Wildlife Management Area
(3 miles N of Spirit Lake off Iowa 276) Hunting, fishing, canoeing, hiking, cross-country skiing, and bird-watching are all popular activities.

### 6. Mini-Wakan State Park
(N shore of Spirit Lake off Iowa 276. 712-337-3211) The park offers swimming and picnicking opportunities. It has a boat ramp but no camping facilities.

### Other Activities
**Biking and hiking** Take the 12-mile-long Spine Trail (from 13th St. in Milford to 10th St. in Spirit Lake), which follows a section of abandoned railroad line through rural, community, and natural areas.

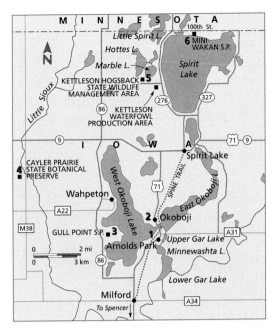

### Annual Events
**January** University of Okoboji Winter Games (W. Okoboji Lake. 712-332-2209 or 888-656-2654)
**May** Blue Water Music Festival (Spirit Lake Community School, 900 8th St., Spirit Lake. 712-336-1370 ext. 219)
**July** Fireworks on July 4th (near Arnolds Park Amusement Park, Arnolds Park. 712-332-2183)

### Lodging
**Fillenwarth Beach** (W. Okoboji Lake, Arnolds Park. 712-332-5646. May–mid-Sept.) Guests at this long-established resort can enjoy free cruises, waterskiing, boating, and heated indoor and outdoor pools.
**Triggs Bay Resort** (E. Okoboji Lake, Arnolds Park. 712-332-2215. May-Oct.) The large, simply furnished, kitchenette suites in this lake resort are perfect for families with children.

**Fillenwarth Beach in Arnolds Park, on West Okoboji Lake**

# NEBRASKA
# Platte River Crossroads

The Platte River, meandering calmly across the Nebraska plains, is actually one of the world's busiest crossroads. Millions of birds, including a mob of majestic sandhill cranes every spring, stop along a 50-mile stretch of the river and put on a show of soaring, preening, and dancing that draws birdwatchers from all over the world. A century and a half ago, earthbound migrants on the Oregon, California, and Mormon Trails met here and followed the Platte west. Some pioneers looked around at Nebraska's rippling grasslands and decided they'd gone far enough. The prairie whispered its song to writers like Mari Sandoz and Willa Cather, and it still sings to visitors today.

Amid the open cornfields of the Nebraska plains, rush hour in the spring begins around twilight. There's more commotion, more honking, more jockeying for position than the most humongous snarl on a Los Angeles freeway. If you happen to find yourself late in the day along the Platte River

**Sandhill cranes on the Platte River, near Kearney**

between Kearney and Grand Island, it's better to sit tight and not try to go anywhere.

Preferably, do your sitting in a wildlife blind along the river: The traffic jam here is for the birds. More than half a million sandhill cranes feast on leftover corn in the fields and congregate every night on the Platte's sandbars. The cranes' feathery-fingered wings extend in long strokes as the birds search the river, calling to each other in a throbbing tremolo. When they hear a familiar call, they float down to rub feathers with friends.

For birdwatchers, the cranes get top billing, but they are not the only avian attraction: Throughout the year, bald eagles, ducks of all varieties, geese, and threatened wading birds such as the piping plover also travel through or nest in the area. Spring, though, belongs mostly to the sandhills, who fatten up in the Nebraska cornfields for their nesting season in the far north. The tasty corn stubble comes at a price: Cultivation has drained both the river and surrounding wetlands, sharply reducing the habitat once enjoyed by migrating fowl. It makes for an incomparable concentration of birds—the world's most "reliably impressive wildlife viewing" as one Audubon Society official put it—but it also creates dangerously narrow corridor for migratory species.

State wildlife officials and conservation organizations are working to save what remains of the habitat. Some land is protected by state and federal laws, while other areas are part of private preserves such as the **Crane Meadows Nature Center** and the National Audubon Society's **Lillian Annette Rowe Sanctuary**. Both of these areas offer educational presentations and blinds for close-up crane-watching. It's a good way to see the birds and to talk to experts about them. You will learn that cranes are the oldest species of birds surviving today; they may have flown when dinosaurs roamed the earth. With a little instruction, you will soon be able to tell the taller whooping crane apart from the sandhill crane, with its red cap and 6-foot wingspan.

### Cather Country

The Nebraska plains strike some visitors as flat and unimpressive, but the region has inspired fine writers by the score: Wright Morris, Mari Sandoz, and Willa Cather among them. Cather was raised well south of the Platte in **Red Cloud.** Anyone who has been moved by *My Ántonia* or *The Song of the Lark* will find her hometown much as she described it almost a century ago, including the house and magical attic room where she first found inspiration. No one captured the spare beauty of the plains quite like Cather. "The red of the grass made all of the great prairie the color of wine-stains…there was so much motion in it; the whole country seemed, somehow, to be running."

Surprisingly, for their size, the sandhill cranes generally weigh less than ten pounds. This explains the physics, if not the aesthetics, of the birds' bizarre dancing, which can sometimes be seen from the Crane Meadows' hillside birdwatching bunker. The birds usually dance in the fields near the river, in pairs or groups. The "dancers" will rush forward, their long necks

**Willa Cather's childhood home, Red Cloud**

stretched near the ground, and then suddenly flare their wings and leap. These graceful acrobatics have often been compared to a ballet.

Field trips with conservation groups are informative and interesting, but many veteran bird fanatics guide themselves using a migration booklet available at local Visitors Bureaus. They watch from the walking bridge at **Fort Kearny State Recreation Area** or stop their cars by the fields where the cranes spend their days. The birds are less spooked by people in cars, it turns out, than they are by people on foot. No one has a problem spotting geese and cranes in the early morning or at twilight, when they blanket the skies.

In between those times, visitors have much of the day to follow in the footsteps of pioneers, whose nation-shaping trek west in the 1840s followed the Platte River. Just as birds of a different feather share a Platte River stopover, the pioneers on various routes came together at the Platte. The Oregon and California Trail came up from Independence, Missouri, while the Mormon Trail came from Omaha in the north and another came from Nebraska City. They merged at the river not far from the site today of **Fort Kearny State Historical Park**. The fort, on the river's south side, was built to protect the pioneers from Indian attacks, and also served as a station stop for Pony Express riders such as young Buffalo Bill Cody in the 1860s. By the 1870s the Indian threat had shifted farther West and railroads had replaced the trails. After a vigorous but futile attempt by locals to make Fort Kearny the nation's capital (because it was halfway between the coasts), the fort was torn down. The stockade and other buildings have been rebuilt at the site, which is far enough from the nearest town or interstate to retain the feel of the frontier when you walk the grounds beneath towering cottonwoods.

After the Civil War, Nebraska settlers began farming their homesteads in earnest, believing that, despite the arid climate, "rain follows the plow." A few wet years in the 1870s gave them hope. The sweeping saga of settling and cultivating the plains is woven from thousands of individual stories; those stories come back to life in the household artifacts on display at the **Stuhr Museum of the Prairie Pioneer**. Adjacent to the modern museum building are a re-created railroad town of the 1880s, an earlier log cabin town, a farm equipment collection, and an Indian artifacts display.

The early sodbusters soon realized that plowing did not seed rain clouds, and after the tragedy of the Dust Bowl years in the 1930s, farmers turned to irrigation. The Platte was dammed and its water diverted to fields, and the fertile soil produced. But the river that had been "a mile wide and a foot deep" became smaller and narrower, and fringed by cottonwoods that floods had previously cleared. That was bad news for sandhill cranes, because for all their airborne grace, they tend to run into such things as trees, power lines, and barns.

Damming the Platte has been similarly hard on the Rainwater Basin south of the river. This collection of clay-lined depressions held water and wetland munchies for ducks, shorebirds, geese, and other waterfowl migrating along the central flyway. Many of the marshes have been drained and planted, but the remaining ones are crowded with wildlife. Maps from the U.S. Fish and Wildlife Service show the way to protected marshes such as the **Funk Waterfowl Production Area**, a favorite of snow geese in March.

Watching the birds along the river, or driving the narrow, empty roads of the Rainwater Basin, you would hardly know that I-80 runs just north of the Platte. Road warriors speeding across the continent may likewise find the surrounding landscape too horizontal to take notice. Too bad for them. They are, after all, part of a long line of travelers. If they took a break here, like the sandhill cranes, snow geese, and pioneers before them, they could take home some frontier history, beautiful images of wings silhouetted by a twilight moon, and maybe a funky new dance step.

—*Geoffrey O'Gara*

# Travel Notes

### Directions
This corner lies along Nebraska's Platte River between Kearney and Grand Island. **By car:** I-80 parallels the Platte River. **By plane:** The nearest major airport is in Omaha; commuter airlines serve Kearney and Grand Island. **By train:** Amtrak stops in Hastings (in the middle of the night).

### General Information
The sandhill crane migration is in full swing during March and April. Generally, the best times for viewing birds are early morning and twilight—hours that can be chilly in the spring and fall, so bring warm clothes. Ask the Visitor Bureaus for the "Spring Migration Guide" by NEBRASKAland Magazine or a

"Crane Watch" brochure. For information contact the Kearney Visitors Bureau *(1007 2nd Ave., Kearney 68847. 308-237-3101 or 800-652-9435)*; Grand Island Visitors Bureau *(309 W. 2nd St., Grand Island 68801. 308-382-4400 or 800-658-3178)*; Stewards of the Platte *(308-382-2521)*, a nonprofit educational organization dedicated to river issues; and the U.S. Fish & Wildlife Service *(Rainwater Basin District. 308-236-5015)*.

### Things to See and Do
**1. Stuhr Museum of the Prairie Pioneer** *(US 34 at US 281, near Grand Island. 308-385-5316. Adm. fee)* This museum has a modern design, but it is surrounded by a moat and holds an excellent collection of sodbuster

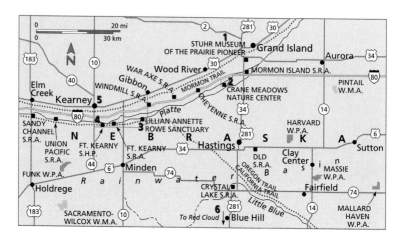

artifacts. Nearby is "Railroad Town," a 40-acre re-creation of an 1880s settlement.

**2. Crane Meadows Nature Center**
*(9775 S. Alda Rd., W of Grand Island. 308-382-1820. Adm. fee)* The center conducts workshops, field trips, and public hikes. It has 7 miles of nature trails and a crane-viewing blind built into a hillside.

**3. Lillian Annette Rowe Sanctuary**
*(Elm Island Rd., off I-80 E of Kearney. 308-468-5282. Headquarters open Mon.-Fri., crane-viewing blind mid-Feb.–mid-April daily; adm. fee)* The National Audubon Society protects key crane habitat here and has field trips to blinds.

**4. Fort Kearny State Historical Park**
*(On Nebr. L50A off Nebr. 10 SE of Kearney. 308-865-5306. Visitor Center open Mem. Day–Labor Day)* Built in 1848 to protect travelers on the Oregon Trail, the fort has been

**Sandhill crane**

rebuilt with a blacksmith shop, stockade, and ammunition storehouse. The museum displays artifacts from the fort's military outpost days and shows a sandhill crane video. Two miles northeast of the park is the **Fort Kearny State Recreation Area** *(Adm. fee)*. This 152-acre preserve has camping, a hike-bike trail, swimming ponds, and an old railroad bridge across the Platte that now serves as a birdwatching post and a canoe launch area.

**5. Kearney** Housed in a handsome Renaissance Revival post office building, the **Museum of Nebraska Art** *(2401 Central Ave. 308-865-8559. Closed Mon.)* holds the state's art collection, including frontier portraits by George Catlin. Headquarted in Nebraska, the major outdoor equipment catalogue company **Cabela's** *(US 30 2 miles E of Kearney. 308-237-7999; or Nebr. 385, off I-80 in Sidney. 308-254-7889)* offers showrooms with a huge selection of equipment, including a "Bargain cave," and dramatic displays of mounted wildlife.

**6. Red Cloud** *(Chamber of Commerce 402-746-3238)* At the **Willa Cather State Historic Site** *(326 N. Webster St. 402-746-2653. Adm. fee)*, five buildings mentioned in the author's works, including her childhood home, have been restored to echo her descriptions and their original late 19th-century appearance. Guides to other Cather sites in and around Red Cloud are also available. South of town, the Nature Conservancy's **Willa Cather Memorial Prairie** *(Nebr. 281. 402-746-2653)* offers more than 600-acres of tallgrass and short-grass prairies. This site is a fine place to explore the country that inspired Cather's prose.

## SOUTH DAKOTA

# Coteau des Prairies

It seems unlikely that anything could hide on the plains of South Dakota. Yet such is the case with the little-known hills, or *coteau,* in the state's northeast corner—an elevated landscape of rolling prairie, tree-filled coulees, glacial lakes, wildlife, and at least one haunted hollow. The hills open a window on the prairies as seen through different eyes—Native Americans, an obscure but important explorer named Joseph Nicollet, and one of America's favorite writers, Laura Ingalls Wilder.

Confronted by open prairie, some feel overawed by the exposure, while others feel embraced. Joseph N. Nicollet, a French surveyor sent by the U.S. government in the 1830s to draw a map of the huge territory between the Mississippi and Missouri Rivers, was one who found emotional comfort beneath the sheltering sky: "One never wearies of it." In particular, he was drawn to what he called the Coteau des Prairies, or "hills of the prairie." The hills reminded him of his native Alps, and although it might seem odd to compare the great peaks of central Europe with these gentle slopes, the

**Sica Hollow State Park**

image makes better sense when you stand on the crest of the coteau on a warm summer evening, gazing at what frontier artist George Catlin called the "blue and boundless ocean of prairies…vanishing into azure in the distance." It feels like the top of the world, perhaps even like the Alps.

The coteau was created during the last ice age when an advancing glacier was split on an ancient highland. After piling up layers of rock and clay, the retreating ice left behind 800-foot parallel moraines that separate the flow of water between the Hudson Bay and the Gulf of Mexico.

People lived in the area at least 9,000 years ago. Unearthed by chance in a gravel pit in 1933, the skeleton of the Browns Valley Man ranks among the oldest human remains ever found in America. When Nicollet arrived, the Dakotah Sioux were living here. They liked him, and called him "The Philosopher," because he came simply to measure and record and appreciate, not seize land or dig for gold; ironically, his excellent maps opened the way for the coming flood of settlement.

The scenic heart of coteau country is at its northern tip near Sisseton. Southward, the highlands broaden to about 40 miles across and continue almost to the Iowa border. Hundreds of lakes dot the rolling terrain, including many with no outlets. Recent wet years, 1997 in particular, have raised their levels, flooding farms and highways and reminding residents that no landscape is permanent.

The Dakotah know all about that. Their oral history and scattered tepee rings tell of times when bison dotted the plains and grasslands stretched unbroken to the horizon. Today, Dakotah people live throughout the coteau, providing a strong cultural presence most visible at events such as the annual *Wacipi,* or powwow, held south of Sisseton.

**Waubay National Wildlife Refuge panorama**

West of Sisseton, S. Dak. 10—the first state highway in Roberts County, and once a major route—is now a pleasant, winding back road that climbs to the coteau summit through a wooded ravine. Just off the route, the **Joseph N. Nicollet Tower and Interpretive Center** is worth a stop. The 75-foot tower gives a view that Nicollet would have appreciated. His fondness for the area, and the importance of his mapping work, is described in the interpretive center.

Some of the prairie Nicollet loved survives on the flanks and summit of the coteau. Because Scandinavian settlers found it hard to plow, the rocky ground has retained its native covering. The same is true of the coulees, which support forests of oak, maple, basswood, and aspen. Finding cover among the trees are white-tailed deer, wild turkeys, beavers, raccoons, minks, and a rainbow of songbirds. **Sica Hollow State Park** (pronounced SHE-cha, and meaning "bad hollow") preserves a particularly fine coulee with a spooky reputation. Legends tell of groaning earth, ghostly lights, and soil bleeding from sorrowful events of the distant past—a strange history for such a welcoming place.

Not far away, **Fort Sisseton State Historic Park** commemorates sorrowful events of a different kind. The Minnesota Indian Uprising of 1862, a conflict between the Dakotah Sioux and white settlers, ended in many deaths but produced no clear resolution of grievances. Fort Wadsworth, later renamed **Fort Sisseton,** was built in 1864 to keep the peace, but no battles were ever fought here. Today the restored fort offers a glimpse of that time through the eyes of the U.S. Cavalry and Infantry. Fourteen original buildings remain, some of them furnished with appropriate antiques. In June, the whole place comes joyfully alive during the Fort Sisseton Historical Festival.

Among the many lakes and wetlands scattered over the hills, **Waubay National Wildlife Refuge** lays claim to several of the best. Its 4,650 acres are the focal point for the region's more than 100,000 acres of protected wetlands and upland areas. The refuge is one of the richest waterfowl nesting areas in the country. Roads and trails provide access, and a 100-foot tower gives a good overview. All five species of grebes nest here, including the rarely seen red-necked grebe. Because of flooding, water now covers large areas that were

## Little Town on the Prairie

"Softly colored in all shades from dark brown to russet and tan, the prairie rolled in gentle swells to the far edge of the sky," wrote Laura Ingalls Wilder in *By the Shores of Silver Lake.* With those words she described her family's homestead site in the 1880s. Her "Pa," Charles Ingalls, brought his family to De Smet, South Dakota, when he took a job with the railroad; they became the community's first permanent—and most famous—settlers. Laura was inspired to write several books about their pioneer adventures. Today her stories have been translated into 40 languages, and each year more than 24,000 people come from around the world to visit De Smet, Laura's little town on the prairie.

**Prairie sunflowers**

once shallow wetlands or farm fields, dramatically changing conditions in the refuge and underlining the value of maintaining a network of protected lands beyond refuge borders.

These wildlands inspired South Dakota artist Terry Redlin. His early paintings were of waterbirds lifting off from autumnal marshes, and deer standing at attention in snowy woods. With time, those themes joined the moonlit cabins and winter village scenes that have made him one of the country's most popular artists. As a gift to the community, Mr. Redlin built the lavish **Redlin Art Center** in Watertown to house his original paintings.

And who can think of prairies without recalling Laura Ingalls Wilder? Near De Smet, on the western edge of the coteau, Charles "Pa" Ingalls built the house made famous by the *Little House on the Prairie* series. De Smet was the town in *Little Town on the Prairie,* and anyone familiar with the Wilder books will have a great time visiting the original locations. Tours begin in the Surveyors' House where the Ingalls family spent their first prairie winter. You can see a reproduction of the schoolhouse shack where Laura taught classes at age 15, and the original house in town built by Pa when he quit farming in 1887. The Little House itself is gone, but a rebuilt version of it as a tiny half-house (the minimum required to prove up a homestead) stands on the original site, a little spot of land on the wide, rolling prairie.

*—Jeremy Schmidt*

# Travel Notes

**Directions**
In the northeast corner of South Dakota, the region is seen on maps as a cluster of lakes. **By car:** I-29 parallels the coteau, but county roads are the best way to see the hills. A state highway map *(South Dakota Department of Tourism 605-773-3301 or 800-732-5682)* provides sufficient detail. Be prepared for detours; flood damage may take years to repair. **By plane:** The nearest airports are in Watertown and Aberdeen.

**General Information**
Summer and fall are the best seasons. A good central source for information is the Glacial Lakes & Prairies Tourism Association *(P.O. Box 244, Watertown 57201. 605-886-7305 or 800-244-8860).*

**Things to See and Do**
**1. Sisseton** Original works, mostly by Dakotah artists such as Paul War Cloud, are shown in the art gallery at the **Tekakwitha Fine Arts Center** *(401 S. 8th Ave. West. 605-698-7058. Mem. Day–Labor Day daily, Tues.-Sun. rest of year; donation).* At the gift shop, you can purchase prints and Native American crafts.
**2. Joseph N. Nicollet Tower and Interpretive Center** *(S. Dak. 10. 605-698-7672.*

*Mem. Day–Labor Day, and by appt.; donation)*
The observation tower overlooks hills and
plains; the interpretive center offers films
and displays on explorer and mapmaker
Joseph Nicollet.

**3. Sica Hollow State Park** *(15 miles NW
of Sisseton off S. Dak. 10. 605-448-5701)* A
wooded coulee is the scene of numerous
Indian legends. The park offers picnic facilities and hiking and riding trails *(call for mountain-bike and horse restrictions).*

**4. Fort Sisseton State Historic Park**
*(25 miles SW of Sisseton off S. Dak. 10. 605-
448-5701. Visitor Center Mem. Day–Labor Day,
park open year-round; adm. fee)* The Visitor Center and 15 original buildings provide a glimpse
of frontier Army life and regional history.

**5. Waubay National Wildlife Refuge**
*(Cty. Rd. 1 off US 12. 605-947-4521. Visitor
Center Mon.-Fri.)* Dedicated to providing habitat for waterfowl, the refuge has a bird list of
244 species. The Visitor Center offers displays, and a 110-foot tower affords a hawk's-
eye view.

**6. Watertown** The original works of Terry
Redlin, a romantic realist and Watertown
native, are displayed in sumptuous surroundings at the **Redlin Art Center** *(US 212 and
I-29. 605-882-3877).* The building also includes
the state's only planetarium *(adm. fee).*

**7. De Smet** This town was the real-life setting for the prairie books by Laura Ingalls
Wilder. Sites at **Little Town on the Prairie**
*(101 Olivet St. S.E. 605-854-3383 or 800-880-
3383. Adm. fee)* include the Surveyors' House

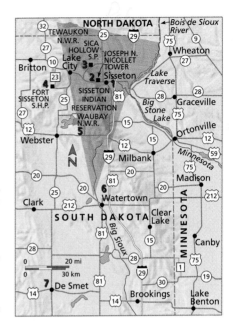

where the family spent its first prairie winter,
and the final home built by Pa in 1887.

## Other Activities

**Trail riding and fishing** are popular
throughout the region. For information on
outfitters and weekly fishing reports, call the
Glacial Lakes & Prairies Tourism Association
*(605-886-7305 or 800-244-8860).*

## Annual Events

**June** Fort Sisseton Historical Festival *(605-
448-5701);* Laura Ingalls Wilder Pageant *(De
Smet. 605-854-3383 or 800-880-3383. Late
June–early July)*
**July** Sisseton-Wahpeton Sioux Tribe 4th
of July *Wacipi* (powwow) *(near Sisseton.
605-698-3911)*

## Lodging

**Lakeside Farm** *(Webster. 605-486-4430)*
Two rooms in the house of a working farm
are available. Guests are welcome, if so
inclined, to wake early and help with chores;
leisurely mornings are also encouraged.
**Prairie House Manor** *(209 Poinsett Ave.,
De Smet. 605-854-9131 or 800-297-2416.
May-Nov.)* This restored Victorian house
next to the Ingalls home originally was built
in 1900 by Col. Thomas Ruth. Its six rooms
sleep from two to six persons.

**Blankets, Fort Sisseton State
Historic Park**

# NORTH DAKOTA
# Lewis and Clark's Land

Although dominated by the vast recreation area of Lake Sakakawea, this area also opens a window on history, when Lewis and Clark camped by the river, and Native Americans grew crops around earth-lodge villages. Several museums help to picture those times, while events such as powwows on the Fort Berthold Reservation celebrate the living native culture.

Nearly two centuries ago, Meriwether Lewis and William Clark set off on their great journey of exploration. They saw the country while bison, grizzlies, wolves, and elk still roamed the prairies in huge numbers. European settlers were scarcely more than a rumor among the Plains tribes. And no one had yet dreamed of putting a dam across the great Missouri River.

Inevitably, dams were built. The Garrison Dam created Lake Sakakawea, submerging 178 miles of river channel. Yet despite the dramatically altered landscape, it is still possible to see country that looks much as it did when the explorers came through. At the lake's upstream end, badlands and wooded coulees give the impression of wilderness untamed. And while

**Bison grazing on prairie grass**

watercraft buzz up and down the reservoir, the shores remain largely wild, with only occasional clusters of summer cabins in sheltered coves.

Below the lake, the river rolls through fertile bottomland thick with cottonwoods and wildlife. **Cross Ranch State Park**, which protects a 589-acre natural area, is a good place to begin a journey of historic imagining. White pelicans fly over the river; deer and coyotes shelter in the forest; and with a little help, you can conjure up an 1804 image. At **Washburn**, the **Lewis and Clark Interpretive Center** provides the needed help through artwork, displays, and objects, including a reproduction of a 28-foot dugout canoe. Surprisingly huge and heavy, it carried about 3,000 pounds. Yet this was the smallest of the expedition's dugouts.

The explorers carved their canoes during the winter of 1804-05, while living in a triangular log stockade near the river. **Fort Mandan Historic Site**, although not on the exact historic location, offers a reproduction of that simple log shelter among the cottonwoods. Twenty-five years later, fur traders built another fort a few miles upstream. Called Fort Clark, it was made famous by Karl Bodmer, a Swiss artist who spent the winter of 1833-34 here. His paintings of the landscape and its people are as detailed as photographs, showing winter camps, bull boats, earth lodges with horses inside, dogs pulling toboggans, and Mandan chiefs in full regalia.

All that remains today at **Fort Clark State Historic Site** are over 200 circular depressions marking locations of Mandan earth lodges, and the fort's barely visible foundation. The story is a sad one: In 1837 a steamboat brought smallpox, and the disease nearly destroyed the Mandan community. Survivors moved north to a village that now lies beneath the lake; for a time, Arikara people occupied the village, but they also moved north when the fort closed.

## Earth-lodge Living

The homes of the Mandan, Arikara, and Hidatsa people were ingenious shelters, perfectly suited to life along the Missouri. Wood frames covered with earth, they varied from 20 to 65 feet in diameter and looked from the outside like small hills. Summer lodges, which formed the villages at Knife River, held from 8 to 30 people, with room left over for horses. Winter lodges, smaller and easier to heat, were built each year at different locations. The choice of winter camp was a critical decision based largely on the availability of firewood.

At **Knife River Indian Villages National Historic Site**, a museum and reconstructed earth lodge help fill in missing parts of the picture. You can't help but admire the simple but efficient architecture of an earth lodge (see sidebar this page). In the early 1800s, five villages stood here, but now only circular depressions remain. At one of these villages the explorers met the fur trader Toussaint Charbonneau, who with his Shoshone wife, Sacagawea, agreed to accompany the expedition. The lake named for her is a long, narrow body of water famous for walleye and lake trout, and popular for water sports. With 1,300 miles of shoreline, numerous side-channels, and many recreation sites, it is an easy place for a visitor to find privacy.

At the lake's eastern end, shoreline marshes of the **Audubon National Wildlife Refuge** were designed to replace wildlife habitat lost beneath the reservoir. Along with other area refuges, it provides a place for more than 200 species of birds. Threatened piping plovers sometimes nest here, bald eagles fly over, and whooping cranes pass through on occasion.

The lake's central part is surrounded by Fort Berthold Indian Reservation, home of the Three Affiliated Tribes: Mandan, Arikara, and Hidatsa. Summer powwows, which feature traditional dancing and drumming, are high-spirited religious and social events where everyone is welcome.

The lake reaches to Williston, but some of the best country is found

**Lake Sakakawea catch**

along the Little Missouri River near the Killdeer mountains—a scenic land with sizable hills and colorful badlands. Back roads cross wheat fields and high prairie, then dive into coulees filled with juniper, ash, oak, and chokecherry, where deer tracks mix with those of coyotes, rabbits, and turkeys. Lewis and Clark might stare in amazement at the huge lake and its jet skiers, but these coulees would cause them to nod in recognition.

—*Jeremy Schmidt*

**Reproduction of Mandan earth lodge, Knife River Indian Villages National Historic Site**

# Travel Notes

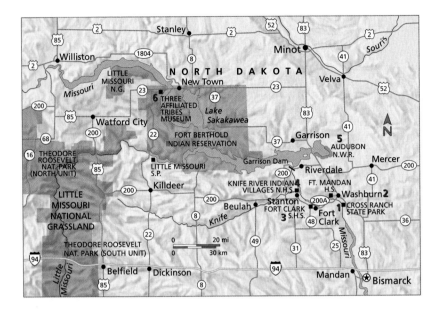

## Directions
The heart of this corner, Lake Sakakawea stretches from Williston to Riverdale. **By car:** From I-94, several state highways go north to the lake. **By plane:** The nearest airport is in Bismarck.

## General Information
Summer and fall are good times to visit. Contact the North Dakota Tourism Department *(604 East Boulevard Ave., Bismarck 58505. 701-328-2525 or 800-435-5663).*

## Things to See and Do
**1. Cross Ranch State Park** *(15 miles S of Washburn off N. Dak. 200A. 701-794-3731. Adm. fee)* Protecting a stretch of wild river bottom, the park offers camping, hiking, wildlife viewing, and a Visitor Center.
**2. Washburn The Lewis and Clark Interpretive Center** *(Jct. of US 83 and N. Dak. 200A. 701-462-8535. Adm. fee)* interprets the expedition of Lewis and Clark; it manages the nearby **Fort Mandan Historic Site**, with its re-creation of the explorers' winter quarters.
**3. Fort Clark State Historic Site** *(N. Dak. 200A. 701-794-8832. Mid-May–mid-Sept.)* The foundations of this 1830s fort are visible beside

the depressions of an earth-lodge village.
**4. Knife River Indian Villages National Historic Site** *(Stanton. 701-745-3309)* An interpretive center near the former site of Mandan and Hidatsa villages features a repro-duction earth lodge complete with furnishings.
**5. Audubon National Wildlife Refuge** *(E end of Lake Sakakawea off US 83. 701-442-5474)* The refuge offers a Visitor Center *(Mem. Day–Labor Day)*, auto tour, and hiking.
**6. Three Affiliated Tribes Museum** *(N. Dak. 23, 4 miles W of New Town. 701-627-4477. Mid-April–Nov.; adm. fee)* The museum exhibits artifacts, history displays, and modern crafts of the Mandan, Arikara, and Hidatsa people.

## Other Activities
**Guided fishing** Call N. Dak. Tourism *(800-435-5663)* for a list of licensed guides.

## Annual Events
**Summer weekends** Fort Berthold Pow-wows *(Reservation communities. 701-627-4781)*

## Lodging
**Robin's Nest B&B** *(101 E. Central Ave., Garrison. 701-463-2465)* This old house offers four guest rooms decorated with collectibles.

# South Central

## TEXAS

# Trans-Pecos Mountains and Desert

West of the Pecos River, the Texas landscape begins to accumulate a new set of adjectives: arid, stark, and lonely, for starters. Harsh, desolate, and barren, some might add—especially Easterners feeling greenery-deprived in this Chihuahuan Desert world of mesquite scrub and sparse grassland. Many people see the area only as a blur through the windshield as they drive by on I-10 or I-20. But if you take time to explore you'll find surprising attractions here, from historic Western towns and picturesque mountains to unexpected oases and diverse wildlife. In time, your own description of the Trans-Pecos no doubt will come to include words such as vast, varied, and beautiful—all entirely appropriate for this part of the Lone Star State.

Just after the time the dinosaurs were dying out, 65 million years ago, volcanic activity began building a mountain range in what is now West Texas. The resulting Davis Mountains stand today as the centerpiece of the Trans-Pecos area, the most extensive of a group of uplands including the Apache, Barrilla, Glass, and Del Norte Mountains. Not only are the Davis Mountains physically dominant in the region, they encompass several of its most intriguing destinations.

In the mid-19th century, thousands of pioneers immigrated to the California gold fields on the San Antonio-El Paso Road, while merchants and

**Madewood Plantation House, Louisiana (see Atchafalaya and Beyond, p. 244)**

stagecoaches passed regularly in both directions. To protect travelers from Apache and Comanche raiders, the U.S. Army in 1854 built a fort in Limpia Canyon and named it for Secretary of War Jefferson Davis (later president of the Confederacy). Today, **Fort Davis National Historic Site** preserves the remains of that outpost, with a restored, refurnished enlisted men's barracks, commanding officer's quarters, and other buildings situated under tall red rhyolite bluffs. As you cross the parade ground here, it's easy to imagine the isolation and danger of a soldier's life when the American West was still young and untamed.

Farther up the canyon, **Davis Mountains State Park** combines stands of pine, oak, and juniper with volcanic rock formations in a setting of striking beauty. A mile above sea level, campers enjoy cool nights year-round in what seems a world apart from the surrounding desert. The park's inviting **Indian Lodge,** built by the Civilian Conservation Corps in the 1930s, is filled with handmade wood furniture and makes a fine base for exploration.

The Big Bend region is truly an immense place: Brewster County alone, just south of the Davis Mountains, is larger than Connecticut. But to put its size into perspective, keep driving up the hills on Tex. 118 from Davis Mountains State Park to the University of Texas' **McDonald Observatory,** where your view will expand to the outer reaches of the universe. Perched atop Mount Locke at an elevation of 6,800 feet, the observatory offers visitors a variety of tours and viewing programs. By continuing on Tex. 118 (the highest paved road east of the Rockies) and turning left on Tex. 166, you'll complete a 74-mile loop, beginning and ending in the town of Fort Davis. Along this scenic drive, one of the best in Texas, you might see wildlife ranging from the common black-hawk (an elegant raptor that despite its name is quite rare in the U.S.) to mule deer and pronghorn.

If you travel north through Wild Rose Pass in the Barrilla Mountains, you'll soon arrive at a desert oasis as historic as it is unexpected. **Balmorhea State Park** centers on San Solomon Springs, which feed a 1.75-acre pool where swimmers share the crystal-clear water with fish, turtles, and other wildlife. Archaeological evidence shows that Native Americans used the springs for thousands of years before European explorers arrived; the Mescalero Apache

## Ancient Reef

The Davis Mountains are igneous—that is, built by the fiery force of volcanic activity—but some nearby ranges have a more unusual origin. The Apache, Glass, Sierra Diablo, and Guadalupe Mountains are actually remnants of a gigantic reef that surrounded an inland sea 250 million years ago, during the Permian period. This horseshoe-shaped reef stretches northward into New Mexico, although most of the formation lies beneath the surface. The reef is unusual because unlike modern coral reefs, it was composed of the skeletons of sponges and algae. The most famous section of exposed reef is the majestic peak called El Capitan, which towers over the desert in Guadalupe Mountains National Park, 110 miles northwest of Fort Davis.

**Lonely Trans-Pecos plains**

once camped at the park's reconstructed *cienega*, or desert wetland.

Mitre Peak rises south of Fort Davis, its 6,100-foot summit seemingly poised to pierce the sky. Named for the triangular hat of a bishop, Mitre may remind you instead of a gigantic shark's tooth protruding from the dry hills. If you're curious about the plants you've been seeing in your travels, the cactus garden at the **Museum of the Big Bend** in its new location in **Alpine** will help you put names to many of them. The museum itself is well presented, with exhibits on regional history and geology.

Nearby **Marfa** attracts more than its share of attention for a town its size (fewer than 3,000 souls). Fans of the iconic actor James Dean visit regularly, for it was to this remote spot that he, Elizabeth Taylor, and Rock Hudson came to make the 1955 movie *Giant*. El Paisano Hotel housed some of the film crew, and still has autographed photos and other memorabilia on display. Marfa is also a mecca for devotees of the unexplained: Since back in the 19th century, travelers have been seeing strange lights moving over the desert here. All sorts of explanations have been offered, but the **Marfa lights** remain a mystery. Wait until dark and take a look for yourself at the viewing station 9 miles east of town on US 67/90.

Like Fort Davis, **Fort Stockton** began as a mid-19th-century Army post, in this instance located at an important water source called Comanche Springs. A few original military structures still stand at **Historic Fort Stockton,** but the town's most interesting spot is the **Annie Riggs Memorial Museum,** which displays local treasures in an adobe hotel built in 1900. The museum is the namesake of Annie Riggs, a divorced mother of ten children whose second ex-husband, a notorious gunslinger, was shot dead by her son-in-law; she used the proceeds of his estate to buy the hotel for $5,000 in 1904, and she operated it nearly until she died in 1931, at the age of 73. She must have had an extraordinary life—but then, only a remarkable life would truly match the history and landscape of Texas west of the Pecos.

—*Mel White*

# Travel Notes

## Directions
The region is located south of I-10 in the area generally bounded by Fort Stockton, Alpine, and Balmorhea. **By car:** From Pecos on I-20 (or from Balmorhea on I-10) take Tex. 17 south. **By plane:** Major airlines serve Midland-Odessa and El Paso. **By train:** Amtrak's *Sunset Limited* stops in Alpine.

## General Information
Spring and fall are the best times to visit; summer heat can be intense. Sources for

**McDonald Observatory**

information include the Texas Travel and Information Division *(800-452-9292)*; the Fort Davis Chamber of Commerce *(P.O. Box 378, Fort Davis 79734. 915-426-3015 or 800-524-3015)*; the Alpine Chamber of Commerce *(106 N. 3rd St., Alpine 79830. 915-837-2326)*; and the Fort Stockton Chamber of Commerce *(P.O. Box C, Fort Stockton 79735. 915-336-2264 or 800-336-2166)*.

## Things to See and Do
**1. Balmorhea State Park** *(Tex. 17 near Toyahvale. 915-375-2370. Adm. fee)* One of

the world's largest spring-fed swimming pools (1.75 acres and more than 3.5 million gallons) offers swimmers, snorkelers, and divers clear water at a year-round temperature of 72°-76°F. The adjacent desert wetland provides habitat for varied birds, reptiles, and other wildlife, including endangered species of fish.

**2. Fort Davis National Historic Site** *(Tex. 17/118 on the north edge of Fort Davis. 915-426-3224. Adm. fee)* Restored structures re-create an Army fort that protected travelers in the second half of the 19th century. African-American calvary troops, known as "Buffalo Soldiers," were important in post operations.

**3. Davis Mountains State Park** *(Tex. 118, 4 miles NW of Fort Davis. 915-426-3337. Adm. fee)* Camping, nature trails, and a scenic drive are highlights of this pretty 2,700-acre park. Encompasses **Indian Lodge** *(See Lodging, p.239)*.

**4. McDonald Observatory** *(Tex. 118. 915-426-3640. Fee for tours)* Visitors are welcome at this mountaintop facility, a historic and still important astronomical research station. Daily tours explain the workings of the observatory's telescopes, and "star parties" at the Visitor Center on Tuesday, Friday, and Saturday nights allow viewing of celestial objects.

**5. Chihuahuan Desert Visitor Center** *(Tex. 118, 4 miles S of Fort Davis. 915-364-2499. April-Aug. daily, Mon.-Fri. rest of year; donation)* Nature trails, a cactus greenhouse, and an arboretum teach visitors about the flora of the Big Bend region.

**6. Marfa** *(Chamber of Commerce 915-729-4942 or 800-650-9696)* The official viewing station for the **Marfa lights** *(US 67/90, 9 miles E of Marfa)* is where people go to look at the strange lights in the desert that have defied explanation for more than a century.

**7. Alpine** *(Chamber of Commerce 915-837-2326)* A cactus garden, items from an old general store, and Indian artifacts are among the displays at the **Museum of the Big Bend** *(Lawrence Hall, Sul Ross State University, US 67/90. 915-837-8143. Tues.-Sun.)*.

**8. Fort Stockton** *(Chamber of Commerce 915-336-2264 or 800-336-2166)* Original and reconstructed buildings at **Historic Fort Stockton** *(300 E. 3rd St. 915-336-2400.*

June–Labor Day daily, closed Sun. rest of year; adm. fee) re-create a portion of a military post active from 1867 to 1886. Still standing is the 1868 guardhouse, with jailer's quarters and holding cells. Also in town is the **Annie Riggs Memorial Museum** (301 S. Main St. 915-336-2167. Adm. fee). This adobe-and-wood structure began as a stagecoach accommodation in 1900, where the first guests paid 50 cents for a bed and walked to Comanche Springs to bathe. One of the rooms displays hotel furnishings from around 1905; others contain local antiques, geological exhibits, Indian arti-facts, and the like.

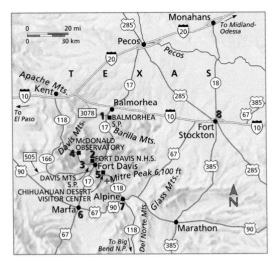

## Other Activities

**Rock collecting** The varied geology of the Trans-Pecos and Big Bend regions makes them a mecca for rockhounds. Most land is private, though, and trespassing is taken seriously in West Texas; collecting is usually forbidden in parks and other public areas. The Woodward Agate Ranch (Tex. 118, 15 miles S of Alpine. 915-364-2271. Adm. fee) allows searching for agates and other minerals.

## Annual Events

**February** Cowboy Poetry Gathering (Alpine. 915-837-8191)

**July** Water Carnival (Fort Stockton. 915-336-2264 or 800-336-2166) Synchronized swim-ming exhibitions are part of the fun during this festival at Comanche Springs Pool.

**September** Marfa Lights Festival (Marfa. 915-729-4942 or 800-650-9696) Annual Labor Day weekend celebration of the mys-terious lights and the notoriety they've brought the town, with dances, a parade, and other festivities.

## Lodging

**Corner House Bed and Breakfast** (801 E. Ave. E, Alpine. 915-837-7161 or 800-585-7795) Six rooms, two with shared baths, in an inn two blocks from the Sul Ross State University campus; home-baked bread is served at breakfast.

**Hotel Limpia** (Town Square, Fort Davis. 915-426-3237 or 800-662-5517) The main build-ing of the Hotel Limpia dates from around

1912. A very good restaurant adjoins the hotel on the town's Main Street.

**Indian Lodge** (Off Tex. 118 in Davis Moun-tains S.P., NW of Fort Davis. 915-426-3254) Built in the 1930s and furnished with handmade furniture and adobe walls 18 inches thick, this pueblo-style lodge sits at a mile-high elevation in the imposing Davis Mountains.

**Prude Ranch** (Tex. 118, 6 miles N of Fort Davis. 915-426-3202 or 800-458-6232) A sprawling ranch that offers cabins, RV hookups, horseback riding, a swimming pool, and a variety of other activities.

**Verandah Country Inn Bed and Break-fast** (210 Court Ave., Fort Davis. 915-426-2233 or 888-383-2847) This historic adobe inn has antique furnishings and gardens.

**Barracks, Fort Davis National Historic Site**

# East Texas

In the stillness of an April dawn, a kingfisher's harsh rattle rings out across a river lined with bald cypress and tupelo. A bobcat, its night of hunting finished, pads silently beneath a flowering dogwood, while in a boggy area nearby a carnivorous pitcher plant stands ready to make a meal of an unwary insect. A swamp rabbit hears the high scream of a red-shouldered hawk and crouches even lower in its hiding place amid a living palette of wildflowers.

This is Texas? Yes, indeed: a region in the east that includes the Piney Woods and the swamplands of Big Thicket, bordering Louisiana and stretching from Arkansas south nearly to the Gulf Coast. Unlike far West Texas, which in some years is lucky to get ten inches of rain, East Texas receives upwards of 50 inches a year, an abundance that helps create the state's most diverse ecosystem. Here you'll find four national forests encompassing varied wilderness areas, an important national preserve, hiking trails and canoeing streams, and parks and museums.

Just as the Piney Woods region is not all pines—hardwoods such as oak, hickory, magnolia, beech, and sycamore make up an important component of the forest—neither is it all woods. Among the cities and towns dotting the area, the most interesting may well be **Jefferson**, in the northern part only 20 miles from Louisiana and Arkansas. Jefferson was a thriving steamboat port on Big Cypress Creek in the mid-1800s, but saw its fortunes decline about one hundred years ago—a reversal that preserved many fine old buildings.

**Yellow trumpets and rough skull-cap, Big Thicket National Preserve**

The 1850s **Excelsior Hotel** stands out among dozens of historic structures; across the street rests the opulent railcar of Gilded Age tycoon Jay Gould, who is said to have predicted the town's demise when citizens spurned his offer of a railroad line. Close by, the **Jefferson Historical Society Museum** is jam-packed with bits and pieces of the past: guns, Indian artifacts, artwork, and much more, displayed in an 1888 building that was once a federal courthouse.

Not far to the east, bald cypress border the waterways of **Caddo Lake State Park,** where bass and crappie tempt anglers. Wood ducks, songbirds, beaver, and an occasional alligator delight wildlife-watchers who walk the park's trails or take a canoe into its backwaters. Boat rides are offered seasonally, providing an easy way to see the

**Bald cypress trees in Turkey Creek, Big Thicket National Preserve**

swamp without having to navigate its confusing channels on your own.

Farther south, travelers who yearn for wilder adventures can explore Texas' four national forests: Sabine, Angelina, Davy Crockett, and Sam Houston, totaling more than 660,000 acres and comprising recreation areas from developed campgrounds to remote wilderness. Two of the forests' prettiest and most rewarding spots are the Sawmill Hiking Trail, on the Neches River near Zavalla in the Angelina National Forest, and the Big Creek Scenic Area, near Shepherd in the Sam Houston National Forest. A walk under towering oaks and pines in either of these areas has the power to renew the spirit and refresh the soul in ways that even the finest museum cannot.

The area of East Texas traditionally known as the Big Thicket is well known to biologists as one of the country's most diverse natural landscapes—it even contains cypress swamps. Much of this once-vast ecosystem has been lost to development, but representative samples are protected within **Big Thicket National Preserve** north of Beaumont. You'll find an excellent and easily accessible nature trail at the preserve north of Kountze, where a quiet ramble will reveal much of the landscape's unique beauty. An international biosphere reserve, Big Thicket includes among its flora a wide variety of wildflowers, including 17 species of orchid and four types of insect-eating plants. The easy Sundew Trail, north of the visitor station, is named for a small plant that traps insects with its sticky leaves, digesting them to provide extra nutrients in poor soil.

The forest that delights naturalists in East Texas today is only a shadow of the wilderness that European settlers found. Since then, timbering has provided thousands of jobs and built entire towns; in **Lufkin,** the **Texas Forestry Museum** dedicates itself to the heritage of logging and sawmills, with tools, equipment, and vehicles from the days when most work was done by hand.

Besides trees, another resource has also had a powerful effect on the region: When wildcatters struck oil in Rusk County on October 3, 1930, they could hardly have known they'd discovered the most productive oil field found anywhere up to that point. Fortunes were made overnight, and boomtowns— lively, dirty, and dangerous—sprang up just as quickly. The **East Texas Oil Museum** in **Kilgore,** one of the state's best small museums, uses innovative exhibits and audiovisual displays to recall that rough-and-tumble era.

Though not as high-tech, several other East Texas museums are well worth an afternoon's visit. In **Henderson,** the **Depot Museum Complex** brings together a collection of restored buildings, including a 1901 rail depot, an 1841 log cabin, and an amazingly elaborate 1908 outhouse.

**Nacogdoches's** Stone Fort Museum, on the campus of Stephen F. Austin State University, houses exhibits on early Texas history in a relocated and reconstructed 1779 building. North of town, **Millard's Crossing Historic Village** re-creates the atmosphere of an early-day settlement, centered on an 1837 boardinghouse and a nicely restored church dating from 1905.

On Tex. 21 a few miles west of Alto awaits the **Caddoan Mounds State Historical Park,** which protects burial and ceremonial mounds of a Caddo Indian town inhabited from about A.D. 800 to 1300. With the help of displays and artifacts in the park museum, as well as a bit of creativity, you can walk through the site of an ancient village and imagine the advanced culture of these Native Americans—although much about their lives, beliefs, and fate remains a mystery awaiting the discoveries of a new generation of archaeologists.

—*Mel White*

# Travel Notes

### Directions
This hidden corner is located in extreme eastern Texas. **By car:** Take I-20 east from Dallas or west from Shreveport, Louisiana, to Marshall or Kilgore. **By plane:** Major airlines serve Dallas and Shreveport. **By train:** Amtrak's *Texas Eagle* stops in Marshall and Longview.

### General Information
The area can be visited year-round, although heat, humidity, and mosquitoes make outdoor activities less pleasant in summer. Sources for information include Texas Tourism *(P.O. Box 12728, Austin 78711. 800-888-8839);* the Marion County Chamber of Commerce *(118 N. Vale St., Jefferson 75657. 903-665-2672);* the Nacogdoches County Chamber of Commerce *(513 North St., Nacogdoches 75961. 409-564-7351);* and the U.S. Forest Service *(701 N. First St., Lufkin. 409-639-8501).*

### Things to See and Do
**1. Jefferson** Housed in an 1888 building, the **Jefferson Historical Society Museum** *(223 W. Austin St. 903-665-2775. Adm. fee)* was once a post office and federal courthouse. It contains local artifacts and historical displays.
**2. Marshall** *(Chamber of Commerce 903-935-7868)* Lady Bird Johnson's ball gown is

one of the assorted items on view at the **Harrison County Historical Museum** (*Washington and Houston Sts. 903-938-2680. Tues.-Sat.; adm. fee*). The restored buildings at the **Starr Family State Historical Park** (*407 W. Travis St. 903-935-3044. Sat.-Sun.; fee for tours*) center on Maplecroft, a house built in 1870; it contains original Starr family furnishings

**3. Caddo Lake State Park** (*Tex. 2198, off Tex. 43, 15 miles NE of Marshall. 903-679-3351. Adm. fee*) Cabins, campsites, hiking trails, and boat tours are features of this picturesque park near 32,000-acre Caddo Lake.

**4. Kilgore** Don't miss the fine **East Texas Oil Museum** (*US 259 at Ross St. 903-983-8295. Tues.-Sun.; adm. fee*), which recounts the 1930 discovery of the "greatest oil field in the world."

**5. Henderson** Both kids and adults will enjoy the **Depot Museum Complex** (*514. N. High St. 903-657-4303. Mon.-Sat.; adm. fee*), whose restored structures include a 1901 Missouri Pacific depot and a "dogtrot" home.

**6. Texas State Railroad State Historical Park** (*US 84, 3 miles W of Rusk. 903-683-2561. June-July Thurs.-Sun., March-May and Aug. and Oct. weekends; fare for ride*) Visitors can take a 4-hour, round-trip ride through the Piney Woods on a restored steam locomotive.

**7. Caddoan Mounds State Historical Park** (*Tex. 21, 6 miles W of Alto. 409-858-3218. Fri.-Mon.; adm. fee*) A small museum on the Caddo Indians stands at the site of a village they occupied more than one thousand years ago.

**8. Nacogdoches** Restored buildings at **Millard's Crossing Historic Village** (*6020 North St. 409-564-6631. Fee for tours*) include an 1837 boardinghouse and a 1905 chapel.

**9. Lufkin** A 100-foot fire tower dominates the grounds of the **Texas Forestry Museum** (*1905 Atkinson Dr. 409-632-9535*), which focuses on the area's timber industry.

**10. Big Thicket National Preserve** (*Visitor Information Station on Tex. 420, just off US*

69/287, N of Kountze. 409-246-2337*) Get advice here on exploring the Big Thicket region, 86,000 acres of which are contained within this National Park.

**Annual Events**
**May** Jefferson Historical Pilgrimage (*Jefferson. 903-665-2672*)
**December** Christmas Candlelight Tour (*Jefferson. 903-665-2672*)

**Lodging**
**Excelsior Hotel** (*211 W. Austin St., Jefferson. 903-665-2513*) In operation since the 1850s, this hotel gives afternoon tours.
**Stillwater Inn** (*203 E. Broadway, Jefferson. 903-665-8415*) This Victorian inn also has a well-regarded restaurant.

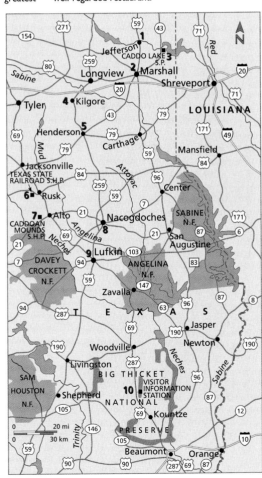

# LOUISIANA

# Atchafalaya and Beyond

Take a hardworking, proud people, persecuted for their differences with European governments, drop them in an unwanted backwater of drenching humidity and hurricane-swept coastline, and immerse for a couple of centuries: That's the recipe for the distinctive "Cajun" culture of the Atchafalaya Basin, which drains southern Louisiana west of the Mississippi. Whether they're lifting alligator eggs from a watery nest or dancing the two-step to an accordion, the people of southern Louisiana are "different" in ways the rest of the world can only envy. And much of who they are is enmeshed in the teeming waters of the swamps and bayous.

Look at a map of Louisiana, and note how the Mississippi River curves around Baton Rouge, past New Orleans and out to the Gulf of Mexico through the toe of the boot-shaped state. Below that curve—the sole of the boot—spreads the low-lying Atchafalaya Basin, a green patchwork of swamps

**Crawfish étouffée**

and sugarcane plantations and bayous. To some, the humid world of moss-hung cypress trees, hyancinth beds, and swamp is just too much *gumbo*, but many more feel the urge to pole off into its mysterious backwaters. There, they'll encounter an almost infinite variety of wildlife, and some pretty wild human life, too.

That variety is greatest toward the coast, where you can travel in an hour from the goopiest alligator swamp to the wave-softened beaches of barrier islands. Such moves are rarely made, however, without a gustatory interlude: In the Atchafalaya, good eating is proof that the Cajuns (see sidebar p. 247) have been blessed by the bountiful bayou...and they like to prove it frequently.

It may have seemed less a blessing back in the 18th century to the Acadians— "Cajun" in Louisiana vernacular—who completed a centuries-long odyssey that had taken them from their native France to Nova Scotia in the early 1600s. The British, having taken control of Acadia in 1713, began *le grand dérangement,* or removal, of the Acadians

**Egrets in mist, Avery Island**

in 1755. They were dispersed to British colonies on the East Coast, the Caribbean, and elsewhere. Eventually several thousand Acadians made their way to south Louisiana, then under French rule. They settled in a forbidding wilderness where the Native Americans, including Houma Indians (who still share the Atchafalaya region), taught them how to survive among the insects and alligators. Cajun people today can remember growing up barefoot on floating, candle-lit "camps" along the bayous where their parents trapped game.

The story of the Acadians is told in displays at the **Wetlands Acadian Cultural Center,** part of the Jean Lafitte National Historical Park system, in **Thibodaux,** an hour's drive from New Orleans. This is a good place to get your historical bearings. Your ear can begin adjusting to the French-tinged Cajun dialect and you'll hear some lilting recorded Cajun music, too. (If you come from the west, the large **Acadian Cultural Center** in **Lafayette** is worth visiting.) Then get out of the museum and follow the bayous. There is plenty of live music in Atchafalaya towns, and the people of the swamps are hospitable to the many outsiders who now want a taste of Cajun life...and perhaps a bite of crawfish étouffée or sautéed alligator.

Alligators live in the swamps, of course, which is half of the natural equation in the basin; the other half being the ocean shore of the Gulf. Visitors enjoying these two intersecting worlds should be aware that a monumental struggle goes on daily between the saltwater and freshwater, with the future health—perhaps even the existence—of southern Louisiana at stake. A labyrinth of islands and cheniers (barrier islands) form a brackish buffer between the Gulf and the freshwater wetlands inland, but 25 square miles of coastal marsh disappear under water each year.

**Moss-draped bald cypress, Lake Verret**

The survival of the Atchafalaya Basin, which ranks as North America's largest river-basin swamp, is worth fighting for, and you'll know it the minute you enter this magical world. Snowy egrets and herons coast gracefully above; alligators nose sinuously through the shallows; nutria slide through the grasses along the banks. You can see some of this from trails and boardwalks in places such as **Wildlife Gardens** in Gibson, but to feel the immensity and seclusion of the swamp, you're better off traveling by boat with a guide. Some local naturalists take small groups out in flat-bottomed boats, identifying colorful flowers and giving swamp survival pointers. Other guides use the noisier and more acrobatic airboat, with a huge propeller in the rear that can lift the boat right out of the water and across a marshy island...or across parking lots, if you ask for a demonstration.

Most of the people in this region live along the bayous, the circulatory system of the basin. "Bayou" is an Indian word for the small streams that connect the swamps and marshes and ocean. Often they are slow-moving and nearly impassable, crowded by trees and vines and throttled by the persistent water hyacinth (a non-native plant). Some, though, have been cleared and channelized between levees to allow small boat commerce. Driving south from Thibodaux along Bayou LaFourche—dubbed "the longest 'street' in the world" because of the houses packed closely along its banks—you'll see shrimp boats with nets like butterfly wings gliding up the bayou, or unloading at docks. Closer to the Gulf, the bayou widens and you see bigger boats, many of which ferry people and gear to offshore oil and gas rigs.

Near the Gulf, dense woods give way to a flat mosaic of canals and marshes, a brackish water world where all the buildings are up on stilts. The footing looks uncertain here, but that doesn't stop the locals from wandering the grassy meanders with a fishing pole (red drum and speckled trout are roadside attractions). More adventurous souls can hire commercial fishing boats in Grand Isle or Cocodrie for a trip out into the Gulf, where they can catch trophy-size marlin and tarpon, as well as good-eatin' redfish and trout. Then again, you might just order the seafood platter at the **Sportsman's Paradise** or one of the other dockside restaurants, and sample delicious soft-shell crab, oysters, and whatever else the boats have hauled in.

At the end of La. 1 is Grand Isle, a thin barrier island with summer houses and a busy sports-fishing marina. The most pleasant spot on the island is **Grand Isle State Park,** where you can walk the beach, fish on a 400-foot pier, swim, and watch for the dolphins that often cruise just offshore. Returning to the mainland, stop at small Cheniere Cemetery by La. 1, a touching reminder of how quickly this peaceful shoreline can turn murderous. Crumbling graves and a plaque commemorate the many who died in a ferocious 1893 storm that destroyed Caminidaville, a fishing port, and the island's hotels as well.

The 1893 tidal surge drove many locals inland, and that's where most travelers return after time on the Gulf—to the inland towns, to relax with a little dancing and, yes, some more delicious food. In places such as **Dula and Edwin's** in Houma, the live music ranges from renditions of Patsy Cline standards to upbeat zydeco music, which, as one local put it, "goes a step beyond the chankedy-chank" of old-time Cajun fiddle and accordian. Newcomers can expect some friendly questions and an invitation—rather emphatic—to get out on the dance floor, where hoofers of all ages, and talents, are enjoying a *fais do do.* If you can't do the two-step and the pretzel, they'll teach you.

### Cajun Cookin'

Despite the world renown of Louisiana cuisine, people are often confused about the difference between Cajun and Creole style. Creole cooking stems from the recipes wealthy Europeans brought to Louisiana back in the 17th century; it's "city" food. Cajun cooking arrived with the exiled Acadians, who showed up in the swamps with not much more than iron cooking pots. Into those pots they tossed the local fish, fowl, and flora. Today their bubbling, slithering concoctions continue to delight (or turn off). Be brave: Try a bowl of gumbo—a rich, spicy soup thickened by sassafras and okra, often with shrimp, sausage, or squirrel. If it's not hot enough, spice it up with some local cayenne sauce, such as the Tabasco from Avery Island.

The dancing, the eating, and the high spirits are a Cajun way of celebrating good fortune. Two centuries ago their ancestors began trickling into a strange land, retreating into the swamps and on the bayous. They learned to live in this teeming wilderness, and soon came to love it. In Cajun country, the celebration is infectious.                                                    —*Geoffrey O'Gara*

# Travel Notes

### Directions
Broadly defined, the Atchafalaya Basin lies between Baton Rouge and Lafayette...and south of there. **By car:** The eastern part of the Atchafalaya Basin is an easy drive from New Orleans, taking US 90 southwest to Raceland (where you can follow La. 1 down Bayou Lafourche) or Houma. **By plane:** Major airlines serve New Orleans.

### General Information
In the summer and early fall a heavy humidity coats the Gulf Coast and the swamps. One of the best times to visit is in March or April when the swamps are in bloom, migrating birds are plentiful, and the swamp wildlife is particularly active. For more information, contact the Louisiana Department of Culture, Recreation, and Tourism *(P.O. Box 94291, Baton Rouge 70804. 504-342-8119 or 800-633-6970).*

### Things to See and Do
**1. Lafayette** *(Convention and Visitors Commission 318-232-3808 or 800-346-1958)* A re-created Acadian-Creole village, **Vermilionville** *(1600 Surrey St. 318-233-4077 or 800-99-BAYOU. Adm. fee)* is worth a stop. It features period houses, craft demonstrations, music, and a restaurant. Also in town is the **Acadian Cultural Center** *(501 Fisher Rd. 318-232-0789),* which offers exhibits, artifacts, and a 40-minute film on the Acadians.
**2. New Iberia** *(Tourist Commission 318-365-1540 or 888-9-IBERIA)* West of the basin, **Shadows-on-the-Teche** *(317 E. Main St. 318-369-6446. Adm. fee)* is a good example of an old plantation estate. The 1834 mansion, a National Trust for Historic Preservation property, has the requisite oaks, dripping Spanish moss, and a white-pillared portico, plus a treasure trove of artifacts.
**3. Avery Island** *(La. 329, S of New Iberia. Toll)* The McIlhenny family that bottles Tabasco pepper sauce *(factory tours and store 318-365-8173. Closed Sun.)* used their wealth to create **Jungle Gardens** *(318-369-6243. Adm. fee),* a 200-acre preserve that includes a

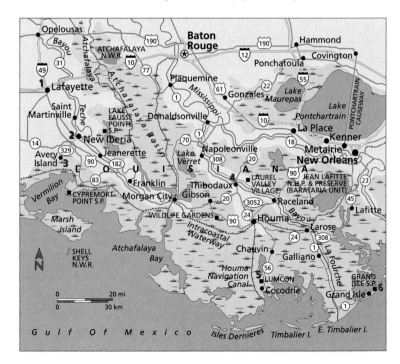

**Swamp lilies, Atchafalaya Basin**

Buddhist temple. This combo is worth a visit.
**4. Thibodaux** *(Chamber of Commerce 504-446-1187)* Informative exhibits at the **Wetlands Acadian Cultural Center** *(Jean Lafitte National Historical Park and Preserve, 314 St. Mary St.. 504-448-1375)* tell the history and culture of the Acadians. There are sometimes craft demonstrations and on Monday evenings Cajun musicians perform. On view at **Laurel Valley Village** *(595 La. 308, 2 miles SE of Thibodaux. 504-447-2902. Closed Mon.)* are an artifact-filled country store and the remnants of a 19th-century sugar plantation, including workers' dwellings.
**5.** LUMCON (Louisiana Universities Marine Consortium) *(8124 La. 56, S of Chauvin. 504-851-2800)* This marine research facility has a tower with a great view of the Gulf Coast and marshes. It also has aquariums and displays on Gulf ecology.
**6. Grand Isle State Park** *(Admiral Craik Dr., Grand Isle. 504-787-2559 or 888-787-2559. Adm. fee)* You can swim, picnic, and fish for redfish or speckled trout from the beach or off a 400-foot pier. An observation tower rises from the Visitor Center, which has history displays.

### Other Activities
**Cajun music** Request the "Louisiana Music Trail" from the state's Office of Tourism *(504-342-8100 or 800-261-9144)*.
**Gulf fishing** Lists of charter guides are available from the travel commissions. In Chauvin, try the Sportsman's Paradise *(6380 La. 56. 504-594-2414)* where the ebullient Connie Scheer provides boats that take anglers to the Gulf and the bayous; or the CoCo Marina *(106 Pier 56. 504-594-6626)*.
**Swamp tours** Among the tours in the Houma area are Atchafalaya Basin Backwater Adventure *(Gibson. 504-575-2371. Closed Dec.-Feb.)*; Bayou Black Swamp Tours *(Gibson. 504-575-2315)*; A Cajun Man's Swamp Cruise *(Houma. 504-868-4625)*; and Alligator Annie Miller's Swamp and Marsh Tours *(Houma. 504-879-3934. Closed Nov.-Feb.)*.

### Lodging
**Bois des Chenes** *(338 N. Sterling St., Lafayette. 318-233-7816)* This beautiful 1820 plantation house still has the tall ceilings and furnishings of its earlier days.
**Madewood Plantation House** *(4250 La. 308, Napoleonville. 504-369-7151 or 800-375-7151)* With white columns and a Greek Revival facade, this mansion is the very picture of the Old South. Completed in 1850, it offers antique-filled guest rooms, as well as public tours *(adm. fee)* of its 21-room interior.
**Wildlife Gardens** *(5306 N. Bayou Black Dr., Gibson. 504-575-3676)* A night in a replicated swamp trapper's cabin and a hearty Cajun breakfast would be enough. But here, for an extra fee, you can also get a walking tour *(Tues.-Sat.)* and a close look at the loggerhead turtles, alligators, and other animals and plants of the swamp.

### Restaurants
**Dula and Edwin's** *(2424 La. 316, Houma. 504-876-0271)* Cajun cuisine and music.
**Sportsman's Paradise** *(6380 La. 56, Chauvin. 504-594-2414)* Seafood specialties.

# ARKANSAS
# Ouachita Mountains

Look out across the Ouachita Mountains of western Arkansas from a high viewpoint and you'll see wooded crests rolling to the horizon one after another like waves in a vast green ocean—a panorama that seems the quintessence of beauty and serenity. A geologist, though, would see something quite different: evidence of a cataclysm so enormous as to reshape our continent. Here, more than 200 million years ago, a long-vanished landmass collided with North America; the slow but powerful impact wrinkled the earth's surface into long east-west ridges separated by narrow valleys. The legacy of that tectonic episode is today's Ouachitas, a rugged land of remote forests and rocky rivers, much of it nearly empty of human population but full of opportunity for recreation and solitude.

A perfect spot for that hawk's-eye view of the landscape is the **Talimena Scenic Byway**, a dramatic drive that begins just outside Mena and winds westward 54 miles to Talihina, Oklahoma. Though the route isn't high compared to, say, the Rockies—it tops out at around 2,600 feet—it rewards travelers with striking vistas. Near the summit of Rich Mountain sits 460-acre **Queen Wilhelmina State Park,** which includes a fine lodge and restaurant as well as camping and hiking trails. The original lodge here was built in 1898 by the Kansas City, Pittsburgh & Gulf Railroad, financed in large part by Dutch interests. Backers named it in honor of the teenage queen of the Netherlands, hoping that she might visit and lend royal cachet to the enterprise. Alas, this attempt at celebrity-fueled publicity failed: Wilhelmina never came to Arkansas, and the lodge closed after only three years.

Nearby, the Talimena Scenic Byway intersects the Ouachita National

## Radio Days

Though the era when folks gathered around the radio for their favorite programs has faded, there's a souvenir of those days near Mena. In 1936 the tiny town of Waters changed its name to Pine Ridge to capitalize on the fame of the radio comedy "Lum 'n' Abner," starring two actors from the Mena area and set in a fictional Arkansas village of that name. Today's real Pine Ridge is the home of the **Lum and Abner Museum and Jot 'Em Down Store** (Ark. 88, 20 miles E of Mena. 870-326-4442. March-Nov. daily, Dec.-Feb. Mon.-Sat.; adm. fee), with memorabilia of the comedians and their show, once one of the most popular in the United States.

**Gnarled red cedars, Magazine Mountain**

Recreation Trail, a 223-mile backpacking route that provides a true wilderness experience for serious hikers. The Ouachita Trail traverses the **Ouachita National Forest**, which encompasses more than 1.6 million acres of western Arkansas and eastern Oklahoma, as well as seven wilderness areas and more than 30 recreation areas. The range of outdoor activities in such a vast area is nearly unlimited, from an overnight hike in the 14,460-acre Caney Creek Wilderness, 25 miles southeast of Mena, to simply sitting beside Little Missouri Falls and enjoying this beautiful series of rocky cascades on the Little Missouri River. White-tailed deer, wild turkey, and a great variety of songbirds inhabit the forests of the Ouachitas, and an extensive network of gravel roads allows exploration far from civilization. Before you set off, though, it's a good idea to pick up a detailed map of the national forest from the supervisor's office in Hot Springs or one of the ranger offices in Mena, Waldron, Mount Ida, Oden, Booneville, or Danville.

A bit farther east, **Lake Ouachita** attracts anglers, water-skiers, scuba divers, and campers aplenty. Despite its popularity, its size—at 48,000 acres, it's Arkansas's largest body of water—nearly always makes it possible to find privacy in a quiet cove.

Several peaks rise alongside the Arkansas River valley just north of the Ouachita Mountains, set apart from the rest of the state's highlands in imposing solitude. Most impressive of all is **Magazine Mountain**, south of

**String of trout**

Paris. Its 2,753-foot summit is Arkansas's highest point, and its steep bluffs provide expansive views of the surrounding forest and farmlands. Visitors can drive to its summit along Signal Hill. Magazine's name probably came from the French word *magasin,* for storehouse or barn.

The newly established **Mount Magazine State Park** is under development on the mountain's summit, a site valued for more than just its recreational value. Several locally and, in some cases, globally rare species of plants and animals are found on the mountain, and environmentalists have been concerned that park activities could endanger its unique ecosystem. Officials have pledged, though, to protect such species as the Diana butterfly, rufous-crowned sparrow, hay-scented fern, maple-leaved oak, and Magazine Mountain middle-toothed land snail. Naturalists both professional and amateur hope that the mountain will endure as one of Arkansas's finest wild places.

Just north of Magazine lies **Paris,** which may not remind you of the city on the Seine but offers several historic buildings and an attractive town square. Dominating the scene is the handsome **Logan County Courthouse,** looking, with its classical columns and cupola, just like an Arkansas courthouse should. Paris was a major coal-producing center from the later 19th century until recent times; it once revolved around a mineworkers' union. Reminders of those days are among the exhibits at the **Logan County Museum,** built in 1886 as the local jail. Arkansas's last execution by hanging took place here in 1914.

Historic structures of a different sort attract visitors to the nearby **Subiaco Abbey and Academy,** an oasis of peace and contemplation that traces its history back to 1878, when three Swiss Benedictine monks moved here from an abbey in Indiana. (Two hundred acres for a church had been donated by the Little Rock and Fort Smith Railroad—not out of piety, but to help attract settlers and increase business.) The abbey buildings were constructed of buff-colored sandstone, and with their medieval-looking towers and arches they seem a part of some Old World city.

Twenty-nine miles east, by way of scenic Ark. 22, is the turnoff to **Mount Nebo State Park,** which covers most of the flat summit of its biblically named, 1,350-foot peak. A twisting road takes you from the lowlands to the top in breathtaking fashion. Views from lookouts are dramatic, as you might expect. Because of Nebo's configuration, hiking trails here are a bit different than at most parks: Concentric paths follow the "bench" (the thick layer of sandstone below the mountaintop), passing springs and the ruins of old structures from the days when this was a well-known resort, complete with a fancy (for its time) mountaintop hotel. The trails pass through attractive woodland, especially pretty in fall, when oaks, maples, blackgum, and other hardwoods turn yellow and orange among the evergreen pines. *—Mel White*

# Travel Notes

## Directions
The Ouachita Mountains are in west-central Arkansas, in the area bounded by Fort Smith, Hot Springs, and Texarkana. **By car:** Take US 71 north from Texarkana or south from Fort Smith, or US 270 west from Hot Springs. **By plane:** Major airlines serve Little Rock. **By train:** Amtrak's *Texas Eagle* stops at Arkadelphia and Malvern, on the eastern edge of the Ouachitas.

## General Information
Winters are fairly mild; summers can be hot and humid, but are the best time for swimming and waterskiing. Sources of information include the Arkansas Department of Parks and Tourism *(1 Capitol Mall, Little Rock 72201. 501-682-7777 or 800-628-8725);* Hot Springs Visitors Bureau *(P.O. Box K, Hot Springs 71902. 501-321-2277 or 800-772-2489);* Paris/North Logan County Chamber of Commerce *(301 W. Walnut St., Paris 72855. 501-963-2244 or 800-980-8660);* Mena Chamber of Commerce *(524 Sherwood Ave., Mena 71953. 501-394-2912);* and Waldron Chamber of Commerce *(P.O. Box 1985, Waldron 72958. 501-637-2775).*

## Things to See and Do
**1. Talimena Scenic Byway** *(Ark. 88 and Okla. 1. 501-321-5202)* This spectacular scenic drive covers 54 miles of hills and curves between Mena, Arkansas, and Talihina, Oklahoma.
**2. Queen Wilhelmina State Park** *(Ark. 88 NW of Mena. 501-394-2863 or 800-264-2477)* Camping, hiking trails, a lodge, a restaurant, and a miniature railroad await in this park on the Talimena Scenic Byway.
**3. Mena** *(Chamber of Commerce 501-394-2912)* A restored 1920s rail depot, the **Mena Depot Center** *(514 Sherwood Ave. 501-394-3817. Closed Sun.)* contains railroad memorabilia and a museum of local history.
**4. Ouachita National Forest** *(Headquarters, 100 Reserve St., Hot Springs. 501-321-*

**Weaving hickory strips**

5202) The oldest and largest national forest in the South, Ouachita encompasses more than 30 recreation areas in Arkansas and Oklahoma, as well as scenic areas, wilderness, and hiking trails.

**5. Lake Ouachita** *(8 miles N of US 270 on Ark. 227, NW of Hot Springs. 501-767-2101)* Campsites, resorts, and marinas ring this sprawling U.S. Army Corps of Engineers reservoir.

**6. Mount Magazine State Park** *(Ark. 309, 20 miles S of Paris. Under development; call Arkansas State Parks at 501-682-1191 or 888-287-2757 for current status)* Arkansas's highest peak offers splendid views, trails, camping, and several rare species of plants and animals.

**7. Ozark National Forest** *(Headquarters, 605 W. Main St., Russellville. 501-968-2354)* Most of this million-acre forest lies north of the Arkansas River. The ranger district south of Paris includes the **Cove Lake Recreation Area,** with camping, boating, fishing, and swimming. A 10.8-mile hiking trail leads to Mount Magazine State Park.

**8. Paris** *(Chamber of Commerce 501-963-2244 or 800-980-8660)* Displays on the local coal industry, railroads, and agriculture are housed in the **Logan County Museum** *(204 N. Vine St. 501-963-3936. Closed Sun.),* a jail built in 1886.

**9. Subiaco** Visitors can take a self-guided walking tour of a former Benedictine monastery, the **Subiaco Abbey and Academy** *(Ark. 22. 501-934-4295).* Set on picturesque grounds, it is now a boarding school.

**10. Mount Nebo State Park** *(Ark. 155, 7 miles W of Dardanelle. 501-229-3655)* Far-ranging views and good hiking trails are the best features of this mountaintop park.

### Annual Events

**September** Arkansas Championship Grape Stomp/Cowie Wine Fest *(Paris. 501-963-3990)*
**October** World Championship Quartz Crystal Dig *(Mount Ida. 870-867-2723)*

### Lodging

**Mount Nebo State Park** *(Ark. 155, W of Dardanelle. 501-229-3655 or 800-264-2458)* This mountaintop park offers rustic and modern cabins, all with bath and kitchen and most with fireplaces.

**Queen Wilhelmina State Park** *(3877 Ark. 88 west, Mena. 501-394-2863 or 800-264-2477)* Fabulous views are one of the attractions at this 38-room lodge near the crest of Rich Mountain on the Ouachita National Forest's Talimena Scenic Byway.

**Stillmeadow Farm** *(111 Stillmeadow Ln., Hot Springs. 501-525-9994)* This New England saltbox-style B&B is set on 70 acres.

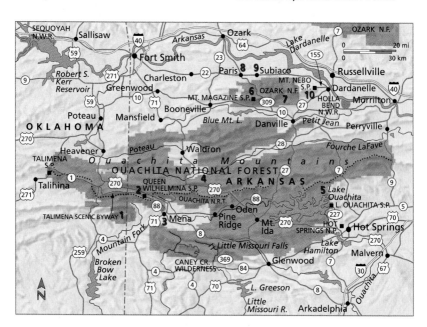

**MISSOURI**

# Ozark Hills and Hollows

The rivers of southeastern Missouri flow peacefully through their rocky valleys—in no particular hurry, it seems, to leave this Ozark mountain country. After a rain they may gather force to hurry through rapids here and there, but mostly their pace is as tranquil as life in the small towns that dot their banks.

Here, just a couple of hours' drive from St. Louis, is a land of rolling hills and clear streams, of woodland and pasture, of beauty and history. Despite being home to some of Missouri's best state parks, an immense national forest, and a scenic river system, this part of the Ozarks remains mostly unknown to those outside the Show Me State, overshadowed by the booming entertainment center of Branson, to the southwest. But the rewards are

**Stream at Amidon Memorial Conservation Area**

**Huzzah Creek, Dillard Mill
State Historic Site**

great for those who follow the winding highways along its ridgetops.

The centerpiece of the region is **Ozark National Scenic Riverways,** where the National Park Service protects 134 miles of the Current and Jacks Fork Rivers: clear, bluff-lined streams. Previous comments about tranquility don't apply to summer Saturdays on these rivers, when the waters are busy with people swimming, fishing, and boating. Those who would like a bit of solitude on their float trip should plan a visit in spring or fall, or on a weekday. The park office can supply a list of outfitters, many of whom are located near **Eminence,** a small town situated along the Jacks Fork, eight river miles below its confluence with the Current.

The Ozark Highlands are an eroded plateau underlain mostly by limestone and dolomite, riddled with caves, sinkholes, and underground streams that discharge at some of the largest springs in the United States. Aptly named Big Spring, on the Current below Van Buren, has an average flow of 276 million gallons of water a day. (To put things in perspective, that discharge would fill up a good-size backyard pool in about six seconds.)

Alley Spring, just west of Eminence, surely ranks among the most picturesque spots in the area. Here, where a major spring surfaces in a small pond at the base of a limestone bluff, stands a partially restored 1894 gristmill—a reminder of an era when this pretty valley was home to a small community including a post office, general store, and blacksmith shop. Nearby you'll find a reconstructed one-room schoolhouse, complete with George Washington's picture on the wall and McGuffey's Readers on the desks.

The abundance of natural water power in the Ozarks made the area home to a great many mills in the late 19th and early 20th centuries. Most have disappeared, but a fine example endures at **Dillard Mill State Historic Site,** located on the banks of Huzzah Creek in Crawford County. Built just after the turn of the century by a Polish immigrant, Dillard Mill continued to grind flour and animal feed until the mid-1950s. Today, visitors can tour its multi-level interior and see its amazingly complicated machinery—gears, leather belts, and sifters—operating just as it did when the mill produced sacks of Ozark Pride flour.

The power of water is displayed in a quite different way at **Johnson's Shut-Ins State Park;** here, the East Fork Black River has worn away at volcanic rocks in a narrow gorge, creating a wondrously rugged riverbed where huge gray boulders split the stream's flow into small waterfalls and rapids. So inviting is the river (for swimming, wading, and just playing-in-the-water), that the number of visitors is limited to protect the park from being harmed; late arrivals in summer may well find the area temporarily closed to entry.

Johnson's Shut-Ins is located in the St. Francois Mountains, a region of ancient rhyolite amid the mostly limestone Ozarks. The most striking illustration of this geology is found at **Elephant Rocks State Park,** where billion-year-old granite boulders and outcrops sit atop a small hill, eroded and deeply fissured in a multitude of shapes. The park's name derives from the resemblance of one series of huge boulders to a train of circus elephants; a 1-mile, paved, interpretive Braille trail encircling the site allows visitors to make up their own fanciful stories.

About 20 miles south, 6,500-acre **Taum Sauk Mountain State Park** encompasses Missouri's highest peak and its highest waterfall—though both natural features come with asterisks, figuratively speaking. Taum Sauk, like many Ozark mountains, has a broad, flat summit; the view is mostly of oaks and rocks, though there are nice vistas from the road to the top. (For even better views, visit Skyline Drive in the Mark Twain National Forest just south of Van Buren.) Mina Sauk Falls drops 132 feet in a series of small cascades, but flows strongly only during rainy spells. To experience the best of Taum Sauk, walk the 3-mile loop trail to Mina Sauk in spring, when the falls are spectacular, the oaks show new green leaves, and the mountainside glades are spangled with wildflowers. In more ways than one, it could be the high point of your trip to the Missouri Ozarks.            *—Mel White*

# Travel Notes

### Directions
Missouri's eastern Ozark mountains are located southwest of St. Louis and east of Springfield. **By car:** From St. Louis, take US 67 south; from Springfield, take US 60 east. **By plane:** Major airlines serve St. Louis; commuter lines serve Springfield. **By train:** Amtrak's *Texas Eagle* stops in Poplar Bluff.

### General Information
Spring, when wildflowers bloom and canoeing is excellent, and fall, when hardwoods turn color, are the best times to visit the Missouri Ozarks. Sources of information include the Missouri Division of Tourism *(P.O. Box 1055, Jefferson City 65102. 573-751-4133 or 800-877-1234);* Missouri Dept. of Natural Resources *(Div. of Parks, P.O. Box 176, Jefferson City 65102. 573-751-2479 or 800-334-6946);* Ozark National Scenic Riverways *(P.O. Box 490, Van Buren 63965. 573-323-4236);* Mark Twain National Forest *(401 Fairgrounds Rd., Rolla 65401. 573-364-*

**Elephant Rocks State Park**

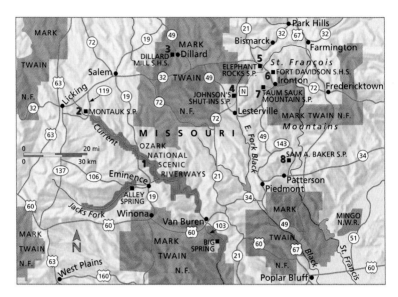

*4621)*; and the Ozark Heritage Tourism Association and Rolla Chamber of Commerce *(1301 Kings Hwy., Rolla 65401. 573-364-3577 or 888-809-3817).*

## Things to See and Do

**1.  Ozark National Scenic Riverways** *(Along the Current River. 573-323-4236)* Operated by the National Park Service, this park protects 80,000 acres and 134 miles of the Current and Jacks Fork Rivers. It offers canoeing, fishing, and swimming.

**2.  Montauk State Park** *(Mo. 119, 21 miles SW of Salem. 573-548-2201)* Good trout fishing in the Current River is found here, along with nature trails, cabins, and a historic gristmill.

**3.  Dillard Mill State Historic Site** *(1 mile S of Mo. 49 near Dillard, follow signs. 573-244-3120)* A restored mill dating from the turn of the century, this is one of the state's most famous historic sites.

**4.  Johnson's Shut-Ins State Park** *(Cty. Rd. N, 8 miles N of Lesterville. 573-546-2450)* Trails wind through beautiful river-carved gorges, or shut-ins, with rock formations; visitors are limited to prevent overcrowding.

**5.  Elephant Rocks State Park** *(Mo. 21, 1 mile N of Graniteville. 573-546-3454)* A paved trail allows easy access to a striking area of billion-year-old granite boulders.

**6.  Fort Davidson State Historic Site** *(Mo. 21 in Pilot Knob. 573-546-3454)* The site

of a bloody 1864 Civil War battle includes a preserved earthwork fort, cannon, and interpretive exhibits in the Visitor Center.

**7.  Taum Sauk Mountain State Park** *(Cty. Rd. CC, 9 miles SW of Ironton. 573-546-2450)* The state's highest mountain and highest waterfall are the attractions at this park.

**8.  Sam A. Baker State Park** *(Mo. 143, 3 miles N of Patterson. 573-856-4411)* This beautiful 5,163-acre park in the St. Francois Mountains offers fine trails, canoeing, cabins, and a nature center.

## Annual Events

**May**  Founder's Day *(Salem. 573-729-6900)*
**July**  Bluegrass Festival *(Sam A. Baker S.P. 573-856-4411)*
**October**  Rose Holland Trout Derby *(Montauk S.P. 573-548-2201)*

## Lodging

**Cedar Stone Country** *(Mo. 19 south, Eminence. 573-226-5656)* This 11-room B&B is set in a log lodge. Activities such as bluegrass concerts and rodeos are held on the grounds.
**Maple Tree Inn** *(Jct. of Mo. 19 and 106, Eminence. 573-226-3644)* This 1890 house offers four rooms. It's located a quarter-mile from the Jacks Fork River.
**Sam A. Baker State Park** *(Mo. 143 N of Patterson. 573-856-4223)* Cabins with bath and kitchen are available April through October in this convenient location, one of Missouri's most popular parks.

# Missouri Vineyards

A surprisingly rich panorama of scenery and history unfolds along the bluffs, hills, and broad valleys of the Missouri River between St. Charles and Hermann. The Missouri Rhineland, a name the western part of this region goes by today, is a legacy of the German immigrants who began cultivating vineyards here over 150 years ago. Earlier, a diverse and almost legendary cast of characters— including a French-born saint, the American frontiersman Daniel Boone, and the explorers Meriwether Lewis and William Clark— left their mark on the area when it was still wilderness.

**St. Charles,** an early settlement on the Missouri River, rises in tiers from the wide, flat bottomlands of the muddy river 42 water miles northwest of St. Louis. Passing St. Charles on the final leg of its 2,315-mile journey south from the Rockies, the river flows north before spilling into the Mississippi.

St. Charles's history extends back to 1769 when French-Canadian settlers called the area Les Petites Côtes, or "the little hills." The **Frenchtown Historic District** is one place outside of New Orleans and Quebec where examples of French architecture still exist. One of the town's early French residents, Rose Philippine Duchesne, was eventually canonized as a saint. Her shrine on the grounds of the **Academy of the Sacred Heart,** which she founded in

**Rooftops of Hermann**

**Lewis & Clark Center, St. Charles**

1818, draws devout visitors from around the world.

South Main Street, with its jostling mixture of small shops, stately mansions, excellent restaurants, streetside plazas, and museums, runs parallel to the river. Nearly all the buildings on this lively, tree-shaded street are brick and date from the early- and mid-19th century. From 1821 to 1826, Missouri's first legislators met in the attached row of brick buildings that is now the **First Missouri State Capitol State Historic Site.**

The history of St. Charles is inextricably linked to the Missouri and the role it played in America's westward expansion. In 1804 it was a point of departure for Lewis and Clark and the Corps of Discovery expedition to the Pacific coast. The mammoth undertaking is explained in exhibits and dioramas at the **Lewis & Clark Center.** Later, the river town grew in importance as pioneers trekked westward toward the start of the Oregon, California, and Santa Fe Trails. (And later steamboats docked near the shores of today's **Frontier Park,** where the last of the great showboats, the nearby *Goldenrod,* is moored today.)

**Bounty of Missouri grapes**

One of the earliest pioneers in the area was Daniel Boone. In 1799 the intrepid frontiersman moved his family to the lushly wooded Femme Osage Valley, a few miles southwest of St. Charles. Near the town of Defiance, Boone helped his son Nathan build the four-story limestone mansion known as the **Historic Daniel Boone Home.** Completed in 1810, the distinguished Georgian-style house sits on some 200 acres adjacent to a cluster of superbly restored mid-19th-century buildings.

Missouri's **Weinstrasse,** or Wine Road, extends from Defiance to Dutzow on the north bank of the Missouri River, passing several vineyards where you can stop and sample the varietals unique to this region. It comes as a surprise to most people that Missouri was once one of the largest wine-producing states in the country. Wine-making is, in fact, one of the area's most time-honored traditions. An important commercial wine industry flourished from the 1850s until 1920, when Prohibition killed it. Replanting began again in the late 1960s.

Augusta, a few miles south of Defiance, became America's first federally designated wine district in 1980, but wine was being produced well over a century ago at Mount Pleasant Vineyards. This sophisticated oasis sits on a breezy hill-top overlooking a broad floodplain created when the Missouri River shifted its course.

Scenic highways follow both the north and south banks of the Missouri River. Lying in the foothills of the Ozarks, the countryside is characterized by steep hills dotted with woodlands and high plateaus overlooking the river's fertile bottomlands. There's a humid, languorous quality to summers here, when cicadas buzz and rasp in the trees and a sultry haze veils the hills.

**Hermann,** on the river's south bank, has been a bastion of German culture since its founding in 1836 by members of the German Settlement Society of Philadelphia. Wide, orderly streets bearing names such as Schiller, Mozart, and Gutenberg are lined with solidly built brick houses.

Touring the buildings that comprise the **Deutschheim State Historic Site** is the best way to gain an overall perspective on Missouri's German past. The Strehly House is a remarkably preserved 1840s residence with an attached winery. The German neoclassic Pommer-Gentner House contains Biedermeyer furniture and a fascinating collection of photographs from the town's earliest days.

### Root of the Vine

In the late 19th century, when Missouri wines began to outclass European vintages in international competitions, French vintners hoped to improve their own products by importing rootstock from Missouri vines. Unbeknownst to anyone at the time, the vines carried phylloxera, a microscopic root louse. The pest had no effect on vines planted in Missouri, but in France it quickly destroyed or damaged nearly every vineyard in the country. A major viticultural catastrophe was averted when two Missourians, a winemaker and a professor, developed a rootstock that was resistant to phylloxera. Their efforts saved the French wine industry from virtual extinction.

Vines cascade down the slopes of several vineyards in and around Hermann, which celebrates autumn with the jubilant, month-long festivities of Oktoberfest. Stone Hill Winery, which was producing award-winning wines as early as 1851, is the oldest and best-known of Hermann's wineries. It's a fitting place to lift a glass and toast vintage Missouri.

—*Donald S. Olson*

# Travel Notes

### Directions
The Missouri Vineyards region is located along the Missouri River, west and north of St. Louis; its towns and wineries are well marked and easily accessible. **By car:** From St. Louis, take I-44 to Mo. 100, which follows the south bank of the Missouri to Hermann. From St. Louis, scenic Mo. 94 heads southwest and follows the north bank of the Missouri. **By plane:** The nearest airport is in St. Louis. **By train:** Amtrak offers service to St. Louis, Washington, and Hermann.

### General Information
Spring, summer, and fall are the best seasons to visit the Missouri Vineyards. The best sources of information are the Greater St. Charles Convention & Visitors Bureau *(230 S. Main St., St. Charles 63301. 314-946-7776 or 800-366-2427)*; and the Hermann Visitor Information Center *(312 Schiller St., Hermann 65041. 573-486-2744 or 800-932-8687)*.

### Things to See and Do
**1. St. Charles** *(Convention & Visitors Bureau 314-946-7776 or 800-366-2427)* Sprinkled with French history, this lively town has many captivating sights. The shrine to Saint Rose Philippine Duchesne lies at the **Academy of the Sacred Heart** *(619 N. 2nd St. 314-946-6127. Donation)*, which she founded in 1818. It was the first free school for girls west of the Mississippi. A self-guided walking tour of the **Frenchtown Historic District**

*(Bounded by N. 2nd, N. 5th, Clark, and French Sts. 314-946-7776)* offers several examples of German and French Colonial architecture. Tour maps are available at the Convention & Visitors Bureau. **Frontier Park** *(500 Riverside Dr. 314-949-3372)* is a pleasantly strollable, 16-acre area located across the street from the historic district alongside the wide Missouri River. The *Goldenrod* **Showboat Dinner Theatre** *(1000 Riverside Dr. 314-946-2020. Fee for tours and shows)* is housed in the *Goldenrod*, a National Historic Landmark. Restored to its bright, original glory, the *Goldenrod* was the inspiration for Edna Ferber's novel *Showboat* and the musical of the same name. Geared to all ages, the compact **Lewis & Clark Center** *(701 Riverside Dr. 314-947-3199. Adm. fee)* focuses on explorers Lewis and Clark and their historic expedition (1804-1806). The **First Missouri State Capitol State Historic Site** *(200-216 S. Main St. 314-946-9282. Tour fee)* is a historic complex featuring the chambers used by Missouri's first legislators, a residence, and a dry goods store. All have been meticulously restored.
**2. Historic Daniel Boone Home and Boonesfield Village** *(1868 Hwy. F, Defiance. 314-789-2005. March-Thanksgiving; adm. fee)* The legendary frontiersman helped build and later died in this distinguished limestone mansion. Adjacent Boonesfield Village is a collection of restored houses and buildings moved

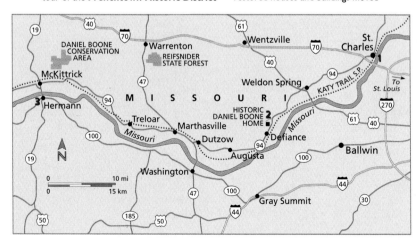

**Wine kegs, Hermann winery**

from various locations around the state.

**3. Hermann** *(Visitor Information Center 573-486-2744 or 800-932-8687)* The culture of Missouri's early German immigrants is preserved at the **Deutschheim State Historic Site** *(Tours start from 109 W. 2nd St. 573-486-2200. Fee for tours)*, with two historic houses, a winery, and a barn. Used as an elementary school from 1871 until 1955, the **German School Building** *(4th and Schiller Sts. 573-486-2017. April-Oct.; adm. fee for museum)* now houses an information center, craft shop, and an engaging series of small-scale historical exhibits.

### Other Activities

**Walking and biking** Katy Trail State Park *(Division of State Parks 800-334-6946)* is a 45-mile section of what will eventually be a 230-mile-long walking and biking trail across Missouri. This linear park stretches from St. Charles to Treloar, following the flat bottomlands of the Missouri River and passing towering bluffs and historic towns on the way.

**Wine-tasting** Missouri's Weinstrasse or wine road *(314-433-2245)* runs from Defiance to Dutzow and includes the Mount Pleasant Vineyards *(314-482-4419)*. Other possibilities are the Sugar Creek, Montelle, Augusta, and Blumenhof Wineries.

### Annual Events

**May** Maifest *(Hermann. 573-486-2744 or 800-932-8687)*; Washington Wine & Art Fair *(Washington. 314-239-1743)*; Lewis and Clark

Rendezvous *(St. Charles. 314-946-7776)*

**July** Light Up the Sky Fourth of July *(St. Charles. 314-946-7776 or 800-366-2427)*

**August** Festival of the Little Hills *(St. Charles. 314-441-4821)*

**September** Goldenrod Ragtime Festival *(St. Charles. 314-946-2020)*; Mosaics, Missouri Festival for the Arts *(St. Charles. 314-946-7776 or 800-366-2427)*; Bluegrass Festival *(St. Charles. 314-946-7776 or 800-366-2427)*; Civil War Reenactment *(St. Charles. 314-946-7776 or 800-366-2427)*; Weinstrasse Fest *(held in wineries along Mo. 94 between Defiance and Dutzow. 314-433-2245)*

**October** Oktoberfest *(St. Charles. 314-946-7776 or 800-366-2427)*; Oktoberfest *(various Hermann wineries. 573-486-2744 or 800-932-8687)*

**December** Candlelight Christmas *(Defiance. 314-789-2005)*

### Lodging

**Boone's Lick Trail Inn** *(1000 S. Main St., St. Charles. 314-947-7000)* The rooms are comfortably inviting, the breakfasts are delicious, and the historic ambience of this expertly run inn, located in a federal-style brick building dating from the 1840s, tickles the imagination.

**The Captain Wohlt Inn** *(123 E. 3rd St., Hermann. 573-486-3357)* Located on a quiet residential street in the heart of historic Hermann, this inn features five bedrooms with private baths located in an 1886 home and three suites in an adjacent building.

# KANSAS
# Flint Hills

People who say that Kansas is flat have certainly never been to the Flint Hills. They've never driven along a Chase County creek bottom bordered by rolling ridgelines, never climbed to the top of one of those ridges and looked out over an expanse of crests and valleys stretching beyond the horizon, never heard the song of a meadowlark fluting across the grassland and cottonwoods. No one who has done those things can ever think of the state as flat cornfields again.

Extending in an irregular band north to south across Kansas nearly from border to border, the Flint Hills were named for the hard flint (or chert) rock interbedded with the predominant underlying limestone. Settlers learned early on that most of this region was unsuitable for farming; the rocky, up-and-down ground resisted the plow, and crop production was poor. But the lush prairie grasses provided fine grazing for cattle, and today—except for scattered small towns and limited agriculture in the bottomlands—nearly all of the Flint Hills is devoted to ranching. History, nature (in the form of a new national preserve), and a strong Western heritage converge in the central part of the area, offering travelers a journey into a singularly intriguing landscape.

**Prairie wildflowers at dusk**

A sense of the past is ever-present in **Council Grove,** a town whose name reflects its historic beginnings. Here the Santa Fe Trail, one of 19th-century America's most important trade routes, crossed the Neosho River amid a grove of oaks and other hardwoods; the trees provided shelter for travelers heading west from Missouri to Santa Fe, as well as wood for wagon repairs. The grove was the site of an 1825 council meeting between U.S. government officials and Osage Indian chiefs, who agreed to allow passage across their land in exchange for $800. The bur oak beneath which the council took place stood on Main Street until it was blown down in a windstorm in 1958; the stump of the Council Oak is preserved today under a small shelter.

**Lush hillside, Flint Hills**

Eventually a thriving settlement grew up at this natural gathering place along the river, and many structures still endure from those pioneer times. The **Hays House 1857 Restaurant** serves home-style food in a building constructed in 1857 by Seth Hays, Council Grove's founder; over the years it's been a post office, courthouse, and church, and now (thoroughly modernized) calls itself the oldest continuously operating restaurant west of the Mississippi. Just down the street, the 1851 stone building at **Kaw Mission State Historic Site** was a school for children of the Kaw, or Kansa, tribe, the Native Americans for whom Kansas was named. For a glimpse even further back into the past, ask locally for directions to a spot about 5 miles west of Council Grove where ruts of the original Santa Fe Trail are still visible. You'll have to use your imagination a bit, but you can definitely see a wide depression across the grassy field here; nearby oil pumps provide fuel for the vehicles that replaced the covered wagons of pioneers.

Stretching for 2 miles along both sides of Kans. 177 north of Strong City, the **Tallgrass Prairie National Preserve** was created in 1996 after many years of often bitter controversy. Conservationists wanted a national park dedicated to preserving a portion of the once vast tallgrass prairie, one of America's most endangered ecosystems; local ranchers fought against government acquisition of Flint Hills grazing land. As a compromise, most of the preserve's 10,894 acres are owned by the private National Park Trust, although the land will be managed by the National Park Service. The preserve is still under development, but visitors can walk its 1.75-mile nature trail, which begins at an 1881 French Second Empire-style mansion built by the original ranch owner and passes the historic, one-room 1882 Lower Fox Creek School.

Dominating the scene in **Cottonwood Falls,** the 1873 Chase County Courthouse rises impressively on the town square, its French Renaissance-style mansard roof topped with an ornate cupola. As imposing as its native limestone exterior is, though, the courthouse's glory is its spiral staircase, made of black walnut cut on the banks of the Cottonwood River and rising three stories in graceful curves, one complete circle for each floor.

Ask locally (try the Chase County Chamber of Commerce, a block north of the courthouse in Cottonwood Falls) for a map that will guide you to back roads that locals call the Sharpe's Creek Drive, a 20-mile route through some of the finest scenery in the Flint Hills. Beginning in the tiny hamlet of Bazaar, the drive heads south and then west, crossing I-35 twice before it ends in the village of Matfield Green. Along the way it passes through open rangeland where ridgetops offer terrific views of prairie. If it's near lunchtime when you complete your backroad tour, head south to the small town of **Cassoday** and the **Cassoday Cafe,** a local favorite where you're likely to see cowboys —real ones, not shiny-boots pretenders—taking a break from herding cattle on nearby ranches. You have to like a place with a sign out front that reads, "Good Food and Gossip—Established 1879."

*—Mel White*

# Travel Notes

**Indian grass stem**

### Directions

The central Flint Hills lie northeast of Wichita, west of Emporia, and south of Council Grove. **By car:** Take I-35 north from Wichita or Kans. 177 south from I-70. **By plane:** Airlines serve Wichita and Topeka. **By train:** Amtrak's *Southwest Chief* stops in Topeka and Newton.

### General Information

Winter can bring very cold temperatures and, rarely, blizzard conditions to the Flint Hills; check with the Kansas Road Condition Hotline *(out of state 785-291-3000, in Kansas 800-585-7623)* before traveling. Sources of information include the Kansas Travel and Tourism Development Division *(700 S.W. Harrison St., Suite 1300, Topeka 66603. 913-296-2009 or 800-252-6727);* Kansas Department of Wildlife and Parks *(3300 S.W. 29th St., Topeka 66612. 913-273-6740);* Council Grove Visitors Bureau *(200 W. Main St., Council Grove 66846. 316-767-5882 or 800-732-9211);* and the Chase County Chamber of Commerce *(P.O. Box 362, Cottonwood Falls 66845. 316-273-8469 or 800-431-6344).*

### Things to See and Do

**1. Council Grove** *(Visitors Bureau 316-767-5882 or 800-732-9211)* Once a stop on the Sante Fe Trail, this town is home to the **Kaw Mission State Historic Site** *(500 N. Mission St., three blocks N of US 56. 316-767-5410. Closed Mon.; donation),* a restored 1851 Indian schoolhouse with pioneer and Native American artifacts. Nearby, the **Hays House 1857 Restaurant** *(112 W. Main St. 316-767-5911. Closed Mon.)* is known as the oldest, continuously operating restaurant west of the Mississippi River.

**2. Tallgrass Prairie National Preserve** *(Kans. 177, 2 miles N of Strong City. 316-273-8494. Donation)* This 10,894-acre preserve is managed by the National Park Service and dedicated to the natural and cultural heritage of the Flint Hills tallgrass prairie.

**Campfire breakfast, Flint Hills**

**3. Cottonwood Falls** *(Chamber of Commerce 316-273-8469 or 800-431-6344)* One of the state's most famous buildings, the 1873 **Chase County Courthouse** *(Broadway and Pearl St. 316-273-8469 or 800-431-6344. Fee for guided tours)* is made of limestone and features a beautiful black walnut spiral staircase inside. Also in town, the **Chase County Historical Society Museum** *(301 Broadway. 316-273-8500 or 316-273-8469. Closed Mon. and Thurs.; donation)* offers local historical items housed in an 1882 bank building.
**4. Cassoday** The **Cassoday Cafe** *(211 Main St. 316-735-4432. Closed Sun. except 2nd Sun. of each month)* is a well-known small-town spot popular with locals and tourists.

**Other Activities**
**Covered-wagon rides** Visitors interested in an Old West-style overnight trip can hop a ride on the Flint Hills Overland Wagon Train *(meet at Cassoday Cafe.*

*316-321-6300. June-Sept. weekends; fare. Reservations required).* After a ride across the prairie in Chase County, there's a campfire meal and cowboy music.

**Annual Events**
**June** Wah-Shun-Gah Days *(Native American festival, Council Grove. 316-767-5882 or 800-732-9211)*; Flint Hills Rodeo *(Strong City. 316-273-8469 or 800-431-6344)*

**Lodging**
**Cottage House Hotel and Motel** *(25 N. Neosho St., Council Grove. 316-767-6828 or 800-727-7903)* This architecturally eclectic hotel began as a cottage and blacksmith shop in 1867.
**Grand Central Hotel** *(215 Broadway, Cottonwood Falls. 316-273-6763 or 800-951-6763)* Elegantly restored (and expensive), this 1884 hotel boasts a highly regarded restaurant.
**Prairie Women Adventures and Retreat** *(P.O. Box 24, Matfield Green 66862. 316-753-3465. Spring-autumn)* For women only, this 5,000-acre cattle ranch provides the opportunity to help with such farm tasks as calving, branding, and fence-mending, depending on the season. Guests stay in a bunkhouse with a wood stove, hot tub, and deck overlooking the Flint Hills.

## OKLAHOMA
# Wichita Mountains

Like a venerable grandfather, the Wichita Mountains of southwestern Oklahoma may not stand as tall as they did in their youth, but we look on them with the respect and admiration that only great age and experience can earn. The granite Wichitas have eroded for more than five hundred million years to their present rounded profile, dotted with huge boulders worn and weathered to an infinitude of rugged shapes.

The sight of the Wichitas rising from the surrounding Great Plains is a compelling one. Today's travelers are naturally drawn to explore these highlands, just as were the Wichita Indians, who considered them sacred, and later the Kiowa, Comanche, and other tribes of the Southern Plains. Nearby attractions reward visitors as well, among them a historic military base, sites celebrating Native American heritage, and a popular state park.

**Wichita Mountains National Wildlife Refuge** ranks among Oklahoma's best natural areas, encompassing diverse terrain and wildlife, with opportunities for recreation ranging from car-window sightseeing to wilderness backpacking. A paved road leads to the top of 2,464-foot Mount Scott for a splendid view of mountains and plains—probably the best first stop in your survey of the region.

The 59,020-acre federal refuge was established as a forest reserve just after the turn of the century. It became home in 1907 to 15 bison, among the few survivors of a species then in serious danger of extinction despite the fact it had roamed the Great Plains in the tens of millions just a half-century earlier. More than 500 bison now thrive on the refuge, thrilling visitors who often get close views of animals alongside the roadway. (And sometimes in it; you'd be wise to obey speed limits here.) Elk and wild turkey, both once extirpated in the Wichitas, have also been reestablished, along with Texas longhorn cattle, the legendary breed that almost died out as more productive types became popular. Other fauna seen around the refuge's oak woodlands, lakes, and grasslands include prairie dogs, white-tailed deer, coyotes, several species of hawks, both bald and golden eagles, waterfowl, and the endangered black-capped vireo, a small songbird with a highly restricted breeding range in the South Central states.

Okla. 115 twists and turns through a scenic part of the Wichita Mountains north of the refuge until the landscape flattens into plains beyond Saddle Mountain. Along the way it passes through **Meers,** a town so tiny it might easily escape notice. At mealtime, though, that would be a serious mistake; the locally famous **Meers Store** serves huge hamburgers made from longhorn beef that have earned praise from around Oklahoma and

**Surveying view from the Wichita Mountains**

beyond. At the turn of the century Meers was a gold-mining boomtown with a population in the thousands, but today its inhabitants can be counted on the fingers of both hands.

Bordering the wildlife refuge on the southeast, sprawling Fort Sill Military Reservation has a long and varied history dating back to 1869, when the Army founded a post alongside the Wichita Mountains from which it could keep the peace between Plains Indians and white settlers. In 1911 the base became the U.S. military's main artillery training center, a role it still proudly plays. The **Fort Sill Museum,** spread through several buildings, recalls its past from frontier days to modern warfare. The Cannon Walk displays dozens of pieces of imposing weaponry; one, "Atomic Annie," fired the world's first nuclear artillery shell in 1953.

This part of Oklahoma (which was then Indian Territory) was opened to white settlement in 1901—not in a frantic land run, as was the case with some areas farther north, but through a lottery in which winners were given 160-acre plots. The city of **Lawton** went from wilderness to a population of 10,000 almost literally overnight, boasting 400 businesses (most housed in tents) and a newspaper; within three months it's said to have had 86 saloons. Growing like Fort Sill, Lawton is now Oklahoma's fourth largest city, and home to the excellent **Museum of the Great Plains,** which interprets both the natural and human history of the region. An extensive collection of Indian artifacts is a museum highlight, along with a reconstructed 19th-century trading post where twice-yearly encampments re-create frontier activities, complete with costumed buffalo hunters, soldiers, and traders.

Several Indian tribes have their headquarters in or near the small town of

**Cloudscape over bison, Wichita Mountains National Wildlife Refuge**

**Anadarko,** which calls itself the "center of Native America." The **Southern Plains Indian Museum** and the adjacent **National Hall of Fame for Famous American Indians** are good places to learn about Native American history. **Indian City, U.S.A.,** while more commercialized, is worth a visit for its re-creations of dwellings of seven different Indian cultures.

The Wichita Mountains don't quite end where they seem to. Forty miles west of the main range, Quartz Mountain rises like a monolith over the plains, a mass of granite with man-made Lake Altus at its base. Popular with nature-lovers, anglers, rock climbers, water-skiers, and golfers, **Quartz Mountain State Park** is also—perhaps unexpectedly for a place so remote—a regional center for the arts. Summer home for the Oklahoma Arts Institute, an arts program for young people, the park's lakeside lodge partially burned in 1995. In 1999, though, a grand new lodge and performance hall will open, providing a home for the students' concerts and artworks in summer, and a center for other arts activities year-round.

For the energetic traveler, the finest experience at Quartz Mountain

may well be the short but somewhat strenuous New Horizon hiking trail to the summit, where the wonderful view takes in lake, foothills, and plains. Late in the day, when the setting sun turns the reddish granite boulders even redder, the Native American belief in the sacredness of the Wichita Mountains seems perfectly understandable. Their enduring presence still has the power to enchant all who take the time to fully experience them.

**Comanche powwow attire**

—*Mel White*

# Travel Notes

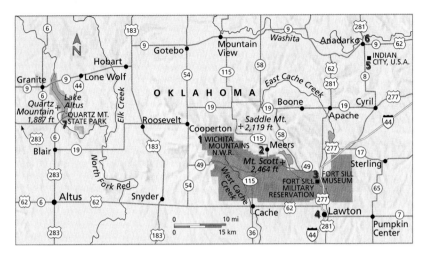

## Directions
The Wichita Mountains lie in southwestern Oklahoma, west of Lawton. **By car:** Take I-44 southwest from Oklahoma City.
**By plane:** Major airlines serve Oklahoma City; commuter lines serve Lawton.

## General Information
Spring and fall bring migrating birds, while bison, elk, and deer are visible year-round. Sources of information include the Oklahoma Department of Tourism and Recreation *(P.O. Box 52002, Oklahoma City 73152. 405-521-2409 or 800-654-8240)*; Lawton Chamber of Commerce and Industry *(P.O. Box 1376, Oklahoma City 73502. 580-355-3541 or 800-872-4540 )*; and Altus Chamber of Commerce *(P.O. Box 518, Altus 73522. 580-482-0210)*.

## Things to See and Do
**1. Wichita Mountains National Wildlife Refuge** *(Jct. of Okla. 49 and Okla. 115, W of Lawton. 580-429-3222. Visitor Center closed Tues.)* This is an expansive wildlife refuge with excellent scenery, hiking, camping, and herds of bison, elk, and Texas longhorn cattle.
**2. Meers** Longhorn burgers are the attraction at the **Meers Store** *(Okla. 115. 580-429-8051)* restaurant, which is located in a former mining town.
**3. Fort Sill Museum** *(437 Quanah Rd., Ft. Sill Military Reservation. 580-442-5123)* Varied

exhibits on this artillery-training base include fort history displays, the Cannon Walk, and Geronimo's grave.
**4. Lawton** *(580-355-3541 or 800-872-4540)* Among the sites in this town steeped in Native American culture is the **Museum of the Great Plains** *(601 N.W. Ferris Ave. 580-581-3460. Adm. fee)*, which offers displays on local history and Native Americans; outside are a 1926 steam locomotive and a re-created 19th-century trading post.
**5. Indian City, U.S.A.** *(Okla. 8, just S of Anadarko. 405-247-5661 or 800-433-5661. Adm. fee)* Re-creations of Indian housing and dance demonstrations are featured here.
**6. Anadarko** *(Chamber of Commerce 405-247-6651)* The **National Hall of Fame for Famous American Indians** *(851 E. Central Blvd./US 62. 405-247-5555)* is an outdoor walk with busts of notable Native Americans. The **Southern Plains Indian Museum** *(715 E. Central Blvd./US 62. 405-247-6221. June-Sept. daily, Oct.-May Tues.-Sun.; adm. fee)* has exhibits and a shop sells Indian-produced items.
**7. Quartz Mountain State Park** *(Okla. 44A N of Altus. 580-563-2238)* This pretty park sits next to 6,260-acre Lake Altus. It has a hiking trail to the top of Quartz Mountain, a golf course, lodge rooms, and cottages.

## Annual Events
**August** American Indian Exposition *(Festival in Anadarko. 405-247-6651)*

# Mountain and Desert States

## MONTANA

# Big Sky and Ghost Mines

Southwest Montana is a spacious landscape filled with historic sites, wildlife, big sky vistas, excellent trout rivers, and lovely mountain ranges. Ranching remains a primary industry, but mining was the business that set the pattern for settlement. Gold started things off, silver played a role, and finally copper made the biggest impact of all. Some early settlements became ghost towns, while others still thrive among the preserved relics of their past. Butte tells an epic hard-rock story all its own.

An August morning in the Big Hole Valley: Mist rises from the river, flows across fields of freshly cut hay, and partially obscures the Bitterroot Mountains. High snowfields ignite with the warm light of dawn. The air is filled with the fragrance of growing things. The sky is a perfect blue, and no one—no creature, no person—seems to be in a hurry.

It is summer, a time of abundance. The trouble is, summer has no lasting power. Fall comes early, winter is long, spring is uncertain. People tell jokes: "Summer? I missed it. I slept late that day."

In truth, summer can stretch out to six weeks or more. This country was designed for summer. Everything feels right, from the meadowlarks on fence posts to the purple lupines bursting across alpine meadows. Even the scale is right. Numerous small ranges—the Tobacco Roots, Pintlers, Pioneers, and others—alternate with sage-covered foothills and green hayfields. The mountains have timber, the ranches have cows, the rivers have trout, and things seem to have been that way for a very long time.

Mining was the foundation of settlement throughout the Rockies, and southwest Montana is a good place to track its development. In the beginning,

**North Rim of the Grand Canyon (see Arizona Strip, p. 317)**

prospectors wandered the countryside, panning for gold. If they found some, other prospectors would pour in. A tent village would appear, and the ground would become a beehive of activity, with men digging and sluicing and sometimes (if Hollywood has it right) yelling "Eureka!" If the gold proved abundant, someone would build a sawmill, and wooden structures—shops, saloons, boardinghouses—would go up on either side of a main street.

Usually, gold discoveries played out fast and hopeful towns withered. The exceptions occurred where deep ore deposits justified underground mining. In those cases, large companies took over, hiring hundreds of men, building mills, railroads, and smelters. Deep mines sometimes lasted long enough for a town to become permanent, with brick buildings, stone churches and plans for a stable future. But even the rich mother lode that gave rise to Butte ran out eventually.

What we see today is a secondary economy. From the beginning, miners needed food, shelter, tools, and clothing. The first Montana ranches sold beef to them. Loggers supplied the mines with timber. Sawmills made lumber. Wagon roads and railroads were needed to carry freight. Growing communities needed laborers, clerks, lawyers, lawmen, tailors, and teachers. When the mines failed, the men and women who served them often stayed on to become the fabric of a more lasting society.

Montana's first major gold strike occurred in 1862 at **Bannack,** now a ghost town and state park. More than 50 buildings survive, most of them standing empty but speaking volumes about frontier conditions. The risks faced and the price paid by miners is evident today in the graveyard, whose stones record many early deaths.

Bannack was quickly overshadowed by the fabulous strike at Alder Gulch. **Virginia City** grew up there and became notorious for its crooked sheriff, Henry Plummer, and the vigilantes who ended his outlaw activities. Plummer managed to become sheriff of both Virginia City and Bannack. Using his position to criminal advantage, he ran a gang of road agents called the Innocents, until the Montana Vigilantes lynched him in Bannack.

From Virginia City, the boom moved on but the town did not die. Its history has been well preserved, to a point where past and present can be difficult to separate. The lower end of Main Street is lined with one of the West's most complete collections of original buildings—wooden structures hastily erected in the 1860s.

## Stacking Hay

The beaverslide haystacker is a Montana invention. It worked well with horse-drawn equipment, and it still works in the age of tractors. The haystacker consists of a high ramp, made from poles, and a sliding rack that can be raised and lowered by pulling on a rope. After the hay has been cut and raked, the stacker is set up against a frame that will hold the house-size haystack. Then, tractors with long forks scoop up piles of hay and dump them onto the sliding rack. Another tractor pulls the rope; the rack runs up the ramp and dumps the hay in the frame.

**Beaverslide haystacker, Big Hole Valley**

As Virginia City faded, **Butte** exploded, dominating the regional economy and environment for a century. Called the "richest hill on earth," it yielded more than 20 billion pounds of copper clawed from thousands of miles of tunnels and shafts and, most visibly, the enormous Berkeley Pit. A hard, two-fisted town now recovering from the closure of its vast mines in the 1980s, Butte is a powerful piece of history. Its story is one of great fortunes and hardship, of immigrants making their first stake in a new land, of mine disasters and labor unrest.

Today, Butte—a National Historic Landmark District—can be called a mining town only in the sense that mining built it and half destroyed it.

The destruction was literal. The Berkeley Pit, opened in 1955, swallowed part of Butte and two neighboring communities. About 7,000 feet long, 5,600 feet wide, and 1,600 feet deep, it is now partly filled with toxic brownish red water that presents a serious cleanup problem.

Like monuments to the past, the headframes of underground mines stand on unreclaimed ground. It's a raw scene, but if you look at the downtown buildings and architectural styles, many of which reflect Butte's early stature and wealth, it's easy to understand why many people consider the headframes valued historic artifacts.

**Methodist church and parsonage, Bannack**

If that seems unlikely, look at neighboring Anaconda, whose smelters have been torn down, leaving only the landmark 585-foot-tall brick smokestack. The wasted landscape, a one-time Superfund site, is now a golf course designed by Jack Nicklaus, where golfers play near brick walls and flues.

South of Anaconda is another smelter remnant, the Mount Haggin Recreation and Wildlife Management Area, 55,000 acres owned by Montana. This place once belonged to the Anaconda Company, whose smelter poisoned the air for miles around. "To avoid controversy," the company bought huge tracts of land around the furnace. Now these tracts have come back to the state, and although the forest is thin, the hills are green and lovely.

Farther south, the **Pioneer Mountains Scenic Byway** follows the Wise River through the heart of the Pioneer Mountains. The byway passes Coolidge, a ghost town and the site of the abandoned Elkhorn Mine. Today visitors who go poking among weathered boards and collapsed houses might find rusted machinery and other mining artifacts.

Just to the west is Big Hole Valley, where ranches date from early gold rush days. Most of the hay is native grass, watered and fertilized and cut for generations. The region has always been good for grazing, and it was well known to Nez Perce who arrived here in 1877 from Idaho. Having crossed the Bitterroot Mountains, the Nez Perce paused to rest, thinking they had left their pursuers behind. But a surprise attack had been planned. The subsequent battle is commemorated at **Big Hole National Battlefield**. Its sad but beautiful ground will help you understand why people love this region so passionately.                     —*Jeremy Schmidt*

**Big Hole National Battlefield**

# Travel Notes

## Directions

This area is located in and around the Beaverhead-Deerlodge N.F. in southwest Montana. **By car:** I-90, running from east to west, and I-15, running from north to south, meet at Butte. US 287 is a good route to follow from Yellowstone National Park to Ennis; then head west on Mont. 287. **By plane:** The closest airports are in Butte and Bozeman.

## General Information

Summer is the best time to visit; good fall weather can extend into October. Contact Montana State Parks (*P.O. Box 200701, Helena 59620. 406-444-3750*); Travel Montana (*1424 9th Ave., Helena 59620. 406-444-2654 or 800-847-4868*); and Gold West Country (*1155 Main St., Deer Lodge 59722. 406-846-1943*), which offers the "Southwest Montana Travel Guide."

## Things to See and Do

**1. Beaverhead-Deerlodge National Forest** (*Headquarters, 420 Barrett St., Dillon. 406-683-3900*) This 3.3-million-acre forest between Missoula and Yellowstone has two wilderness areas; several mountain ranges; many lakes, streams, trails, and campgrounds; and the **Pioneer Mountains Scenic Byway.**

**2. Bannack State Park** (*25 miles W of Dillon via Cty. Rd. 278. 406-834-3413. Adm. fee*) More than 50 buildings survive on the site of Montana's first major gold strike and its first territorial capital.

**3. Virginia City** (*Chamber of Commerce 406-843-5555 or 800-829-2969*) The town is filled with the spirits and history of the Alder Gulch gold rush. Many original buildings have been preserved with their contents; they stand beside busy shops and restaurants.

**4. Nevada City** (*Chamber of Commerce 406-843-5555 or 800-829-2969. May-Aug.; adm. fee*) Several historic buildings were moved here from around the region and reconstructed on the site of an 1860s mining town. This collection of buildings is jammed with artifacts, making it one of the best museums of its kind.

**5. Big Hole National Battlefield** (*10 miles W of Wisdom, on Mont. 43. 406-689-3155. Adm. fee*) Here, on August 9, 1877, U.S. government forces fought Nez Perce Indians, who were fleeing into Montana from Idaho. The Visitor Center and battlefield trails tell the story.

**6. Butte** (*Chamber of Commerce 406-723-3177*) Located at the site of the Old Orphan Girl Mine, the **World Museum of Mining and Hell Roarin' Gulch** (*W end of Park St. 406-723-7211. April-Oct.; adm. fee*) presents mining history and hardware, mineral displays, and a reconstructed mining town from 1889. The **Berkeley Pit** (*Viewing platform off Continental Dr. 406-723-3177. Spring–early fall*) is the major landmark in Butte. Although abandoned and partly filled with water, the pit is an amazing sight.

**7. Sheepshead Mountain Recreation Area** (*Just N of Butte off I-15. 406-494-2147*) Designed for wheelchair accessibility, the area has 5 miles of paved trails around Maney Lake, and picnic and recreational facilities.

**8. Red Rock Lakes National Wildlife Refuge** (*Off I-15, 28 miles E of Monida on unpaved Centennial Valley Rd. 406-276-3536*) The refuge is a nesting place for trumpeter swans and home for a wealth of wildlife. It

**Widlflowers brightening lush buttes**

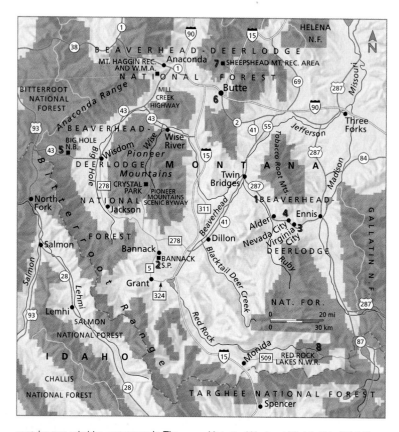

contains two primitive campgrounds. The rough road running through the refuge is a historic and scenic back way to Yellowstone N.P.

## Other Activities

**Float-fishing** The Big Hole, Madison, Ruby, and other Montana rivers are famous among trout fishers. Contact local Chambers of Commerce for more information.

**Rockhounding** Many places allow a little prospecting. Check with Forest Service or BLM offices. Call the BLM office in Butte (406-494-5059) for a brochure. Crystal Park (26 miles S of Wise River on the Pioneer Mountains Scenic Byway) lets you dig for amethysts and quartz crystals. For information, call Beaverhead-Deerlodge National Forest (406-683-3900).

## Annual Events

**June** Gold Rush Fever Day (Virginia City. 406-843-5555 or 800-829-2969)
**July** Butte Vigilante Rodeo (Butte. 406-723-3177); Bannack Days (Bannack. 406-834-3413);

Victorian Weekend (Virginia City. 406-843-5555 or 800-829-2969)
**August** Battle of the Big Hole Commemoration (Big Hole National Battlefield. 406-689-3155); Smelterman's Heritage Day (Anaconda. 406-563-2400)
**October** Butte Heritage Days (Butte. 406-782-0742)

## Lodging

**Copper King Mansion B&B** (219 W. Granite St., Butte. 406-782-7580) A brick Victorian built in 1884 by "Copper King" William A. Clark, the mansion offers five guest rooms with some original furnishings.
**Horse Prairie Ranch** (3300 Bachelor Mt. Rd., W of Dillon off Mont. 324. 406-681-3160) In the foothills of the Bitterroots, where the explorers Lewis and Clark met the Shoshone relatives of Sacagawea, one of the area's oldest ranches offers modern accommodations (three-day minimum stay) and a glimpse of ranch life.

# IDAHO
# Craters to Mountains

From the eerie moonscapes of the Snake River Plain to the ripsaw backbone of the Sawtooth Range, the heart of central Idaho presents a magnificent cross section of the state's geologic wonders. Scenic back roads cross lava beds dotted with young volcanic cones, valleys lined by snowy peaks, and rugged mountains that cup sparkling alpine lakes. The area encompasses a national monument and recreation area, as well as national forestland, with the population concentrated in a sprinkling of tiny towns that survived the mining booms of the late 19th and early 20th centuries. This is a land of elbowroom, of wide open spaces that can take your breath away with their emptiness and stark beauty.

**Ballooning by the Sawtooth Range, near Stanley**

Roughly a rectangle defined by the towns of Arco, Hailey, Stanley, and Challis, the area rises from a sagebrush desert of 5,000 feet to a series of northwest-southeast mountain ranges that crest above 12,000 feet. About 15,000 years ago, volcanoes erupted, spewing prodigious amounts of lava and ash and scarring the land with deep crevices, tunnels of twisted black basalt, and mountains of dark cinders and lava bombs. The eruptions continued until a mere 2,000 years ago and likely will happen again.

You can explore the ruins of this cataclysm in the 83-square-mile **Craters of the Moon National Monument.** A 7-mile road loops past monument highlights and walking trails, giving you an intimate look at a wound in the earth. You can walk along ropy sheets of basalt and piles of lava bombs.

Here and there a gnarled limber pine has sprouted in the wasteland, and cinder gardens with delicate plants grow amid black piles of rock. Nearly everyone stops to climb Inferno Cone, its arched back neat against the sky. In another area, you may enter lava tubes and get a sense of how the magma flowed across the land, hardening into glassy scabs and tunnels.

Shoshone and other tribes lived in remote high-country meadows to the north, fishing for salmon, hunting sheep, and quarrying basalt for tools. Fur trappers arrived in the 1820s, and the discovery of gold in 1860 brought thousands of miners into the mountain fastnesses. The gold rush died out in a few years, but it lasted long enough to build towns like Challis and **Hailey;** the later arrival of farmers and ranchers kept the towns going.

In 1983 a 7.3 magnitude earthquake struck near Borah Peak, and just east of US 93 you can see a giant rip in the earth, running 24 miles along the base of the Lost River Range. Accentuating the basin and range topography, the quake added a foot to Borah Peak, Idaho's highest mountain, while dropping the valley some 4 feet. The fault zone itself, now dotted with sage and yellow-flowering rabbitbrush, is 50 to 60 feet wide in places. At 12,662 feet, Borah Peak often floats in the clouds along with other peaks in the Lost River Range, named for rivers that flow more than 100 miles before disappearing into porous lava beds and replenishing the vast aquifer of the Snake River Plain. Borah Peak hikers must ascend 5,100 feet in less than 3.5 miles and be prepared for tough scrambles up a snowfield and rock face well above timberline. Contact the Salmon-Challis National Forest (208-588-2224) for trail information and weather conditions.

### Hemingway Was Here

Invited by the statesman Averell Harriman, Ernest Hemingway began coming to Sun Valley in 1939. He wandered the mountains, fished the Big Wood River, hunted in the nearby valleys, drank at the Casino and the Alpine Club (now Whiskey Jacques), and worked on *For Whom the Bell Tolls* at the Sun Valley Lodge. After visiting on and off over the years, he returned to live in 1959. Two years later, depressed and in bad health, the Nobel and Pulitzer Prize-winning author shot himself dead. Hemingway is buried in the Ketchum cemetery, and a memorial stands about a mile away, in view of his beloved mountains.

**Ketchum townscape**

While US 93 makes an easy ride along the Big Lost River Valley, Idaho 75 climbs into the highlands of the Sawtooth Range. At the southern end of these mountains, the friendly town of **Ketchum** sprang to life in the 1880s as a silver- and lead-mining center. But its present fame stems from neighboring **Sun Valley,** started by railroad executive Averell Harriman in 1936. The first destination ski resort in the West, Sun Valley immediately attracted the rich and famous—Clark Gable, Gary Cooper, Ernest Hemingway (see sidebar p. 280), and others whose pictures line the halls of Sun Valley Lodge. Champion skiers and skaters train here, and movie stars continue to drive up real estate prices. Yet the area remains relatively uncrowded, especially in the off-season, and the year-round population of Ketchum is still under 4,000. Though Sun Valley may feel like an ersatz village of tiny shops and eateries, Ketchum maintains an Old West charm, its original brick buildings housing bars, boutiques, art galleries, and bookstores.

**Salmon River rafting**

The best and easiest view of the Sawtooth Range lies to the north on Galena Summit. From an 8,450-foot overlook here you can behold the snowcapped pinnacles, then look down into the valley where the Salmon River is born. Thousands of sockeye and chinook salmon used to make the annual 900-mile migration from the ocean up the Columbia, Snake, and Salmon Rivers to spawn and die. Local lore says that the Salmon once ran so thick that fish flopped out onto the banks to find room. In 1991 four sockeye returned, and a few years later…none. Eight dams and their hydroelectric plants have made migration nearly impossible for salmon and steelhead trout. The **Sawtooth Fish Hatchery** captures returning chinook and sockeye, rears juveniles, and releases the young into the river or area lakes.

In the region's northwest corner, Redfish, Stanley, and scores of other lakes nestle among the sharp peaks of the **Sawtooth National Recreation Area.** Glaciers are no longer active here, but perennial ice patches and snowfields lie a tantalizing distance above the timberline. The air is cool even in summer, and the alpine meadows are stippled with purple asters, fireweed, and lacy yarrow. Hiking, fishing, and horseback riding are wonderful ways to explore the lakes and mountains. Idaho 75 (Sawtooth Scenic Drive) follows the Salmon River around the heights and passes through the town of Stanley, base of several white-water rafting outfitters. Several hot springs are nearby. Ranging from 89° to 160°F, these natural baths make for a welcome soak after a long day.　　　　　　　　*—John M. Thompson*

# Travel Notes

### Directions
The area is roughly bounded by US 20, US 93, and Idaho 75. **By car:** From Boise take Idaho 21 northeast; from Twin Falls take US 93/Idaho 75 north; from Idaho Falls take US 20 west. **By plane:** Airports are in Boise and Idaho Falls.

### General Information
Summer and winter are best for mountain visits. Spring and fall are the best times to visit the lower country around Craters of the Moon N.M.; summer temperatures can soar above 90°F. The loop road is closed in winter, but makes a good cross-country skiing trail. Contact Stanley/Sawtooth Chamber of Commerce *(P.O. Box 8, Stanley 83278. 208-774-3411)*; the Sun Valley/Ketchum Chamber of Commerce *(P.O. Box 2420, Ketchum 83340. 208-726-3423 or 800-634-3347)*; and the Lost River Valley Visitor Center *(P.O. Box 46, Arco 83213. 208-527-8977)*.

### Things to See and Do
**1. Craters of the Moon National Monument** *(18 miles W of Arco, on US 20/26/93. 208-527-3257. Adm. fee)* Hiking trails and a 7-mile drive wend past lava flows and volcanic vents 2,000 to 15,000 years old.

**2. Hailey** Housed in an 1883 building, the **Blaine County Historical Museum** *(N. Main St. 208-788-2700. Mem. Day–Labor*

**Palominos, Wood River Valley**

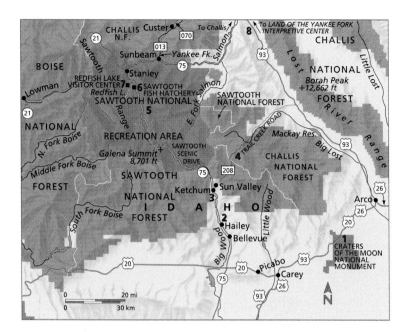

Day Wed.-Sun.) features a mine tunnel reproduction, antique political campaign buttons,
and a corner on native poet Ezra Pound.
**3. Ketchum** Among the displays at the
**Ketchum/Sun Valley Heritage & Ski
Museum** (Washington Ave. and 1st St. 208-
726-8118. Closed mid-April–late May) is a
memorabilia collection of Gretchen Fraser,
one of the first American women to win an
Olympic gold medal.
**4. Trail Creek Road** (Cty. Rd. 208 bet. Sun
Valley and US 93) Ascending the Pioneer
Mountains, this 40-mile road climbs through
a narrow valley to a 7,896-foot summit, then
descends along the Big Lost River. The middle 20 miles are unpaved and not recommended for passenger vehicles.
**5. Sawtooth National Recreation Area**
(N of Ketchum, on Idaho 75. 208-727-5013) A
756,000-acre tract of the Sawtooth National
Forest holds 4 mountain ranges, more than
1,000 alpine lakes, the Sawtooth Wilderness,
and 750 miles of hiking trails.
**6. Sawtooth Fish Hatchery** (5 miles S of
Stanley, on Idaho 75. 208-774-3684) A self-
guided tour of traps and ponds shows how
the hatchery helps restore fish populations.
**7. Redfish Lake Visitor Center** (3.5
miles S of Stanley, Idaho 75. 208-774-3376.
Mid-June–Labor Day) The facility offers interpretive displays, films, and a nature trail

along Fishhook Creek.
**8. Land of the Yankee Fork Interpre-
tive Center** (Idaho 75 and US 93, 2 miles S
of Challis. 208-879-5244. Closed weekends mid-
Nov.–April) Photographs, mineral displays, and
an 18-minute slide show detail the area's mining history and ghost towns.

### Annual Events
**August** Northern Rockies Folk Festival
(Hailey. 208-788-2700)
**October** Sun Valley Swing 'n' Dixie Jazz
Jamboree (Sun Valley. 208-344-3768)
**December** Christmas Eve Torch Light
Parade (Sun Valley. 208-622-2248)

### Lodging
**Idaho Country Inn** (134 Latigo Ln.,
Ketchum. 208-727-4000) This spacious log
and river-rock guest house has 11 rooms;
full breakfast is included.
**Sun Valley Lodge** (1 Sun Valley Rd., Sun Valley. 208-622-4111 or 800-786-8259) Opened
in the mid-1930s, the grand lodge and adjacent
chalet-style inn form the resort's centerpiece.
**Wild Horse Creek Ranch** (20 miles NE of
Sun Valley, just off Trail Creek Rd. 208-588-2575)
This charming guest ranch in the Pioneer
Mountains features landscaped grounds,
modern Western decor, a swimming pool,
and gourmet dining. Trail rides offered.

# WYOMING

# Bighorn Mountains

Set apart from the main Rocky Mountains, the Bighorns are often overlooked. They should not be. Rising above north-central Wyoming, their granite crags anchor a wilderness of rocks, alpine lakes, and snow. Their meadows and forests are filled with flowers and wildlife. Their steep flanks are cut by spectacular canyons. The west slope is a land of colorful sedimentary rocks, fossilized dinosaur bones, and a spectacular canyon reservoir. The east side is rich in Old West history, from Native American conflicts to the ranching era—and even Butch Cassidy's Hole-in-the-Wall hideout.

## Legendary Gold

In Western mythology, the Bighorns may hold lost gold. Several versions of the Lost Cabin Mine legend are told, and one of them describes seven prospectors working the eastern slopes of the mountains in 1865. The men found placer gold so abundant that in three days, they gathered $7,000 worth. As the legend tells it, they could have had even more gold if Indians hadn't found them, evicted them, and killed five of the party. The two survivors could not recall where the gold came from, and no one else has ever found the place.

The Bighorn Mountains have a way of ambushing travelers driving west across the plains. Headed for Yellowstone National Park or the Tetons, visitors come across a 30-by-120-mile range almost 200 miles from the main Rocky Mountain chain. Its highest point is **Cloud Peak,** whose 13,166-foot summit presides over a cluster of crags and alpine lakes. The high granite core is 2.8 billion years old. Like an elephantine molar, it pushes up through the younger layers of sandstone, dolomite, shale, and limestone that now flank the range in steeply angled slabs. On the east side of the mountains is the Powder River Basin, famous cattle country and the last stronghold of the Plains tribes. To the west lies the buff-colored expanse of Bighorn Basin, a kingdom of raw tilted sediments colored by the chemicals and events of their long history and filled with oil deposits and dinosaur bones.

High above them rolls the Bighorn montane forest. Except for its craggy heart, it is a gentle terrain of rolling forest and meadows strewn with lupine, American bistort, harebells, purple asters, and pasqueflowers. Trout streams meander beneath weathered granite outcrops, and in the pools lurk native cutthroat and introduced species, such as lake, brook, rainbow, golden, and brown trout, and grayling.

**Bighorn Mountains**

It is an uplifted, uplifting land that has inspired people for thousands of years. At 9,642 feet, on the wind-blasted ridge of Medicine Mountain, lies one of the area's most appealing mysteries: the **Medicine Wheel**, a stone circle 74 feet in diameter, with 28 spokes. Archaeologists think it was built between A.D. 1200 and 1700. Crow legend says it existed when their people first came to the area, and while its meaning is unclear, it holds an important place in Native American cultures. Said to resemble the structure of a Sun Dance lodge, its stones may also mark astronomical turning points, such as the solstice.

Close by are the less enduring remains of Fortunatis Gold Mine, operated near Bald Mountain City in the late 1800s. The gold grades were never high enough to justify the effort, and only a few relics survive.

The flanks of the range rise like ramparts broken by rugged canyons. As US 14 climbs southwest out of Dayton, you pass numerous scenic overlooks where you can view the increasingly distant plains. And when you get to the top, there's no easy way down. US 14A *(closed in winter)* drops 3,600 vertical feet in 10 miles of dizzying switchbacks, while US 14 finds its precarious way through Shell Canyon. The Cloud Peak Skyway (US 16) makes a similar crossing of the range, climbing from Buffalo to Powder River Pass, then burning the brakes on a steep descent through Ten Sleep Canyon.

The west side is a desertlike place of red and yellow rocks, where irrigated hayfields splash brilliant green across the valley bottoms. If the weather is dry, you can spend a dusty but pleasant day rattling along the foothills at the base of sandstone slabs dotted with juniper trees and prickly pear cactuses. In the canyons you won't find cliff dwellings, but you can see pictographs on an overhanging cliff at **Medicine Lodge State Archeological Site**.

Near Lovell, the Bighorn River has carved a deep canyon, now partly filled by the rock-rimmed reservoir of **Bighorn Canyon National Recreation Area.** You stand a fair chance of seeing bighorn sheep on the cliffs above the lake, and a better chance of seeing wild horses on the adjacent Pryor Mountains Wild Horse Range. By some accounts, the first horses came here in the 1700s, and today's wild horses resemble early Spanish breeds.

On the east side of the range, the Powder River Basin is a greener land. Cattle country for more than a century, it was once prime bison range fiercely contested by Indians, ranchers, and homesteaders. Near **Fort Phil Kearny,** one of three Army posts set up to guard the Bozeman Trail, Red Cloud and his warriors killed 81 soldiers and civilians in December 1866. Months later, trying to repeat that success, they were themselves surprised and defeated. Conflict between cattle barons and small-time cattlemen culminated in the deadly Johnson County Cattle War. West of Kaycee, along the Middle Fork Powder River, was the Hole-in-the-Wall hideout of Butch Cassidy and the Sundance Kid. This place is one of the prettiest and least-known areas in a range that is itself a hidden corner.

*—Jeremy Schmidt*

# Travel Notes

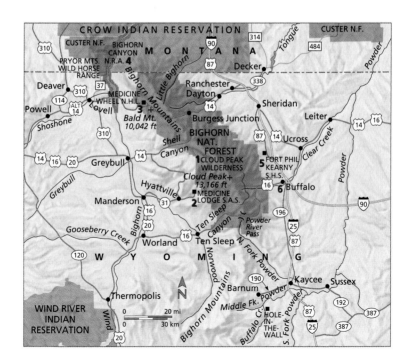

**Pryor Mountains Wild Horse Range**

## Directions
The Bighorns are in north-central Wyoming.
**By car:** I-25 and I-90 meet at Buffalo. US 14
and US 16 cross the range and provide access
to the high country. US 14A is closed in winter.
**By plane:** The nearest airport is in Sheridan.

## General Information
Summer usually begins in late June; snow closes
the high country in October. The Bighorn
National Forest *(headquarters, 1969 S. Sheridan
Ave., Sheridan 82801. 307-672-0751)* manages
most of the mountain land. The Buffalo Chamber of Commerce *(307-684-5544 or 800-227-
5122)* and the Sheridan County Chamber of
Commerce *(307-672-2485 or 800-453-3650)*
offer general information about the area.

## Things to See and Do
**1. Cloud Peak Wilderness** *(W of Buffalo
via US 16. Buffalo Ranger District, Bighorn
National Forest. 307-684-1100)* The wilderness includes the highest peak in the Bighorns
and offers hiking and horseback riding trails.
**2. Medicine Lodge State Archeological
Site** *(6 miles NE of Hyattville. 307-469-2234)* A
cliff wall is covered with prehistoric paintings.
The park offers camping, picnicking, hiking,
biking, and a Visitor Center *(mid-May-Oct.).*
**3. Medicine Wheel National Historic
Landmark** *(E of Lovell off US 14A. 307-548-
6541)* The stone circle on Medicine Mountain
is reached by a 1.5-mile walk. Interpreters are

on duty from 7 a.m. to 7 p.m. in the summer.
**4. Bighorn Canyon National Recreation
Area** *(E of Lovell. Visitor Center, US 14A. 307-
548-2251. Adm. fee)* The area offers boating,
hiking, camping, and superb scenery.
**5. Fort Phil Kearny State Historic Site**
*(US 87 exit off I-90, 12 miles N of Buffalo. 307-
684-7687. Site open year-round, museum open
April–mid-May and Oct.-Nov. Wed.-Sun., mid-
May–Sept. daily; adm. fee)* The fort stood for
two violent years. When the Army was forced
to leave in August 1868, the fort was burned
by Cheyenne warriors. No buildings survive,
but the site is interpreted at a Visitor Center.
**6. Buffalo** The **Jim Gatchell Memorial
Museum of the West** *(US 16 and Main St.
307-684-9331. May-Oct., and by appt.; adm.
fee)* holds 15,000 artifacts from battlefields,
cowboys, famous outlaws and lawmen, and
Native Americans.

## Annual Events
**July** Sheridan Rodeo *(307-672-9084)*; Kaycee
Sheepherders Rodeo *(307-738-2301)*; Bozeman
Trail Days *(Fort Phil Kearny. 307-684-7687)*
**August** Johnson County Fair and Rodeo
*(Buffalo. 307-684-7357)*

## Lodging
**T-A Guest Ranch** *(13 miles SE of Buffalo on
Wyo. 196. 307-684-5833 or 800-368-7398)*
The Johnson County Cattle War ended at
what is now a dude ranch and B&B.

# Green River Basin

This triangular slice of Wyoming is bounded by the Wind River Range on the east, the Wyoming Range on the west, and sagebrush-covered desert on the south. It's a land of high elevation, hard winters, and short summers. It offers prime mountain scenery, complete with forests, lakes, craggy peaks, and narrow canyons—good country for hiking, riding, fishing, and white-water rafting. History comes alive through the still visible wagon ruts of the Oregon Trail, a mining ghost town, and the haunts of the mountain men.

Wyoming is known for Yellowstone National Park and the Tetons. But ask any cowboy, and he'll say that classic Wyoming, the real Wyoming, is a wide-open land with few trees, a little barbed wire, plenty of sagebrush, and wind so strong that sometimes it's hard to notice much else. And always, there must be snowy mountains hanging on the horizon, close enough to admire but not so close as to make a person feel crowded.

The Green River Basin is classic cowboy Wyoming, a big triangle of open country in the embrace of two mountain ranges—the towering Wind River

**Arrowhead Lake, Wind River Range**

and the gentler Wyoming. The two ranges form a vee, open to the south but joined at the north. More than just pretty to look at, the mountains are essential to life in the basin. They provide water to feed numerous streams and hayfields. They provide summer range for cattle and offer excellent, uncrowded touring routes. And the wind doesn't always blow. There are sweet summer evenings, breathless and fragrant, when sandhill cranes clatter in the marshes and common snipe perform exuberant, buzzing, mating dances overhead. Those are the times you remember most. They are precious and fleeting.

One of the best places to get a feel for the past is near Cora, where mountain men gathered along the Green River for their annual whoop-up trading spree. In what they called the rendezvous, hundreds of trappers and Native Americans met traders bringing wares from the east. But the high times came to an end when beaver hats went out of fashion and the beavers themselves became scarce.

Between 1841 and 1869, several hundred thousand people traversed the Green River Basin on their way to the promised lands of California, Oregon, and the new Mormon settlement of Salt Lake City. You can still see the ruts worn by their wagon wheels, and in a few places you can find the names of pioneers carved into stone outcrops. Nearly everyone crossed the Green River near today's **Seedskadee National Wildlife Refuge,** a long stretch of bottomland that looks much as it did in the days of wagon trains. Seedskadee means "river of the prairie hen," or sage grouse, which is a fairly common bird in these parts. The refuge is home to great blue herons, sandhill cranes, and coots.

One branch of the **Oregon Trail,** called the Lander Cutoff, went farther north, crossing the Wyoming Range between Marbleton and Afton. Authorized by Congress in 1857, it was the first military road west of the Mississippi. You can follow parts of it now in a car. The old trail is marked by small concrete monuments and occasional graves. One of the more poignant sites is the resting place of Elizabeth Paul, who died along LaBarge Creek in July 1862. Thirty-two years old, she died giving birth to a daughter who died two days later. The tall pine beneath which she was buried still stands in a sagebrush- and lupine-covered meadow.

At the northern end of the basin, you can see why wagon trains stayed

### Hard Traveling

Of the nearly half a million emigrants who made their way along the Oregon Trail from 1841 to 1869, some 20,000 died. Sickness was the major killer, followed by injuries, accidental gunshots, bad weather, drowning, and conflict with Native Americans. Some people on the trail gave great aid and comfort to less fortunate travelers. Bernard Reid and his companions, for example, came across a 17-year-old girl nursing her cholera-stricken brother in their wagon. The parents of the two had died, their oxen had strayed, and their party had abandoned them. Reid, a knight in shining homespun, found a doctor for the boy, collected money for new livestock, and set the pair on the trail again.

**Cirque of Towers, Wind River Range**

south. Five mountain ranges—the Wind River, Wyoming, Gros Ventre, Teton, and Snake—come together in a confusion of crumpled valleys and canyons. It's here that the Snake River, having traveled a spectacular but easy route from Yellowstone past the Tetons, turns west and cuts a deep furrow on its way to the volcanic plains of Idaho. The furrow is called Snake River Canyon, which despite its rugged character is the only natural weakness through the mountains for many miles. In winter, avalanches often stop traffic on the major highway following the canyon; in summer, river rafts barreling through big frothy waves draw the attention of passersby. You just have to stop and watch, and maybe join in. There are bald eagles, ospreys, moose, and sometimes black bears in the canyon, but river running dominates the scene, and no one comes here expecting solitude.

Privacy is not far away though. The **Greys River Valley,** just to the south, is a local secret, blessed with many of the Snake River Canyon's attractions—bald eagles, elk, moose in the willow flats, trout in the river. But the valley is served only by a rough gravel road. Greys River is a smaller stream that tumbles over boulders and gravel bars beneath gentle, forested mountains. It is a quiet, peaceful place conducive to slow-speed wandering with many stops.

The other side of the basin is the same kind of place, but on a far more dramatic scale. The towering granite pinnacles of the Wind River Range include Gannett Peak, at 13,804 feet the highest point in Wyoming. Nearby summits are scarcely lower and no less impressive. Mostly wilderness, the high country is the domain of mountaineers and backpackers, but even the trailheads are outstanding. Locations such as Green River Lakes, Elkhart Park, Fremont Lake, and Big Sandy will reward any visitor with a Forest Service map and the inclination to wander.

—*Jeremy Schmidt*

**Gas station, Daniel**

# Travel Notes

### Directions

The area is between Rock Springs and Jackson. **By car:** From the south, leave I-80 on US 191 from Rock Springs, or on US 189 from Evanston. The roads meet west of Pinedale and continue north to Jackson. From Idaho Falls, US 26 leads to Jackson via the Snake River Canyon. **By plane:** The nearest airports are in Jackson and Idaho Falls, Idaho. Salt Lake City, Utah, is about a four-hour drive to the southwest.

### General Information

Summer and fall are good for visits. Spring can be unsettling; the high country often stays snowbound through June. To get started, contact the Wyoming Division of Tourism (*I-25 at College Dr., Cheyenne 82002. 307-777-7777 or 800-225-5996*); also Bridger-Teton National Forest Headquarters (*340 N. Cache St., Jackson 83001. 307-739-5500*).

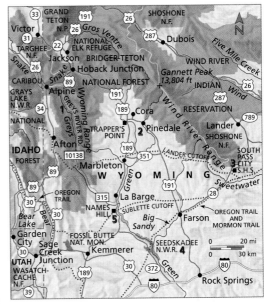

### Things to See and Do

**1. Greys River Road** (*Forest Rd. 10138 from Alpine, joining other roads. 307-886-3166*) Rough in places, this scenic route follows the river through mountains and forests, past numerous campsites, trailheads, and fishing streams. A national forest map is essential.

**2. Pinedale** The **Museum of the Mountain Man** (*700 E. Hennick St. 307-367-4101. May-Sept. daily, Oct. weekends, and by appt.; adm. fee*) tells how the fur trade contributed to history and exploration. Exhibits include Jim Bridger's rifle. Six miles west of Pinedale, near Cora, is **Trapper's Point.** Above the lush Green River bottomland, a monument marks the place where mountain men gathered six summers between 1825 and 1840 to trade furs for merchandise, but also to drink, gamble, fight, and plot their trapping strategies.

**3. South Pass City State Historic Site** (*South Pass City off Wyo. 28. 307-332-3684. Mid-May–Sept.; adm. fee*) The remains of a gold rush boomtown include 27 buildings, many artifacts, and a Visitor Center.

**4. Seedskadee National Wildlife Refuge** (*W of Farson on Wyo. 28. 307-875-2187*) The refuge stretches along 35 miles of the Green River and provides habitat for more than 200 species of birds and other wildlife. Seedskadee offers auto-tour routes, hiking, boating, and fishing.

**5. Names Hill** (*5 miles S of LaBarge on US 189*) Travelers on the **Oregon Trail** and other pioneers carved names and dates in this limestone formation. Many names have been obscured by recent additions.

### Other Activities

**White-water rafting** For information, contact the Jackson Chamber of Commerce (*307-733-3316*).

### Annual Events

**February** International Rocky Mountain Stage Stop Sled Dog Race (*area sites. 307-733-7388*)

**July** Green River Rendezvous (*Pinedale. 307-367-4101*)

### Lodging

**Box Y Guest Ranch & Hunting Lodge** (*30 miles SE of Alpine, on Greys River Rd. 307-654-7564*) The ranch offers horseback riding, fishing, hunting, pack trips, and more.

# COLORADO
# North Park

Surrounded by snow-fringed peaks, North Park is some 30 miles wide and 45 miles long, a tremendous arena of grass and sage, cattle and wild animals. From the middle of this north-central Colorado rangeland, the Rockies form a jagged cyclorama on the horizon, and the sky stretches like a vast canvas from one side to the other. The area's few roads connect a handful of dot-size towns; the rest is all wide-open space, most of it off-the-beaten-track public lands for grazing and recreation. A national wildlife refuge and surrounding national forests are full of opportunities for hiking and scenic driving. They also include plenty of places where visitors can spot moose, elk, grouse, and other animals.

The "park" in North Park refers not to a designated recreation area but to a geologic entity—an intermountain glacial basin, in this case the most northern one in Colorado. Scoured of trees long ago by enormous glaciers that rolled across the land, the grassy area made a perfect feedlot for big game. North Park essentially follows the Jackson County lines and measures 1,628 square miles, or more than a million acres. Rich with meadows irrigated by the North Platte River and its tributaries, the area must have looked like a land of plenty only a few hundred years ago, with great herds of bison mowing the meadows and thousands of deer and antelope roaming the rises. No wonder the Ute Indians called it the Bull Pen. With the coming of colder weather in fall, man and beast found themselves together here, trying to escape the chill of higher elevations.

As late as 1855, an Irish hunter in North Park boasted of killing thousands of bison, deer, and antelope. But soon after, game declined as miners and prospectors came West in search of mineral riches and green pastures. In

## Altitude Adjustment

Before you go tackling those alpine meadows and snow-capped peaks, bear in mind that Acute Mountain Sickness can occur at 8,000 feet. With lower oxygen and humidity, you may feel nauseated, have headaches, and experience lethargy or shortness of breath. The quickest solution is to descend 1,000 feet and stay there for at least a day. Better yet, you can avoid these symptoms by being prepared. Come to the high country in good physical condition, then plan to spend the first couple of days doing almost nothing. Also: Drink fewer alcoholic beverages and more glasses of water.

**Feeding cattle, Steamboat Springs**

1879 a stockman drove 3,000 Texas steers into the area to graze; others followed, and by the late 1880s all of the best land along the rivers was taken by ranchers. Cattle and sheep now graze where bison, bighorn sheep, and bears once foraged in freedom.

The game population has begun to stabilize, though. In the 23,267-acre **Arapaho National Wildlife Refuge**, raptors, prairie dogs, waterfowl, and pronghorn find the peace and quiet that they need for feeding, resting, and raising their young. From the short nature walk or the 6-mile driving loop, you'll almost certainly see wildlife or signs of wildlife: Look for tracks and scat along the marshy bottoms, or for tree stumps chewed by beavers on riverbanks. On clear days you can see 20 miles or more to the Medicine Bow Mountains, in the east, and the Never Summer peaks, with their mantle of snow, to the south.

In the late 1970s, the Colorado Division of Wildlife released two dozen moose into North Park. The animals have done so well that their population is now between 550 and 600, making North Park—and more specifically Walden—the moose viewing capital of the state. One of the best places to catch a glimpse of a moose is in **Colorado State Forest State Park** near Gould. Moose browse on willows or shrubs along streams and ponds, particularly in the early morning and at dusk. The observation deck off Colo. 14 overlooks perfect habitat for moose. But be sure to remember to keep a safe distance from these very large creatures, because they can suddenly become aggressive if they feel threatened. If for some reason you

**Elk at sunset**

miss seeing a live moose, you can take a look at one made out of barbwire at the Visitor Center. This life-size structure took a team of three local artists 700 hours to make.

The dusty little town of **Walden** serves as the county seat and the center for area recreation; the Cache la Poudre-North Park Scenic Byway (Colo. 14), which starts 101 miles to the east, in Fort Collins, ends here. Walden also anchors one of the richest hay-producing centers in the state, and almost all of the hay is the native mountain variety.

Visitors to Walden usually make a quick trip to the **North Park Pioneer Museum** to view its collection of artifacts. The town also has motels, a bar, a café, and a few stores. A small but well-stocked Chamber of Commerce has useful information for visitors, including a brochure about all the wildlife-watching spots in North Park. One such spot, the Walden Reservoir, sits on the west edge of town, and this sizable wetland is a convenient place to view ducks, Canada geese, and avocets honking and dabbling across the area.

If you prefer a little more upscale nightlife, you need to cross the mountains to the ski and spa town of **Steamboat Springs.** On the way over, you'll cross Rabbit Ears Pass, visible from miles away for its twin volcanic plugs. The hike up to the 100-foot-tall "ears" could be the highlight of your visit to North Park, offering crisp views of the basin and its surrounding stockade of peaks.

—*John M. Thompson*

# Travel Notes

## Directions
North Park centers on Jackson County, near the Continental Divide northwest of Denver. **By car:** From Denver, take I-70 W, then US 40 and Colo. 125 north, or follow the Cache la Poudre-North Park Scenic Byway from Fort Collins. **By plane:** The closest major airport is in Denver.

## General Information
Summer and fall are the best seasons for a visit. Winter brings heavy snowfall, but roads are plowed and there are miles of snowmobile and cross-country ski trails. Contact the North Park Chamber of Commerce *(517 Main St., P.O. Box 68, Walden 80480. 970-723-4600).*

## Things to See and Do
**1. Rabbit Ears Peak** *(20 Miles E of Steamboat Springs, off US 40)* A 5-mile round-trip hike winds through meadows and forests to the base of twin peaks. Views from the top take in North Park to the east and the Mount Zirkel Wilderness to the north. For trail information, contact the Routt National Forest, Hahns Peak Ranger District *(925*

*Weiss Dr., Steamboat Springs. 970-879-1870).*
**2. Arapaho National Wildlife Refuge** *(S of Walden, off Colo. 125. 970-723-8202)* The refuge offers abundant wildlife, a 6-mile driving loop *(late March–mid-Oct.),* a half-mile foot trail, and expansive views of North Park.
**3. Walden** Displays at the **North Park Pioneer Museum** *(465 Logan St. 970-723-4711. Mid-June–mid-Sept. Tues.-Sat.)* include a pioneer kitchen, a re-created early schoolroom, a pool hall, and a music room.
**4. Colorado State Forest State Park** *(Colo. 14 near Gould. 970-723-8366)* The 72,130 acres of this park encompass meadows, streams, and sub-alpine terrain; activities include fishing, camping, and hiking.

## Annual Events
**February** Winter Carnival *(Steamboat Springs. 970-879-0695)*
**July** Never Summer Rodeo *(Walden. 970-723-4344)*

## Lodging
**Steamboat B&B** *(442 Pine St., Steamboat Springs. 970-879-5724)* This erstwhile church *(1890s)* offers antiques and Victorian charm.

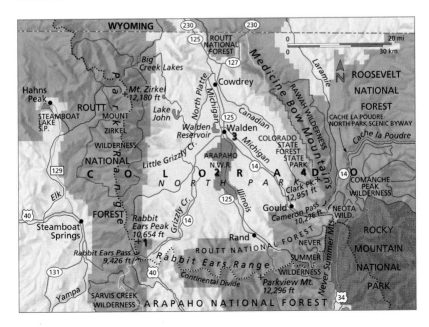

# Black Canyon of the Gunnison

The Black Canyon of the Gunnison National Monument embraces 12 miles of the Gunnison River, which sloshes through a defile so deep and narrow that shadows are the rule, sunlight the exception. In this deep gash in the earth, raptors ride the updrafts and time is frozen into dark walls of stone. The monument and adjacent Curecanti National Recreation Area in west-central Colorado anchor the vast Gunnison River territory—more than 85 percent of it public land. Drives over high mountain passes to the north unveil magnificent scenery and wind around to ghost towns and mining towns whose old buildings are now museums and inns.

Standing at the rim of the **Black Canyon,** you can see more than 2,000 feet down to the frothy green Gunnison River. Fins and spires of cold dark rock plummet sharply from a plateau of stunted trees down to a Land of Mordor, a netherworld of shadowy plinths and parapets. There are canyons that are deeper and canyons that are narrower, but "no other canyon in North America combines the depth, narrowness, sheerness, and somber

**Black Canyon of the Gunnison National Monument**

countenance of the Black Canyon," wrote geologist Wallace Hansen. This startling combination of dimensions and textures creates a natural wonder that rivals even the Grand Canyon in beauty. While the Colorado River was carving through soft shale and sandstone to create the multicolored Grand Canyon, the Gunnison was chiseling into schist and gneiss. The result is a canyon that has not yielded easily to time. Sheer walls with stripes of pink granite and teetering splinters of stone rise like monuments to resistance. At the basement level you can see metamorphic rock more than 1.5 billion years old.

It is difficult to say which overlook along the 6-mile **South Rim** drive is the most spectacular, because each offers a slightly different vantage. High Point, at 8,289 feet, is the highest one; a three-quarter-mile stroll from here takes you to Warner Point, offering stunning views of the west canyon and the farmlands near Montrose. The South Rim is not at all crowded—a few cars per overlook—but if you want the whole place to yourself, drive (about 90 miles from Montrose, including 12 on dirt) to the isolated **North Rim**—the unpaved rim road here offers similarly breathtaking views.

Because much of the monument is a designated wilderness, there are no developed trails into the canyon. Rangers can suggest routes for the adventurous, who must obtain a permit for all inner-canyon activities. The distance to the river is only about a mile, but with an elevation drop of at least 1,800 feet and long pitches through scree and loose dirt, the "hike" is a heart-racing, one-hour slide going down and a hand-over-hand haul coming out. At the bottom, you can lie on flat boulders and watch the cliffs towering above you like skyscrapers on Wall Street.

## Movie Time

While in Montrose, treat yourself to an old-fashioned cinema. Although it has gone triplex, the 1929 **Fox Theatre** (*27 S. Cascade St. 970-249-8211. Fee*) still claims the largest screen in western Colorado. Updated in the 1970s and early '80s, the Egyptian-style movie house sports Mexican tile worth $100,000, as well as paintings by a local artist, including one of Jane Fonda. A gold lamé curtain shimmers over the old stage, while stained-glass accents and 387 plush, roomy seats put movie viewers in the lap of luxury.

The canyon and its waters have long daunted travelers. A few arrowheads and early campsites have been found, but the Ute Indians generally avoided the canyon. Likewise, explorers found ways to go around it rather than face the unknown perils within. Even Capt. John W. Gunnison, for whom the river and canyon are named, made a crossing just north of the canyon. John C. Frémont followed Gunnison's trail, and the Hayden geological expedition in the 1870s declared the canyon inaccessible. Finally, in the winter of 1882-83, a railroad survey crew explored the length of the canyon, climbing down each morning and back out in the afternoon. Within a month, half of the crew had quit. The rest soldiered on, finishing after 68 days. Not until 1901, 32 years after Maj. John Wesley Powell's

**Stone and log barn, near Crawford**

historic trip through the Grand Canyon of the Colorado, did a party of two men make it all the way through the Black Canyon by raft.

The early 20th-century explorations showed that the Gunnison's power could be tapped. Farther upriver, to the east, windsurfers and sailboats now glide among rough-hewn mesas and canyons, thanks to three dams that hold water for irrigation and hydroelectric power. **Blue Mesa Reservoir,** the largest of the three lakes, makes an impressive if unexpected sight up in canyon country, its tentacles groping into erstwhile washes and creeks. There are plenty of hiking trails, camping sites, boat tours, and water sports to enjoy here; the winter brings ice fishermen and snowmobilers to the lake. On a pair of cross-country skis you can share the quieter side-pockets of the lake area with the elk and bighorn sheep that come down from the mountains during the cold weather.

To the north spread the alpine timberlands of Gunnison National Forest, home of more than 20 peaks that top 13,000 feet. You can make a fun auto loop if you take Colo. 135 north from Gunnison to Crested Butte, then follow an unpaved road west over Kebler Pass (*closed in winter*) and down to Colo. 133. From there you can return via Colo. 92 and US 50. Hunkering in the lee of its namesake peak, the funky little town of Crested Butte started in the 1880s as a coal-mining camp. Stroll the few blocks of downtown along Elk Avenue, a main street of saloons, cafés, and laid-back art galleries. Weathered wooden buildings with metal roofs, many of them from the 19th century, lend the town a never-say-die rusticity. While the mining era died out in the 1940s, downhill skiing has turned the area into a small boomtown. Condos and chalets cluster a few miles up the road, at the foot of the mountain. The locals are determined to keep the town of Crested Butte from becoming another chic Aspen. So far they have succeeded.

The road over Kebler Pass is unpaved, but it is not especially cruel on two-wheel-drive cars. A gradual ascent to the 9,980-foot summit allows visitors to take in pleasant views of alpine meadows, gorgeous stands of aspen and spruce, and the snowy crags of mountains that thrust up several thousand feet above the road. If you turn north on Colo. 133 you can explore Redstone, a village that was built at the turn of the century by industrialist John Cleveland Osgood. Its main purpose was to extract the area's coal. The little town's one road is now chockablock with B&Bs, cafés, and shops selling ice cream, jewelry, and antler art. The 35-room, red-roofed **Redstone Inn** was built to house bachelor miners; Osgood's mansion, Redstone Castle, is now a bed-and-breakfast.

A worthwhile side trip will take you up the Crystal River to the town of Marble, where high-quality marble was quarried for use in the Lincoln Memorial, in Washington, D.C. The ruins of a marble mill stand on the bank of the river, and huge slabs of the precious white stone lie scattered amid the weeds.

*—John M. Thompson*

# Travel Notes

### Directions
This area is in west-central Colorado, near US 50 between Montrose and Gunnison. **By car:** From I-70 at Glenwood Springs, take Colo. 82, 133, and 92 south. **By plane:** The nearest airports are in Montrose and Gunnison. **By train:** Amtrak has service to Grand Junction and Glenwood Springs.

### General Information
The climate features much sun and little humidity; expect -5°F to 30°F in January, and 35°F to 85°F in July. Contact the Black Canyon of the Gunnison National Monument (*P.O. Box 1648, Montrose 81402. 970-641-2337 or 970-249-1915*); Montrose Chamber of Commerce (*1519 E. Main St., Montrose 81401. 970-249-5000 or 800-923-5515*); Gunnison Chamber of Commerce (*P.O. Box 36, Gunnison 81230. 970-641-1501 or 800-274-7580*); or the Crested Butte Chamber of Commerce (*P.O. Box 1288, Crested Butte 81224. 970-349-6438 or 800-545-4505*).

### Things to See and Do
**1. Black Canyon of the Gunnison National Monument** (*14 miles NE of Montrose, via US 50 and Colo. 347. 970-641-2337* or *970-249-1915. Adm. fee*) The 20,766-acre monument holds the steepest 12 miles of the Gunnison River gorge. A rim drive on both sides offers bracing views. Free backcountry permits, available at the Visitor Center, are required for all inner-canyon activities.

**2. Montrose** The **Montrose Historical Museum,** in the old Denver & Rio Grande Depot (*21 N. Rio Grande Ave. 970-249-2085.*

**At the Glenwood Hot Springs Pool**

*Mid-May–Sept. Mon.-Sat.; adm. fee),* harbors farm machinery, a homesteader's cabin, a country store, and Indian artifacts.

**3. Ute Indian Museum** *(4 miles S of Montrose, on US 550. 970-249-3098. May-Oct. daily, Nov.-April Thurs.-Mon.; adm. fee)* On the farmsite of Chief Ouray, this facility has dioramas, a medicinal garden, and exhibits on the Ute and early explorers. Ouray's wife is buried on the grounds.

**4. Curecanti National Recreation Area** *(Along US 50 bet. Montrose and Gunnison. 970-641-2337)* The area offers fishing, swimming, hiking, and camping *(fee).* Boat tours of Morrow Point Reservoir are available in summer *(970-641-2337).* The Cimarron Visitor Center *(20 miles E of Montrose. Mem. Day–Labor Day)* has an outdoor narrow-gauge railway display; a 1-mile drive from here takes you to the 469-foot-high Morrow Point Dam. Overlooks and information centers are located at the 20-mile-long **Blue Mesa Reservoir.**

**5. Gunnison** The **Pioneer Museum** *(US 50. 970-641-4530. Mem. Day–Labor Day Mon.-Sat.; adm. fee)* has antique cars, a narrow-gauge train, and farm tools.

**6. Glenwood Springs** *(Chamber of Commerce 970-945-6589)* Bathers at the **Glenwood Hot Springs Pool** *(I-70 and Grand Ave. 970-945-6571. Adm. fee)* soak in two tremendous mineral hot springs pools. A water slide, athletic club, and restaurant round out the offerings. At **Yampah Spa Vapor Caves** *(709 E. 6th St. 970-945-0667. Adm. fee)* natural geothermal steam baths heated by a 125°F mineral spring have been used by area inhabitants for centuries. Guests sit on marble benches in dimly lit grottoes; massages and other spa treatments are available.

### Other Activities

**Rafting** Among companies running trips on the Gunnison are Gunnison River Expeditions *(Montrose. 970-249-4441)* and Three Rivers Outfitting and Rafting *(Almont. 970-641-1303).*

### Annual Events

**June** Strawberry Days *(Glenwood Springs. 970-945-6589)*

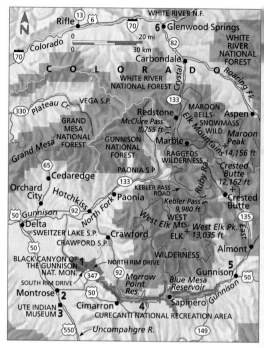

**July** Cattlemen's Days *(Gunnison. 970-641-1501)*

**August** Black Canyon Horse and Mule Race Meet *(Montrose. 970-249-5000)*

**September** Native American Lifeways *(Ute Indian Museum, Montrose. 970-249-5000)*

### Lodging

**Cristiana Guesthaus** *(621 Maroon Ave., Crested Butte. 970-349-5326 or 800-824-7899)* This European-style inn features a hearty continental breakfast served fireside; an outdoor hot tub and sauna soothe sore muscles.

**Elk Mountain Lodge** *(2nd and Gothic Sts., Crested Butte. 970-349-7533 or 800-374-6521)* Dating from 1919, the 3-story lodge offers 19 rooms with full breakfast and indoor hot tub.

**Hotel Colorado** *(526 Pine St., Glenwood Springs. 970-945-6511 or 800-544-3998)* Host to presidents, socialites, and gangsters, this imposing Italianate hotel opened in 1893 opposite the renowned hot springs. Twin campaniles and a piazza grace the exterior; guest rooms are furnished with antiques.

**Redstone Inn** *(82 Redstone Blvd., Redstone. 970-963-2526)* This 1901 Swiss-style inn has swimming, tennis, elegant dining, and cross-country skiing.

## UTAH

# Uinta Basin and South

Utah is not all slickrock canyons and empty desert. Up in the northeast corner of the state, the Strawberry and Duchesne Rivers thread fertile valleys lush with alfalfa and rolling ranchlands, and towns such as Roosevelt and Duchesne wave the banner of small town cheer. Land of pioneers, Native Americans, and outlaws, this is the Uinta Basin, drained by the Green River to the east and walled by the rugged Uinta Mountains on the north. Harboring Utah's highest peaks, the Uintas rank as the largest east-west range in the contiguous United States. The largest designated wilderness in the state lies within that formidable range. Elsewhere in the area are an Indian reservation, two national forests, a lakeside state park, and a little-known canyon marked with thousands of ancient petroglyphs and pictographs.

**Storm clouds over Nine-Mile Canyon**

**A hunter's mural, Fremont Culture petroglyphs, at Nine-Mile Canyon**

President Abraham Lincoln proclaimed the western two-thirds of the Uinta Basin an Indian reservation in 1861, and for about 40 years a few hundred Native Americans inhabited the vast area. Then, Theodore Roosevelt reversed Lincoln and opened up parts of the reservation to homesteaders. According to some writers, a Ute elder commented: "When the Americans came, they came by the many manys, they came nose to tail like a string of black ants crossing the sand."

But most of them moved on through, leaving the area the quiet corner it remains today. In its northern reaches, the **High Uintas Wilderness Area** beckons with 460,000 acres of solitude and untamed beauty. Trails for hiking and horseback riding ascend from river valleys lined by willow and aspen through forests thick with spruce, fir, and lodgepole pine. Lakes and ponds, brimming with trout, lie like hidden treasures in the higher elevations, while above the 10,000-foot tree line hulking masses of gray-brown rock jut 1,000 feet above alpine meadows. The beauty here is more rough-hewn than in some alpine landscapes; it is more about brute strength than well-worn refinement. The forces of mountain building are new, raw, and very evident—you may even hear the thunderclap of landslides when huge blocks of quartzite and sandstone topple onto the talus slopes below.

Down among the gentle valleys around Roosevelt and Duchesne, rippled hills stubbled with sage and rabbitbrush seem draped in velour. Though Roosevelt—named for the president who opened the area to white settlement—has been hurt by the recent closure of its oil refinery, it remains a prosperous little agricultural community. While tourism promotion is on the rise, it remains low-key in these parts, with most efforts geared toward serious outdoorsmen and visitors interested in Indian culture. Near Duchesne is the handsome **Starvation State Park**, a haven for campers and boaters. Situated on the 3,310-acre Starvation Reservoir, the park extends its watery arms into the pinyon-and-juniper-studded hills. Some people fish here, but you'll have better luck at the **Strawberry Reservoir** to the west. One of the country's first reclamation reservoirs, the 17,160-acre sheet of water dates from 1906 and offers some of the finest trout fishing in the West.

On the southern edge of the Uinta Basin, the land becomes redder and rockier with pinyons and junipers spreading across the high desert bluffs and canyon ledges. Down in this hidden pocket, prehistoric Indians found an area perfect for year-round hunting and home building. **Nine-Mile Canyon**, with its yellow-and-brown valley and its high rock ledges, was home to early Native Americans for thousands of years. They must have found the living good, because they took time to mark the sandstone walls with so many petroglyphs and pictographs that the canyon has one of the highest concentrations of rock-art sites in the United States. A dirt road winds deep into the backcountry—you'll need about a day to really explore it. But when you come across an animal or a mysterious figure etched in stone, you are rewarded with a feeling of discovery. Sure, most of the art has been seen before, but not by many people. Bring water and food and a tankful of gas, because there are no services along the 78 miles from Wellington to Myton. And bring a good sense of adventure—that's what this area is all about.

—*John M. Thompson*

### Indian Exodus

Why were the ancestral Pueblo all gone from Utah by A.D. 1300? At least five theories have been put forward. Tree-ring analysis suggests they left during a prolonged drought; other studies point to war, disease, crowding, and religion. Like the interpretation of their rock inscriptions and paintings, the true answer is that no one knows for sure. Where the mysterious people ended up is more certain: Modern Pueblo, Zuni, and Hopi on the mesas of Arizona and New Mexico claim descent from the ancestral Pueblo, or Old Ones.

# Travel Notes

### Directions
About 100 miles east of Salt Lake City, the area is bounded by the Uinta Mountains and the Green River. **By car:** Take I-80 E and US 40 south from Salt Lake City. **By plane:** The closest airport is in Salt Lake City. **By train:** Amtrak has service to Helper.

### General Information
Spring and fall are best for visits; temperatures reach 100°F in summer and dip below zero in winter. Contact Ashley National Forest *(355 N. Vernal Ave., Vernal 84078. 435-789-1181)*; Wasatch-Cache National Forest *(8236 Federal Bldg., 125 S. State St., Salt Lake City 84138. 801-524-5030)*; Duchesne County Area Chamber of Commerce *(50 E. 200 South St., P.O. Box 1417, Roosevelt 84066. 435-722-4598)*; Castle County Travel Bureau *(90 N. 100 East St., P.O. Box 1037, Price 84501. 435-637-3009).*

### Things to See and Do
**1. High Uintas Wilderness Area** *(E of Utah 150. Duchesne Ranger Dist. 435-738-2482)* Hike, go horseback riding, or fish for trout in 460,000 acres of alpine landscapes.

**2. Strawberry Reservoir** *(S of US 40, about 40 miles W of Duchesne. Heber Ranger Dist. 801-654-0470)* The lake offers excellent trout fishing.

**3. Starvation State Park** *(4 miles W of Duchesne, on Old Hwy. 40. 435-738-2326. Adm. fee May-Oct.)* A 3,500-acre park offers boating, picnicking, and lakeside camping *(summer only).*

**4. Helper** Exhibits at the **Western Mining and Railroad Museum** *(296 S. Main St. 435-472-3009. May-Sept. Mon.-Sat., Oct.-April Tues.-Sat.; donation)* include historical photographs, videos, and mining equipment.

**5. Nine-Mile Canyon** *(12 miles NE of Wellington)* See thousands of examples of Native American rock art. Call the Castle County Travel Bureau for self-guided tour booklets.

### Lodging
**U Bar Wilderness Ranch** *(N of Neola, end of Uinta Canyon Rd. 435-645-7256 or 800-303-7256)* The ranch offers cabins, hearty meals, fishing, hunting, and packhorse adventures.

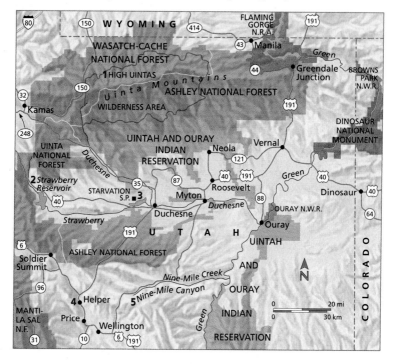

# Grand Staircase-Escalante National Monument

A sign at a Boulder Mountain overlook says that Connecticut or Luxembourg could fit into the space spread out below you. As far as the eye can see—100 miles or more on a clear day—are white cliffs and banded mesas. Set aside in September 1996, the new Grand Staircase-Escalante National Monument encompasses 1.7 million acres of sandstone canyons, gullied plateaus, and weird rock formations in the high desert of southern Utah. Here you can lose yourself in the presence of boundless blue skies, intense sunlight, and an immense silence broken only by faint breezes.

The size of this space is hard to grasp, even when you are staring in awe from Utah 12 on Boulder Mountain, nearly 9,500 feet up. A vast wilderness

**Reflection pool on an Escalante River tributary**

surrounded by yet more wild country, the **Grand Staircase-Escalante National Monument** extends from the Glen Canyon National Recreation Area and the Arizona border to **Bryce Canyon National Park** and Dixie National Forest. After Death Valley and Yellowstone, it is larger than any other park or monument in the contiguous United States.

The name of the monument derives from two major geologic features— a series of sandstone plateaus that rise more than 5,000 feet from the Colorado River to Bryce Canyon, and the Escalante River, which runs from the town of Escalante to the Colorado. One of the last rivers in the United States to be explored, the Escalante was named for Friar Silvestre Vélez de Escalante, who passed through the area in 1776 after failing to find a route from Santa Fe to the Spanish missions in California (see sidebar p. 307). Coincidentally, Escalante derives from a word meaning "to climb up."

The rugged and unforgiving terrain was crossed by a cavalry detachment in 1866, then rediscovered in 1872 by a team sent by explorer John Wesley Powell. Team geologist Clarence Dutton wrote a description that still holds: "It is a maze of cliffs and terraces lined off with stratification, of crumbling buttes, red and white domes, rock platforms gashed with profound cañons, burning plains barren even of sage—all glowing with color and flooded

**Pariah River ghost town**

with blazing sunlight." Dutton was not altogether accurate, however, or perhaps 125 years have altered the landscape somewhat. In fact, there is sagebrush—lots of it—as well as gnarled junipers, pinyons, cactus, delicate wildflowers, and many other desert plants.

Today's explorers have a road to get them started. Snaking along the north edge of the monument, Utah 12 has been called one of the most scenic roads in the country. From Escalante to Boulder, it weaves along red-rock cliffs and through slickrock canyons, at times following a knife-ridge with sheer drop-offs and spectacular views on either side. Pull-offs give you a chance to savor the scenery and relax your white knuckles. The section of the road that crosses the forbidding Aquarius Plateau was not completed until 1940 and was paved only in 1971, thus allowing Boulder to make the claim that it was the last town in the United States to have mule train mail delivery. An even more recently completed stretch is Utah 12 from Boulder up to Torrey. It was paved in the mid-1980s and runs through an area every bit as gorgeous, high among the pine and aspen forests on Boulder Mountain. This section makes a particularly vivid impression in autumn when the aspens turn gold and shimmer in the wind.

Beyond this main corridor are several smaller roads, most of them dirt and gravel, some suitable only for four-wheel-drive or high-clearance vehicles. The roads peter out to foot trails, and the trails eventually give out, leaving you an explorer in a potentially dangerous area. Names such as Carcass Canyon and Little Death Hollow are powerful reminders that nature is still sovereign here. Heed the warnings and check on road and weather conditions before you set out. Some roads are impassable when wet. In addition, summer flash floods can make instant rivers out of dry washes and arroyos, pouring across the roads and leaving you stranded (see sidebar p. 308). That said, try to get out at least a short distance into the backcountry to experience the kind of splendid isolation for which the monument was established.

A wonderful road missed by most visitors, the Burr Trail Road heads southeast from the town of Boulder through some of the most magnificent countryside in the entire Southwest. If it were designated a scenic drive in a national park, the road would be a stream of traffic. But only a small sign marks the entrance, so you may have the whole road to yourself. The first

### Domínguez-Escalante Expedition

While the American Revolution was going on back East, two Franciscan missionaries, Friars Francisco Atanasio Domínguez and Silvestre Vélez de Escalante, set out on a bold journey. They had intended to go from Santa Fe to California, but the winter of 1776-77 forced them to loop south by way of the Grand Canyon. A persistent problem for the ten-man outfit was food and water. On at least one occasion they had to eat one of their horses; locals gave them little more than pine nuts, grass seeds, and cactus fruit. But they all survived, making it back home after five months on the trail.

30 miles are paved, the road twisting through a canyon so narrow that the sky is just a wedge of blue way up between the walls. The landscape becomes a giant's palace with huge pillars, temple gates, and archways, and drivers find it impossible to resist motoring on to see what lies around the next bend. Be sure to watch the road, too; piles of fallen rock are common. Beyond the monument are 6 miles of unpaved road crossing **Capitol Reef National Park,** then another 15 miles to Glen Canyon National Recreation Area. Just inside the park you find yourself wrapped in limitless scenery, with magnificent views of Capitol Reef's **Waterpocket Fold,** the Circle Cliffs, and the Henry Mountains far beyond. Plateaus extend for miles and miles, like continental shelves, before dropping off into a sea of canyons. Tilted buttes with crewcuts of red rock thrust skyward, while distant thunderstorms angle down on the horizon.

Hiking trails stem from many of the roads. Off the Burr Trail Road, the Deer Creek Trailhead becomes a scramble around rock tunnels and side canyons within a mile or so. You cross cascading pools good for sore feet and skirt high rock slopes that scratch against the sky. If you have a couple of days, you can follow the canyon all the way to the Escalante River. A more sociable and easy walk, the **Calf Creek Trail** makes a gentle climb through a desert and riparian ecosystem and ends at a 126-foot-high waterfall. The water cascades down a mineral-streaked wall of Navaho sandstone to a cool, misty pool popular with swimmers. The 5.5-mile round-trip hike also passes a striking example of Fremont rock art, the large paintings still bright red after 1,000 years.

## Flash Floods

From late summer to early fall is prime time for flash floods in canyon country, but they can occur at any time. Making a sound like a jet engine, a wall of water and mud as much as 15 feet high suddenly hurtles down a previously dry wash. When you are driving or hiking in narrow canyons, pay attention to the weather and check the forecast. If rain starts to fall, move to higher ground or begin hiking out—a little extra caution could save your life.

Another good hike lies off the Cottonwood Canyon Road in **Kodachrome Basin State Park.** Named by the National Geographic Society in 1949, the park switched its name to Chimney Rock in 1962 to avoid a lawsuit. But, recognizing a promotional opportunity, Kodak gave permission to use the trademark name. The arches, spires, and sandpipes of ocher and sienna shot through with rusty red make this area look like a miniature Bryce Canyon. Yellowstone-type geysers were once active here, but over time they clogged with sediment, solidified, and eroded into the shapes you see today. Formations bear such fanciful names as Ballerina Spire and Mama Bear.

Beyond Kodachrome, Cottonwood Canyon Road becomes a graded, dry-weather road—in other words, it turns to mud in the rain. If the weather is good, it's well worth the 10-mile drive down to Grosvenor Arch, a rare double-arch formation standing out against a big sky. And the drive through the canyon is a photographer's joy.

Escalante and Boulder are the area's main towns, both of them small and friendly and not yet overrun with tourist development. Escalante was known as Potato Valley in 1875, for the native tubers. Early Mormon settlers came here looking for a gentle climate to grow their vegetables, fruits, and black walnuts. Having no American flag to celebrate July 4, 1876, locals raised a striped Navaho blanket and christened the town in honor of the 1776 journey of Friar

**Evening primrose**

Escalante. Ma-and-pa motels, cafés, a grocery store, and rock shops line the wide, four-block Main Street. Boulder claims a total population of 100. Locals, however, forecast a bigger Boulder, and not everyone is pleased. While the creation of the monument opened a large potential market in tourism, it spelled a sudden curtailment of grazing and mining permits. At any rate, the area will not be the same in a few years. Eat a meal in one of the cafés and catch the latest buzz on the monument.

*—John M. Thompson*

# Travel Notes

### Directions
The area lies east of Bryce Canyon National Park and west of Glen Canyon N.R.A., in southern Utah. **By car:** Utah 12, the monument's main road, is accessible via I-70 and Utah 72, or via I-15 and US 89. **By plane:** The closest airports are in Cedar City and St. George; and in Page, Arizona.

### General Information
Spring and fall are the most moderate seasons. Summer temperatures can top 100°F, though the nights often cool to 60°F or below. Late summer brings frequent thunderstorms. Winter snowfall is light; humidity is low. Contact Escalante Interagency Office *(755 W. Main St., P.O. Box 246, Escalante 84726. 435-826-5499)*. There are no services in the monument backcountry. Always bring food, water, a full tank of gas, and emergency supplies.

### Things to See and Do
**1. Grand Staircase-Escalante National Monument** *(Off Utah 12. Escalante Interagency Office 435-826-5499)* Follow Utah 12 for a scenic drive through this vast wilderness, or you can hike any of several trails.

**2. Capitol Reef National Park** *(Visitor Center, Utah 24, Fruita. 435-425-3791. Entrance fee)* White rock domes, red ridges, and hidden canyons cluster along a 100-mile-long buckle in the earth called the Waterpocket Fold.

**Negotiating a slickrock slot canyon**

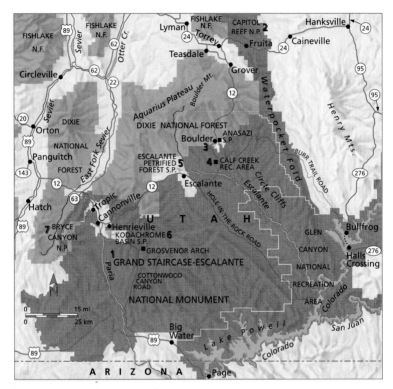

**3. Boulder** (*Escalante Chamber of Commerce 435-826-4810*) A short trail in **Anasazi State Park** (*460 N. Utah 12. 435-335-7308. Adm. fee*) winds around the excavation of a 900-year-old Indian village and a 6-room pueblo replica. The museum contains artifacts excavated on-site.

**4. Calf Creek Recreation Area** (*15 miles E of Escalante, on Utah 12. 435-826-5499. Parking fee*) A 5.5-mile round-trip nature hike goes to lovely Lower Calf Creek Falls; picnicking and camping facilities are available.

**5. Escalante Petrified Forest State Park** (*2 miles W of Escalante, off Utah 12. 435-826-4466. Adm. fee*) A 1-mile nature trail loops around a hillside littered with petrified wood.

**6. Kodachrome Basin State Park** (*8 miles SE of Cannonville, on Cottonwood Canyon Rd. 435-679-8562. Adm. fee*) The 2,241-acre park preserves sandstone spires and petrified geysers. Some 9 miles of trails explore the area.

**7. Bryce Canyon National Park** (*Visitor Center, Utah 63, W of Tropic. 435-834-5322. Adm. fee*) Eroded pillars of sandstone form castles, fins, and spires. A 34-mile (round-trip) scenic drive along the canyon rim reaches 9,115

feet in elevation and offers spectacular views; 61 miles of hiking trails explore the canyon.

**Other Activities**

**Guided tours** Escalante Canyon Outfitters (*Boulder. 435-335-7311 or 800-326-4453*) offers four- to six-day horse-supplied walking treks into the backcountry. Rainbow Country Tours (*Escalante. 435-826-4567 or 800-252-8824*) leads hikes and full- and half-day off-road tours.

**Annual Events**

**June** Annual Wide Hollow Fishing Derby (*Escalante. 435-826-5499*)
**July** Pioneer Days (*Escalante. 435-826-4810*)

**Lodging**

**Boulder Mountain Lodge** (*Utah 12 and Burr Trail Rd., Boulder. 435-335-7460 or 800-556-3446*) Nestled beside a wetland bird sanctuary, this elegant new lodge has 20 guest rooms with tasteful furnishings.
**Pine Shadows** (*195 West 125 South, Teasdale. 435-425-3939 or 800-708-1223*) This new facility offers six clean, comfortable bungalows with kitchenettes and mountain views.

# NEW MEXICO
# Pueblo Country

As you drive the Ancient Way or walk the dusty roads of Acoma and other pueblos, you notice a stillness as big as the land itself. Looking out across ancient lava flows, you can see the Continental Divide and the Zuni Mountains, where ragged clouds gather like smoke signals, taking on the pink hue of the valley floor. Ravens glide like black arrows against the unbelievably blue sky. On the high mesas, the air is thin, the sun intense, the sky very close.

**Mission of the Pueblo of Laguna**

The pueblo country south of I-40 between Albuquerque and the Arizona border does not startle you with its beauty. Instead, the high desert and its scattered mesas offer a subtly changing scene of tones and shadows, while the brown and white adobe buildings of centuries-old Indian villages cut neat patterns against the bright blue sky.

Ultimately it is the cultural presence, interwoven with the land, that becomes the guiding spirit when you are traveling along the back roads, through the pueblos, by the hidden lakes, and across the two national monuments. Subtle but always felt, dwarfed by the scenery but a part of it, the Indian communities are nearly as integral to this ancient landscape as the flat-topped mesas pushing against the sky.

### Navajo Train

Looking for a quick and easy way to see the pueblo country? Sit back and let Amtrak take you across the countryside, with an added feature: The train from Albuquerque to Gallup carries Navajo guides who interpret area history and culture. The *Southwest Chief* leaves daily at 5:15 p.m. for the two-hour, 20-minute trek; call 800-872-7245.

Both Zuni and Acoma claim to be the oldest continually inhabited settlement in the country; both are nearly a thousand years old. The Zuni and Acomites had been enjoying a settled, agricultural lifestyle for several centuries when the Spanish came looking for the Seven Cities of Cibola in 1539. Perhaps tricked by the play of sunlight on adobe walls, scouts spread reports of cities made of gold, and the following year Francisco de Coronado led an expedition to see for himself. He found only mud walls and, after killing a few Indians, returned to Mexico City. But the Spanish persisted. Within the next hundred years, pueblos all along the Rio Grande had mission churches.

In today's village of **Zuni**—one of New Mexico's largest pueblo communities—smoke rises from adobe ovens, roosters crow, old dogs lie sleeping on dirt lanes, and multistoried dwellings of board and cinder block bear the look of Third World resourcefulness. In the hot sun, few people are out and about; they are cordial but reserved. Near the plaza is **Our Lady of Guadalupe of Zuni,** the 1629 brown adobe church with stark bell and cross; it was wrecked during the Pueblo Revolt of 1680. The Spanish had tried to force Christianity and obedience on the Zuni and other pueblo people, punishing the recalcitrant ones by burning their kivas (ceremonial pits), beating them, and hanging them. The Indians finally orchestrated a rebellion, killed hundreds of Spaniards, routed them, and remained free for 12 years. No other North American Indians were as successful against European encroachment.

The Zuni mission, a casualty of the rebellion, has been undergoing restoration since the 1960s, and if you are lucky you may get to look inside. Spectacular 50-foot murals present a colorful procession of life-size kachinas—deified ancestral spirits believed to visit the pueblos and bring them luck. Their presence is an affirmation of the Indians' ability to blend both old and new traditions. A family of local artists keeps the work going despite lack of funding. If the church is closed, you can visit the village museum and adjacent arts-and-crafts shop, which sells turquoise and shell jewelry and carved animal fetishes. You may also go to the tribal headquarters for permission to drive the 10-mile dirt road south to the ruins of Hawikuh, the village visited by Coronado.

The nearby pueblo of **Acoma** has a similar history of dominance by the Spanish, a rebellion, and a gradual acceptance of Catholicism. But three things immediately strike the visitor as different from Zuni: The setting is more spectacular, the church was never destroyed, and Acoma attracts more tourists. Called Sky City, Acoma began around A.D. 1150 on a well-protected mesa 367 feet above a valley. The approach to the pueblo on Indian Rd. 38 makes a steady climb and tops out at an overlook of the valley and mesa. Down at the Visitor Center and museum you board a bus that takes you and a small group up to the mesa for an informative one-hour walking tour. The **San Esteban del Rey Mission** dates from 1629, its simple white walls and hard-packed dirt floor adding eloquence to a spacious interior. Walking about, you see Acoma women selling painted

**Inscription Rock, El Morro National Monument**

pottery and fry-bread while chatting to each other in the native Keresan. If the pueblo seems strangely quiet, it's because only about 30 people still live on the mesa (which has no plumbing or electricity); the other Acomites live elsewhere on the reservation.

To the north, Laguna Pueblo stands on a hill above the interstate, its squat houses and dusty roads uplifted by the presence of a blinding white mission church. Dating from 1699, the Mission of the Pueblo of Laguna was built with beams carried by Indians from the mountains 30 miles away. On the ceiling above the altar, an unusual painting on animal skin represents the sun, moon, stars, and rainbow, surrounded by Christian symbols. As at Acoma, the people speak Keresan and make similar pottery.

## Camel Corps

When the U.S. Army was looking for a mode of desert travel superior to the water-guzzling mule and horse trains, they thought of camels. In the 1850s, the Army imported animals from Egypt and Turkey and began training in Texas. It was not long before a caravan of 41 camels came swinging through New Mexico, amazing the locals. The name of an expedition leader, P. Gilmer Breckinridge, can be seen among the carvings on Inscription Rock. The camel experiment was a great success, but the Civil War put a quick end to the Camel Corps. For years afterward, wild camels were reported from Mexico to Arkansas.

**Isleta** is another interesting pueblo. It lies south of Albuquerque, just off I-25, and is known by the Navajo as "tribe by the water" because it straddles the Rio Grande. Most of Isleta's people now work in the city, but some still farm the fertile bottomlands. They also produce fine pottery, jewelry, woven belts, and embroidery work. The Mission of San Agustin de Isleta, built in 1613 by Fray Juan de Salas, was burned down during the Pueblo Revolution and restored after the 1692 reconquest. It now has a decidedly modern interior with a clean carpet, stained-glass windows, and oil paintings. Outside, yellow school buses pass through the plaza, a reminder of Isleta's ties to the big city. All around the mission, though, is a 19th-century town of low-slung adobe buildings and dirt roads. An Isleta legend honors the long past: "After we emerged, the world was flat and life was too easy. We soon forgot about our makers. So they created the mountains, mesas and valleys to make us humble and make us repentant. That is what our fathers tell us."

Before there were Indians, the land was playing out its own drama. Over some three million years, volcanoes covered the area with hot rivers of rock and clouds of ash. About 3,000 years ago, lava was reshaping the landscape yet again. From high points in **El Malpais National Monument and National Conservation Area,** you can see remnants of at least a dozen of the area's more than 20 volcanoes, some now overgrown with pines and aspens. The monument holds miles of trails along the badlands created by lava flows, and you can behold spatter cones and lava tubes, one of them 17 miles in length. On the monument's east side rises La Ventana, a freestanding sandstone arch, the largest such formation in the state.

The **Ice Cave and Bandera Volcano** offers a close-up look into a volcanic crater about 1,200 feet wide and 750 feet deep; a short trail winds through an otherworldly landscape of pumice and 500-year-old trees to a small cave that has been floored with ice for more than 3,000 years.

Today we frown upon leaving our mark on the natural landscape, but for centuries wayfarers who passed the white sandstone bluff called El Morro left so much graffiti that it became known as Inscription Rock. **El Morro National Monument** preserves the bluff and ruins that were vacated in 1375 by people who had carved a gallery of animals and geometric designs into the cliffs. By the late 1500s, Spanish expeditions had found the site while following the old trade route called the Ancient Way (roughly paralleled by N. Mex. 53). New Mexico's first governor, Don Juan de Oñate, carved his name on the rock in 1605, and after that, scores of travelers did the same. The carvings at El Morro date from before 1906, the year it became a national monument. If you can walk 2 miles at 7,200 feet elevation, take the trail that loops 200 feet higher to the top of the rock. The badlands, the sky, the colorful sandstone, the quiet, and the wildflowers bending in the breeze conspire to create a landscape that still looks young.

*—John M. Thompson*

# Travel Notes

### Directions
Located in northwest New Mexico, the area encompasses the 150 miles between Albuquerque and Gallup. **By car:** Most points of interest lie south of I-40. **By plane:** The closest airports are in Albuquerque and Gallup. **By train:** Amtrak has service to Albuquerque and Gallup.

### General Information
The area is mostly high and dry, with summer temperatures reaching the upper 80s and winter lows dipping below freezing. Spring and fall are delightful. The best sources of information are the Gallup Convention & Visitors Bureau *(701 Montoya Blvd., Gallup 87301. 505-863-3841 or 800-242-4282)*; Grants/Cibola County Chamber of Commerce *(100 Iron Ave., Grants 87020. 505-287-4802 or 800-748-2142)*; and the Albuquerque Convention & Visitors Bureau *(20 First Plaza N.W., Suite 20, Albuquerque 87102. 505-842-9918 or 800-733-9918)*.

### Things to See and Do
**1. Red Rock State Park** *(8 miles E of Gallup, off I-40. 505-722-3839)* A 640-acre parcel of red sandstone cliffs and canyons features a museum with exhibits on Southwestern Indians, a rodeo arena, and hiking trails to the cathedral-shaped Church Rock.
**2. Zuni Pueblo** *(37 miles S of Gallup, via N. Mex. 602 and 53. 505-782-4481)* Though visitors may no longer view the masked dances, you can still wander the pueblo, see

**Acoma potters**

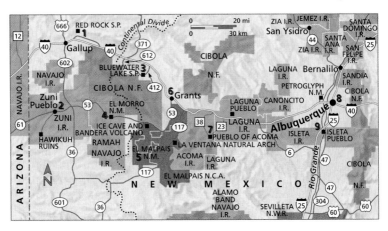

the museum and mission church, and buy gifts. (You must obtain permission to take pictures at the tribal offices on Main St.)

**3. Bluewater Lake State Park** (28 miles W of Grants via I-40 and N. Mex. 412. 505-876-2391. Adm. fee) On the north flank of the Zuni Mountains, this 2,105-acre park offers fishing, boat rentals, hiking trails, and camping.

**4. El Morro National Monument** (43 miles SW of Grants, via N. Mex. 53. 505-783-4226. Adm. fee) The 1,278-acre monument preserves Inscription Rock, a 200-foot-tall sandstone bluff that bears ancient petroglyphs as well as signatures from early 17th-century Spanish explorers and later travelers. Two trails take in the sights.

**5. El Malpais National Monument and National Conservation Area** (S of I-40, via N. Mex. 53 or N. Mex. 117. 505-285-4641) Some 376,000 acres of volcanic badlands include lava tubes, spatter cones, mesas, and sandstone arches. Hiking trails explore lava tube caves, some of which have collapsed. Visit the **Ice Cave and Bandera Volcano** (30 miles S of I-40, on N. Mex. 53. 505-783-4303. Adm. fee). Short trails lead to a cave rimed with ice and to a crater some 10,000 years old.

**6. Grants** An excellent little museum, the **New Mexico Museum of Mining** (Santa Fe and Iron Aves. 505-287-4802 or 800-748-2142. Adm. fee) limns the history of uranium mining in the area; an elevator descends to a realistic model of a uranium mine.

**7. Pueblo of Acoma** (13 miles S of I-40 via Cty. Rd. 23, or 15 miles S of I-40 via Indian Rd. 38. 505-470-4966 or 800-747-0181. Adm. and photography fees) One of the oldest settlements in the country, this sky-high pueblo resisted the 16th-century Spanish for nearly

100 years. Indian labor was used to build the **San Esteban del Rey Mission.** Access to the mesa-top is by guided one-hour tour only.

**8. Albuquerque** (Convention & Visitors Bureau 505-842-9918 or 800-733-9918) Visit the **Indian Pueblo Cultural Center** (1 block N of I-40, at 2401 12th St. N.W. 505-843-7270 or 800-766-4405. Adm. fee) to see a museum that outlines the history and culture of the state's 19 pueblos. On the city's outskirts is **Petroglyph National Monument** (3 miles N of I-40. Visitor Center, 4735 Unser Blvd. N.W. 505-899-0205. Adm. fee). The new park preserves about 17,000 petroglyphs, most carved between A.D. 1300 and 1650.

**9. Isleta Pueblo** (17 miles S of Albuquerque via I-25 and N. Mex. 47. 505-869-3111) People here speak a southern Tiwa language.

### Annual Events

**May** La Fiesta de Colores (Grants. 800-748-2142)

**August** Gallup Inter-Tribal Indian Ceremonial (Red Rock S.P. 505-863-3896 or 800-233-4528); Zuni Tribal Fair and Arts and Crafts Expo (505-782-4481)

**September** Harvest Dance and Annual Feast of San Estevan (Acoma. 505-252-1139); Festival of San Jose de Los Lagunas (Laguna. 505-552-6654)

### Lodging

**El Rancho Hotel and Motel** (1000 E. 66 Ave., Gallup. 505-863-9311 or 800-543-6351) This historic Spanish Colonial-style property is located on old Route 66. Hollywood film crews and movie stars galore stayed here from the 1930s to '60s; their photographs line the building's walls.

# ARIZONA

# Arizona Strip

Miles and miles of trackless desert and rangeland, unencumbered by signs of civilization, roll ever onward to the plateaus and peaks of the far horizons. The few dirt roads that crisscross this vast acreage are as noteworthy as stray threads on a carpet. The land is what matters here. Welcome to the Arizona Strip, an American outback, the no-man's land between the Grand Canyon and Utah. Harboring more than 8,000 square miles, the northwest corner of Arizona is home to a few thousand souls, nearly all of whom live in Fredonia or Colorado City. The rest of the land lies open like a lonely frontier, with one scenic highway nipping along the eastern portion through a luminist landscape of cliffs and buttes, meadows and forested plateaus.

As far back as 10,000 B.C., people came here to hunt and gather. Ancestral Pueblo people appeared around the time of Christ and raised corn, beans,

**North Rim of the Grand Canyon**

and squash to supplement their diet of wild plants and game. Spanish friars Domínguez and Escalante became the first Europeans in the area in 1776 (see sidebar p. 307), but after their expedition not much changed for a hundred years. Then the Mormons began extending their reach from Utah to remote corners of the desert; they grazed their stock and set up tiny communities in the Strip. In 1893 the Grand Canyon Forest Reserve was established within the Strip's south and east portions, which became the **Kaibab National Forest** and **Grand Canyon National Park.**

As whites began to settle the area, they encountered the relatives of the Kaibab Paiute, who live today on the remote Kaibab Indian Reservation. Within the reservation, the stamp-size **Pipe Spring National Monument** preserves a spring that was highly valued by Native Americans and pioneers in the 1800s. If you climb the short nature trail on the hill behind the 1870s rock fort and ranch, you will see the kind of relentless terrain those early travelers faced. You can also appreciate the beauty of this little oasis. But from a modern pair of eyes, the view is all the other way—outward to a vast plain, to cloud shadows floating atop the baked mesas, to buzzards drifting in a steel blue sky, and to the Kaibab Plateau 50 miles away.

Beyond lies an early traveler's nightmare: the Grand Canyon. Of course, today people go out of their way to see it rather than avoid it. The canyon is just two hours away in the air-conditioned comfort of your car. If you're willing to sacrifice some comfort, you can head out across the barren width of the Arizona Strip on a 60-mile dirt road for a private view of the spectacular canyon. (The road is not marked, so be sure to ask for directions. Drive it only in dry weather; a high-clearance vehicle is recommended.) The drive crosses an uninhabited land of severe beauty and ends at Toroweap Overlook, a narrow twist of the canyon with sheer walls dropping nearly 3,000 feet. You could stack New York's two World Trade Center buildings atop each other here and still have room at the top. The view is down, hundreds of millions of years, into some of the earliest layers of rock in earth's history.

The colors of the Arizona Strip are of the earth and the sky—the purples and reds of the cliffs, the greens and yellow-browns of the scrub desert, the oranges and pinks and whites of the rocks, and the blues of the distant mountains. In the waning days of fall, the sun casts long shadows of the Kaibab Plateau out across the desert. Up in the cool forest of the plateau, quaking aspens flame bright yellow against the dark green backdrop of

### John Wesley Powell

When one-armed Civil War veteran John Wesley Powell led the first successful expedition down the Colorado River in 1869, he became an American hero and a lecture-circuit star. The river back then was an untamed demon that could easily devour the wooden boats of the day. But Powell was no mere guide: A dedicated geologist and ethnologist, the self-taught explorer learned the area from scratch, then put his skills to the test. His publications became the early standards of conservation literature.

**Indian paintbrush, Paria Canyon, Vermilion Cliffs Wilderness**

ponderosa pines. And in winter, 4 to 8 feet of snow blanket the high country. Though the road from the town of **Jacob Lake** to the North Rim of the Grand Canyon is closed in winter, you can stay overnight at the Jacob Lake Inn and experience a pristine wonderland on snowshoes or cross-country skis. If you don't care for the noise of snowmobiles, stay east of Ariz. 67 where they are not allowed.

The **Kaibab Plateau** is the highest of the five plateaus that make up the North Rim of the Grand Canyon. It tops 9,000 feet and collects a lot more wind and moisture than the lower areas of the Strip. If you take US 89A and Ariz. 67 south toward the North Rim, you'll be ascending the plateau. The zigzag route is slow, but you will have majestic views of the Strip area.

The **North Rim,** while no longer the secret it was several years ago, still attracts far fewer people than the canyon's South Rim and is the main reason for most excursions into the Arizona Strip. Of the nearly five million annual visitors to the Grand Canyon, only about 400,000 come to the North Rim. But its visitors are generally serious about the outdoors; they intend to get out and hike around and into the canyon. Views from this side are a little different: The canyon walls are higher and more dramatic. Walking along a short, paved trail from the **Grand Canyon Lodge** to Bright Angel Point gives you a dizzying feel for the canyon's depth and width. To get away from the people, try the delightful Widforss Trail, a 10-mile round-trip through a ponderosa forest to another overlook along the rim. You might spot a tufted-eared Kaibab squirrel, found only on the plateau, or a mule deer. In the early 1900s, hunters killed hundreds of mountain lions and nearly eliminated the area's wolves in a misguided effort to control predators of game species. The result: Within 20 years, the population of deer exploded; the deer stripped the plateau of its vegetation, then died of starvation by the thousands.

A newly reintroduced scavenger is back after about a 70-year hiatus. Nineteen California condors were released on the Vermilion Cliffs northeast of the Grand Canyon in 1996 and 1997. With wingspans of up to 9.5 feet, these rare raptors again soar the heights over the Arizona Strip. You may have a chance of seeing one along US 89A as you pass the 3,000-foot-high escarpment that glows pink and orange around the edges of the day.

In Marble Canyon, you can see how the Colorado River and thousands of years of erosion have separated the cliffs by more than 2 miles. Head to **Lees Ferry**, at the end of Marble Canyon Road, and watch expeditions gearing up to run the Colorado River. After waving goodbye to the river rafters, you will have the stark and lonely beauty of this desert outpost all to yourself.                                                   —*John M. Thompson*

# Travel Notes

### Directions
The isolated Arizona Strip is in the state's northwest corner, between the Grand Canyon and Utah. **By car:** It is more than 150 miles from Las Vegas and 120 miles from the South Rim of the Grand Canyon. From I-15 in St. George, Utah, take Utah 9 and 59 southeast to Colorado City. US 89A crosses the Strip's northeastern part, with access to the North Rim via Ariz. 67.
**By plane:** The nearest airports are in Page; Las Vegas, Nevada; and St. George, Utah. **By train:** Amtrak provides service to Flagstaff.

### General Information
The weather varies depending upon location, season, and time of day. On the high plateau, expect a heavy winter, late spring, and pleasant summer. On the lower desert areas, summer temperatures can rise above 100°F; nights are cooler. Contact Kaibab National Forest *(430 S. Main St., P.O. Box 248, Fredonia 86022. 520-643-7395)*; Grand Canyon National Park *(P.O. Box 129, Grand Canyon 86023. 520-638-7888)*; or Page-Lake Powell Chamber of Commerce *(644 N. Navajo Dr., Page 86040. 520-645-2741 or 888-261-7243)*.

**Blacksmith paraphernalia, Pipe Spring N.M.**

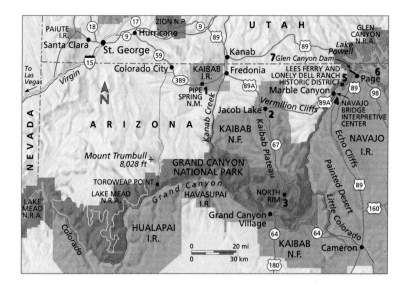

## Things to See and Do

**1. Pipe Spring National Monument**
*(14 miles W of Fredonia, on Ariz. 389. 520-643-7105. Adm. fee)* An 1870 fort and a re-created historic garden and orchard make this pioneer oasis a worthwhile stop. Admission includes guided tours of the fort and self-guided walking tours on the half-mile nature loop.

**2. Jacob Lake** At the **Kaibab Plateau Visitor Center** *(US 89A and Ariz. 67. 520-643-7298. April-Oct.),* you can pick up maps and information on the Kaibab National Forest.

**3. North Rim of the Grand Canyon**
*(S end of Ariz. 67, Grand Canyon N.P. 520-638-7888)* Walk out to spectacular views. Forest trails offer adventure and quiet time.

**4. Navajo Bridge Interpretive Center**
*(US 89A, Marble Canyon. 520-608-6404. Mid-May–mid-Oct.)* Now a pedestrian bridge beside the new highway bridge, the 1928 span runs 834 feet across the Colorado River.

**5. Lees Ferry and Lonely Dell Ranch Historic District** *(Lees Ferry Rd., 6 miles N of Marble Canyon, off US 89A. 520-608-6200)* These sites preserve the remnants of an 1870s river crossing. Tours of homestead dwellings and ferry buildings are self-guided.

**6. Page** Exhibits at the **John Wesley Powell Museum and Visitor Information Center** *(Lake Powell Blvd. and N. Navajo Dr. 520-645-9496. Mid-Feb.–mid-Dec.; call for hours)* outline area geology and history.

**7. Glen Canyon Dam** *(Just N of Page, off US 89, Glen Canyon N.R.A. 520-608-6404)*
Guided and self-guided tours take in the gargantuan dam that created Lake Powell.

## Other Activities

**River rafting** Wilderness River Adventures *(520-645-3279 or 800-528-6154)* runs float trips from Glen Canyon Dam to Lees Ferry *(March-Oct.).* Grand Canyon National Park *(520-638-2901)* will send you a list of some 20 concessioners running the rest of the river.

## Annual Events

**July** July 4th Fireworks Display *(Lake Powell. 520-645-2741)*
**December** Festival of Lights Boat Parade *(Lake Powell. 520-645-1001)*

## Lodging

**Grand Canyon Lodge** *(Ariz. 67, North Rim. 303-297-2757. Mid-May–mid-Oct.)* Perched on the edge of the canyon, this 1930s lodge has a high-ceilinged restaurant, a saloon, and large windows with sweeping views. There are 201 rooms and cabins.
**Jacob Lake Inn** *(Ariz. 67 and US 89A, Jacob Lake. 520-643-7232)* Simple cabins and motel rooms provide an alternative to the North Rim. Facilities include a dining room, gift shop, and gas station.
**Marble Canyon Lodge** *(US 89A, Marble Canyon. 520-355-2225 or 800-726-1789)* In the shadow of the Vermilion Cliffs, this full-service facility offers modern motel units and a rustic 1929 stone-and-log lodge.

# NEVADA
# Pony Express Territory

Pony Express riders who galloped through Nevada in the early 1860s, each carrying a revolver, a Bible, and a mailbag, couldn't slow down long enough to take in the silent grandeur of the basin-and-range country. But you can. Amid the "miles and miles of miles and miles" along US 50, you'll also discover Native American rock art, a sand mountain, fossils of fishlike dinosaurs, ruins of Pony Express stations, and scattered friendly towns such as Fallon and Austin.

You stand in terra incognita—mystery territory. It's sunset at **Grimes Point,** where 7,000 years ago unknown people pecked designs into basalt boulders on the desert. No one alive knows the meaning of the abstract patterns, although some people think that shamans may have made them to ensure good hunts or harvests. You bend down, touch a carved rock, and feel the presence of something ancient.

And then the silence shatters, as a low-flying military jet screams toward the naval air station at nearby **Fallon,** quickly catapulting you into the here and now. In only a few moments you've twice met the unexpected, and

**US 50 near Austin**

realized that this part of Nevada can be summed up in one word: Surprise! What's more surprising is that absolutely *nothing* is supposed to be happening out here! *Life* magazine once dubbed US 50 "the Loneliest Road in America." It runs through isolated country, a last stand of the Old West, where vast skies of pure light shine above stony mountains and broad valleys, where cattle wander on open range. Along this highway, you will not encounter traffic gridlock or shopping malls. But you will find plenty of elbow room and history.

The Pony Express route, later followed by Overland stagecoaches, parallels the highway. Near Sand Mountain you'll see the ruined stone walls of a **Pony Express station**, one of 157 relay stations used by the plucky service that delivered mail from St. Joseph, Missouri, to Sacramento, California, for $5 a half ounce (see sidebar). Life at the station and along the route was no picnic. British traveler Sir Richard Burton, who followed the Pony Express route in 1860, wrote in his diary that this station was "roofless and chairless, filthy and squalid...[with] the walls open to every wind and interior full of dust."

Today, Pony Express horses have been replaced by dune buggies as the steeds of choice. Off-roaders swarm over **Sand Mountain**, a 600-foot-high dune shaped from the windblown sand of an ancient inland sea—now called Lake Lahontan—whose waters covered this area about 10,000 years ago.

A locale that is much quieter and far more serene is the **Stillwater National Wildlife Refuge**. Each year, thousands of migrating birds swarm to this wetland area on the Pacific flyway. The refuge offers a temporary home to more than 200 species, including American white pelicans, swans, pintail and canvasback ducks, and white-faced ibises.

## Mail Service

The Pony Express lasted just 18 months—until the transcontinental telegraph put it out of business in October 1861—but that was long enough for its riders to make it into the history books. Brave young men galloped in relays almost 2,000 miles from Missouri to California to deliver the mail. They crossed the Nevada Territory, where 21 stations let them change horses and sometimes grab a bite, such as it was: Meals contained desert grit, and water had so much alkali that only a shot of vinegar could make it "drinkable."

Migratory motorists also can find a temporary home out this way, at the old mining town of **Austin**. They enjoy a friendly cup of java at Carol's Country Kitchen (which has been called "a combination yard sale and café") and see stone and brick buildings that include Nevada's oldest Catholic church (1866) and a Methodist church that was paid for through a mining stock scheme promoted by the minister. A hilltop stone "castle," built by a mining financier, gives a panoramic view of the Reese River Valley.

Austin sprang up in 1862 after an employee of the Overland Mail and Stage Company accidentally struck silver while looking for stray horses. Once Nevada's second largest city, with a population of more than 10,000,

Austin has dwindled to fewer than 300 people. Residents will happily tell you the tale of frontier store-keeper Reuel Gridley, who lost a bet and had to carry a 50-pound sack of flour clear across town. He auctioned it off—and kept auctioning it across the country until he'd raised $275,000 for the forerunner of the Red Cross. His 1860s Gridley Store still stands on Main Street.

South of Austin rises the Toiyabe Range, whose forests and streams offer plenty of opportunities for hiking, fishing, and camping; one 50-mile stretch never dips below 10,000 feet. Also down that way is **Berlin-Ichthyosaur State Park,** which preserves two bizarrely unrelated pieces of the past. The first are fossils of prehistoric "fish lizards" (ichthyosaurs). Up to 60 feet long, with eyes as big as auto hubcaps,

**Darkened cross against the sky**

these strange-looking creatures were deposited here, covered by mud, and petrified into fossildom. The second bit of history preserved at the park is a former 1890s boomtown: Berlin. It boasts a ruined mill, an assay office, and a hard-rock tunnel where you can still see ore carts and feel a tingle of the old gold fever when you spy the yellow metal glittering amid the quartz.

Berlin makes a nice place for visitors to rest a spell and contemplate the immense span of time that is revealed in this hidden corner of Nevada. Here you can step from the age of dinosaurs into the era of gold prospectors, all in just one spot. Surprise!

—*Jerry Camarillo Dunn, Jr.*

**Austin street scene**

# Travel Notes

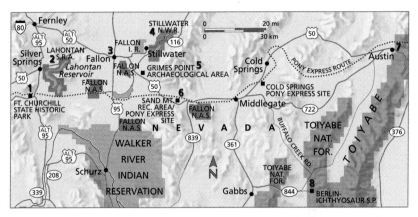

## Directions

This hidden corner lies in west-central Nevada and, in general, extends eastward from Fallon to Austin. **By car:** US 50 leads to or near most sites. **By air:** An airport is in Reno, the nearest large city. **By train:** Amtrak serves Reno.

## General Information

Visit the area year-round; spring and fall have the best weather. Contact the Nevada Commission on Tourism *(Capitol Complex, Carson City 89710. 800-NEVADA-8)*; Division of State Parks *(Capitol Complex, Carson City 89710. 702-687-4384)*; and the Austin Ranger District, Toiyabe National Forest *(100 Midas Canyon Rd., Austin 89310. 702-964-2671)*.

## Things to See and Do

**1. Fort Churchill State Historic Park** *(8 miles S of Silver Springs on US 95A. 702-577-2345. Adm. fee)* Nevada's first Army base (1860) guarded settlers from Indian raids and was a Pony Express stop. The park includes a Visitor Center and areas for picnics and camping.

**2. Lahontan State Recreation Area** *(18 miles W of Fallon on US 50. 702-867-3500. Adm. fee)* Popular for fishing, swimming, boating, picnics, and camping, Lahontan Reservoir has 72 miles of shoreline.

**3. Fallon** *(Tourism office 702-423-4556 or 800-874-0903)* The **Churchill County Museum** *(1050 S. Maine St. 702-423-3677. April-Dec. daily, Fri.-Wed. rest of year; donation)* has exhibits on Native Americans, the Pony Express, and pioneer life. Tours visit Hidden

Cave *(2nd and 4th Sat.)*, a storage cache for prehistoric migratory tribes.

**4. Stillwater National Wildlife Refuge** *(US 50 to Stillwater Rd., 20 miles N of Fallon. 702-423-5128)* This marshy area may be visited annually by 450,000 birds.

**5. Grimes Point Archaeological Area** *(US 50, 11 miles E of Fallon. 702-885-6000)* A trail leads through an area where petroglyphs were carved on boulders as early as 5000 B.C.

**6. Sand Mountain Recreation Area/ Pony Express site** *(US 50, 25 miles E of Fallon. 702-885-6000)* A huge sand dune attracts off-road vehicles. You can see ruins of the Sand Springs Pony Express station.

**7. Austin** *(Chamber of Commerce 702-964-2200)* This old mining town has pioneer churches and the 1897 Stokes Castle.

**8. Berlin-Ichthyosaur State Park** *(Nev. 844, 22 miles E of Gabbs. 702-964-2440. Tours Mem. Day-Labor Day daily, Sept.-mid-Nov. Sat.-Sun.; adm. fee)* See marine fossils, a ghost town, and an old mine. Camping *(fee)* is available; call for reservations.

## Annual Events

**June** Gridley Days *(Austin. 702-964-2200)*
**September** Hearts of Gold Cantaloupe Festival *(Fallon. 702-423-4556 or 800-874-0903)*

## Lodging

**The Pony Express House** *(115 N.W. Main St., Austin. 702-964-2306)* This 1860s adobe house has two bedrooms, a kitchen, and Western decorations.

# Pacific States

## CALIFORNIA

# San Diego Backcountry

It may surprise you that behind coastal San Diego—the nation's sixth largest city, with 1.2 million people—there's backcountry that stretches eastward into virtual emptiness. First come ranchland and forested mountains, where the western falsefront town of Julian rests among historic gold mines and apple orchards. Then come the raw grit and empty spaces of Anza-Borrego Desert State Park. The San Diego backcountry achieves this startling change of personality—from the palm-lined Pacific to stark desert—in less than a hundred miles. Scattered around the region are such attractions as a battlefield of the Mexican-American War, San Diego Wild Animal Park, and a segment of the Pacific Crest National Scenic Trail—surely enough variety for anyone.

Hills of gold. Venerable oak trees. Huge sandstone boulders. Shy mule deer. This is the San Diego backcountry, which you enter as the land climbs away from the Pacific coastline. Once this was the realm of the Kumeyaay Indians, whose summer acorn-gathering territory is preserved in the 25,000 acres of **Cuyamaca Rancho State Park.** To the Indians the river that flows here was *Ah-ha-coo-muik,* renamed later by the Spanish as the *Aqua Dulce.* Both translate to an English name still used today: the Sweetwater River. Close your eyes and listen to the water's music, accented by the notes of spring songbirds. Acorn woodpeckers flit among some of the biggest canyon live oaks in California. At dusk keep an eye out for coyotes and raccoons, while night brings out mountain lions. Atop Cuyamaca

**Samuel H. Boardman State Scenic Corridor, Oregon (see Banana Belt, p. 348)**

and Stonewall Peaks you'll discover views across remarkable distances—eastward to the desert and the Salton Sea, westward to the Pacific Ocean, southward to Mexico. On days of warm sunshine, the air fills with the tang of incense cedars and ponderosa pines. Up here you come to understand the old expression, "feeling on top of the world."

In 1857 an American bought some of today's Cuyamaca park for a hay ranch to feed horses that pulled Butterfield Overland stagecoaches. Another phase of California history unfolded at the park's **Stonewall Mine site.** After a gold strike in 1870, miners dug a main shaft 630 feet deep and hauled up $2 million in ore. (The shaft still remains beneath your feet.) More than 500 people lived in adjacent Cuyamaca City, and on Sundays folks came from miles around to dance to the music of the "Cuyamaca Horticultural Band." (One imagines corncobs for flutes and pumpkins for drums.) Today grass and trees have reclaimed the old town site, leaving only faint traces of a boomtown gone bust—scattered stone foundations, a few rusty ore buckets and other mining equipment. Still, it's a pleasant place to let your imagination fill in the sights and sounds of the miners, the clattering wagons, and the saloons.

### Desert Bighorn Sheep

In Anza-Borrego Desert State Park (*borrego* is the Spanish word for lamb), you just may spot one of these elusive sheep. About the size of small deer, the light brown animals are seen occasionally in remote areas on rocky slopes or near waterholes. During mating season, from August through October, they may be bolder. Look for a flash of white belly and curved horns in the wilderness.

Mining also built the town of **Julian** in the late 1800s, a period reflected in the falsefront buildings and wooden sidewalks along Main Street. After mining around Julian had produced $4.5 million in gold, the town's hot streak cooled in the 1930s. But at least twice a year things come back to life again: in spring, when colorful wildflowers bloom across the countryside, and in autumn, during the apple harvest. Settlers first planted orchards here in the 1870s, and Julian apples won blue ribbons at the 1893 Chicago World's Fair. Nowadays the aroma of fresh-baked pies fills your nose, tempting you to wolf down a thick wedge at one of the pie shops along Main Street. Also redolent of the past is the street's architecture. Among the historic buildings are the former jail and the Julian Drug Store, whose marble-topped soda fountain serves up sparkling sarsaparilla. The wood-frame Julian Hotel was founded by a freed Georgia slave a century ago. The 1886 Levi-Marks store was erected with 100,000 locally made bricks. Old-fashioned shops are chockablock with country crafts and Western arts, while the Julian Cider Mill presses fresh apple cider.

Keep traveling east and suddenly, everything looks dry. Trees thin out, and now the roadside is lined with spindly, red-flowered ocotillos and yuccas, with their creamy yellow blossoms. The only signs of man are occasional telephone poles. You've entered **Anza-Borrego Desert State Park,** a realm of 600,000 acres with pink and yellow badlands, rocky peaks, and

**Font's Point and Borrego Valley, Anza-Borrego Desert State Park**

eroded canyons. Like the landscape itself, the cactuses seem to have popped right out of a *Roadrunner* cartoon—especially barrel cactuses that inflate like water balloons to hold precious rainfall. Also comical are beavertail and hedgehog cactuses, as well as rare elephant trees (*Bursera microphylla*), whose bark resembles wrinkled hide on a short, fat trunk.

After a while, though, you grow more accustomed to the desert's sheer oddness. You begin to look deeper, past the weird shapes and into the earth's history book. Here our planet's pages have turned—at a pace that is geologic in its slowness and majesty—millennium after millennium, leaving a record that's fairly easy to read. Along the .25-mile Narrows Earth Trail, for instance, you see granitic rocks that were formed about 100 million years ago.

Mountain building and erosion have shaped the park. In fact, the raw, young Santa Rosa Mountains are still rising along one of California's most active fault zones, the San Jacinto. All over the park you see alluvial fans, great sprawls of rocks and sand that spread below mountain flanks where rain has washed down everything loose. In the Borrego badlands, powerful storms have carved gullies and knifelike ridges.

The desert may be rough company, but it's not empty and alone. Keep your eyes open for some of the 60 mammal, 225 bird, and 60 reptile and amphibian species that live here. Among the strangest are survivors from the last ice age, tiny pupfish that developed remarkable adaptations in order to live in the harsh desert environment. Saltwater or fresh, near freezing temperatures or 108°F—it makes no difference to the hardy pupfish, which live in ponds dotting the park.

Human beings have managed to survive here for thousands of years, too, leaving their testimony on the rocks. Pictographs of black and red, their meanings lost, still remain as they were painted, probably by Native American shamans. Some of the park's rocks contain mortar holes where Indians ground seeds for food. Next came passing Spanish settlers in the de Anza party in 1774. (The park is named after expedition leader Juan Bautista de Anza.) Kit Carson scouted along the Southern Emigrant Trail, followed by argonauts heading for the California gold fields and by travelers on the Butterfield Overland Stage. At Foot and Walker Passes you can set your feet in the ruts of stagecoaches that passed by in the 1850s.

To the west the **Pacific Crest National Scenic Trail** runs northward from Campo (near the Mexican border), passing near Cuyamaca and Julian on a path that leads hikers all the way to Canada through isolated territory. But this hidden corner of California isn't all a remote province of mountain and desert. It includes busy Escondido, where an undistinguished hillside is labeled **San Pasqual Battlefield State Historic Park,** site of the fiercest battle of the Mexican-American War; in 1846 proud *Californios* overcame U.S. soldiers. (The victory, however, didn't prevent the American conquest of California.)

A nearby attraction in the San Pasqual Valley, the **San Diego Wild Animal Park** has about 3,200 creatures roaming on sunbaked hills and dusty plains that simulate Africa, Asia, and other habitats. In this expansive environment, animals such as antelope and zebras forage, bear their young, and behave pretty much normally. (Except, of course, for eating each other; the vegetarians and carnivores are separated.) From your seat aboard a monorail, you'll see elephants, tigers, cranes, and scimitar-horned oryx, which are often pictured in ancient Egyptian art with their twin horns arching downward. The park's most important role is as a pioneer in captive breeding, with notable successes including the southern white rhino and nearly extinct California condor.

Perhaps the condor—with a nine-foot wingspan to carry it high enough to scan all the San Diego backcountry—can serve to remind us that seeing California unspoiled is worth the journey. This hidden corner is a good place to start.

—*Jerry Camarillo Dunn, Jr.*

### Star Gazing

The 200-inch Hale telescope at Palomar Observatory (*Cty. Rd. S6, Pauma Valley. 760-742-2119. Adm. fee*) can peek into the hidden corners of the cosmos, at distances more than one billion light-years away. Its 13-story white dome shines near the summit of Palomar Mountain, in the corner's northern realm. Visitors can't peer through the 530-ton instrument, the nation's largest optical telescope, but they can admire it and the photographs it takes of faraway galaxies, nebulae, and our own starry neighbors in the Milky Way.

# Travel Notes

## Directions
This backcountry lies east and northeast of San Diego. **By car:** From San Diego take I-8 east, then Calif. 79 north to Julian and Calif. 78 east toward Anza-Borrego Desert State Park. **By plane**: San Diego has an international airport. **By train**: Amtrak serves San Diego.

## General Information
The region is a year-round destination; however, summer temperatures at Anza-Borrego Desert State Park can blow the top off a thermometer at over 100°F. For general information contact the San Diego Convention & Visitors Bureau *(401 B St., Suite 1400, San Diego 92101-4237. 619-236-1212).*

## Things to See and Do
**1. Cuyamaca Rancho State Park** *(4 miles N of I-8, at 12551 Calif. 79. 760-765-0755. Adm. fee)* This domain of mountains, forests, streams, and meadows has more than 100 species of birds, many animals, four kinds of pines, and over 100 miles of trails, including the 3.5-mile hike up Cuyamaca Peak. At park headquarters are exhibits on the Kumeyaay Indians and early Spanish explorers; an interpretive trail leads to a Kumeyaay village site.

**At Anza Borrego Desert State Park**

The **Stonewall Mine site** has a re-created miner's shack with displays on the local gold rush of the late 1800s. The park has picnic areas and campgrounds, and Lake Cuyamaca offers trout and bass fishing.
**2. Julian** *(Chamber of Commerce 760-765-1857)* Gold and apples built this small getaway town, which makes a good overnight stop with its B&Bs and hotels. The **Julian Pioneer Museum** *(2811 Washington St. 760-765-0227. April-Nov. Tues.-Sun., weekends only rest of year; donation)* is the town's communal attic, with Native American artifacts, pioneer clothes and lace, Ulysses S. Grant's china cabinet, Julian's first bathtub, and a 1920s permanent wave machine often compared to an electric chair. At the **Eagle** and **High Peak Mines** *(Eagle Mining Company, off C St. 760-765-0036. Adm. fee),* one-hour guided tours explore a 1,000-foot mine tunnel and reveal how gold is extracted. The nearby 2,325-acre **Vulcan Mountain Wilderness Preserve** *(Farmer Rd. 760-765-0650)* has popular hiking trails.
**3. Anza-Borrego Desert State Park** *(Visitor Center, Borrego Springs. 760-767-5311)* With expansive desert scenery (rocky peaks,

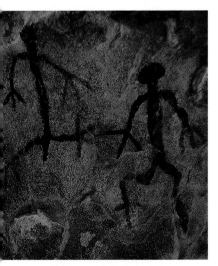

**Carrizo Canyon pictographs, Anza-Borrego Desert State Park**

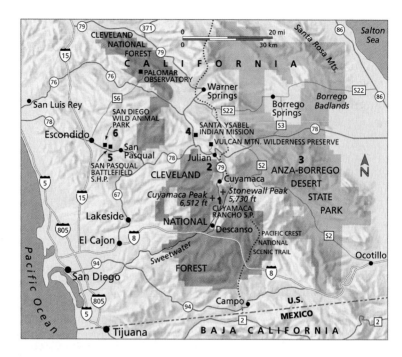

badlands, canyons, palm groves), wildlife, Native American rock art, historic trails, and an intriguing subterranean Visitor Center, the 937-square-mile park offers a living lesson on California. Surprisingly, this "barren" desert boasts streams, animals, and birds. Wildflowers bloom February through March; phone for updates. There are developed campsites, some with electricity, water, and sewer hookups (reservations 800-444-7275); also primitive camping and a horse camp.

**4. Santa Ysabel Indian Mission** (Calif. 79, 8 miles NW of Julian. 760-765-0810) This outpost of Mission San Diego de Alcala was founded in 1818 to serve Indian neophytes, and the reconstructed chapel (1924) still draws worshipers from nearby Indian reservations. There are history exhibits, including one on the "mystery of the lost bells of Santa Ysabel."

**5. San Pasqual Battlefield State Historic Park** (Calif. 78, 8 miles E of Escondido. 619-220-5430. Fri.-Sun.; adm. fee) See the location of a fierce 1846 encounter of the Mexican-American War, which is interpreted at the Visitor Center.

**6. San Diego Wild Animal Park** (Off I-15, 30 miles NE of San Diego. 619-234-6541. Adm. fee) Exotic animals of Africa and Asia

roam 2,200 acres divided into five habitats, including plains and waterholes; monorail ride, educational animal shows, petting corral, "safari" walk.

### Other Activities

**Hiking** The Pacific Crest National Scenic Trail cuts through this hidden corner on its way north to Canada; call the Pacific Crest Trail Association (916-349-2109 or 888-728-7245) for information.

### Annual Events

**March-April** Peg Leg Liar's Contest (Borrego Springs. 760-767-5555 or 800-559-5525) **May** Wildflower Show (Julian. 760-765-1857) Desert and mountain floral arrangements are showcased.
**October** Apple Days (Julian. 760-765-1857) Cider fest, arts festival, and more celebrate a tradition dating back to 1909.

### Lodging

**Julian Goldrush Hotel** (Main and B Sts., Julian. 760-765-0201 or 800-734-5854) Victorian fixtures distinguish this 1897 gold rush hotel, with a porch and an antique-filled parlor.

# Old California

There is scenery here—mountains cradle the region—but what you'll remember is its ambience of earlier times: Spanish missions where bells have rung for nearly two hundred years, landscapes little changed since the era of missions and land grant ranchos. This is backroad country, where any turn off a busy highway onto a county two-lane leads to farming plains, humble wineries, and backwater towns, quiet pastorales where novelist John Steinbeck found inspiration for much of his Nobel Prize-winning work.

**Pinnacles National Monument**

How much longer this bucolic anteroom of California's Middle Kingdom will remain untouched by inexorable suburban sprawl is anybody's guess. For now, however, its mountainous coastal forests, hills of wild grass and oak savanna retain the look of Old California. The white fences of cattle and thoroughbred horse ranches embroider grassy Gabilan Range valleys east and south of **Salinas,** where the writer John Steinbeck grew up among rural folk of the kind immortalized in his Dust Bowl epic, *The Grapes of Wrath.*

Busy US 101 divides this hidden corner lengthwise, following the route of the 18th-century Spanish Colonial *El Camino Real* ("Royal Road") from Mexico to San Francisco. Along the way are three of the Franciscan missions that anchored *Californio* life in the early 1800s. Mission Nuestra Senora de la Soledad is little more than an enchanting ruin, but **Mission San Antonio de Padua** still functions as a parish church. Franciscans carry on their religious traditions at **Mission San Miguel Arcángel,** whose sanctuary's hand-painted interior walls are unchanged since 1821.

The friars' original charter was to convert *Alta California's* natives to Christianity and create a rural labor force loyal to Spain. The souls they sought here came from the Salinan people and various tribes who lived in the Santa Lucia Mountain foothills. The beauty of the Lucias—best known for the spectacular Big Sur headlands—still belies difficult terrain; few roads link the coast's heavily traveled Calif. 1 with the great green basin of the **Salinas Valley,** self-styled the "Salad Bowl of the World" for its huge lettuce, broccoli, and artichoke crops, and the setting of Steinbeck's novel *East of Eden.*

Monterey was a center of Californio culture during the Spanish and Mexican eras, but the city's elite drew part of their wealth from huge inland ranchos such as El Portrero de San Carlos. Privately owned, its 37-room hacienda, forests, and meadows flank Robinson Canyon Road south of Carmel Valley Road in a setting that is virtually unchanged since its original grant of 1839.

## Mission Legacies

Once romanticized as a halcyon time, the mission era, which lasted from 1769 to 1864, was anything but idyllic. The Franciscans' policy of forced native labor sparked periodic rebellions, and Spanish *Californios* resented the padres' royally-granted monopoly on prime ranchlands. After Mexico broke free of Madrid in 1821, it ordered the missions to distribute their holdings among Native converts and Spanish settlers. No longer self-supporting, most missions failed. Some, like Nuestra Senora de la Soledad, were looted for building materials. Others languished through the 19th century as picturesque ruins, their beauty kindling mistaken notions of a storybook past.

The somnolent Middle Kingdom of the padres' time lives on along Nacimiento Fergusson Road, one of the few east-west routes across the Lucias. It winds for 27 miles between Mission Road south of Mission San Antonio de Padua and the Big Sur coast below Lucia, climbing from rolling oak woodlands into forests of redwood and fir. Time was when stagecoaches

**Mission San Antonio de Padua**

changed horses in Jolon, which still supports itself welcoming travelers who venture west off US 101. There's even less going on in Adelaida, where a crossroads hamlet once stood in the barley-growing country west of Paso Robles. In this instance, however, the pleasure lies not in the destination but in the journey, a loop west on County Rd. G14 from US 101 north of Paso Robles, forking left on Adelaida Road to Vineyard Drive, which curves back to little Templeton and its wineries.

In *East of Eden*, Steinbeck described the Gabilan Range as "full of sun and loveliness and a kind of invitation." Calif. 146 accepts the invite and climbs from Soledad to nearby **Pinnacles National Monument**, a labyrinthine pile of volcanic stone. Between Salinas and Pinnacles lies more vineyard country, where in summer and autumn the usual breeze carries the aroma of ripening grapes. Follow Calif. 25 south toward San Miguel and you'll voyage across rolling hills of oak and grass, landscapes of the early 1800s, when the first generation of *rancheros* put out cattle to graze on them, and proudly declared themselves Californios.

—*Mark Miller*

# Travel Notes

## Directions

Bounded roughly by the north-south trending Santa Lucias and the easterly Gabilan Range, this area extends from Salinas to the latitude of Morro Bay. **By car:** From San Francisco, follow US 101 south to Salinas, then do your best to avoid US 101 thereafter. From Los Angeles, take I-5 to Calif. 46 west. **By plane:** The closest major airports

**Mission votives, San Antonio de Padua**

are San Jose, Oakland, and San Francisco. Commuter airlines serve the Monterey Peninsula Airport. **By train**: Amtrak's *Coast Starlight* passenger train stops in Salinas.

## General Information

Central coast "summers" are vexed by sudden ocean fogs and stiff chilly breezes; however, you'll find the weather generally glorious between November and April: cool, clear days, moderate temperatures, and, except for Pacific storms, little of the Monterey Peninsula's ubiquitous fog. For information contact the California Division of Tourism (*801 K St., Suite 1600, Sacramento 95814. 916-322-2881 or 800-862-2543*); the Monterey County Travel and Tourism Alliance (*137 Crossroads Blvd., Carmel 93932. 408-626-1424 or 888-221-1010*); or the Salinas Valley Chamber of Commerce (*119 E. Alisal St., P.O. Box 1170, Salinas 93902. 408-424-7611*).

## Things to See and Do

**1. Salinas** John Steinbeck was born in 1902 in this agricultural town. First editions, letters, and photographs at the new, 37,000-square-foot **National Steinbeck Center** (*1 Main St. 408-753-6411. Adm. fee*) detail the Nobel Prize-winning author's literary accomplishments; changing exhibitions explore Salinas Valley history and heritage. Steinbeck's prim, two-story Victorian birthplace is preserved as the **Steinbeck House** (*132 Central Ave. 408-424-2735. Closed Sun.*), where you'll find memorabilia and interpretive information, and a pleasant luncheon restaurant. Salinas' oldest building (1844-46), the **José Eusebio Boronda Adobe** (*333 Boronda Rd. 408-757-8085. Closed Sat.; donation*) largely typifies rural *Californio* haciendas of the pre-Gold Rush era; period furnishings fill its cool rooms.

**2. King City** At the **Monterey County Agricultural and Rural Life Museum** (*San Lorenzo County Park, 1160 Broadway St. 408-385-8020*), the Salinas area's surprisingly genteel turn-of-the-century farming culture is brought back to life by relocated vintage buildings including a barn, a one-room 1887 schoolhouse, a farmhouse, a working blacksmith shop, and an 1887 railroad depot.

**3. Pinnacles National Monument** (*Visitor Center, near east entrance off Calif. 25. 408-389-4485. Adm. fee*) Thirty miles of trails snake through the eroded wreckage of a primordial volcanic mountain jutting from rolling hills and chaparral, forming craggy spires and eerie caves.

**4. Mission San Antonio de Padua** (*Hunter Liggett Military Reservation, via Cty. Rd. G14/Jolon Rd., 23 miles SW of US 101. 408-385-4478. Donation*) Founded in 1771, this was California's third mission. The adobe church, gristmill, and tannery retain their original appearance. A small museum is devoted to the history of the mission and of the Central Coast's native tribes.

**5. San Miguel** Unlike many of California's 21 Catholic missions, **Mission San Miguel Arcángel** (*775 Mission St. 805-467-3256. Donation*) and its attendant buildings (beside US 101) were never abandoned, and the painted walls of its sanctuary and other interior decorations haven't changed since 1821. Brown-robed Franciscans are still in residence here. Once a humble inn and stage stop, the nearby **Rios-Caledonia Adobe** (*700 S. Mission St. 805-467-3357. Donation*) is typical of mid-19th-century rural haciendas. It welcomed travelers along the *El Camino Real* from about 1868 to 1890. Period furnishings evoke the simple life of early California.

### Other Activities
**Wine-tasting** Wineries dot the Central California landscape. For wine-tasting and tour information, contact the Monterey County Vintners and Growers Association *(408-375-9400)* or the Paso Robles Visitors & Conference Bureau *(805-238-0506 or 800-406-4040)*.

### Annual Events
**May** Salinas Valley Fair *(Salinas Valley Fairgrounds, King City. 408-385-3243)*
**June** Fiesta of Mission San Antonio de Padua *(Mission San Antonio de Padua. 408-385-4478)*
**July** California Rodeo *(Salinas Sports Complex, Salinas. 408-757-2951 or 800-771-8807)*
**August** Steinbeck Festival *(National Steinbeck Center, Salinas. 408-753-6411)*
**September** Festival of Mission San Miguel Arcángel *(San Miguel. 805-467-3256)*; Salinas Valley International Mariachi Festival and Conference *(Salinas. 408-758-7387)*; California International Air Show *(Salinas. 408-754-1983. Late Sept.–early Oct.)*

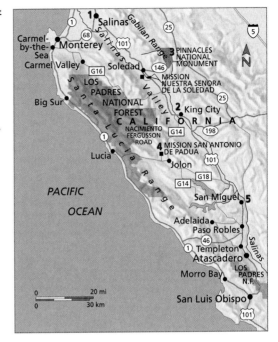

### Lodging
**StonePine Estate Resorts Inn** *(13 miles E of Calif. 1, at 150 E. Carmel Valley Rd., Carmel Valley. 408-659-2245)* This luxurious, 1920 stone château and its Paddock House overlooking the Carmel River's deep canyon form a secluded 330-acre estate; the acclaimed dining room has a 5-course menu.

**Salinas Valley farmland**

# Lakes Basin

When your thoughts are on finding gold, you don't pay attention to the beautiful evergreen forests or sparkling lakes surrounding you. When you're hammering away at a vein of quartz, you might not appreciate the granite peaks raking the azure sky above. So it wasn't until a few decades ago, in the twilight of the Lakes Basin's 60-year mining boom, that people began to appreciate this out-of-the-way corner of California's northern Sierra Nevada for its greatest resource: high country scenery that is often flat-out spectacular. For all the digging and logging, the Lakes Basin still looks pristine. Its old mining towns keep themselves up well enough to evoke bygone days, when miners are said to have relaxed in winter by riding ore buckets up mountains and sliding down on 16-foot-long skis. Skiers have been joined by hikers, trail bikers, and anglers, and folks who dine amid the rustic luxury of old-style lodges. Ask most Californians where the Lakes Basin Recreation Area is, and odds are few will know. But now you will.

**Upper Sardine Lake reflection of Sierra Buttes**

Within a few months of the discovery of gold in 1849, prospectors over-ran California's central Sierra foothills. They ranged north and south, driven up every creek and draw by rumors of nugget-filled lakes and veins of gold thick as a horse. In 1851 a band of fortune-seekers scouring 7,447-foot-high Eureka Peak (then called Gold Mountain) found something close, a quartz outcropping filigreed with gold, silver, and lead. Mining companies arrived and hired men to tunnel into the hills. Shacky little mining towns sprang up, sweat and whiskey flowing as the valleys echoed with the thunder of stamp mills crushing ore.

The gold boom sprouted two-fisted, hard-drinking towns such as Jamison City and **Johnsville,** the capital of the basin's mining district, preserved within the 5,000-acre **Plumas-Eureka State Park** at the basin's northern fringe. The park's prime attraction is a superb museum where artifacts and exhibits illustrate the region's mining history and forest wildlife. They've shut down the old five-story Mohawk Stamp Mill, where 60 massive drills pulverized 150 tons of ore a day, but the park's blacksmith shop occasionally fires up for demonstrations of old-style ironworking. There's more about mining at the Sierra County Historical Society's **Kentucky Mine Museum** near **Sierra City,** on the site of a gold-mining operation that fired up in 1853 and dug away for a century.

Ever present in the tumult of discovery were the Lakes Basin's Maidu people, who shared the Sierras' western slope with the southerly Yokut and the Miwok. Like their neighbors, they were hunters who summered in the high country and retreated to lower elevations in winter. As settlement spread, the Maidus' world shrank. They abandoned hunting for work as miners and ranch hands and railroaders. Over time, the region's gold petered out, the miners disappeared, and the Lakes Basin was forgotten by most. Still eclipsed by Lake Tahoe's attractions, the basin remains one of California's favorite out-of-the-way places, where people return year after year for summer idylls far from Lake Tahoe's traffic and shoreline crowds.

When Congress gave the Middle Fork Feather River wild and scenic status a generation ago, the photographers and wilderness enthusiasts who flocked to Blairsden and Mohawk for access to the isolated stream found much more: over three dozen perfectly gorgeous lakes, lofty granite peaks, and wild forests of pine and fir flanking the Feather's three splashy, trout-filled forks through the Lakes Basin. They discovered that a stretch of the

### Golden Lake Mystery

Tom Stoddard was one of a group of prospectors in the Lakes Basin area in the fall of 1849. One day he stumbled across a glorious, gold-rimmed lake. He quickly began filling his pockets with treasure, but was disturbed by Indians and fled. The next spring, Stoddard led a party of 25 who paid him abundently for leading them to the golden lake. Alas, all the ravines and streams looked the same, and he couldn't find it again. The group went on to strike it rich elsewhere, and the golden lake's location remains a mystery.

**North Fork Feather River**

mile-high **Pacific Crest National Scenic Trail** crosses Calif. 49 just east of Sierra City and follows the high country north through the lordly **Sierra Buttes,** soaring spires resembling the Swiss Alps, and among the handsomest peaks in the entire Sierra Nevada range.

The news of this latter-day discovery spread slowly, and the best spots are still pretty much secret. But those in the know are treated to a splendid array of wilderness treasures. Hikers one day can trek to the top of the Sierra Buttes for majestic views over the Sierras and beyond; then wander the next day to the Sardine Lakes, Gold Lake, Long Lake, or a couple of dozen other granite-ringed alpine beauties. Anglers will find prize trout darting in pellucid shallows of the Feather River forks, one of California's great trout fly-casting streams. And horseback riders can traipse through pine-scented forests that prospectors from long-ago would still recognize.

But let's say you prefer to reconnoiter the wilderness first from the window of your car. You can venture along the Feather River's equally pretty North Fork, which is shadowed by the Feather River National Scenic Byway (Calif. 70). The route joins the Feather's northernmost branch just northeast of Oroville and follows it nearly to **Quincy.** These red-soil forests—the rusty hue is from an abundance of iron oxide—were once the domain of the vanished Maidu, who gaze out of the past from old photographs collected in the **Plumas County Museum** in Quincy.

And for those looking for a less adventuresome experience, there's **Graeagle,** where you're likely to hear the whack of golf balls more often than the resonant ring of a weekend prospector's pick. The old lumbering town is the basin's unofficial hub, a sociable village situated near a half-dozen courses that dogleg through forest. The most challenging is the 18-hole course at Plumas Pines Golf Resort, where wide shots remind you why this country is called the Lakes Basin.

At the end of the day, Lakes Basin visitors unwind at one of the region's several lakeside lodges, where drinks are served overlooking mountain-ringed, mirrory waters, and hearty dinner tables are set before snapping fireplaces. As you watch the sun set behind the sawtooth ridgelines, the end to another glorious day, you will surely toast yourself for venturing off the beaten path to this high-altitude Sierra hideaway.

—*Mark Miller*

# Travel Notes

### Directions

The Lakes Basin lies in the Sierra Nevada northwest of Lake Tahoe. **By car:** From I-80, Calif. 89 meanders northwest from Truckee into the heart of the basin. Calif. 49 leaves I-80 at Auburn for a slower scenic byway climb through Gold Country foothills. **By plane:** The closest major airport is in Reno, Nevada. **By train:** Amtrak trains stop in Reno and Truckee.

### General Information

Typically, the basin's most comfortable weather lasts from mid-May through October, although snowfalls have occurred in every month. Warm summer days are often followed by very cool nights. Good information sources include the California Division of Tourism (801 K St., Suite 1600, Sacramento 95814. 916-322-2881); the Sierra County Visitors Bureau (Main St., Downieville 95936. 530-289-3507 or 800-720-7782); and the Plumas County Visitors Bureau (91 Church St., P.O. Box 4120, Quincy 95971. 530-283-6345 or 800-326-2247).

### Things to See and Do

**1. Quincy** (Plumas County Visitors Bureau 530-283-6345 or 800-326-2247) At the **Plumas County Museum** (500 Jackson St. 530-283-6320. May-Sept. daily, Oct.-April Mon.-Fri.; adm. fee), displays on gold-mining, logging, and railroad history provide a glimpse into the basin's past. Nearby stands the 1878 **Coburn-Variel Home** (137 Coburn St. 530-283-6320. Call for hours; adm. fee).

**2. Portola** (Eastern Plumas Chamber of Commerce 530-832-5444) At the **Portola Railroad Museum** (1 mile S of Calif. 70 on Cty. Rd. A15. 530-832-4131. May-Sept. daily, call for winter schedule; adm. fee) awaits an outdoor collection of more than 100 railcars and locomotives. Historical exhibits shed focus on Far West railroading.

**3. Plumas-Eureka State Park and Museum** (Off Calif. 89 6 miles W. of Graeagle, at 310 Johnsville Rd./Cty. Rd. A-14, Blairsden. 530-836-2380. Park open year-round, museum May-Oct.; adm. fee for museum) A monument to Lakes Basin mining lore, this 6,000-acre state park surrounds the town of **Johnsville.** You can see where it all started by climbing the arduous 3-mile loop trail up **Eureka Peak.** Housed in a restored miners' boardinghouse, the museum interprets the gold-mining legacy with mining tools, photos,

**Feather Falls, Plumas National Forest**

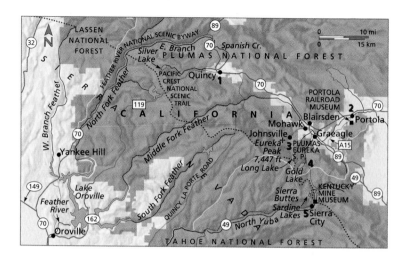

and mining machinery models; just outside stand the Mohawk Stamp Mill, a blacksmith shop, and a miner's house.

**4. Gold Lake** *(7 miles S of Graeagle via Gold Lake Rd. Gold Lake Lodge 530-836-2350)* The basin's biggest lake offers a surfeit of scenery, hiking trailheads, and boat rentals. Come evening, if you have a reservation, the launch of the Gold Lake Beach Resort *(530-836-2491)* will ferry you across the water for dinner.

**5. Sierra City** *(Sierra County Visitors Bureau 530-289-3507 or 800-720-7782)* The Sierra Buttes tower 4,000 feet over the Main Street of this tiny gold-rush town. One mile east of town, the **Kentucky Mine Museum** *(Calif. 49. 530-862-1310. Mem. Day–Sept.; adm. fee)* offers a well-curated account of Sierra County's history, plus exhibits of Maidu artifacts.

### Other Activities

**Golf** Among the area's several golf courses is Plumas Pines Golf Resort *(402 Poplar Valley Rd., Graeagle. 530-836-1420. May–Oct.; fee).*
**Hiking** Call the Pacific Crest Trail Association *(916-349-2109 or 888-728-7245)* for information on hiking this popular trail. Gold Lake Lodge *(530-836-2350)* has several trailheads, including the 0.4-mile, interpretive Red Fir Nature Trail, which introduces you to the towering trees that dominate the Lakes Basin; and the popular Round Lake Loop Trail, which connects many of the Lakes Basin's prettiest ponds including Silver Lake. The Beckworth Ranger District of Plumas National Forest *(530-836-2575)*

offers additional trail guidance.
**Horseback riding** For horse rentals and information on trail rides and pack trips, contact Graeagle Stables *(Calif. 89, Graeagle. 530-836-0430. May-Oct.)*; Gold Lake Pack Station and Stables *(Gold Lake Rd. bet. Graeagle and Gold Lake Lodge. 530-836-0940. Mid-June–mid-Oct.)*; or Bucks Lake Stables *(10 miles W of Quincy on Bucks Lake Rd. 530-283-2532. July-Aug.).*

### Annual Events

**January-March** Historic Longboard Revival Series *(Plumas Eureka Ski Bowl, Johnsville. 530-283-6345 or 800-326-2247)*
**June-August** Living History Days *(Plumas Eureka S.P., Johnsville. 530-836-2380)*
**July-September** Kentucky Mine Summer Concert Series *(Sierra City. 530-862-1310)*
**August** Portola Railroad Days *(Portola Railroad Museum, Portola. 530-832-4131)*

### Lodging

**Gold Lake Lodge** *(7 miles S of Graeagle via Gold Lake Rd. 530-836-2350. Mid-June–Sept.)* Perched on a 6,620-foot mountain summit, this rustic lodge was built in 1912 as the Lakes Basin's first tourist lodge.
**Gray Eagle Lodge** *(5 miles south of Graeagle at 5000 Gold Lake Rd. Mem. Day–mid-Oct. 530-836-2511 or 800-635-8778)* An upscale retreat of 18 handsome, comfortably furnished cabins in a timbered creekside setting, established in 1923. Its log lodge holds one of the basin's most praised restaurants.

# Shasta's Halo

Where the Sierra Nevada range ends in California's timbered northeast corner, the Cascades begin at Lassen Peak, southern marker of a vast and geologically restless region of grassy plateaus, steep river valleys, splashy streams, trout-filled lakes, eroded canyons, jagged ridges, and glacial mountains such as 14,162-foot Mount Shasta, crowned "king" of the Halo's peaks by Sierra Club founder John Muir. The volcanism that shaped the region still seethes amid the ash and lava landscapes of Lassen Volcanic National Park. Scattered across the region are the railroad, lumber, and mining towns of the Far West's final frontier, where newcomers now seek the priceless intangibles of wilderness adventure.

Barely over a half-day's drive from the tony pleasures of San Francisco, this quiet region of small towns and sparsely populated backcountry retains the look of the mid-1800s, when gold brought fortune-seekers along the Sacramento River on the central California Trail. That's not likely to change, for the Halo country is a mosaic of mostly public lands: national forests, wilderness, state parks, wildlife refuges, and 30,000-acre Shasta Lake, California's largest man-made reservoir.

**Mount Shasta**

**Indian rhubarb fringing McCloud River, Shasta National Forest**

Even as railroaders spiked their way north along modern-day I-5's route, and loggers first cut its trees, California's wilderness poets were extolling the region's dramatic landscapes. Joaquin Miller wrote of Mount Shasta's "sudden and solitary" rise from "great black forests." Muir called the dormant volcano the "grandest" of California's "fire-mountains."

Most travelers race through Halo country on I-5, unaware of the enormous wilderness flanking the highway. Those who hunt, fish, or hike, however, are probably rushing to a freeway exit, like a good many who return annually to Shasta Lake to idle through the Halo's hot summer days aboard rented houseboats. Things get crowded at the marina, but the lake's serpentine 365-mile shoreline (longer than San Francisco Bay's) hides most of the pleasure fleet. Hikers have a smorgasbord of trails from which to choose—including the short trail halfway up **Mount Shasta**; beginning from the Everitt Vista Turnout, it meanders through pine-scented woods to a lava outcrop overlooking the green and gold patches of McCloud Valley.

In winter, skiers come to the slopes below Mount Shasta's five glaciers, overnighting in the picturesque towns of **Mount Shasta** and

**McCloud,** the last an 1890s lumber company town with board sidewalks and vintage peaked-roof wooden buildings.

Shasta's conical shape betrays the region's volcanic nature, dormant here since the late 1700s but still very much alive in **Lassen Volcanic National Park.** You'll know you're getting close to the park by the sulfurous scent of hissing steam vents and boiling "mud pot" cauldrons, and the headless throat of decapitated Mount Tehama. Lassen Peak, the Cascades' southern-most peak, grew off the flank of long-gone Tehama, a volcano that collapsed perhaps 11,500 years ago, leaving treeless Lassen looking to Miller "lonely as God and white as a winter moon." Take Calif. 89's scenic meander through the park's western reach past dramatic geothermal features, including Lassen Peak itself, which last erupted between 1914 and 1921.

Glaciers finished off what remained of Mount Tehama, but managed only to bevel the soaring granite steeples of **Castle Crags State Park,** a splendidly pristine wilderness hiking and camping area with a stretch of the **Pacific Crest National Scenic Trail** corkscrewing through. The Sacramento River provides a needed respite in summer. Ever dominating Halo country, lordly, snow-dusted Mount Shasta rises dramatically in the distance from the park's scenic overlook.

Venture east on Calif. 89 over 4,533-foot Dead Horse Summit to the sunrise slope of the Cascades. Looking east from the summit, there's just so much land out there! Some of it's ranching country, with little hamlets whose main occupation is selling hardwares and feed. There's a sense of aridity out there, but not in **McArthur-Burney Falls Memorial State Park,** where subterranean springs spew from fissures in precipitous basalt formations. One creates Burney Creek, which plunges nearly 130 feet from a cliff in two feathery cascades into a jade-green pool. When the sun shines, their misty curtains make rainbows.

### John Muir

The literary avatar of the High Sierra was 56 when his first book, *The Mountains of California,* appeared in 1894. Born in Scotland, raised by Calvinists on the Wisconsin frontier, John Muir developed a religious reverence for nature. Temporarily blinded by an industrial accident, his recovery at age 29 left him determined to see all he could of the "gardens of God." A cross-country odyssey led to the Sierra Nevada, where the cheerful ascetic climbed its peaks wearing ordinary shoes and without equipment, and reveled in the beauty of his beloved "Range of Light."

As you roam the Halo country, don't be surprised to find yourself thinking about coming back. John Muir returned often, climbing Mount Shasta many times. Initially preoccupied by the peak's ponderous geology, he eventually found greater pleasure in the beauty of its magnificent setting. "Far better than climbing the mountain," he wrote, "is going around its warm fertile base, enjoying its bounties like a bee circling around a bank of flowers." Trust Muir: A bouquet of wonders awaits you.

—*Mark Miller*

# Travel Notes

### Directions

This corner lies south of Mount Shasta in northeastern California. **By car:** I-5 is the main north-south entry. Excellent and scenic state highways thread the region, but require considerable driving time and are often closed in winter. **By plane:** Commuter airlines serve Redding and Chico; the closest major hubs are Reno, Nevada, and, about 6

hours away by car, San Francisco. **By train:** Amtrak trains serve Dunsmuir and Redding.

### General Information

Northeastern California weather is unpredictable, although late spring through fall is generally moderate at lower elevations. Summer is the peak season, with very hot days. The Shasta Cascade Wonderland Association's California Welcome Center *(Deschutes Rd. exit off I-5, at 1699 Calif. Hwy. 273, Anderson 96007. 800-326-6944)* offers an excellent free travel guide to the region.

### Things to See and Do

**1. Shasta State Historic Park** *(Calif. 299. 530-243-8194)* The 13-acre park preserves the brick ruins of Shasta, an 1850s-era

gold-mining town gone bust. The general store survives, along with the cemetery, jail, and the **Courthouse Museum** *(Wed.-Sun.; adm. fee)*, which showcases a classic collection of early California paintings and regional artifacts.

**2. Shasta Dam** *(16349 Shasta Dam Blvd., Shasta Lake. 530-275-4463)* The photogenic 3,460-foot-long hydroelectric dam is the water-engine of central California's colossal breadbasket. Form and function compete here at its spillway, America's tallest, nearly triple the height of Niagara Falls.

**3. Castle Crags State Park** *(Castle Creek Rd., Castella. 530-235-2684. Adm fee)* The oldest peaks in Shasta's Halo, upthrust over 200 million years ago, are among its most picturesque, surrounded by woodlands, lakes, and evergreen forests.

**4. Dunsmuir** *(Chamber of Commerce and Visitor Center 530-235-2177)* Railroading built this riverside town, still a whistle-stop. Old-time gandy dancers pose proudly in historical photos at the **Dunsmuir Museum** *(4101 Pine St. 530-235-0733. April–Labor Day Tues.-Sun.; donation)*, which also has railroading artifacts.

**5. Mount Shasta** *(Visitors Bureau 530-926-4865 or 800-926-4865)* This outfitting center beside its namesake peak is a fine jumping-off place for white-water rafters, hikers, and mountain bikers. The retired **Mount Shasta Fish Hatchery** *(1 N. Old Stage Rd. 530-926-2215)*, built in 1888, has been replaced by a modern hatchery behind it. The old building houses the **Sisson Museum** *(530-926-5508. April-Dec.)*, which treats Halo geology and its equally turbulent human history. The Sacramento River's northernmost source flows from the Big Springs lava tube in wooded **City Park** *(Off N. Mount Shasta Blvd.)*, outside town.

**6. Mount Shasta** *(Mount Shasta Ranger Station 530-926-4511)* Take the Everitt Memorial Highway 11 miles up to the timberline at 7,800 feet and ponder the glacial wilderness above. The fresh-air diorama sweeps from

Lassen Peak to Castle Crags.

**7. McCloud** *(McCloud Business and Professional Chamber of Commerce 530-964-3113)* The downtown historic area includes the **Heritage Junction Museum** *(320 Main St. 530-964-2604. May-Oct.; donation),* which dotes on the company town's history: from Native Americans, early fur trappers, and homesteaders to logging, milling, and skiing.

**8. McArthur-Burney Falls Memorial State Park** *(24898 Calif. 89, Burney. 530-335-2777. Adm. fee)* The falls are only a short stroll from a parking area. Enjoy the scenic 1-mile loop hike in Burney Creek Canyon or watch for bald eagles over nearby Lake Britton; call ahead *(800-444-7275)* to reserve a bucolic camping spot.

**9. Lassen Volcanic National Park** *(Headquarters, 38050 Calif. 36, Mineral. 530-595-4444. Mon.-Fri. Park open year-round, but road closes late Oct.–early June; adm. fee)* The southern end of Lassen Park Road is close to the best fumaroles, boiling springs, and boiling "mud pots." If you want to know why this otherworldly landscape gurgles and hisses and smells like rotten eggs, visit the **Loomis Museum** *(Lassen Peak Rd. 530-595-4444 ext. 5180. Mid-June–Sept. daily, late May–mid-June Sat.-Sun., closed rest of year),* which also serves as a Visitor Center. The museum is perched on Manzanita Lake, a pretty picnic spot.

### Other Activities

**Boating** All kinds can be found on area lakes and rivers. Especially popular is houseboating on Shasta Lake; call the Redding Convention & Visitors Bureau *(530-225-4100 or 800-874-7562)* or the Shasta-Trinity National Forests *(530-246-5222).*

**Fishing** Anglers seek bass and trout in the area's rivers and lakes.

**Hiking** The Pacific Crest National Scenic Trail is one of a multitude of trails that run through the region. For more information contact the Shasta-Trinity National Forests *(530-246-5222)* or Lassen Volcanic National Park *(530-595-4444).*

### Annual Events

**April** Kool April Nites Classic Car Show *(Redding. 530-225-4100 or 800-874-7562);* **May** Shasta Art Fair and Fiddler Jamboree *(Redding. 530-225-4100 or 800-874-7562)* **June** Shasta District Fair *(Anderson. 530-378-6789)* **August** McCloud Heritage Days

**Potem Falls, Shasta National Forest**

*(McCloud. 530-964-3113)* **September** Cool Mountain Nights, including Blackberry Music Festival *(Mount Shasta. 530-926-4865 or 800-926-4865);* Redding Museum Art and Craft Fair *(Redding. 530-243-8801)*

### Lodging

**McCloud Hotel Bed-and-Breakfast** *(408 Main St., McCloud. 530-964-2822)* The lumber barons who owned McCloud and paid its citizen-workers in scrip redeemable at the company store favored this restored 17-room 1916 hotel. A full gourmet breakfast is served up in the lobby.

# OREGON
# Banana Belt

Old-growth conifer forests plunge to driftwood-strewn beaches where pieces of the continent rise offshore, marooned by Oregon's oversize surf. Thanks to a banana-shaped weather trough, this southwest corner enjoys a temperate clime that extends inland over timbered mountain wilderness to somnolent bee-buzzed farming valleys. Logging and gold mining once paid the bills. Today fishing, white-water boating, flower-growing, and wine-making reflect a growing appreciation of the Banana Belt's extraordinary beauty and nurturing weather.

**Along the Samuel H. Boardman State Scenic Corridor**

Bounded by the Pacific Ocean, the California state line, US 199, and a winding scenic road from Grants Pass to Gold Beach through the Wild Rogue Wilderness, the Banana Belt is mostly forest and stream, meadow and river. A good part of its oceanfront—arguably Oregon's most picturesque—lies within **Samuel H. Boardman State Scenic Corridor** along US 101, where forested headlands, wide beaches, and wave-battered sea stacks give the appearance of a continent breaking up under the relentless onslaught of a mercurial sea. Lofty viewpoints along the Cape Sebastian State Scenic Corridor present sweeping panoramas.

You'll find it more serene, and probably warmer, too, in the Siskiyou National Forest, where trails enter a vast sap-scented garden of Noble and Douglas-fir, Jeffrey and knobcone pine, tanoak, and madrone. Some of the Northwest's largest hardwoods and Douglas-fir trees grow along the 1-mile loop of the **Schrader Old Growth Trail** about 30 minutes east of **Gold Beach.** The silent grandeur among these giants is so profound, you might consider staying for a while at the nearby Lobster Creek Campground.

Gold Beach straddles the mouth of the Rogue River—one of America's first eight Wild and Scenic rivers, a location so difficult to access that a small fleet of commercial jet boats has arisen, making it possible to voyage in shameless comfort from either Gold Beach or the "white-water capital" of Grants Pass. In Grants Pass, outfitters ferry anglers down the Rogue in double-ended dorylike Mackenzie riverboats and nature buffs in jet boats or rafts. Whichever way you choose, you'll not find more splendid evergreen wilderness, nor soon forget the river's 1,000-foot-deep canyons.

## Whale Spotting

Thousands of gray whales migrate along the Oregon Coast, which has 29 "Whale Watching Spoken Here" viewpoints in or near state parks, highway turnouts, and lighthouses. The great creatures travel south in December and January, returning between March and May with their newborn calves. Oregon has a resident population of up to 500 grays, who feed a half-mile offshore from June to October. Bring binoculars and a camp chair, and watch for their feathery spouts.

One of the Belt's few truly pristine evergreen wilds reachable by auto is the **Kalmiopsis Wilderness,** part of which is just south of sleepy Agness along the bucolic Illinois River Valley. This dense preserve of over 180,000 acres is one of Oregon's undiscovered destinations with numerous hiking and camping opportunities. For a sampler of primordial Northwest coastal conifer forest, you can enter the Kalmiopsis via the Eight Dollar Mountain Road off US 199 between Selma and Kerby. Inside the Kalmiopsis, footpaths wind into its rugged ups and downs, where hikers search for the tiny rhododendron-like *kalmiopsis leachiana*, a flower blooming here since the Ice Age.

Around **Brookings**, growing flowers—lilies in particular—is big business. One of the better-known, big-volume commercial operations is Flora Pacifica, where you can buy plants and bulbs, or just enjoy the colors when the lilies bloom. In **Azalea Park,** from April through June, five varieties of wild azaleas put on a dazzling display, rivaling Portland's rose gardens for the title of Oregon's prettiest flower patch.

Before the flower industry sprang up here, Brookings was foremost a commercial fishing port and a logging community. The old timber-cutting days are chronicled at the **Chetco Valley Historical Museum.** For a first-hand look at the kind of forests that covered Oregon's coastal region before the arrival of the saw, spend an hour in **Alfred A. Loeb State Park.** The short **Riverview Trail** follows the Chetco River through groves of old myrtlewood trees, whose fragrant, luminous wood inspires hundreds of south coast craftspeople. The Forest Service's nearby Redwood Nature Trail loops for a mile among the northernmost stands of *Sequoia sempervirens.*

While Oregon's timber industry has its ups and downs, Brookings still earns a decent living from the sea. Stroll along the waterfront and you'll find an armada of fishing boats rigged for catching salmon, tuna, shrimp, and crab. Not surprisingly, seafood restaurants abound here. Study the menus posted along the road in every little coastal hamlet, make your choice, order up a glass of a Rogue River appellation wine, and toast yourself for finding your way to this out-of-the-way Oregon jewel.

—*Mark Miller*

**Wild Rogue Wilderness**

# Travel Notes

## Directions

The Banana Belt is located in Oregon's south-western corner, bounded by US 199, the Rogue River, the Pacific Ocean, and the California state line. **By car:** US 199 offers a scenic but roundabout route from Grants Pass into the Banana Belt—you must follow it south into California before joining US 101 north. **By air:** The nearest major airport is in Portland, 250 miles north of Grants Pass via I-5.

## General Information

The region's gentle clime makes for comfortable visits year-round. Spring is cool and rainy; summer and autumn days can be hot. Winter brings rain and occasional storms. Sources of advice are the Southern Oregon Visitors Association *(P.O. Box 1645, Medford 97501. 541-779-4691)*; Brookings-Harbor Chamber of Commerce *(16330 Lower Harbor Rd., Brookings 97215. 541-469-3181 or 800-535-9469)*; Gold Beach Visitor Center *(29279 Ellensburg Ave. #3, Gold Beach 97444. 541-247-7526 or 800-525-2334)*; and Grants Pass Chamber of Commerce *(P.O. Box 970, Grants Pass 97528. 541-476-7717 or 800-547-5927)*.

## Things to See and Do

**1. Kalmiopsis Wilderness** *(Chetco Ranger District, Siskiyou National Forest 541-469-2196)* The wilderness has more than 12 established trailheads accessible from multiple locations; maps are available for purchase from the Chetco Ranger District.

**2. Schrader Old Growth Trail** *(North Bank Chetco River Rd., Gold Beach Ranger District, Siskiyou N.F. 541-247-3600)* An easy half-hour amble along this footpath brings you face-to-face with primeval Oregon. Take Jerry's Flat Road/Forest Rd. 33 to the national forest boundary at Lobster Creek Campground, turn right onto FR 090. The trailhead is exactly 2 miles ahead on the right. Also near Lobster Creek Campground is the **Myrtle Tree Trail** (FR 3533), which features the world's largest known myrtle tree.

**3. Gold Beach** The charming little **Curry County Historical Museum** *(29410 Ellensburg Ave./US 101. 541-247-6113. June-Aug. Tues.-Sat., Sept.-May Fri.-Sat.; donation)* tells the rough-and-tumble stories of old-time Banana Belt gold mining, logging, and the

**Insect-eating pitcher plants**

Rogue River Indian War.

**4. Samuel H. Boardman State Scenic Corridor** *(Off US 101 Mile 9 through 21. 503-469-2021. Adm. fee.)* Take advantage of convenient parking along this linear 13-mile stretch of coastline to beachcomb. Twelve points provide access to the coastal trail running the park's length.

**5. Brookings** *(Brookings-Harbor Chamber of Commerce 541-469-3181 or 800-535-9469)* In this south coast town, the historical exhibits at **Chetco Valley Historical Museum** *(15461 Museum Rd. 541-469-6651. May-Sept. Wed.-Sun., Oct.-April Fri.-Sun.; donation)* are what you'd expect in a region whose economy was once based on logging. The star attraction is Oregon's biggest Monterey cypress, a gnarled behemoth with a 27-foot circumference, standing 100 feet tall. If time permits, plan a picnic at lovely **Azalea Park** *(Left on Old County Rd. off Constitution Way. 541-469-2163)*.

**6. Alfred A. Loeb State Park** *(North Bank Chetco River Rd. 541-469-2021)* An excellent spot for a riverside idyll beside the Chetco. If you stroll the **Riverview Trail,** be sure to take along an interpretive booklet.

**7. Kerby** Even if old logging, farming, and mining equipment don't make your heart race, you'll find the photographs exhibited at the **Kerbyville Museum** *(US 199. 541-592-2076. Adm. fee)* as charming as an old family album.

## Other Activities

**Deep-sea fishing** Brookings has many licensed charter boat operators whose packages include equipment, bait, and food for half- and full-day trips. Contact the Brookings-Harbor Chamber of Commerce *(541-469-3181 or 800-535-9469).*

**Hiking and camping** Two good information sources are in Brookings: the Brookings-Harbor Chamber of Commerce *(541-469-3181 or 800-535-9469);* and the US Forest Service Chetco Ranger District headquarters *(541-469-2196).*

**Horseback riding** For horse rentals and information on rides and trips, contact Hawk's Rest Ranch Stables and Trail Rides *(Pistol River. 541-247-6423);* or the Agness-Illahe Historical Center *(Agness. 541-247-2014).*

**Rogue River boat trips** Outfitters offer trips of varying lengths and destinations into the Rogue's Wild and Scenic section from Gold Beach to Grants Pass. Two leading Gold Beach outfitters are Jerry's Rogue Jets *(541-247-4571 or 800-451-3645)* and Rogue River Mailboats *(541-247-7033 or 800-458-3511).*

**Whale-watching** *(Oregon Parks 541-563-2002)* Excursion boats depart from most harbor towns between March and October.

**Wine tasting** The Banana Belt's climate produces superb varietal wines. You can taste them at Bridgeview Vineyard and Win-

**Two-Mile Rapids, Rogue River**

ery *(2 miles E of US 199 off Oreg. 46, at 4210 Holland Loop Rd. 541-592-4688),* and nearby Foris Vineyards Winery *(off Holland Loop Rd. at 654 Kendall Rd., Cave Junction. 541-592-3752 or 800-84-FORIS).*

## Annual Events

**May** Azalea Festival *(Brookings. 541-469-3181 or 800-535-9469. Mem. Day weekend);* Boatnik *(Grants Pass. 541-476-7717 or 800-547-7927)*

**June** Jet Boat Marathon *(Gold Beach. 800-525-2334);* Pistol River Wave Bash *(Pistol River. 541-247-4153)*

**September** Festival of Quilts *(Gold Beach. 800-525-2334)*

## Lodging

**Chetco River Inn** *(21202 High Prairie Rd., Brookings. 541-670-1645 or 800-327-2688)* The Chetco River coils around three sides of the 35-acre tract of private forest surrounding the homey oak- and cedar-built hotel.

**Tu Tú Tun Lodge** *(96550 North Bank Rogue, Gold Beach. 541-247-6664)* This rustic and luxurious riverside wilderness lodge 7 miles up the Rogue offers gourmet *prix fixe* dinners and a three-meal plan that features local fare such as Chinook salmon. Imagine a forest retreat you might build; this is it.

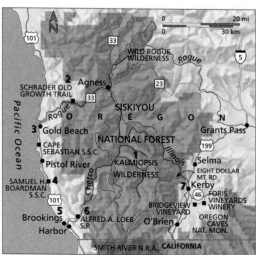

# OREGON
# High Desert

Surprises abound in southeast Oregon. That such an area even exists in Oregon is perhaps the biggest surprise. Erase those images of grand conifer forests and rocky seashores. Instead, picture sagebrush grasslands, cattle ranches, and pocket towns that wouldn't seem out of place in a Zane Grey novel. Within this unexpected high desert realm, many particular surprises await, including duck-filled marshlands, a mountain ridge nearly 10,000 feet high, and a herd of pronghorn. Southeast Oregon may be far from civilization, but it's far from empty.

A 70-mile-long massif, **Steens Mountain** lies at the heart of Oregon's high desert. On the west it slopes up gently from the sagebrush flats; on the east it rises precipitously, a basalt rampart towering a mile above the plain below. Whether travelers ascend from the west via the loop road or rock climb up with the bighorn sheep from the east, they reach the same 9,700-foot-high ridge from which most of southeast Oregon is visible. Though

**Looking up Big Indian Gorge, Steens Mountain**

you can see thousands of square miles, the only signs of human occupation are a few widely dispersed ranch buildings. The remoteness simultaneously unnerves and exhilarates.

The Steens, as locals call the mountain, is more than a massive platform from which to view the rest of the region. Is there a better way to spend an hour than to sit against a gnarled mountain mahogany above Big Indian Gorge, watching hawks ride the thermals? During summer the Steens's western slope riots with wildflowers: Indian paintbrush, wild geranium, and penstemons as blue as a mountain lake. At dusk in the juniper woods, hikers often hear a deep, hollow thrumming: the sound of courting nighthawks.

Did somebody mention birds? People come from all over to watch birds at **Malheur National Wildlife Refuge.** Surrounded by miles and miles of mostly arid terrain, Malheur's 186,000 acres of lakes, marshes, and wet meadows act as a magnet to birds, especially during the spring and fall migrations. More than 300 species have been sighted here over the years, including birds that you might expect, such as western meadowlarks and golden eagles. But you'll also come across species that seem out of place in the desert, including white pelicans, sandpipers, and 29 species of waterfowl.

Wildlife also is the raison d'être of southeast Oregon's other refuge, the **Hart Mountain National Antelope Refuge.** Established in 1936 as one in a series of national measures to bring the pronghorn back from near extinction, the refuge harbors a summer herd of about 2,000 of the antelope-like creatures. (Though people call pronghorn "antelope," they're not related to the true antelopes of the Old World.) Because they're here to breed, it's possible to see gawky pronghorn fawns gamboling about as they learn to run—you'll spot them mainly on the open flats on the refuge's east side, but don't neglect the mountainous western section.

The eponymous Hart Mountain rises above 8,000 feet and an imposing fault-block wall almost as long and high as the Steens marks the western boundary. The deeply incised terrain offers hikers some dramatic rifts to explore, such as De Garmo Canyon. A path winds up along De Garmo Creek, following the lush riparian tangle of alder, willow, aspen, and dogwood. The canyon's tumultuous terrain harbors animals that thrive in vertical landscapes, such as bighorn sheep and prairie falcons.

After seeing so much wildlife and driving back roads that go 100 miles without a gas station, travelers may conclude that humans have no place in southeast Oregon. Not so. Native Americans lived here for centuries. In the late 1800s and early 1900s, cattle barons, homesteaders, and Basque sheepherders settled in this area. Some of their artifacts can be seen at the **Harney County Historical Museum,** a pleasing grandma's attic of a museum in **Burns.** Travelers also should visit some of the scattered historical sites, such as the **Pete French Round Barn State Heritage Site.** Peter French was a king among cattle barons; his domination of southeast Oregon ended abruptly in 1897, when a disgruntled homesteader shot him in the head.

These days shots generally are directed at road signs, not at people, but in less lethal ways the frontier era still appears. In Diamond, the next person to walk into the local café easily could be a cowboy, complete with hat and handlebar moustache. Up in Crane, children attend one of the nation's few public boarding schools; their remote ranch and farm houses make daily travel impractical. Frenchglen serves as something of a regional center, what with its store, two-room school, gas station, and small historic hotel, yet its population could fit inside a couple of minivans.

**Pronghorn, Hart Mountain National Antelope Refuge**

It's not that people in southeast Oregon don't live in the 1990s; they use cell phones and pull in *Frasier* on their satellite dishes. But they also ride horses and spend time on generous front porches. Past and present blur. The same holds true for the natural world. Overgrazing and irrigation withdrawals have altered the landscape; and people long ago decimated some of the wildlife populations. Yet many habitats, animals, and plants remain, giving travelers a glimpse of the original natural bounty. .And southeast Oregon's grand beauty remains unimpaired. You still can marvel at the imposing escarpments, horizonless vistas, and bright stars that blaze in clear night skies.                                   —*Bob Devine*

**Ducks in flight at the Malheur National Wildlife Refuge**

# Travel Notes

### Directions

Oregon's High Desert is located in the southeast corner of the state, bounded by US 20 and US 395. **By car:** Travelers coming from Bend, 130 miles west, can follow US 20 east to Burns.

### General Information

The best weather occurs in spring, summer, and fall, but consider other seasonal factors: The road up the Steens typically is open from mid-July to mid-October; the bugs in Malheur are pretty bad in the spring; and the pronghorn high season runs from June through September. For information, contact the Harney County Chamber of Commerce *(18 W. D St., Burns 97720. 541-573-2636).*

### Things to See and Do

**1. Burns** *(Chamber of Commerce 541-573-2636)* The jam-packed **Harney County Historical Museum** *(18 W. D St. 541-573-5618. April-Sept. Tues.-Sat.; adm. fee)* displays some Native American items and some mounted birds from Malheur N.W.R., but its strong suit is its collection of pioneer artifacts.

**2. Malheur National Wildlife Refuge** *(Off Oreg. 205. 541-493-2612. Refuge and museum open daily, Visitor Center Mon.-Fri. year-round and some weekends in spring and summer)* A remarkable variety of birds and other animals find sanctuary on the refuge's marshes, lakes, and wetlands. The excellent museum features hundreds of mounted birds.

**3. Diamond Craters Outstanding Natural Area** *(Map available at Bureau of Land Management, US 20/395 W of Hines. 541-573-4400)* Hidden amid the sagebrush-covered hills lies this impressive assemblage of craters, lava tubes, and other volcanic features.

**4. Pete French Round Barn State Heritage Site** *(Off Oreg. 205, about 13 miles N of Diamond)* Cattle baron Pete French needed a constant supply of horses for the cowboys who worked his vast "P" Ranch in Harney County, so he had this and two other round barns built in the early 1880s to break and exercise the animals during the winter.

**5. Steens Mountain** *(Information and maps available at Bureau of Land Management, US 20/395 W of Hines. 541-573-4400)* A 55-mile gravel-and-dirt loop road (rough and rocky in places) takes travelers past meadows, aspen groves, and broad glacial valleys to the 9,700-foot ridgeline of this fault-block mountain.

**6. Alvord Desert** *(E of the Steens)* You can walk or even drive out onto this otherworldly landscape of dried, cracked mud dusted white and devoid of vegetation.

**7. Hart Mountain National Antelope Refuge** *(E of Plush. Information available at refuge headquarters, off Frenchglen Rd. 541-947-3315)* This haven for pronghorn and other wildlife also features dramatic canyons, high mountains, and huge desert vistas.

### Lodging

**Frenchglen Hotel** *(Oreg. 205, Frenchglen. 541-493-2825. Mid-March–mid-Nov.)* The small, plain, well-kept 1920s hotel offers pleasant family-style dinners and a front porch that looks into the Malheur N.W.R. **Hotel Diamond** *(Diamond. 541-493-1898. Mid-March–mid-Nov.)* The last four digits of the phone number reveal the date when this historic hotel was built. A recent restoration should carry this gem well into the 21st century.

# WASHINGTON

# Sasquatch Country

Like a mute and frozen ghost from ages past, glacier-mantled 14,410-foot Mount Rainier watches over the Seattle-Tacoma metropolis from some 40 miles southeast atop the rugged spine of the Cascade Range. Among the world's most potentially hazardous volcanoes, inactive since the late 1800s, Rainier and still-active Mount St. Helens 50-odd miles south remind the cities' populaces that this is the Pacific Northwest, and that the primordial wild is closer than they might think. Indeed, anyone hiking the shadowy depths of the region's lush forests will understand how the myth of Sasquatch—the legendary apeman—has persisted over the years.

The eruption of **Mount St. Helens** in 1980 focused national attention on the Cascades, which march in close-order drill from Lassen Peak in

**Mount St. Helens National Volcanic Monument**

northern California into Canada, their volcanic tendencies repressed until the cataclysmic blast flattened about 200 square miles of the **Gifford Pinchot National Forest**. About a cubic mile of mountain shot over 12 miles high that May morning, creating the cinder-gray moonscapes of 110,000-acre **Mount St. Helens National Volcanic Monument**. The devastation will inevitably cause you to direct uneasy glances at the steaming peak, but the greater wonder here is nature's indomitable life force. At first, plants and wildflowers led by pink-red fireweed poked through the ashes, as if to reconnoiter. After awhile, the resurgent greenery brought animals back into the incinerated habitat, along with curious visitors lured by the region's scenic roads.

## Sasquatch, phone home!

Legends die hard, particularly when there is an "authentic" home movie capturing the tall, hairy, apelike biped in full stride, and "genuine" plaster casts of its giant "footprints." Native Americans, who named Sasquatch, believed absolutely in the creature, and considered it merely elusive. Reported sightings throughout the Pacific Northwest have diminished in recent years, fueling speculation that the real "Bigfoot" hung up his gorilla suit and is somewhere chuckling over his hoax. Others, however, think Sasquatches may have simply become extinct.

The word "scenic" is used to death, admittedly, but here it carries a full set of credentials: grand forest—trees 200 feet tall—plunging canyons, serene meadows, naked crags, leafy woods, and always the towering Cascades. "Scenic" designations appear on most highways to and through the Sasquatch country: Wash. 7, 161, and 410 from the Seattle-Tacoma area; Wash. 12 between I-5 and Yakima, and especially Wash. 504, the road to the monument from Castle Rock. If you haven't time for the 43-mile drive up along the North Fork Toutle River to the **Coldwater Ridge Visitor Center** (which has impressive views and a pleasant restaurant), at least take in the monument's Visitor Center beside **Silver Lake**, where exhibits detail the ominous geologic stirrings preceding the awful blast.

The first outsiders to probe this wilderness were 17th-century fur trappers who came for beaver and otter pelts. They traded amiably with the region's native tribes, mostly nomadic hunters and river salmon fishermen who summered in the Cascades. Native American names are everywhere on your map: Snohomish, Nisqually, Chehalis, Puyallup. Gold and silver strikes accelerated settlement, forcing the retreat of Native Americans to reservations. Farmers followed the prospectors into coastal lowlands and interior basins, but Sasquatch country was left alone until the 1880s, when the timber industry left depleted Great Lakes forests for the Cascades. By the 1920s, logging trains chuffed through their forests of fir, pine, hemlock, and spruce, supplying the nation's ever-growing demand for lumber.

What's the old saying? Find where big trucks are parked and the eating's good? Barely 1,100 people live in the logging town of Morton, but there are times when it appears that every one of them drives a logging truck and parks it on Morton's main street, where you'll find real "Logger Breakfasts," with calorie counts triple the population, served up by a half-dozen excellent eateries.

Before diesel trucks came along, logs were hauled through these parts by standard-gauge steam locomotives. Most are museum pieces now, but in tiny **Elbe** you'll find one fired up and hooked to refurbished vintage passenger coaches, doing business as the **Mount Rainier Scenic Railroad.** Scenic its 14-mile run is, through conifer stands and over snow-fed streams to piney **Mineral Lake.** Elbe was named by its German immigrant majority, seeking to honor pioneer settler Henry Lutkens, who was born in Germany's Elbe River Valley. Old-country hymns occasionally rise inside the quaint roadside Evangelische Lutherische Kirche, built in 1906 by Elbe's Lutheran faithful.

**Carbon River Rain Forest, Mount Rainier National Park**

You might have to pull over for a lumber company truck now and then, but logging roads—generally paved and well-maintained—lead to many lovely backwoods destinations far from the snarl of chain saws. One of the most appealing is the Indian Heaven Wilderness just east of Mount St. Helens, where wild huckleberries grow in profusion, sugaring up from late July through September. If you catch glimpses of 12,276-foot Mount Adams, centerpiece of its namesake wilderness area to the east, you're looking at the western boundary of the vast Yakama Indian Reservation.

You might not sense it among the evergreens, but you're actually on the fringe of Washington's sagebrush ranching country. That's plain to see in nearby Glenwood, which amounts to little more than the Shade Tree Inn, a roadside restaurant where patrons sport working Western garb. Ask for their free map, which points out the area's waterfalls and camping spots, and provides information on fishing and white-water rafting. In nearby Trout Lake, you'll feel like you've found one of the most out-of-the-way mail drops in the Cascades. In reality, you're barely a half-hour north of the Columbia River Gorge National Scenic Area and its lovely drive west to Portland—as painless as a leave-taking from this splendid getaway can be.

—*Mark Miller*

# Travel Notes

### Directions
Sasquatch Country is located in south-central Washington, roughly bounded to the north by Mount Rainier N.P., to the south by the Columbia River, and to the west and east by Mount St. Helens N.M. and the Yakama Indian Reservation respectively. **By car:** I-5, I-84, and I-90 permit quick approaches from Seattle and Portland. **By plane:** Airports in Portland and Seattle are both 40 minutes away. **By train:** Amtrak serves Portland and Seattle, and several stops in between.

### General Information
Winter snows close roads at higher elevations, and linger into July. Summer days are warm, with exuberant wildflower blooms in July and August. Mount Rainier and Mount St. Helens are popular destinations, so weekend traffic may be heavy at any time, especially in summer. A national forest map, available at most ranger and visitor stations, is essential for backcountry driving. Five Visitor Centers along Wash. 504 offer general information for the area; or contact the Mount St. Helens National Volcanic Monument Visitor Center (*3029 Spirit Lake Hwy., Castle Rock 98611. 360-274-2100*).

### Things to See and Do
**1. Mount Rainier National Park**
(*Entrances off Wash. 706, 123, and 165. 360-569-2211. Adm. fee*) Entering from the west

**Autumn colors at Mount Rainier N.P.**

via Wash. 706 leads quickly past the museum at **Longmire** to the vistas of the Henry M. Jackson Memorial Visitor Center at **Paradise** (Early May–mid-Oct. daily, weekends rest of year). The park has many self-guided nature trails and roadside exhibits, and free naturalist-led tours from all four Visitor Centers. Vine maple, mountain ash, and hemlock peak in late September to early October.

**2. Elbe** The **Mount Rainier Scenic Railroad** (Wash. 7. 360-569-2588 or 888-783-2611. Mid-June–Labor Day daily, Labor Day–Sept. weekends; fare) offers a choice between restored vintage coaches and open-air cars for the 1.5-hour trip to **Mineral Lake.** Ask about 4-hour Sunday evening "dinner" train rides.

**3. Pioneer Farm Museum** (3 miles N of Eatonville, at 7716 Ohop Valley Rd./Wash. 7. 360-832-6300. Mid-June–Labor Day daily, March–mid-June and Labor Day–Thanksgiving weekends; adm. fee) Urban sprawl has erased most relics of the coastal region's early rural culture, when dairy cattle grazed among evergreens. The museum's 1880s-era farmstead is a re-creation, but so well done you'll feel like you've come to a housewarming, not a living history center.

**4. Gifford Pinchot National Forest** (Headquarters, 10600 N.E. 51st Cir., Vancouver. 360-891-5000. Information Stations in Packwood, Amboy, Randle, and Carson. Camping June-Oct.) There's little in the way of outdoor recreation you can't find here, where weather is more moderate than that in northerly Mount Rainier National Park. The 1.25 million-acre reserve holds seven designated wilderness areas.

**5. Mount St. Helens National Volcanic Monument** (40 miles E of Silver Lake on Wash. 504. 360-247-3900. Adm. fee) Five Visitor Centers along Wash. 504 offer close-up views of the recovering forests flattened by the 1980 eruption. The **Coldwater Ridge Visitor Center** (360-274-2131), only 7 miles from ground zero, has impressive views of the crater's bulging lava dome.

### Other Activities
**Backcountry hiking** Contact the National

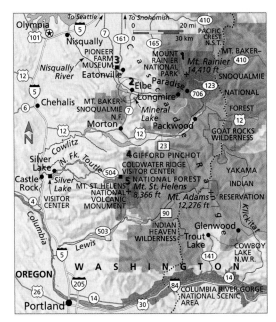

Forest Service and National Park Service Outdoor Information Center in Seattle (206-470-4060) for information on trails, including the Pacific Crest National Scenic Trail.

**Climbing** The adventure requires preparation, conditioning, and professional guides. The Visitor Center at Paradise (360-569-2211) can recommend companies that conduct guided climbs up Mount Rainier. For information on climbing Mount St. Helens, call the hot line at 360-247-3961.

### Annual Events
**August** Logger's Jubilee (Morton. 360-496-6086)
**September** Western Washington State Fair (Puyallup. 253-845-6755 or 253-841-5045); Historic Homes Tour (Snohomish. 360-568-2526)

### Lodging
**The Farm** (490 Sunnyside Rd., Trout Lake. 509-395-2488) Antiques and quilts fill the rooms of this 1890 farmhouse.
**Paradise Inn** (Off Wash. 706, Paradise Historic Area, Mount Rainier N.P. 360-569-2275. Mid-May–early Oct.) Rustic, cozy, and lofty—at 5,400 feet elevation—the venerable 116-room stone-and-carved cedar lodge, completed in 1917, faces Rainier's southern slope and its glaciers.

# The Okanogans

Silence and solitude reign in this mountain-and-steppe realm of northeastern Washington, named for the tribe of Native Americans who once ranged along the valley of their namesake river from the Columbia River to British Columbia. Thinly settled, its rural hamlets modest and unprepossessing, the Okanogan region appeals most to contemplative travelers, especially those who paint or photograph. Apples and wheat flourish in the Okanogan River valley, which gives way to rolling sagebrush grasslands and then arid forests that wrap the mountains of the Okanogan Highlands like buffalo robes. The mountains' gray cockscomb pinnacles give no hint of the serene alpine plateaus beyond, where snowfields water verdant meadows and deep cold lakes offer some of the Evergreen State's finest camping and trout fishing.

## Tribal Tongues

French traders rarely spoke the Salish language of Eastern Washington's tribes. Often, when pronunciation of tribal names defied their tongues, French substitutes were coined. Probably the most well-known example: Idaho's Sahaptin-speaking Nimiipu became the Nez Perce ("pierced nose"). The roots of other tribal names are harder to trace, but there is surely French influence in the names of the San Poil, who lived in the state's northeastern portion, and the Palouse, who called the Palouse River valley home. Those who seem to have escaped the French connection include the Okanogan, the Methow, and the Wenatchee, whose names live on throughout the region.

People often come to this corner without plans and wander randomly, knowing they can't go wrong even if they get lost. They're right; they can't help but find charming little towns to explore, and picturesque roads meandering overland through farmlands and woods, and scores of opportunities to win next year's photography contest. What they also can't avoid is utter peace—the sigh of wind through larch and lodgepole pine, its wheezy whispers in juniper and sage.

Newcomers to the region are surprised to find much of it not forested, claimed instead by the rugged, sparse, rolling terrain of the Columbia Basin steppe. It's not truly desert; strictly speaking the area is too wet for that, though its hot dry summers, occasional bursts of cactus, scuttling lizards, and elusive rattlesnakes perpetuate the notion. Steppe it is, however, too dry for trees but wet enough to grow a perennial carpet of wild grass tufted with threetip sagebrush. These wild, rumpled meadows rise into rolling rocky uplands spiked

**Alpine meadow in mist**

with broken granite spires rising to 8,000 feet. Follow a network of hiking trails over their crests and you'll find gentle bowls of alpine turf and heath, stippled with wildflowers and wild herbs whose names have a fanciful, Wind-in-the-Willows sound: the coil-beaked lousewort, snowbed cinquefoil, Alpine pussytoes.

None of this interested the first Oregon Trail migrants of the 1800s, who bypassed northeastern Washington for the fertile Willamette River valley beyond the Cascades. The Homestead Act encouraged the next generation of Northwest sodbusters and ranchers to venture into the wilds west of Spokane and north of the Columbia River to "prove out" land claims on the "Late Frontier," sometimes called Washington's Old West.

In the 1860s, hundreds of Canada-bound cattle drives raised hopes along the Cariboo Trail, a route paralleling modern-day US 97, but many ranches still failed. Northeastern Washington is littered with the wreckage of these broken dreams: rusting metal tripods where windmills spun, marooned equipment, abandoned barns, and farmhouses with windows empty as the eyes of a skull. Some, like Hiram Smith, fared well. In 1854, near Oroville, Smith seeded one of eastern Washington's first apple orchards, "proving out" not only his homestead but also the Okanogan River valley's hidden promise, realized today through extensive irrigation, as one of the Evergreen State's top producers of apples, pears, peaches, and cherries.

Before the farmers came fur trappers, prospectors, and missionaries; and, before them all, the region's Indian tribes, a baker's dozen whose stories are woven together at the riverside **Okanogan County Historical Museum** in

**Okanogan River valley**

Okanogan. Boosters once promoted the town, established in 1888, as the Okanogan River's head of navigation, preferring not to mention that the stream ran deep enough to float a riverboat only in May and June. You'll find the region's history, a saga with as many players as in a James Michener epic, lucidly summarized in exhibits at the Fort Okanogan Interpretive Center near Brewster.

If your travels start anywhere near **Omak**, a bricky early-century lumber and apple growing town, spend a few minutes at the **Visitor Information Center,** where maps and information will help you choose destinations corresponding to your interests. Among the more curious is the old mining town of Molson, forced to relocate from a mile down the road when a mix-up involving title claims delivered its land to a farmer. "Old" Molson's outdoor museum features antique mining equipment, and the nearby Molson School museum holds another historical archive. Until recently, nearby Nighthawk was a bona fide ghost town in the humble pastorale of the Similkameen River valley. You'll find some 40 old buildings here, and the countryside dotted with the remnants of old mines. Today, local entrepreneurs are betting on vineyards to supply Washington's ever-burgeoning premium wine industry.

It's another world entirely within the huge **Colville Indian Reservation,** where many of the region's original tribes now reside under a single banner.

The epic odyssey of the legendary Nez Perce leader Chief Joseph ended here. Rather than submit to internment on a reservation, Joseph led a tribal band on a 1,500-mile fighting retreat from the U.S. Cavalry toward Canada before surrendering in 1877. His tale ended in lifelong exile from his homeland at the reservation, where he died in 1904. You'll not soon forget the faces (including Joseph's) gazing at you out of time at the **Confederated Tribes of the Colville Reservation Museum.**

As you travel the Sherman Pass Scenic Byway (Wash. 20) between Republic and Kettle Falls, indisputably northeastern Washington's most scenic drive, you'll rise and fall over rolling sagebrush hills, then climb through forests of fir, pine, and larch to 5,575-foot Sherman Pass. **Republic** sprang to life during a gold rush in the 1890s, and still digs for the yellow metal. Many local hearts race faster over the town's rich fossil beds, which yield the stony imprints of plants and insects buried in volcanic ash and mud some 50 million years ago. Prize finds are exhibited at Republic's **Stonerose Interpretive Center**, named for an Eocene-epoch rose leaf unearthed here—most appropriate for a region of painterly panoramas where the main recreational pursuit is smelling the flowers.

*—Mark Miller*

# Travel Notes

### Directions
The Okanagans area is roughly bounded by the Canadian border, by US 97 on the west, the Columbia River to the east, and the Colville Indian Reservation on the south. **By car:** Coming from the west on I-90, which links Spokane and Seattle, take US 97 north from Ellensburg through Wenatchee to Wash. 17 and Omak. Travelers starting from Spokane may take US 395 north to Kettle Falls, where Wash. 20 offers a splendidly scenic drive west into the region. **By air:** The closest airport is in Spokane. **By train:** Amtrak serves Spokane.

### General Information
Spring, summer, and fall are the Okanagans' most hospitable seasons, with the nod going to autumnal months. Winters tend to be gray and, of course, very cold. Omak's Visitor Information Center *(401 Omak Ave., Omak 98841. 509-826-4218 or 800-225-6625)* and the Oroville Visitor

Information Center *(1728 Main St., P.O. Box 536, Oroville 98844. 509-476-2739)* are excellent resources.

### Things to See and Do
**1. Okanogan** At the **Okanogan County Historical Museum** *(1410 N. 2nd Ave.*

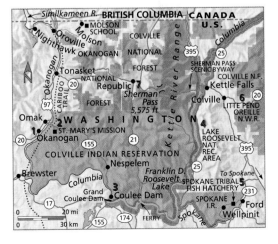

**Northern spotted owl**

509-422-4272. Mid-May–mid-Sept.; adm. fee), the fine exhibition of historical photographs, Indian artifacts, and relics from early farming and ranching days imparts a vivid sense of the region's cultural heritage, adding to your appreciation of its peculiar rural charm.

**2. St. Mary's Mission** (Omak Lake Rd., off Wash. 155, about 5 miles E of Omak. 509-826-2097. Donation) The exceedingly pretty granite canyon cradling this recently restored 1915 missionary church is alone worth the drive. Register at the Pascal Sherman Indian School office first, then ask for directions to the nearby waterfall, where rocks are adorned with petroglyphs.

**3. Coulee Dam** The small but evocative collection at the **Confederated Tribes of the Colville Reservation Museum** (512 Meadway St. 509-633-0751. April-Dec. Mon.-Sat.; adm. fee), housed in an old Catholic missionary church, features artifacts of 19th-century tribal culture, including cedar-strip basketry, and a haunting photographic archive.

**4. Lake Roosevelt National Recreation Area** (Headquarters, 1008 Crest Dr., Coulee Dam. 509-633-9441) Wash. 25 follows the scenic upper eastern shoreline of 150-mile-long Franklin D. Roosevelt Lake, created when the Grand Coulee Dam blocked the Columbia and the Spokane Rivers. Millions of migratory birds rest and roost here, along with resident eagles.

**5. Spokane Tribal Fish Hatchery** (Off Martha Boardman Rd., 2.5 miles W of Ford/Wellpinit jct.. near Wellpinit. 509-258-7297) In a scenic setting, interpretive exhibits of local Native American history and culture adjoin natural springs where salmon

and rainbow trout are raised for release into the upper Columbia River system.

**6. Little Pend Oreille National Wildlife Refuge** (11 miles SE of Colville, off Wash. 20. 509-684-8384) Rough back roads make this side trip best taken in a 4-wheel-drive vehicle, but the rewards are considerable: Pine forests are home to deer, bears, wildcats, squirrels, and birds.

**7. Republic** Visitors to the **Stonerose Interpretive Center** (15 N. Kean St. 509-775-2295. Mid-June–mid-Sept. Tues.-Sun., May–mid-June and mid-Sept.-Oct. Tues.-Sat.; fossil hunting fee) may also tour and rent tools to scour the center's unprepossessing but well-studied paleontological site for 50-million-year-old fossils of plants, insects, and fish.

## Annual Events

**May** Sunflower Festival (Omak. 509-826-1880) Traditional Native American foods and celebrations are featured.

**June** Prospector's Days (Republic. 509-775-2704) Displays of vintage equipment, and manly competitions such as log-rolling and tree-topping celebrate local logging and mining history.

**August** Omak Stampede and Suicide Race (Colville Reservation, Omak. 509-826-1880) This four-day top-ranked rodeo includes Indian music, drumming and dancing competitions, and break-neck horse races including a horse-rider swim across the Okanogan River; Spokane Falls Northwest Indian Encampment & Pow Wow (Riverfront Park, Spokane. 509-625-6685)

## Lodging

**Amy's Manor** (435 Rte. 153, 4.5 miles N of Pateros. 509-923-2334) Nearly 180 acres of woodland, orchard, and grassy meadow surround this casual, homey riverside country place in a charming 1928 shuttered stucco residence near Lake Chelan. Breakfast fare draws from the inn's organic garden and adjoining orchard.

**Hidden Hills Guest Ranch** (18 miles S of Tonasket off US 97, at 104 Hidden Hills Ln. 509-486-1890 or 800-468-1890) Mountain views and a setting of meadows and pine trees add to the charm of this pretty Victorian country inn, whose 10 guest rooms are decorated in Gilded Age style.

## ALASKA
# Kenai Peninsula

An extraordinarily scenic sampler of Alaska's great wild begins
minutes south of Anchorage, as you confront the Kenai Peninsula's
towering topography, pristine vistas, and myriad wildlife. The
Kenai hangs from an isthmus cut by ice age glaciers that once sub-
merged its 13,000-foot mountains. Their descendants, perpetually
renewed by 12-foot snowfalls, still sculpture the peninsula's frozen
canyons into long alpine valleys, and spew silt-laden "glacial milk"
into fast-running streams that splash through dark forests. Along its
rocky shores, fishing settlements make a living by welcoming
travelers, and Native Alaskan communities preserve the vestigates
of 19th-century Russian immigrants on their own timeless past.

**Seward Small Boat Harbor**

Look across the windy waters of Cook Inlet at the dark serrations of the Alaska Range, North America's tallest mountains, some with vertical rises greater than Mount Everest's. Twenty miles distant, you say? Try 80 miles, and chalk the illusion up to Alaska's crystalline air. But forgive yourself, for in 1778 no less of a savvy dead reckoner than Captain James Cook sailed halfway up the channel, believing it might be the fabled Northwest Passage. Despite its proximity to Anchorage, the Kenai Peninsula remains largely a wilderness. Most of its 48,000 people live by the sea, leaving the interior to outdoor enthusiasts and its peaceable kingdom of moose, bear, Dall's sheep, lynx, beaver, eagles, and water birds.

Just south of Anchorage, water birds populate the mudflats of the Anchorage Coastal Wildlife Refuge, and 3-foot-long, 40-pound Chinook salmon cruise the pellucid waters of **Potter Marsh**, a splendid bird nesting habitat created in 1916 when the Alaska Railroad laid a track to Seward, damming a stream that empties into Turnagain Arm. In spring, look for Canada geese, trumpeter swans, and mallards among the reeds.

While the heavy sunlight broils your bare head, the chill from **Portage Glacier** will raise goose bumps on your arms. In the August spawning season, pools at the glacier's Visitor Center complex roil with bright-red salmon. Portage is shrinking, however, and many consider **Exit Glacier** in **Kenai Fjords National Park** a more memorable introduction to these blue-ice behemoths. Exit Glacier's flow ends 13 miles northwest of the bustling sport-fishing town of **Seward** on Resurrection Bay. An easy .75-mile stroll leads to the glacier's 150-foot-high turquoise-hued spires, known as seracs. If you're fit and have the time, an arduous full-day 3,000-foot climb up the 3.5-mile Harding Icefield Trail rewards you with a spectacular sight: Harding Icefield, Exit Glacier's source, a nearly 700-square-mile ice field—the largest entirely within the United States.

## Whittier Cut-off

One of Alaska's most unusual side trips begins at Portage at the bottom of Turnagain Arm. Here, motorists drive onto Alaska Railroad flatbed cars for a scenic but lurching 12.4-mile ride to Whittier, a World War II-era military port. From here, visitors can board their cars onto an Alaska Marine Highway ferry to the pipeline oil port of Valdez—a memorable ride that crosses Prince William Sound, skirting the Columbia Glacier, whose perpetual winter sends sunbathing passengers scurrying for overcoats. Call 907-265-2494 or 800-544-0552 for information.

Many travelers inadvertently bypass the Kenai's west coast, where early 19th-century Russian missionaries, traders, and fishermen founded colonies among Native Alaskan settlements on Cook Inlet. The 143-mile Sterling Highway (Alas. 1) leaves the Seward Highway at Tern Lake junction and winds through the 2-million-acre **Kenai National Wildlife Refuge**, whose lakes teem with moose and beaver. From spring through fall, the refuge's lowland forests echo with the bleat of trumpeter swans.

The name of Soldotna reflects Alaska's Russian bloodlines, but the hamlet has lost most signs of it to growth. You'll appreciate **Kenai** for sweeping visits of Cook Inlet (an excellent spot for binocular-aided whale-watching) and the 1894 **Holy Assumption of the Virgin Mary Russian Orthodox Church,** which holds religious artifacts brought by the Russian émigrés.

The Russian imprint remains vivid in the coastal village of **Ninilchik,** whose lovely beach is known for excellent clamming. Grigorri Kvasnikoff, a lay missionary from the Moscow area, arrived here in 1847. The village—whose local telephone directory is sprinkled with names like Resoff, Leman, Oskolkoff, and Kompkoff—is still strongly Russian Orthodox, and venerates the photogenic **Holy Transfiguration of Our Lord Russian Orthodox Church.** The interior isn't open for tours, but if you walk up the trail from the Village Cache Store to the shrine's bluff-top location, you'll find a 45-mile view across Cook Inlet; ancient Redoubt and Iliamna

**Holy Assumption of the Virgin Mary Russian Orthodox Church, Kenai**

**Brown bear**

Volcanoes rise 10,000 feet above the water.

**Homer** is Alaska's Greenwich Village, an eccentric, fun-loving end-of-the-road creative colony with a literate newspaper and a thoughtfully programmed public radio station. The much-touted Homer Spit, a 4.5-mile gravel bar extending into Kachemak Bay, often suffers from RV overload. Better to spend your time roaming Homer's "downtown," chockablock with art galleries and appealing if odd shops. Much of the best local artwork is exhibited along with historical artifacts at the **Pratt Museum.** There's plenty to see and do here—more than enough to fill even a 19-hour day.

*—Mark Miller*

# Travel Notes

## Directions
The Kenai Peninsula lies south of Anchorage. **By car:** Two well-maintained highways link the Kenai with Anchorage: the 127-mile Seward Highway—Alas. I and Alas. 9—to Seward; and the 143-mile Sterling Highway from the Seward's Tern Lake junction, which follows Alas. I to Homer. **By air:** The nearest major airport is in Anchorage. **By sea:** Many of Alaska's visitors arrive by cruise ship or ferry via the Inside Passage, the channel between Vancouver Island and the British Columbia mainland. Alaska Marine Highway ferries embark from Bellingham, Washington, and Prince Rupert, British Columbia, connecting with the Alaska Highway system at Skagway and Haines. Motorists who want to continue their travels from Whittier, Homer, or Seward aboard Alaska Marine Highway ferries *(fare)* should call 907-235-8449 or 800-382-9229.

## General Information
Summer—June through August—is Alaska's high season, sometimes hot, occasionally rainy and cool, with 19-hour days that go directly from twilight to dawn. Highway traffic is heavy in summer. Advance reservations for lodging are strongly advised and imperative for passage on Alaska Marine Highway ferries. The best official source of information is the Alaska Division of Tourism *(333 Willoughby St., 9th floor, P.O. Box 110801, Juneau 99811-0801. 907-465-2010).*

## Things to See and Do
**1. Potter Marsh** *(Seward Hwy. Milepost 117.4. 907-269-2556)* An extensive boardwalk across the marsh permits close-up viewing of bald eagles, nesting trumpeter swans, Canada geese, and other waterfowl.
**2. Potter Section House State Historic Park** *(Seward Hwy. Mile 115. 907-345-5014)* A small museum in an old seaside Alaska Railroad section house documents the lonely life of early railroaders.
**3. Portage Glacier** *(Off Seward Hwy., Chugach National Forest. Begich, Boggs Visitor Center 907-783-2326)* Learn why glacial ice is blue at the Visitor Center.
**4. Kenai Fjords National Park** *(Visitor Center, Alas. 9 just outside the park's eastern boundary. Mem. Day–Labor Day daily, Mon.-Fri. rest of year. Park headquarters 907-224-3175.*

*Adm. fee)* Be sure to ask about ranger-led hikes to the towering base of **Exit Glacier.**

**5. Seward** *(Chamber of Commerce 907-224-8051)* Stop by the Information Cache *(3rd and Jefferson Sts. 907-224-3094)* for self-guided walking tour maps of the town's Victorian-era houses. The $52 million **Alaska Sealife Center** *(Railway and 4th Aves. 907-224-6300 or 800-224-2525. Adm. fee),* open in mid-1998, includes underwater looks at coastal sealife.

**6. Kenai National Wildlife Refuge** *(Visitor Center, Ski Hill Rd. off Sterling Hwy., Soldotna. 907-262-7021)* Four thousand lakes and 300 campsites make this one of the peninsula's most popular spots for sylvan sojourns.

**7. Kenai** *(Visitor Information 907-283-1991)* The peninsula's largest city (population approximately 7,000) dates from 1791, when Russian fur traders built a fort here. The **Holy Assumption of the Virgin Mary Russian Orthodox Church** adjoins the site of the Army's **Fort Kenay,** put up in 1869.

**8. Ninilchik** *(Visitor Information at the Village Cache Store, Village Rd. near Sterling Hwy. Mile 135.1)* The decaying fishing village of old Ninilchik *(Village Rd. Pick up information at Village Cache Store)* and the nearby cemetery and Russian Orthodox church of the **Holy Transfiguration of Our Lord** offer a chance to win photography prizes. The ocean-level **Deep Creek Recreation Area** *(Sterling Hwy. Mile 137.3)* is one of the peninsula's finest camping spots.

**9. Homer** *(Chamber of Commerce/Visitor Center 907-235-7740)* Start your tour at the **Pratt Museum** *(3779 Bartlett St. 907-235-8635)* for a historical overview of the town. Homer appears less sophisticated than it is; here are several of the state's more interesting restaurants, including the **Two Sisters Bakery** *(106 W. Bunnell Ave.).*

### Other Activities

**Bicycling** Check local guides for rental companies. One of the nicest rides is Homer's 6.7-mile Homestead Trail *(Information 907-235-5263),* abloom with wildflowers in spring and summer.

**Birding** Birders praise the Kenai's heavy late spring and autumn migratory bird traffic. See local event calendars for tours.

**Camping** Campsites and forest cabins available. Contact the Chugach N.F. *(907-224-3374 or 800-280-2267. Camping fee).*

**Kayaking** Rental companies come and go; check local ads.

### Annual Events

**May–Labor Day** Homer Jackpot Halibut Derby *(Homer. 907-235-7740);* Kachemak Shorebird Festival *(Kachemak. 907-235-7740)*

**July** Fourth of July Mountain Marathon *(Seward. 907-224-8051)*

**August** Silver Salmon Derby *(Seward. 907-224-8051)*

### Lodging

**Ballaine House Lodging** *(437 3rd Ave., Seward. 907-224-2362)* Clean, attractively furnished rooms and an excellent breakfast distinguish the moderately priced inn from dozens of earnest competitors.

**Driftwood Inn** *(135 W. Bunnell Ave., Homer. 907-235-8019)* A rustic exterior belies the modern, spiffy rooms inside, complete with ocean view and appealing guest lounge.

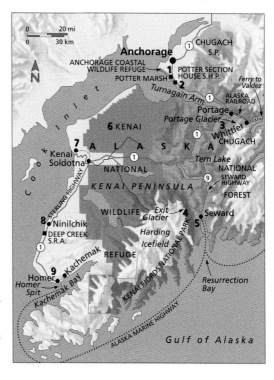

# HAWAII

# Secret Shangri-las

Want to step back in time and glimpse the Hawaii of old? Modern life has hardly touched Waipio Valley, one of seven valleys that cleft the Big Island's Hamakua Coast. Guarded by 2,000-foot cliffs, Waipio was once the legendary home of Hawaiian chiefs, gods, and supernatural beings. To please the gods, temples made of black lava rocks ran red with human sacrifices. Today, Waipio's few residents still feel ancient *mana,* or power from the spirit world, in certain places around the valley. Waipio is also one of Hawaii's prettiest places to visit, with farmers tending taro patches as in the old days. There are only two ways in: by foot or four-wheel-drive vehicle. And for those who yearn for even more isolation, rough trails led hikers to more remote Waimanu and Pololu Valleys.

**Tulip trees and royal palms, Hamakua Coast**

Traveling northwest along the Hamakua Coast, you reach the end of the road: the **Waipio Valley Overlook.** Below you lies a green gash in the earth, a valley a mile wide at the shoreline and 6 miles deep—small, but a world unto itself. The view takes in a curved fringe of surf and a black sand beach. Just inland are high dunes and then patches of taro. Guava and breadfruit trees rustle in the breeze. Everything is hemmed in by nearly vertical valley walls.

Some travelers gazing down on this tropical hideaway feel they've discovered Shangri-la. And perhaps they're right: While too many lovely spots in the Hawaiian Islands have been commercially developed beyond recognition, Waipio still evokes an unspoiled Eden.

Appropriately, it's not a simple task to enter the valley. A four-wheel-drive shuttle plies a wrenchingly steep, narrow access road. Hardy folks can hike down, but should realize that the thousand-foot drop must be negotiated on the way up, too. Because the valley floor is an alluvial plain, walking there is rough going; it's basically a swamp.

Instead, most visitors choose to tour on the shuttle or by horseback or wagon. Local guides spin tales of Waipio and may even take you to see their taro patches. You'll stop to pick wild fruit—coconuts, mango, guavas, limes—and perhaps shampoo ginger, whose egg-shaped bulb holds sweet-smelling liquid that's great for washing your hair. Pink and white impatiens festoon the cliff walls. Ponds and streams teem with prawns. A Shangri-la, indeed.

About 75 wild horses roam the valley, the descendants of Spanish stock brought by Chinese rice farmers in the late 1800s to transport crops up the hill. When most residents abandoned the valley after a 1946 tsunami, the Chinese left their horses behind, where they bred in the wild.

Waipio has been occupied for nearly a thousand years. To truly understand the valley, though, you must gaze back through history into the mists of legend. In Waipio, it's said, the god Lono slid down a rainbow to wed Kaikilani, a lovely maiden who lived in a breadfruit grove near the 1,300-foot Hiilawe Falls. Along Waipio Beach lay the legendary doorway to the underworld of the dead, called Milu. At night local residents report seeing the spirits of fallen warriors and nobles marching in processions by torchlight.

In Waipio, myth and history weave together like the roots of a monkeypod tree. Milu, for instance, was also the name of one of Hawaii's earliest kings, who lived in Waipio. Indeed, the valley ranks as a Hawaiian

## Nanaue: The Shark Man

In old times the Waipio Valley was home to Nanaue, the shark man. The son of a shark god and an earthly mother, he had a shark's mouth on his back, which he concealed under a cape. He spent his days sitting on a rock at Nanaue Falls. When people passed on the way to the sea, Nanaue would warn them of sharks, then arrive first by swimming downstream. In the ocean he devoured a victim, then went back to his waterfall to await the returning mourners. When the people of Waipio uncovered Nanaue's identity and bad deeds, they burned the shark man alive.

**Taro cultivation, Waipio Valley**

homeland. Beginning around A.D. 1100, Polynesian voyagers from Tahiti settled Waipio. With rich soil and 100 inches of rainfall annually, the valley made a fertile garden for cultivating taro, which is pounded to make the Hawaiian staple dish, poi (see sidebar p. 375). Waipio's crops and pigs supported a population of up to 10,000 people in the period before contact with Europeans.

Food for the body, food for the soul: Waipio was also a great religious center, scattered with six important temples called *heiau*. Most important was Pakaalana; now destroyed, it stood by the beach on the left-hand side of Wailoa Stream as you face the ocean. The site had two functions—as a place of human sacrifice and, paradoxically, as a "place of refuge" (*puuhonua*) that gave sanctuary to taboo violators, defeated warriors, and the sick. In the center of a large enclosure stood the Hale o Liloa (House of Liloa), which held the sanctified bones of famous chief Liloa.

More human sacrifices were offered at Moaula Heiau, which has also disappeared with time. It is said that during sacrifices "the god Ku came down from the heavens in a black cloud and in a rainbow and licked up the offering with a tongue of fire." Similar occurrences were reported at Honuaula Heiau, which stood in the center of the beach. In 1919 its ruined platform was measured at 210 feet long and 90 feet wide.

Waipio remained an important religious and political hub into the era of Kamehameha the Great, the imposing warrior who began conquering and uniting the Hawaiian Islands in the 1790s. Waipio was his stronghold, but it was invaded by his rival, Keoua, who destroyed valuable fish ponds and taro patches. Later, Kamehameha and his war canoes, in league with two Americans whose ship had cannons, defeated chiefs from Oahu and Kauai in the first modern naval battle in Hawaiian history. Taking place just north of Waipio, the battle was named *Kepuwahaulaula*, or "Red-Mouthed Gun."

Despite Waipio's former importance, the valley today is virtually deserted, with fewer than 50 residents. Most families left after the 1946 tsunami erased their taro patches, knocked down their houses, and destroyed temples. When the wall of water hit Pakaalana Heiau, it scattered the rock walls like pebbles. A flood in 1979 inflicted further damage on the valley, as well as chasing out "back to nature" hippies who began moving in during the late 1960s. Surprisingly, no one was killed in either disaster. Many locals say they feel mysteriously protected in Waipio, perhaps by the mana of the Hawaiian chiefs buried here, or by the spiritual power remaining from the old temples.

Today Waipio is a popular weekend spot for island residents, who surf, picnic, and camp. At times there may be more than a hundred people on the beach, with their four-wheel-drive vehicles parked nearby.

To *really* get away from it all, physically fit hikers can head for **Waimanu Valley** over a difficult 8-mile trail along an ancient footpath from Waipio. The hiker's reward is to discover a largely unspoiled natural paradise. Five major waterfalls tumble down the valley's western wall. Much of the flat valley bottom is wetland, where you'll see black-crowned night-herons and endangered Hawaiian ducks, or *koloa*. The open water supports colonies of floating aquatic ferns. Prawns, mollusks, and fishes thrive in the estuary. Hawaii's only native land mammal—the endangered hoary bat—can be seen flying in the sunset skies.

Like Waipio, this valley was formed by volcanic faulting followed by stream erosion that created rich soil. In the early 1800s about 200 people lived in Waimanu Valley, growing taro and fruit and raising fish in rock enclosures. Not a soul remains, but you'll see traces of their lives—house sites, terraces, irrigation ditches, heiau ruins.

The 12-mile stretch of the Hamakua Coast from Waipio to Pololu is carved with 7 remote valleys. You must drive to reach **Pololu**, the northernmost valley, where a trail descends into the former realm of taro farmers. The valley is now abandoned—except by surfers and campers who pick wild fruit and try their hands at fishing on shore. A black sand beach stretches for half a mile; the view seems to go on forever.

—*Jerry Camarillo Dunn, Jr.*

## Poi

The main crop of Waipio Valley has always been taro, which Mark Twain characterized as a "bulbous sweet potato." When its corm, or underground stem, is cooked and pounded into a purplish paste, it becomes poi, a staple food still eaten in many Hawaiian households. The flavor of this starchy, glutinous food is undeniably bland; it looks (and tastes) something like library paste. Fermenting it adds a sour or acid zing. Poi's consistency is measured by how many fingers it takes to get it to your mouth—i.e., "two-finger poi" and "three-finger poi."

# Travel Notes

## Directions

Waipio and the other remote valleys of the Hamakua Coast lie on the north shore of Hawaii (aka the Big Island). **By car:** To Waipio Valley: From Kailua, take Hawaii 190 northeast to Waimea, then Hawaii 19 northeast to Hawaii 240; turn northwest to the end of the road at the Waipio Valley Overlook. From Hilo, take Hawaii 19 northwest to Hawaii 240; continue northwest to the Waipio Valley Overlook. To the Pololu Valley Overlook: From Kailua, take Hawaii 19 north to Hawaii 270; follow this road through Hawi and Kapaau to the dead-end at the Pololu Valley Overlook. From Hilo: Take Hawaii 19 to Waimea, then take Hawaii 250 north to Hawaii 270 east; follow this road to the Pololu Valley Overlook. **By air:** Hawaii is accessible by air from other islands, with airports at Kailua and Hilo.

## General Information

The Big Island has generally warm weather year-round; the rainiest period is December to March. The Kailua side is hotter and drier, the Hilo side rainier and more lush. For travel information, contact the Big Island Visitors Bureau *(250 Keawe Street, Hilo 96720. 808-961-5797; and 75-5719 W. Alii Dr. Kailua 96740. 808-329-7787).*

## Things to See and Do

**1. Waipio Valley** Of the several different ways to see the Edenesque but remote Waipio Valley, the easiest is probably aboard a 4-wheel-drive van. **Waipio Valley Shuttle Tours** *(Office at Waipio Valley Artworks in Kukuihaele, on Hawaii 240. 808-775-7121. Mon.-Sat.; fee)* bring you down the steep access road to see the valley on a 1.5-hour tour. Your local driver-guide knows Waipio lore and natural history. You'll see waterfalls, taro patches, wild fruit trees, and a big view of the valley on the way down; however, the tour doesn't go to the beach *(see Hiking below)*. Another popular way to see the valley is by horseback, with the help of **Waipio Naalapa Trail Rides** *(45-3626 Mamane St./Hawaii 240, Honokaa. 808-775-0419. Mon.-Sat.; fee. Reservations required).* The tours begin with a 4WD descent to family-owned stables deep in the valley. There you mount surefooted local horses that can cross swampy ground and afford a clear, elevated view of the surroundings. The two-hour tour ventures where vehicles can't, while the guide, raised in the valley, tells legends and family stories as you go. The route takes in waterfalls, a heiau site, burial sites, taro patches, and lotus ponds. A different way to visit the valley is with a **Waipio Valley Wagon Tour** *(Last Chance Store on Hawaii 240, Kukuihaele. 808-775-9518. Mon.-Sat.; fee).* After a 4WD descent, you board a mule-powered wooden wagon that plies the central valley's roads (such as they are). On the one-hour tour, guide Hanalei, a showman, tells tales, plays ukulele, and sings songs for passengers as they view valley sights.

## Other Activities at Waipio Valley

**Camping** The Kamehameha School's Bishop Estate *(808-776-1104)* owns a section of the beach where it allows unimproved camping. Call well ahead for requirements and a free permit.

**Hiking** You can hike into the valley, but beware: The road in is a steep mile. On the valley floor, trails are rough and poorly marked, if at all; it's easy to get lost. (No signs say, "This way to the beach.") Reaching the beach means crossing slippery ground and muck holes. Hiking deeper

Pacific Ocean
Hamakua Coast
Makapala
Kukuihaele — 240
POLOLU VALLEY OVERLOOK
Pololu Valley
KOHALA FOREST RESERVE
Honopue Str.
Waikilikahi Str.
Waimanu Valley
Muliwai Trail
Waipio Valley
WAIPIO VALLEY OVERLOOK
Waipio
Hiilawe Falls
Wailoa Str.
Waiulili Str.
KOHALA FOREST RESERVE
KOHALA FOREST RESERVE
H A W A I I
PUU O UMI NATURAL AREA RESERVE
Waipio Stream
Kohakohau Str.
19
250 Str.
Keawewai Str.
0    2 mi
0    3 km
Waimea
19    190

**Waipio Valley, Hamakua Coast**

into the valley means crossing streams and slippery boulders. Much of the land is private property. The terrain appeals to adventurous hikers, but many visitors are more comfortable seeing the valley on a guided tour *(see above)*. **Swimming** Waipio's black sand beach stretches a mile and has long been a surfing spot. Swimmers should beware of dangerous rip currents and strong waves.

**2. Waimanu Valley** Hiking is the only way into the valley. The 8-mile **Muliwai Trail** starts at the bottom of the Waipio Valley's west wall. It climbs 1,200 feet in less than a mile and then winds in and out of a dozen gulches to reach Waimanu Valley. The way is steep, rutted, and narrow. After heavy rains, footing becomes slippery, falling rocks pose a danger, and swollen streams and flash floods are potentially fatal. A hikers' shelter stands about two-thirds of the way along the trail.

*Other Activities at Waimanu Valley*
**Camping** Reserve campsites (no earlier than 30 days in advance) and obtain a free permit through the Division of Forestry and Wildlife *(808-974-4221)*. Don't fail to treat drinking water (including spring water) before

use. Centipedes that inflict painful bites are common in the campsite area; check your tent and bedding. Outhouses available.

**3. Pololu Valley** It's a 20-minute walk from the Pololu Valley Overlook *(at the end of Hawaii 270)* to the valley floor on a trail that is well-maintained but slippery in wet weather. Cattle and horses graze in the valley; the slopes are a forest reserve. The beach often collects great mounds of driftwood. Beware of hazardous rip currents and high surf.

Lodging
**Tom Araki's Hotel** *(Waipio Valley. 808-775-0368)* Live like a local with simple accommodations facing a taro patch on the valley floor. No electricity (kerosene lamps instead); bring your own food for the communal kitchen. Reserve three weeks ahead; if no one answers the phone, you'll have to just walk in.
**Waipio Tree House** *(Waipio Valley. 808-775-7160)* Perched 30 feet high in a monkey-pod tree facing a thousand-foot waterfall, this unusual place has skylights and a panoramic view. It offers tours and study of taro raising. Electricity, refrigerator, and hot plate provided; bring your own food.

# Illustrations Credits

Cover, Michael Melford. 1, David Epperson/Tony Stone Images. 2-3, David Muench/Tony Stone Images. 4, Byron Jorjorian/Tony Stone Images. 5 & 10, Michael Melford.

## Northeast

12, Fred Hirschmann. 15, Joel Sartore. 16, David Hiser. 19, B. Anthony Stewart. 20, David Hiser. 21, Luis Marden. 22, David Alan Harvey. 23 & 24, Scott Goldsmith. 26, Lee Snider. 27 & 28, Sandy Felsenthal. 30, Bruce Alexander. 31, Jim Wark/Peter Arnold, Inc. 32, Courtesy, Bailey's Country Store. 33, G. Frederick Stork/ Folio, Inc. 35 & 36, Gail Mooney. 39, Richard Cheek. 40 & 42 (upper), Dick Swanson; 42 (lower), James L. Amos. 45-47 (all), Walter Bibikow/Folio, Inc. 49-52 (all), Scott Goldsmith. 53, Walter Bibikow/Folio, Inc. 55, James L. Amos/Peter Arnold, Inc. 56 (both), Michael Melford. 60, Kenneth Garrett. 61, Melissa Farlow. 62, Dan McCoy/The Stock Market. 66, Wendy Neefus/Earth Scenes. 67 & 68, Mary Ellen Kretz. 69, Alex Hargrave. 71, Carol Owens. 72 (upper), Nellie Pennella; (lower), Endless Mountain Visitors Bureau. 75, Mark Andermann. 77-79 (all), Bill Luster. 82, Robert P. Ruschak. 84, Bob Woodward/The Stock Market. 86, Ted Spiegel. 87-91 (all), Michael Melford. 93, George Schupp/ Delaware Bay Schooner Project. 94, Gail Mooney. 95, Robert Villani/ Peter Arnold, Inc. 97, Jonathan S. Blair. 98 (upper), Fred J. Maroon/Folio, Inc.; (lower), Stephen G. St. John/NGS Image Collection. 102, Fred Hirschmann. 104, Michael Ventura/Folio, Inc. 105, Joseph Sohm/Uniphoto. 107 & 108 (upper), David W. Harp/ Folio, Inc.; (lower), Everett C. Johnson/Folio, Inc. 110, Ira Wexler/Folio, Inc.

## South

112, Michael Melford. 114, Kevin Fleming. 115, Kenneth Garrett. 117, Linda Richardson. 118, David Alan Harvey. 119, Mike Pierry, Jr. 120, Tal McBride/Folio, Inc. 121, Michael Ventura/Folio, Inc. 122 (upper), Linda Bailey/Earth Scenes; (lower), Fred Hirschmann. 124, Kenneth Garrett. 127, Jean Anderson/The Stock Market. 128 (upper), Jim Brandenburg; (lower), Wendell Metzen/Bruce Coleman, Inc. 131-134 (all), Tony Smith Photography. 137, Galen Rowell/Mountain Light. 138, Bob Thomason/Tony Stone Images. 139, Roger Manley.

142 (upper), James Randklev/Tony Stone Images; (lower), Gail Mooney. 143, James Randklev/Tony Stone Images. 145, Michael Melford. 147, Jeanne Rawlings. 148, John Moran/The Gainesville Sun. 149, Joe McDonald/Bruce Coleman, Inc. 151, Fred J. Maroon/Folio, Inc. 152 (both), Fred Hirschmann. 155, David Muench/Tony Stone Images. 156, David Muench. 158, Len Rue, Jr./Earth Scenes. 161, William Albert Allard, NGP. 162, Raymond Gehman. 164, Steve Walls. 167, Larry Ulrich/Tony Stone Images. 168, Joseph F. Viesti. 169 & 170, Priit J. Vesilind/NGS Image Collection. 171, Greg L. Ryan-Sally A. Beyer/Tony Stone Images. 172, David Muench. 174, Pete Souza.

## Great Lakes and Plains

176, Greg L. Ryan-Sally A. Beyer/Tony Stone Images. 178 (upper), Phil Schermeister; (lower), Fred Hirschmann. 181-183 (all), Phil Schermeister. 185, Terry E. Eiler/Folio, Inc. 187, Kelly Faris/Eastern National. 190-192 (all), Bill Luster. 193, Harrison County Chamber of Commerce. 195, Courtesy, Saint Meinrad Archabbey. 196, Courtesy, Squire Boone Village. 199, Peter Pearson/Tony Stone Images. 200 (upper), Sam Abell, NGP; (lower), Lyntha Scott Eiler/Folio, Inc. 201, Sam Abell, NGP. 203, Jeremy Schmidt. 204, Ken Nardius/The Picture Cube. 206 & 207, Jeremy Schmidt. 208 (upper), Maxwell Mackenzie/Tony Stone Images; (lower), Jeremy Schmidt. 210, Phil Schermeister. 212, Michael Lewis. 213, A.B. Sheldon/Earth Scenes. 214-219 (all) Michael Lewis. 220, Michael Melford. 222, T. Dietrich/H. Armstrong Roberts. 224, Randy Olson. 225 & 226, Jeremy Schmidt. 228, Jim Brandenburg. 229, Gary Withey/Bruce Coleman, Inc. 230, Fred Hirschmann. 232 (both), Jeremy Schmidt.

## South Central

234, Bill Luster. 237, Robert P. Carr/Bruce Coleman, Inc. 238, Matt Bradley/Bruce Coleman, Inc. 239-241 (all) Fred Hirschmann. 244, John Burwell. 245, Philip Gould. 246, John Eastcott & Yva Momatiuk. 249, James P. Blair. 251, David Muench. 252, Bill Luster. 253, Mike Clemmer. 255 & 256, Kevin Sink/Midwestock. 257, C.C. Lockwood/ Bruce Coleman, Inc. 259 & 260 (upper), Bruce Mathews/ Midwestock; 260 (lower),

Sue Vanderbilt. 263, Jim Hays/Midwestock. 264 & 265, Phil Schermeister/Tony Stone Images. 266, Bern Ketchum. 267, Jim Brandenburg. 269, Richard Olsenius, NGS. 270 (upper), George F. Mobley; (lower), David Alan Harvey.

## Mountain & Desert States

272, Gary Yeowell/Tony Stone Images. 275 (upper), Jeremy Schmidt; (lower), Tom Dietrich. 276, Jeremy Schmidt. 277, Ron Sanford/Tony Stone Images. 279 & 281 (upper), Michael Melford; 281 (lower), Steve Bly/Tony Stone Images. 282, Michael Melford. 285, Tom Bean/Tony Stone Images. 287, Dick Durrance. 288, David Schultz/ Tony Stone Images. 290 (upper), John MacMurray; (lower), Jeremy Schmidt. 293, Paul Chesley/Tony Stone Images. 294, Aldo Brando/Tony Stone Images. 296, David Muench/ Tony Stone Images. 298, Fred Hirschmann. 299, D. Kjell Mitchell. 301-305 (all), Fred Hirschmann. 306, Tom Till/Tony Stone Images. 309 (both), Fred Hirschmann. 311, David Muench/Tony Stone Images. 313, Fred Hirschmann. 315, Danny Lehman. 317, Tom Bean/Tony Stone Images. 319, Larry Ulrich/Tony Stone Images. 320, Fred Hirschmann. 322 & 324 (upper) Galen Rowell/Mountain Light. 324 (lower), Ron Sanford/Tony Stone Images

## Pacific States

326, John MacMurray. 329, David Alan Harvey. 331 (upper), David Muench/Tony Stone Images; (lower), Marc Solomon. 333, Roger Ressmeyer. 335 & 336, Marc Solomon. 337, David J. Gubernick. 338, Keith J. Sutter. 340 & 341, David Hiser. 343, Fred Hirschmann. 344 & 347, Larry Ulrich/Tony Stone Images. 348, Jim Corwin/Tony Stone Images. 350, John MacMurray. 351, Larry Ulrich/Tony Stone Images. 352, John Marshall/Tony Stone Images. 353, John MacMurray. 355 (upper), Jim Brandenburg; (lower), David G. Allen. 357, Jack Dykinga. 359, Fred Hirschmann. 360, Stuart Westmorland/Tony Stone Images. 363, Art Wolfe/Tony Stone Images. 364, William Thompson/Tony Stone Images. 366, Greg Vaughn/Tony Stone Images. 367, Fred Hirschmann. 369, Larry Ulrich/Tony Stone Images. 370, Tom Walker/Tony Stone Images. 372, Larry Ulrich/Tony Stone Images. 374, Chris Johns, NGP. 377, Greg Vaugn/Pacific Stock.

# Index

Composition for this book by the
National Geographic Society Book Division. Printed and bound by R.R. Don-
nelley & Sons, Willard, Ohio. Color
separations by CMI Color Graphix,
Huntingdon Valley, Pennsylvania. Cover
printed by Miken Companies, Inc.
Cheektowaga, New York.

**Library of Congress Cataloging-in-Publication Data**

National Geographic's guide to America's hidden corners / prepared by
the Book Division, National Geographic Society.
p.  cm.
Includes index.
ISBN 0-7922-7211-0(reg). —ISBN 0-7922-7210-2 (dlx)
1. United States—Guidebooks.   I. National Geographic Society
(U.S.).  Book Division.
E158.N262 1998
917.304'929--dc21                                              98-4637
                                                                  CIP

Visit the Society's Web site at
http://www.nationalgeographic.com